Work and Labour in Canada

Praise for
Work and Labour in Canada, Critical Issues

"This book is very readable, and provides good coverage of a range of key
issues affecting workers in the Canadian labour market and the global economy.
Particular strengths include the balanced way topics are introduced
(e.g., inequalities in the labour market), the coverage of a number of significant
debates in the field (e.g., whether there is a future for unions in Canada),
and the helpful material included in the recommended readings."
— **Lee Chalmers**, Department of Sociology,
University of New Brunswick

"This book offers a perspective that puts workers front and centre.
It covers the key issues affecting work in Canada in a clear and accessible manner."
— **Ursule Critoph**, Educational Studies,
Centre for Work and Community Studies,
Athabasca University

Work and Labour in Canada

Critical Issues

Second Edition

Andrew Jackson
Foreword by Wallace Clement

Canadian Scholars' Press Inc.
Toronto

Work and Labour
By Andrew Jackson

First published in 2009 by Canadian Scholars' Press Inc.
180 Bloor Street West, Suite 801
Toronto, Ontario
M5S 2V6

www.cspi.org

Canadian Scholars' Press Inc. gratefully acknowledges financial support for our publishing activities from the Government of Canada through the Book Publishing Industry Development Program (BPIDP), and the Government of Ontario through the Ontario Book Publishing Tax Credit Program.

Library and Archives Canada Cataloguing in Publication

Jackson, Andrew, 1952–
    Work and labour in Canada : critical issues / Andrew Jackson. — 2nd ed.

Includes bibliographical references and index.
ISBN 978-1-55130-366-6

        1. Labor—Canada—Textbooks. 2. Labor movement—Canada—Textbooks. I. Title.

HD8106.5.J32 2009   331.0971   C2009-903655-X

Cover design by Colleen Wormald
Text design and layout by Brad Horning and Stewart Moracen

Printed and bound in Canada

Canad**ä**

MIX
Paper from
responsible sources
FSC
www.fsc.org   FSC® C004071

This book is dedicated to
Karen, Caitlin, and Emma

Table of Contents

List of Tables and Figures

List of Boxes

Foreword

Work life is fundamental to how we experience life in general. Most of us work to live but many of us also live to work. We gain our quality of life, identities, and much of our sense of meaning from our work lives. And, the link between work life and family life and/or leisure and education is also shaped by the quality of our work lives — our hours of work, its rewards, self-esteem, and social interactions. It is important to have a holistic view of work — that it is embedded in a series of economic, political, social, and cultural forces. Equally important is what we call "work" — whether for pay or not (volunteer, domestic work, etc.) — and recognize that the essential reproduction of citizens through care work is to be valued. How we understand work in terms of how we frame it as a value for individuals and societies matters. Work does not just happen. It is created, conditioned, and destroyed by the political economy in which it is embedded.

For these reasons, it is important to acknowledge the contribution of Andrew Jackson's *Work and Labour in Canada*. It is a book designed to inform and educate its readers. Clearly, he has done a great deal of thinking about the right questions to ask and how to frame our understanding. He offers fresh ways to think about changing times by locating his analysis of Canada in a comparative context. At the base of his analysis is his penetration of struggles over whose views and/or interests prevail in the construction of work, such as his detailed account of conflicts over the implications of the debate about social spending versus tax cuts.

Work is embedded in a variety of processes and developments. Andrew Jackson reveals many of the links between work, jobs, and employment in Canada as outcomes of broader forces and practices. I say practices because these are not simply anonymous forces of capitalism at play. They are also practices by capitalists and political leaders and, to a lesser extent, labour and social leaders.

Fundamental to any understanding of work includes what it means to live in a capitalist market society; that is, the capitalist market for the most part sets the standard for wages and entitlement, although not entirely. The state sector, at least in Canada and most other countries with the possible exceptions of the United States and recently Japan, still is important as an employer and site for organized labour. In Canada, the public sector includes the Canadian Union of Public Employees, the Public Service Alliance of Canada, municipal workers, teachers, and nurses. The public sector is strongly connected to the quality of work available, especially for women.

Knowledge is power, so it is said. More likely, knowledge can be empowering and this is clearly Andrew Jackson's purpose—to put knowledge about the world of work into the hands of workers, social activists, and students who wish to impact the quality of work available in Canada.

In what at first glance appears to be a highly empirical book, it is really a book about framing public issues concerning wages and the quality of work. It is an intervention into public discourse on the quality and availability of work while understanding the processes or forces transforming these conditions and experiences for Canadian workers. A good deal of the book can be looked upon as a resource encouraging readers to pursue issues in greater depth and providing them with the means to do so through extensive references and web links.

The book is a specific account of the current crisis in terms of economics, politics, consumption, job markets, and job quality, presented in clear, accessible terms. Andrew Jackson raises issues about the legitimacy of current practices, and challenges the current hegemony in terms of evidence documenting increased income inequality and widening gaps between the wealthy and everyone else, all in an attempt to create much needed political space.

There is a specific discussion of changes in living standards with a strong grasp of the literature produced nationally and internationally on wage distributions and distortions arising from neo-liberal practices. This includes an important discussion of family structures and the effects on single earners, divorced couples, and dual-earner families. Lifelong learning also receives attention, addressing the implications of low-skill traps for individuals and society by addressing real productivity. The link between health and work is also presented, not only in terms of stress but also the link with work-life balance and benefits like extended medical coverage and sick leave.

In terms of the characteristics of workers, specific chapters are dedicated to women, heritage, older and younger people. Each discussion is accessible. For women, Andrew Jackson documents the persistence of the "double ghetto," characterized so aptly by the Armstrongs in the 1970s, with some recent modifications. If anything, women's burden is doubled even more with increases in paid labour without commensurate reduction of unpaid work, including working full time and continuing on later in life. Women in Canada at mid-life (25–54 years of age) have an 86 percent labour force participation rate, with women contributing a third of overall household incomes in dual-earner households, while continuing to bear primary responsibility for "managing" complex family lives. Still, gender pay gaps persist and will continue to do so given the stealth dismantling of pay equity practices embedded in the Conservative recovery budget and the ongoing precariousness of so much of the work available to women.

The changing face of immigration and its characteristics (including more temporary migration without full rights) is unlike earlier generations of immigration. The current immigrants are not matching native-born earnings, although exceeding this population in education levels. Heritage is also addressed in terms of Aboriginal employment and their diversity of experiences, including for far too many abysmal labour market conditions.

Andrew Jackson's primer on pension erosion is eye-opening. He documents the erosion from defined benefit to defined contribution plans based on "the market." He notes that only a third of private-sector employees are covered by employer pension plans. No wonder there are such increases in labour force participation by older workers, especially women. Youths are discussed in terms of school-to-work transitions. The primary issue identified is the quality of the labour market for entry-level jobs and its impact on families.

As one might expect given Andrew Jackson's day-job as Director of Social and Economic Policy at the Canadian Labour Congress, there is a strong primer on unions and a reminder about the significance of unions for political, social, and economic rights. The future of unions is thoughtfully reflected upon in terms of their declining political strength and new challenges, such as work-life balance issues. The cornerstone of unions is now in public and social services with a dramatic decline in the private sector (less than a fifth organized), with only 13 percent of all union membership now in manufacturing. The decline in Canada's manufacturing is analyzed in terms of globalization and the continued reliance upon resource exports, as they have been strengthened by the global financial crisis, which sees Canadian finance flourishing while other sectors suffer. Canada's trade outside North America has been characterized by manufacturing imports and resource exports, but is now in an overpowering deficit position, which contributes to our current employment crisis.

Finally, consistent with his overall framing of the book in the world-comparative context, Andrew Jackson concludes by invoking the Scandinavian experience with social democracy as opposed to the neo-liberalism of Canada, the United States, and the United Kingdom, our typical comparators. He notes that social democracy is itself being transformed in this neo-liberal era, yet he documents the possibility of high employment, good wages and working conditions in small, advanced capitalist nations. It is always good to be reminded that there are other ways to think and act than those that have become so dominant in our "no-other-choice" political discourse.

Wallace Clement
March 2009

Preface to the Second Edition

Much of the material in the first edition of this book was originally produced, often in a very different format, as research papers for the Canadian Labour Congress (CLC). The CLC is the major trade union federation in Canada, representing some three million workers who belong to its affiliated unions.

The CLC has consciously tried for a number of years to contribute to and shape the public debate on work, employment, and incomes through a close factual analysis of trends in employment and unemployment, wages and working conditions, incomes of working families, the situation of equality-seeking groups, and inequality and poverty.

It would seem to be obvious that wages and the quality of work are central aspects of the economic and social well-being of Canadians and should be at the centre of public debate on how our economy is performing, but it still seems to take constant effort to push these issues to the forefront and to the attention of policy-makers.

The CLC has tried to highlight forces and trends affecting all working people and not just union members, and to earn a reputation for informed analysis of current issues. Theory and experience show that the social forces behind an argument are often decisive in politics and policy-making, but the force of an argument is important as well. Special thanks go to the CLC elected officers, especially current President Ken Georgetti and former President Bob White, for their recognition of the importance of economic and social research in trade union work.

Much of the analytical work of the CLC is undertaken by the Department of Social and Economic Policy. Thanks are due to Bob Baldwin, my predecessor as Director, who contributed material on pensions and older workers to the first edition of this book. More importantly, Bob has held up the other side of a 20-year-long ongoing conversation on work, labour, and social and economic policy issues. Very special thanks goes to my assistant, Judy Cerra, for her highly skilled work in pulling my text into a comprehensible format, not once, but twice.

My research work has involved frequent collaboration with trade union colleagues. Hugh Mackenzie, formerly of USW, Jim Stanford (CAW), and Jane Stinson and Toby Sanger (CUPE) deserve special thanks for grounding my work in labour perspectives on work and workers. I also owe a lot to my contact over the years with John Evans, General Secretary of the Trade Union Advisory Committee to the Organisation for Economic Co-operation and Development (OECD), and colleagues in the global labour movement.

Many of the papers that form the basis for chapters in this book were presented to academic conferences, and some have appeared in different forms in academic publications. Maintaining a link between union and academic research hopefully provides the reader with some assurance of credibility, and certainly provides for constant stimulus. Particular thanks in shaping the material in this book, either through conversation and direct input or through their own work, go to Keith Banting, Wallace Clement, Jane Jenson, Pradeep Kumar, Gregor Murray, John Myles, Lars Osberg, Charlotte Yates, Leah Vosko, and, especially, Rianne Mahon of the Institute of Political Economy at Carleton University to which I am affiliated as a research professor. Thanks to Wallace Clement for reading over both editions of the manuscript.

From the world of policy institutes, I have worked with and learned a lot from Bruce Campbell and Armine Yalnizyan of the Canadian Centre for Policy Alternatives; Ken Battle of the Caledon Institute; Andrew Sharpe of the Centre for the Study of Living Standards; and Katherine Scott, who was a colleague at the Canadian Council on Social Development during my sojourn there as director of research from 2000 to 2002.

Much of the material that follows is highly empirical, drawing heavily on data and analytical studies undertaken by Statistics Canada. The Analytical Studies Branch makes an incredibly important contribution to understanding Canadian economic and social trends, and has consistently devoted a great deal of attention to work, income, and labour (though we still badly need a national survey of working conditions and identifiers for workers of colour on the *Labour Force Survey*!). This book draws heavily on data from the *Labour Force Survey*, much of it obtained from special tabulations by Statistics Canada or directly from public-use microdata files. For that reason, some data tables are simply referenced to the survey rather than to published sources.

Finally, thanks to Megan Mueller of Canadian Scholars' Press Inc. for encouraging me to write this book and for so capably helping me to pull it together.

A Note on the Second Edition

The second edition of this book was mainly written over the Summer of 2008, and updated trends to that point (mainly using an end date of 2007 for annual data). All of the chapters were substantially revised and added to, not just updated, especially Chapter 11 ("Canadian Workers in a Changing World: The Impacts of Globalization and Free Trade"), which places much more emphasis than the original on "globalization" as opposed to North American economic integration. Chapter 8 on young workers is new, and Chapter 6 was substantially revised to add more material on persons with disabilities and to place more emphasis on the fortunes of racialized Canadian-born workers as opposed to recent immigrants. The thrust of the argument on older workers was changed to reflect a quite dramatic increase in the participation rate of older workers and the erosion of the pension system. Chapter 2 focuses on key trends in the period of economic expansion, 1997–2007, which saw a steady decline in unemployment to low levels, albeit combined with some much more troubling trends in the job market. The economic crisis of 2008 marked the return of high unemployment, and a brief note on the causes of the crisis and its roots in the labour market has been added to Chapter 1.

A Note from the Publisher

Thank you for selecting the second edition of *Work and Labour in Canada: Critical Issues* by Andrew Jackson. The author and publisher have devoted considerable time and careful development (including meticulous peer reviews) to this book. We appreciate your recognition of this effort and accomplishment.

Introduction

The central purpose of this book is to evaluate the quality of work and jobs in Canada from a critical perspective, and to open up a discussion about how conditions might be improved for working people. A substantial amount of detail is provided on recent trends in employment, unemployment, and the quality of jobs; on how the job market serves the needs of particular groups of workers; on the role of Canadian unions; and on how conditions in Canada are rooted in global developments and compare to those in other countries.

Part I, "Working People and the Canadian Workplace," is divided into four chapters. These cover the importance of jobs, recent trends in the job market and Canadian workplaces, and two important aspects of job quality—access to training and healthy working conditions.

Chapter 1 discusses why jobs are important from the perspective of working people, and highlights the importance, not just of wages, but also of the quality of work. It looks at some key forces shaping the nature of jobs and work. Chapter 2 provides a detailed overview of conditions in the job market and in workplaces, and key trends over the past decade or so. While Canada has done very well on some fronts and has recently had a very high rate of employment, including in jobs requiring higher levels of education, other, more negative, trends are of concern. These include growing inequality in wages, job prospects, and family incomes, and the growing problem of low wages and unstable or precarious work.

Chapter 3 focuses on opportunities for access to training and on-the-job learning, and Chapter 4 surveys workplace conditions that have implications for both the physical and mental health of workers.

Part II, "Inequalities and Differences: Gender, Race, Ability, Age," takes an in-depth look at the labour market and work experiences of specific groups: women, racialized workers, persons with disabilities, Aboriginal Canadians, and older and younger workers. The job market is marked by deep inequalities and differences along lines of gender, race, ability, and age, all of which intersect with differences in wages and the quality of employment.

Chapter 5 details the job experiences of women and shows that there are still deep and systematic differences of pay and job quality based upon gender. Chapter 6 looks at the experiences of recent immigrants, workers of colour, Aboriginal Canadians, and persons with disabilities. Despite huge differences, all these groups have some vulnerability to and experience discrimination in the job market. Chapter 7 looks at the situation of older workers and paths from work to retirement, also highlighting some differences between generations and what has come to be known as the changing life-course. Chapter 8 looks at some of the barriers facing younger workers as baby boomers continue to predominate in good jobs.

Part III, "Contemporary Canadian Unions," looks at the role of unions in Canada and in other advanced industrial countries, and at the potential future of unions as a force for improving pay and working conditions and promoting greater equality in the job market. Chapter 9 examines union impacts on wages, low-wage jobs, benefits, and access to training, and discusses how unions affect the way in which the economy and the labour market operate. Chapter 10 looks at changes in union membership, and challenges facing unions in attempting to organize and represent workers in today's job market.

Part IV, "Canada in a Global Perspective," looks at how Canada's greater integration into the global and North American economy has changed the labour market and the world of work, and the extent to which the forces of free trade and global economic integration may limit our choices in terms of shaping how the labour market works. Chapter 11 focuses on the impacts of globalization, and Chapter 12 compares and contrasts Canada's labour market and workplace institutions to those of some European countries, noting that advanced industrial societies exist in different forms, which have major implications for the quality of jobs and the well-being of workers.

This final chapter encourages the reader to think about the ways in which Canada's labour market model might be changed in order to improve the quality of jobs, and to address some of the many problems of work outlined in the book as a whole.

Relevant websites are identified in the introductions to each part of the book, and suggested readings follow each chapter. Questions for critical thought are available at www.cspi.org.

Working People and the Canadian Workplace

This part of the book provides an overview of conditions in the job market and in workplaces today, and a summary of trends over the past 15 years. It focuses on wages, unemployment, forms of employment, opportunities for education and training, and workplace conditions. Differences in the experience of different groups of workers, particularly by gender and age, and of Canadian workers compared to those in other countries are briefly noted, setting the stage for further analysis later in the book.

Chapter 1, "Why Jobs Are Important: Thinking About Work and Labour in Tumultuous Times," sets out some of the key characteristics of jobs that are important to working people, including not just wages but also the quality of work along a number of dimensions, such as stability of employment, working conditions, and opportunities for promotion and training. Some key forces shaping the nature of jobs and work, such as government economic policies, industrial restructuring, and unions, are also highlighted.

Chapter 2, "Work, Wages, and the Living Standards of Canadian Working People," provides a detailed, statistically based analysis of trends in wages, employment, unemployment, and the quality of new jobs created over the past 15 years or so. Canada has done well on some fronts. We have recently had a very high rate of employment, and there has been a shift toward better jobs requiring higher levels of education. However, there are some negative trends as well. The chapter highlights inequality in the job market, and the growing problem of low wages and precarious work—that is, the problem of low-paying and insecure jobs. Links are drawn from trends in the job market to a disturbing trend toward greater inequality in the wider society. This chapter also draws some attention to the different experiences of women and men, providing some background for the more detailed analysis in Part II.

Chapter 3, "Taking Lifelong Learning Seriously," focuses on one key aspect of job quality: opportunities for access to training and on-the-job learning. This is increasingly seen as crucially important to both individual workers and to the economy in a knowledge-based economy. A key dimension of precarious jobs is that they provide limited, if any, access to training and ladders to better jobs. It is disturbing that most opportunities for on-the-job training and career development go to higher paid managers and professionals, compounding their relatively advantaged position in the job market.

Finally, Chapter 4, "The Unhealthy Canadian Workplace," surveys workplace conditions that have implications for both the physical and mental health of workers. The focus here is on physical hazards at work, and on work and stress. Work can be, and often is, very stressful because of the pace and demands of the jobs and the low degree of control exerted by employees, and also because of conflict between work and family and community life.

Related Websites

- Canadian Policy Research Networks (www.cprn.ca) is an Ottawa-based policy think-tank that involves academics and others in policy-related research work. The Work Network has been one of the major streams of activity, and literally scores of articles and research papers are available on trends and changes in Canadian work and workplaces. Many papers produced by the Family Network are also relevant to understanding change in work and workplaces.
- Department of Human Resources and Skills Development (www.hrsdc.gc.ca). The federal government department charged with responsibility for Canada's skills agenda and for labour market and labour issues provides information and research papers on a wide range of issues, including changes in the job market, what kinds of training are needed for different careers, government programs, and trends in workplaces and collective bargaining.
- European Foundation for the Improvement of Living and Working Conditions (www.eurofound.europa.eu/). The Foundation is a European Union body, one of the first to be established to work in specialized areas of E.U. policy. Its role is to provide information, advice, and expertise on living and working conditions and industrial relations. It is especially rich in studies relating to the quality of work and access to training.
- International Labour Organization (ILO) (www.ilo.org/global/lang--en/index.htm). The International Labour Organization is a United Nations agency, uniquely governed not just by governments but by representatives of employers and workers. It describes itself as "devoted to advancing opportunities for women and men to obtain decent and productive work in conditions of freedom, equity, security, and human dignity. Its main aims are to promote rights at work, encourage decent employment opportunities, enhance social protection, and strengthen dialogue in handling work-related issues." The website is a portal to statistics, studies, and reports on trends in work and working conditions around the world.
- Job Quality (www.jobquality.gc.ca) is a sub-site of Canadian Policy Research Networks that contains a wealth of current data on the quality of jobs in Canada.
- Statistics Canada (www.statcan.ca). The website of Statistics Canada, Canada's national statistical agency, has a wealth of free data and research papers on a huge range of employment, income, and social issues, almost all of which provide separate data for women and men. Many free Internet publications are listed under "Our Products and Services" under the subhead "Labour." The latest *Labour Force Survey* data are readily available on *The Daily* sub-site. Also, the quarterly publication *Perspectives on Labour and Income* provides accessible research papers.

CHAPTER 1

Why Jobs Are Important: Thinking about Work and Labour in Tumultuous Times

Introduction

This chapter describes the fundamental importance of good jobs to well-being, flags some major changes in the Canadian workforce and the nature of work over recent decades, summarizes some key forces shaping the quality of jobs, and describes the relevance of labour market issues to current economic challenges.

Jobs and a Changing Workforce

The vast majority of Canadian families and households depend upon jobs and the labour market for their well-being. In 2008, almost eight in 10 of all people aged 15 to 64—including 90% of those aged 25 to 54, and 66% of those aged 15 to 25—participated in the paid workforce. This means that they were either working, or unemployed but actively seeking work. This is one of the highest participation rates among the advanced industrial countries, a bit higher than in the U.S., and only a little below the very high rates in the Scandinavian countries. Participation is understandably lower for teens and older workers, and participation and employment rates vary by gender as shown in Chapter 5, but very few working-age Canadians other than the very marginalized have no attachment at all to the job market.

Earnings from employment make up the lion's share of all Canadian household income. In 2007, Canadian households had a total income of just over $1 trillion, about two-thirds (67%) of which came from employment, with another 8% coming from unincorporated small business earnings (Data from Statistics Canada National Accounts). Income transfers from governments—mainly public pensions, employment insurance, and welfare payments—contributed 13% of total income, with most of that amount going to retirees as Old Age Security and Canada Pension Plan payments. Just 11% of household income came from investments. Some very affluent Canadians do collect very large amounts of dividend, capital gains, and interest income from their investments, but even the very affluent rely very heavily on employment and self-employment income for their livelihood.

In the 1950s and into the 1960s, the Canadian norm was for families to depend on the wages of an adult male breadwinner who worked from leaving school until retirement at age 65 to support his wife and children. A lot has changed, and several chapters in this book focus on the changing workforce. The importance of paid work over the life-course has shifted forwards and backwards. Well over one-half of all young people now complete some kind of post-secondary education. This has delayed entry into the permanent workforce for many young adults. However, the great majority of students work part-time and/or for part of the year, and increasingly rely on earnings to finance their studies. Meanwhile, the normal age of retirement has fallen from 65 a generation ago to just above age 60 today. However, the dream of "Freedom 55" is receding with the crisis of pensions and the increased interest of some older workers in continuing to work for non-monetary reasons (see Chapter 7). Many more older women work today than was the case a few years ago, simply because more women have been in the paid workforce for most of their lives.

By the mid-1970s, half of all women with employed spouses were working, and today that figure has risen to over 80%. The vast majority of women now want to participate in the paid workforce—perhaps with some time out for maternity and parental leaves—and their incomes make up a high and rising proportion of family incomes. Women have made substantial progress, but there are still huge gaps between women and men in terms of earnings and the quality of jobs. The nature of women's work and differences between the work experiences of men and women are explored in Chapter 5. Because male wages have stagnated for so long, families have become increasingly dependent on the earnings of women and on debt in order to maintain their living standards, as documented in the next chapter.

Today, Canada has one of the most diverse populations in the world, and one of the highest rates of immigration. New immigrants make up a high proportion of the workforce, and will—with Aboriginal Canadians—account for virtually all net job growth in the years ahead. New immigrants and racialized workers born in Canada are more highly educated than the Canadian-born, yet their earnings and job chances fall far short of equality. Race and class are closely connected. These issues are discussed in Chapter 6.

To summarize, the great majority of Canadians work for a living and paid work is absolutely central to the economic well-being of individuals and families. Some of our income comes from government transfers, and some of our basic needs—such as education for school-age children and health care—are met through government programs. But, the fundamental reality is that we live in a market or capitalist society. We must work to live, and our income from work centrally determines our standard of living. This is true in both absolute terms and as compared to our fellow citizens. The kinds of jobs we hold and the wages we earn largely determine the kind of homes and neighbourhoods in which we live, the extent to which we can buy the goods and services we want, the extent to which we can provide our children with opportunities, and our ability to balance work with family and community life and opportunities for leisure. As documented in Chapter 2, it is trends within the job market that have driven the ever-increasing polarization of Canadian incomes and Canadian society between rich and poor, and that have lowered the level of economic security enjoyed by many working Canadians and their families.

Without devaluing in any way the contribution and importance of unpaid work in the home and in the community, paid work is also a critical source of meaning and purpose in the lives of most Canadians, and a major source of personal identity. Jobs connect us to the wider society, and provide us with a sense of participation in a collective purpose. Many people define themselves largely by what they do at work. Trade unions seek to construct workers as a social movement. Good jobs in good workplaces are needed if individuals are to be able to develop their individual talents and capacities to the full, to actively participate in society, and to enjoy a broad equality of life chances. On the other hand, unemployment and bad jobs give rise to poverty and low income, stress, ill health, and alienation from the wider society in which we live.

Despite the central importance of paid work to our lives, Canada's progress as a country tends to be measured mainly on the basis of two key indicators: growth of Gross Domestic Product or GDP, and the unemployment rate. GDP is the sum total of all income in the country, and the sum total of all output. The unemployment rate is the proportion of people in the labour force who want to work, but cannot find any work at all. The level of GDP is certainly important, and economic growth will usually lower unemployment and raise incomes, and thus directly benefit working people. But, it is important to go beyond the economic growth and unemployment numbers to ask the critical question: How is work working for people? This can be measured along many dimensions, including income, job security, security of employment, and the quality of jobs at the workplace level.

GDP growth and low unemployment tell us nothing about the adequacy of wages or how earnings are distributed among households and families. One disturbing trend over the past 25 years and more has been rapidly increasing inequality in the distribution of earnings. Wages and incomes from employment have risen for those at the very top, stagnated for those at the middle, and fallen for those at the bottom. Many Canadians work in very low-wage jobs. These trends have increased income gaps between families, and kept poverty at high levels even in an economic recovery.

Trends in employment and earnings also raise important issues of equality between women and men, between the white majority and racialized minorities, and between generations. Inequalities in terms of access to good jobs marginalize many Aboriginal Canadians and persons with disabilities.

Economic growth and unemployment numbers also tell us little about the security of employment and earnings. Many jobs are short-term and unstable, and government supports for frequently unemployed and lower paid workers have been cut back. The cuts to Employment Insurance in the mid-1990s cut off access to the system for many, and lowered the level of benefits for those who did qualify. Low unemployment is obviously a good thing, but a low unemployment rate can and does hide the fact that many people—especially women and racialized workers—are working in low-wage jobs, or are working in temporary jobs, or are working in part-time jobs even if they want to work full-time. Just having a job is a good thing, but there is a big difference between having a survival job and a job that offers a real ladder to better jobs. Economic growth and unemployment numbers also tell us nothing about the quality of jobs in terms of the pace and intensity of work, access to training and career ladders, and the consequences of jobs for our health. This book reviews all of these issues.

For all of its central importance to economic, social, and individual well-being, critical study of the labour market and work is relatively underdeveloped as an academic enterprise (Shalla 2007; Green 2006). Economists view work as a disutility or deprivation of leisure time which is endured to gain income in order to consume, rather than as a sphere for the development of human capacities and well-being. Sociologists tend to have a more critical perspective, stressing that human beings develop their individual potential and enter into social relationships through their labour. However, many academics and management gurus have romanticized the post-industrial workplace as a sphere of liberation of individual talents and capacities. It is primarily critical sociologists working in the traditions of Marxism and Canadian political economy who have charted growing inequality in the job market, the intersections of such class-based inequalities with gender and race, and have also drawn attention to power relations in the workplace and the subordination of the labour process to managerial and competition-driven imperatives. Chapters 3 and 4 look critically at today's workplaces in terms of how they meet basic human needs, especially the need to develop and use skills, and to employ them in a non-stressful, dignified work environment. Of course, what happens in the labour market and in workplaces is not driven just by the needs and interests of employers, but also by the resistance of workers. Chapters 9 and 10 look at the impact and role of unions in shaping labour markets and workplaces, and Chapter 12 looks at the impact of government policies on the functioning of labour markets and workplaces from the perspective of workers.

Green (2006) stresses that job quality should be assessed primarily from a worker perspective, and draws on a growing wealth of survey evidence (much of it sadly lacking for Canada) to show that the quality of work has been in decline for the past 25 years and more along several dimensions. Not only have many workers experienced decreasing job security and stagnant wages due to economic restructuring, work effort

---

Box 1.1: What Is a Good Job?

Most of us would agree that a good job is defined, in part, by the level of pay. However, other dimensions are actually much more important. Prospects for promotion and learning are likely to be particularly important to younger workers, and lower paid jobs may be taken in preference to higher paid jobs if they are more interesting, provide greater security, more acceptable hours, better working conditions, and so on. International survey evidence suggests that job security, having an interesting job, opportunities for advancement, and being allowed to work independently—cited by 59%, 49%, 34%, and 30% of respondents respectively—rank well ahead of high pay (Clark 1999).

An Index of Job Desirability was developed for the U.S. in the late 1980s based upon the weights given to different characteristics of jobs by workers. Non-monetary characteristics of jobs were, in combination, found to be twice as important as earnings, with access to training, low risk of job loss, and characteristics of the job (non-repetitiveness and autonomy) ranking particularly highly and in that order. Other characteristics of jobs examined were hours of work, control of hours, and whether the job was "dirty." The ranking of desirable job characteristics was found to differ little between men and women or by age.

A striking finding of this study was that occupation is a limited indicator of job quality, since variation within occupational groupings was found to be as great as that between groupings. It was also found that job quality differences between women and men are much greater than earnings differences (Jencks et al. 1998).

---

and overqualification for jobs have grown in most countries. There has been a steady increase in the skills of the workforce, and even in the use of skills in the workplace, but the contemporary workplace is also marked by tight control of worker discretion on the job and by much greater stress due to the intensification of work. There is little persuasive evidence that new technologies and the so-called knowledge-based economy have significantly improved the quality of working life even for those at the top of the education and skills ladder, and there is a lot of evidence of deteriorating conditions and increased insecurity for those at the bottom of the job ladder. These issues are considered in depth in Chapter 4.

Key Forces Driving the Quantity and Quality of Jobs

Macroeconomic Conditions

In a market or capitalist economy, the great majority of jobs are created by private-sector employers. Workers are hired in order to produce goods and services, and workers are hired or laid off depending upon demand at home and outside Canada for those goods and services. In a downturn, many workers lose their jobs, but the biggest impact comes from the fact that employers stop hiring. In Canada, deep recessions resulted in very high unemployment in both the early 1980s and the early 1990s.

Box 1.2: Decent Work for All

The primary goal of the International Labour Organization—a tripartite (government, employers, labour) United Nations agency based in Geneva—is to promote opportunities for women and men to obtain decent and productive work, in conditions of freedom, equity, security, and human dignity. The ILO defines decent work as follows:

> Decent work sums up the aspirations of people in their working lives—their aspirations for opportunity and income; rights, voice and recognition; family stability and personal development; and fairness and gender equality. Ultimately these various dimensions of decent work underpin peace in communities and society. Decent work reflects the concerns of governments, workers and employers, who together provide the ILO with its unique tripartite identity.
>
> Decent work is captured in four strategic objectives: fundamental principles and rights at work and international labour standards; employment and income opportunities; social protection and social security; and social dialogue and tripartism. These objectives hold for all workers, women and men, in both formal and informal economies; in wage employment or working on their own account; in the fields, factories and offices; in their home or in the community.
>
> Decent work is central to efforts to reduce poverty, and is a means for achieving equitable, inclusive and sustainable development. The ILO works to develop Decent Work-oriented approaches to economic and social policy in partnership with the principal institutions and actors of the multilateral system and the global economy.
>
> Progress requires action at the global level. The ILO is developing an agenda for the community of work, represented by its tripartite constituents, to mobilize their considerable resources to create those opportunities and to help reduce and eradicate poverty. The Decent Work Agenda offers a basis for a more just and stable framework for global development.

Source: www.ilo.org/global/About_the_ILO/Mainpillars/WhatisDecentWork/lang--en/index.htm.

To some degree, these downturns are part of the normal workings of the business cycle. However, government economic policies have also contributed to periodic high unemployment and ongoing slack in the job market.

Most orthodox economists believe that there is a natural or non-accelerating inflation rate of unemployment. The basic idea is that if unemployment falls too low, below about 7% in the case of Canada, wages will increase too fast, driving up the rate of inflation. In both the early 1980s and early 1990s, the Bank of Canada raised interest rates very sharply to deliberately slow down the economy, fearing that inflation was rising or about to rise too fast because of low unemployment. Critics argue that central banks tend to move too fast, too soon, and that the deliberate use of unemployment to fight even low rates of inflation is very costly (Maclean and Osberg 1996).

A wider issue at stake is how to make sure that very low unemployment does not result in wage-driven inflation. Virtually all economists would agree that, over time, the growth of wages must reflect improved worker productivity or higher output per hour. Mainstream economists think that this will result if labour markets are highly flexible. They take a critical view of the role of unions, minimum wages, and government income supports for the unemployed, all of which are seen to be possible sources of wages that are too high and too rigid. Other economists argue that some countries with strong unions have been able to achieve low inflation and low unemployment, basically because businesses and unions are able to agree on the right level of wages. Chapter 12 details the success of some countries in achieving low unemployment while maintaining a strong floor of labour rights and standards.

The important point in the case of Canada is that our job market usually runs with a bit of deliberate slack, which is with an unemployment rate of at least 6%, and often with a lot more slack. At any given time, there are more workers looking for jobs than there are available jobs. This means that jobs are hard to find, particularly for workers whose skills and education are not in very high demand and for young people and new immigrants who lack Canadian job experience. The degree of slack in the job market is a huge influence upon employer investment in training for the unskilled, attention to the unrecognized skills and credentials of new immigrants, relative pay levels by skill, and employer willingness to balance demands of work and family. The very low unemployment rates reached in the U.S. after 1995 significantly reduced low pay and earnings inequality, as well as pay and opportunity gaps based upon race (Mishel et al. 2003), and there is no doubt that falling unemployment since the mid-1990s also had positive impacts in Canada. Still, as argued in Chapter 2, even when unemployment fell to 6%, there remained some significant degree of slack in most of the job market.

Economic and Industrial Restructuring

Capitalism thrives on what the famous economist Joseph Schumpeter called "creative destruction." The Canadian economy is always adapting to changing economic circumstances. Some sectors and regions expand, while others shrink. This means that many workers must change jobs, often having to move in search of new work, and it means that workers must often gain new qualifications and learn new skills. Constant change and flux is disruptive for people and communities, but it is often a good thing, contributing to economic growth and higher productivity. But, it is better if labour adjustment measures and income supports are in place to help workers adapt. Employment security—continued employment through a series of job changes—is a more realistic social goal than job security in the sense of holding a job for life.

Canada was highly dependent upon international markets long before anyone coined the term globalization. Our resource industries, the auto industry, and most of the manufacturing sector were driven by export markets long before the Canada–U.S. Free Trade Agreement (FTA), the North American Free Trade Agreement (NAFTA), and the huge recent increase in trade with developing countries, especially China. We have long imported a huge share of what we consume. Nonetheless, trade deals in North America and the global shift of manufacturing to developing countries have posed significant adjustment challenges, including the loss of many relatively good jobs in manufacturing. Some of the impacts are examined in Chapter 11. Our economy has also been restructured by the ongoing shift from goods production to services, and by technological and organizational changes in how both goods and services are produced. Chapter 4 looks at some of the implications of change in workplaces for employees, and Chapter 5 examines some of the differences between jobs of women and men that have been shaped by economic restructuring.

Over time, there have been major shifts in the structure of occupations, with some movement toward jobs requiring higher levels of formal education and skills. However, the new economy hype has glossed over the fact that change is not new, or even more rapid, and that many jobs still don't look terribly different from those of a generation ago. New occupations and new industries have certainly been produced by the information technology revolution and by growth in professional occupations. The share of all jobs in professional occupations has risen modestly from a bit under one in five in the 1980s to almost one in four today. (This includes: professional occupations in business and finance; jobs in the natural and applied sciences; professional occupations in health; teachers and professors; jobs in social sciences and government; and jobs in arts, culture, and recreation.) But, about four in 10 men still work in blue-collar manufacturing, utilities, and construction jobs, and almost one-third of women still work in pink-collar clerical, secretarial, and administrative jobs in offices. One in five men and almost one in three women works in sales and service occupations: mainly lower paid and often part-time jobs in stores, hotels, restaurants, and jobs as security guards, building cleaners, and so on. A low-wage, low-skill, private service sector is very much a feature of Canada's new economy, to a greater extent than in many European countries.

Education and Lifelong Learning

Almost everybody seems to agree that education and skills are at an increasing premium in today's knowledge-based economy. Many of the working poor lack the skills sought by employers, or, in the case of recent immigrants, their credentials and skills are unrecognized. People who leave the education system early face a high risk of being trapped in low-wage and insecure jobs. While the public education system is absolutely key, employees who face restructuring or who just want to gain the skills needed to climb job ladders need access to workplace training and lifelong learning. These issues are discussed in Chapter 3.

Unions and Labour Market Institutions

In Canada, about one in three employees is covered by union agreements, double the level in the U.S. Union coverage in the private sector has been slowly falling, but collective agreements still play a major role in shaping wages and other dimensions of employment of many workers. The role of Canadian unions is examined in Chapters 9 and 10.

All of the advanced industrial countries are, with small differences of degree, exposed to the big structural forces of technological change and globalization. But, they differ profoundly in terms of the ways in which the job market is regulated or shaped by governments, employers, and unions. In most of continental Europe, the wages and employment conditions of the great majority of workers are still set by collective bargaining between unions and employers, with some intervention by governments in the form of minimum wages and employment standards legislation. These labour market rules make a big difference to the distribution of earnings and to the quality of jobs (OECD 2006). For example, about one in four full-time workers in Canada is low paid—defined as earning less than two-thirds of the average national wage—compared to just one in 20 in Sweden, and only one in eight in Germany and the Netherlands. Differences in the distribution of earnings, in turn, have big impacts on level of income inequality and poverty between countries. In the United States, the top 10% of the population are more than five times better off than the bottom 10%, but in Sweden, the top 10% are less than three times better off than the bottom 10%.

It is commonly argued that more regulated job markets with stronger unions and better job and income protections come at the price of economic growth and job creation, resulting in major differences in the economic performance of North America and Europe. It is true that unemployment has been very high in some of the major European economies for much of the past 20 years, and this is a very serious problem. But some smaller European countries, such as the Netherlands and Denmark, recently have been able to achieve low unemployment along with higher job quality and more income equality than in North America. The main factors at play have included a strong tilt to job creation in social services rather than private services, high levels of training for unemployed and low-wage workers, and close partnerships between governments, employers, and unions. This experience, which may hold some lessons for Canadians, is discussed in the final chapter. It remains an open question whether a more regulated job market will survive tough economic times.

What Lies Ahead? Canada and the Global Economic Crisis

The rapid descent of the global economy in late 2008, into what even the International Monetary Fund has begun to call a Depression, will see very rapidly rising unemployment in Canada and around the world, likely to the double-digit levels not seen since the recession of the early 1990s. Given that it takes economic growth of about 2% per year to offset annual increases of about 1% in the working-age population and in productivity (output per hour worked), unemployment tends to rise rapidly in downturns, and to take a long period of time to fall even after an economic recovery begins.

This crisis is rooted in significant part in the deregulated or so-called flexible labour markets created by governments in thrall to neo-liberal economic doctrines and employer interests, and the negative impact of the downturn upon Canadian workers will be greatly worsened by the deregulation of labour markets, which has intensified since the last major downturn in the early 1990s. Moreover, the downturn is likely to be deep and long if the labour market is not re-regulated to a significant degree. In short, the economic crisis demands a fundamental and critical re-examination of the kind of labour market we have in Canada, which is analyzed in this book.

Box 1.3: "The Falling Stock of Workers"
By Rick Salutin

Blinding moments of insight often come in asides, parentheses or (among academics) footnotes; what seems overbold gets slipped past fast. This happened in a recent *Globe and Mail* column by Murray Campbell on the decline of Ontario's economy: "The long-term trend toward globalization" (here it comes, pay attention) "—seeking out lower-cost jurisdictions—." And it's gone. But he said it. All the glam theory and rhetoric on globalization and free trade came down to one thing: businesses taking work from here and shipping it to where people will do it more cheaply.

Notice that he doesn't even specify *what* the lower costs apply to in those "jurisdictions." It must be an economic factor that dare not speak its name. So I'll name it: workers. Labour. When workers appear in news about the current crisis, it's mostly as victims, collateral damage to impersonal forces like the economy, credit freezes or globalization.

What a comedown from the heyday of classical economics. All the greats, from Adam Smith to Marx, called *labour* the source of wealth and value. Workers were the core of the economic process, not vulnerable bystanders.

This is why the sad hallmark of this week's federal budget is its failure to restore the wasted employment insurance system for those out of work. It's the hallmark because of what it says about our attitudes toward the economy.

When unemployment insurance began, during the Depression of the 1930s, it was built on the idea of a right to work, like other basic rights, and not just a need to survive. Also on the dignity of work. UI was meant to tide the jobless through bad patches so that they needn't grab any shabby job offer that came along for the sake of survival. It reflected a sense of work as the heart of social and economic life, in a society where left-wing parties, ideologies, writers and, above all, unions, voiced this sense.

When UI became EI in 1996, what a difference. Workers were expected to take gratefully whatever came their way as jobs bled elsewhere; to "turn on a dime," as a government booklet said, because "change is good" and they were part of an exciting new globalized world in which industrial production was de-emphasized or shut down. EI was drastically cut back and restricted, to discipline them to this new reality. In fact, EI today remains *insurance*, bought and paid for by workers who can no longer access it readily, or amply. But many people seem to see it as an equivalent to welfare.

So the shift didn't just happen; it's part of a "globalization" strategy that involved destroying a culture built around productive work and reliable jobs in order to increase profits. On Monday, drug maker Pfizer spent $68-billion (U.S.) to buy Wyeth and simultaneously laid off 8,000 people. (The company has 1,400 employees in Canada.) Globalization is a good way to obscure not just the human debris but this new economic culture. What typifies it? The way that finance supplants goods. Fifty years ago, the finance sector provided 2 per cent of U.S. corporate profits; now it's 40 per cent. Comprehensible production of real stuff is replaced by illusory financial "products"—which works for a while, till it doesn't, like any illusion.

Nothing in this budget alters that pattern, including fiscal "stimulus." Once you strip an economy of its productivity, you can't restore it with infrastructure. What are you going to move on those repaved roads? Stuff imported from abroad? How will you pay for it? With more of the debt that created this mess?

The globalization model was never meant to build an actual global economy to serve people; it was a tawdry, short-sighted, long-winded scheme to increase profits by intimidating workers (and their unions), and replace a real economy with "devices" and "instruments." The point now isn't to inject money into our economy; it's to inject some *economy* back in it.

Source: Rick Salutin, "The Falling Stock of Workers," *Globe and Mail*, January 30, 2009, A11.

The immediate causes of the global economic crisis lie in the deregulation of finance, especially in the U.S. and the U.K., and a massive failure on the part of regulators to reign in rampant speculation and excessive risk-taking. As of early 2009, the International Monetary Fund estimated that total bad loans on the books of the global financial system flowing from the U.S. financial crisis stood at over $2 trillion—or $2,000 billion. Part of these toxic assets originated in the explosion of bank-lending to finance so-called subprime mortgages in the U.S.; that is, loans to high-risk borrowers. U.S. and U.K. banks also allowed many homeowners to use their houses as ATMs as a "housing bubble" developed out of cheap credit, further swelling the total volume of household debt to record levels.

The originators of high-risk debt, mainly the big investment banks, sliced and diced their loans into complex mortgage and credit card-backed securities, which were in turn sold to other investors, such as banks and hedge funds and pension funds, often with (supposed) guarantees against default. When the housing bubble burst in the U.S., the U.K., and other countries such as Ireland and Spain, the whole house of cards collapsed, leaving most large U.S., U.K., and European banks saddled with huge amounts of bad debt which pushed them into or to the brink of insolvency. Even worse, the use of complex financial derivatives, such as credit default swaps, meant that no one was sure just who in the closely connected global financial system was ultimately on the hook for the bad debt. As a result, in 2008, banks were reluctant to do business with each other, and tightened up greatly on new lending, choking off the economy from its needed oxygen of credit.

The financial crisis was a regulatory failure in the sense that governments generally stood by while financial institutions dealt themselves into insolvency by making highly risky loans, often financed by borrowing other people's money, and by spreading the risks through new financial products that virtually no one understood. (Luckily, here in Canada, the federal government resisted calls from financial players to allow banks to merge and to reduce barriers to the entry of foreign banks, which kept our financial system relatively safe even though unexciting to those who wanted to take similarly huge risks.) Many of the key players who fuelled the crisis, such as hedge funds, were not regulated at all, and more than a few were not so much reckless as out-and-out fraudulent. In the wake of the crisis, there have been many calls for and indeed even some action to tighten up regulatory controls and make sure that it never happens again. Unfortunately, financial crises caused by the unwinding of speculative bubbles seem to be an enduring feature of capitalist economies.

All that said, and as compelling as the story of the financial crisis is, the roots of the global economic crisis lie much deeper in the model of neo-liberal or deregulated global capitalism as it developed since the last recession. The financial system not only drove speculative booms in real estate and shares (as in the dot-com boom, which crashed in 2000), it generally failed to finance real productive investments in the advanced capitalist countries. In Canada, as in the U.S. and much of Europe, investment in productive capacity—new plants, machinery and equipment, and so on—lagged despite record high corporate profits. Instead, real investment mainly took place in developing countries, especially China and developing Asia.

One result of rapid Asian industrial development, described in Chapter 11, was the manufacturing job loss crisis and downward pressures on wages in the advanced industrial countries, including the U.S. and Canada. The profits of transnational corporations rose to record levels as did the incomes of the top 1% of the workforce, but the wages of the great majority of the workforce rose only because families worked longer hours. As detailed in Chapter 2, between 1992 and 2004, the incomes of the top 1% of earners rose by 60% in real or inflation-adjusted terms, while the median wage went up by only 9%. Household spending kept the economy growing, but this spending was driven by higher and higher levels of household debt (averaging 130% of family income by the end of the boom), rather than higher wages driven by higher productivity, driven in turn by new investments in the real economy.

Perversely, capital has flowed not from the rich countries to the poor countries, but from the poor countries to the rich countries, notably the U.S. The huge trade surplus of China with the U.S. was recycled into Chinese and other developing country central bank purchases of U.S. financial assets, keeping the lopsided relationship between the two countries going. Japan and, to a lesser extent, Germany benefited by selling enough sophisticated machinery and equipment and production inputs to the developing low-wage countries to keep their manufacturing trade roughly in balance, and the resource boom helped offset the crisis in Canadian manufacturing to some degree. Meanwhile, the U.S. ran a huge and continuing trade deficit of about 5% of its national income over the past decade, keeping the global economy going, but at the price of ever-rising national debt, much of it held by U.S. households.

So-called free trade and liberalization of investment flows, as noted, put downward pressures on the bargaining power of workers and of trade unions. (See chapters 9 and 10 on the role of unions and forces working against unions.) Adding to this, following the prescriptions of the Organisation for Economic Co-operation and Development Jobs Study of the early 1990s and most mainstream economists, many advanced country governments consciously tried to make their labour markets more flexible and less inflation prone by weakening the bargaining power of labour. Trade union rights came under attack. Once relatively insulated parts of the job market, such as public services and regulated industries, like the airlines and trucking, were opened up to lower wage competition through privatization and deregulation. Minimum wages were not increased in line with inflation. Income support programs, such as unemployment insurance, were scaled back, increasing the pressure on unemployed workers to take pay cuts to get a new job.

Here in Canada, the employment rate rose to very high levels in the economic expansion of the past decade, and unemployment fell to very low levels. However, the proportion of the workforce in the most insecure forms of employment remained steady at about one in five workers. (In 2007, 10% of men and 12% of women were in temporary jobs, and 12% of men and 8% of women were in the most insecure form of self-employment, so-called own-account jobs, which are often disguised jobs that offer no security and low pay.) The proportion of workers in low-wage jobs (one-quarter of adult women and one in 10 adult men) has remained virtually constant, at a level second only to the U.S. in the advanced industrial world. High levels of precarious employment and low pay—especially for women and racialized workers—explain why poverty has not fallen significantly in the supposed good times. Indeed, the proportion of adults who are in working poor families has risen. Despite low unemployment, many working Canadians were far from secure, even in the good times.

In late 2008, Canada entered a recession—more likely a Depression—not only with a higher proportion of precarious employed workers than in the 1980s, but also with much weaker private sector unions. Minimum wages were raised in some provinces at the end of the expansion period, but remain well below the level of the 1980s when adjusted for inflation. Social assistance benefits were slashed deeply in the 1990s in Ontario and Alberta, and have not been raised in line with inflation elsewhere. Social assistance benefits fall well below the poverty line for almost all family types in all provinces, and can usually only be accessed by exhausting almost all financial assets. And, unlike previous recessions, any increase in provincial social assistance caseloads will have to be paid for by provincial taxpayers, since federal shared cost-sharing was eliminated in 1994.

Box 1.4: Editorial by Raymond Torres, Director, International Institute for Labour Studies
From the International Labour Organization *World of Work Report*, 2008, Geneva

The financial crisis is hitting the world of work ...
The financial crisis which developed over the past year and erupted last August represents one of the most significant threats to the world economy in modern history. The credit crunch and collapse of stock markets are starting to affect firms' investment decisions as well as workers' incomes and jobs. Several major developed economies have practically entered into recession and unemployment is on the rise. Economic growth in emerging economies and developing countries has slowed down, in some cases significantly.

Ongoing attempts to overcome the financial crisis are of course welcome and, in principle, should help avoid another Great Depression. Important as rescue packages are, however, it is crucial to address the structural dimensions of the crisis as well. As this *World of Work Report* shows, the widening of income inequalities that occurred before the crisis is especially instructive in this respect.

... and happens in the face of income inequalities which are widening ...

While the costs of the financial rescue packages will be borne by all, the benefits of the earlier expansionary period were unevenly shared.

Between the early 1990s and the mid-2000s, in about two-thirds of the countries for which data exist, the total income of high income households expanded faster than was the case for their low income counterparts (Chapter 1). Similar trends have occurred when looking at other dimensions of income inequality, such as labour income vis-à-vis profits, or top wages vis-à-vis wages of low paid workers. In 51 out of the 73 countries for which data are available, the share of wages in total income declined over the past two decades. Likewise, during the same period, the income gap between the top and bottom 10% of wage earners increased in 70% of the countries for which data are available.

This was a period of relatively rapid economic growth and strong job creation. In 2007, world employment was almost one-third higher than in 1990. In short, the gains from the expansionary period which ended in 2007 benefited more high income groups than their medium and low income counterparts.

... at a pace which has probably been excessive

Wider income inequality can be helpful. It can signal stronger rewards to work effort, innovation, and skill development. This, in turn, will improve economic prospects for all, rich and poor. Conversely, an overly compressed income differential may affect job prospects—for instance because the labour market is not sufficiently attractive to would-be workers. Too little income inequality may also weaken the incentive to take risk or invest in human capital, thereby adversely affecting economic growth prospects.

However, there are instances where wider income inequality is both socially harmful and economically problematic.

There is evidence that social conflict grows when inequalities are perceived to be rising excessively. Social support for pro-growth policies will be eroded if low income groups and the middle class believe that such policies do little to improve their situation or that of their children, while benefiting high income groups. Surveys suggest a declining tolerance among respondents vis-à-vis growing inequality.

The report also shows that, prior to the financial crisis, there were already signs that observed trends in income inequality might not be sustainable. In the face of strong wage moderation, workers and their families became increasingly indebted in order to fund their housing investment decisions—and sometimes consumption decisions as well. This has sustained domestic demand and economic growth in some countries, and was made possible by financial innovations. However, the crisis has underlined the limits to this growth model.

It is therefore crucial for policymakers to ensure that income inequality does not rise excessively. At the same time, any action in this area should take into account the need for sustaining employment. But the report shows that it is possible to fulfil both employment and equity objectives...

... second, steep increases in executive pay de-linked from firm performance ...
Developments in global corporate governance have also contributed to perceptions of excessive income inequality. A key development has been the use of so-called "performance pay systems" for chief executive managers and directors.

The result has been a steep increase in executive pay. In the United States for example, between 2003 and 2007, executive managers' pay grew in real terms by a total of 45% compared with a real pay increase of 15% in the case of the average executive and less than 3% for the average American worker. Hence, by 2007, the average executive manager in the 15 largest U.S. firms earned more than 500 times the average employee in the United States compared with over 300 times in 2003. Similar patterns can be observed in other countries, such as Australia, Germany, Hong Kong (China), the Netherlands, and South Africa.

Importantly, empirical studies show only very moderate, if any, effects of these systems on company performance. Moreover, large country variations exist, with some countries displaying virtually no relation between performance-pay and company profits. Though more research is clearly needed in this area, a plausible explanation behind observed trends is that executives are in a dominant bargaining position with respect to company owners, something which is facilitated by the institutional set-up.

Altogether, evidence suggests that developments in executive pay may have been both inequality-enhancing and economically inefficient. This suggests a role for policy action. In this regard, several options are being considered at present, but it is too early to assess the pros and cons of each of them.

... third, institutional change and weaker redistribution policies
Domestic labour, social and tax policies, too, have contributed to observed outcomes. Labour institutions continue to play a redistributive role in the majority of countries under analysis, despite the decline in trade union density documented in Chapter 3. In particular, high trade union density, a more coordinated collective bargaining structure, and greater coverage of collective bargaining agreements tend to be associated with lower inequality. However, it is difficult for these institutions to counteract the global trends arising from globalization. Overall, the bargaining position of employees has weakened, even in countries where labour markets have been tight.

Another important factor has been the rising incidence of non-standard employment observed over the past 15 years or so in the majority of countries (Chapter 4). Indeed, non-standard jobs pay significantly less than their standard counterparts. More fundamentally, the changing employment patterns may have also contributed to weakening the bargaining position of workers, especially the low skilled.

Finally, taxation has become less progressive in the vast majority of countries and thus less able to redistribute the gains from economic growth. This reflects a cut in taxes on high incomes (Chapter 5). Between 1993 and 2007, the average corporate tax rate (for all countries for which data exist) was cut by 10 percentage points. In the case of top personal income tax rates, the cut was of three percentage points over the same period. Chapter 5 also shows that declining tax progressivity has generally not been offset by social policy.

Cutting taxes on high incomes or profits can be justified on economic efficiency grounds. They may even meet equity objectives in certain cases—the lifting-all-boats effect. However, there are other cases where such tax cuts produce sub-optimal results, even when considering efficiency-equity trade-offs. Likewise, stronger social protection, if well-designed, can serve employment objectives. The report gives examples of such policies among countries at different levels of economic development. The use of conditional cash benefits provides an interesting innovation in this respect.

It is therefore time to move ahead with the Decent Work Agenda

But evidence presented in this *World of Work Report* shows that if policymakers are concerned about excessive inequalities in their country while also sustaining employment, they have at their disposal an effective tool. Countries that do well in terms of both employment and inequality are characterised by relatively strong tripartite institutions, well-designed labour regulations and social protection, and respect for basic workers' rights (Chapter 6). Indeed, this is the essence of the Decent Work Agenda.

Moving ahead with the Agenda would help address the social consequences of the financial crisis. Together with a reform of the financial architecture, it would also contribute to achieve a more balanced, sustainable economy.

Source: Editorial by Raymond Torres, Director, International Institute for Labour Studies, from the International Labour Organization *World of Work Report*, 2008, Geneva.

The Employment Insurance system, the first line of defence for workers losing their jobs, was "reformed" in the mid-1990s. Maximum benefits in 2009 are $447 per week, down from more than $600 per week in today's dollars before the cuts. The average benefit is much less, just over $300 per week. Access to the system and the length of benefits vary on the basis of a complex grid based on the local area unemployment rate. Less than half of all unemployed workers—and just one-third of unemployed women—qualify for benefits. To get in, a worker has to have essentially worked six months at full-time hours in the recent past (the 910-hour hurdle that has to be jumped by new entrants to the workforce, such as youth, recent immigrants, and women returning to work after an extended leave), and as many as 710 hours in the period immediately before a claim. The entrance requirement disqualifies many precariously employed workers, including half of all part-timers. Once qualified, benefits last for as few as 19 weeks and as many as 50 weeks, with the maximum being generally applicable only to those who lost full-time permanent jobs in a higher unemployment region.

The key point is that Canada entered a period of high unemployment with many more insecurely employed workers than in previous recessions, with a weakened labour movement, and with a significantly reduced social safety net. The prospect is for the economic crisis to lead to a rapid increase in poverty and widespread economic insecurity. The prospect is also for workers to be forced into intense competition for the jobs that continue to exist, putting much more intense downward pressures on wages and working conditions.

There are economic and not just social dangers ahead. Economists rightly fear the prospect of deflation, an extended period of falling prices. Since interest rates cannot fall below zero, deflation can mean high real interest rates, reducing the willingness of households and businesses to borrow. And consumers will hold off spending on big-ticket items like cars if they know they can buy them for less in the future, particularly if they fear they may lose their jobs.

If and when wages start to fall, a country can enter a deflationary spiral. That is what happened in the Great Depression of the 1930s. Bank-lending and business investment came to a halt. Facing falling sales and falling prices, businesses tried to slash costs, including labour costs. The spiral came to an end only when governments began to invest, and only when the labour market found a floor. The fair wage legislation of the New Deal, plus the rise of industrial unions like the Autoworkers and Steelworkers, set the stage for the recovery. Ultimately, unions helped resolve the crisis by ensuring that wages would rise in line with productivity growth, driving consumer spending and then new business investment to meet higher demand.

As of early 2009, Canadian governments did not seem very concerned about the prospect of wage deflation. To the contrary, the federal Budget imposed a limit of just 1.5% on federal wage settlements, and government Ministers were calling on the CAW to cut auto sector wages. The common sense of much of the media was that workers should tighten their belts in a recession, and accept wage cuts if demanded by employers.

The federal Budget also failed to make significant improvements to the Employment Insurance system (beyond extending benefits by up to five weeks) and instead doubled the Working Income Tax Benefit which tops up very low earnings. This cushions the working poor against the impact of a downturn to some degree, but also allows employers to pay very low wages. Labour organizations have generally called for supplements to very low wages to be twinned to higher minimum wages.

In the context of a deep economic downturn, the focus has to be on stabilizing the job market by reversing a slide into mass unemployment, and also by setting a floor to the job market. This would be best done by raising minimum wages, dramatically improving access to EI benefits as well as the level and duration of benefits, and encouraging unionization, particularly among lower paid workers (as may yet happen under President Obama).

In short, the labour market issues raised in this book are highly relevant to understanding the unfolding economic crisis, in terms of causes, consequences, and solutions.

Conclusion

The quality of employment along a number of dimensions is critical to our individual and collective well-being. Yet, insufficient attention is usually paid to job quality issues. The quality of jobs is shaped by many forces, including the overall state of the economy and industrial restructuring. It is also strongly influenced by the role of governments and unions. Labour market issues lie at the heart of the global economic crisis that began in 2008, and hopefully this book will help spur critical thinking about the centrality of labour market institutions and policies to the well-being of Canadians.

Appendix: "How It All Began"
By Sinclair Stewart and Paul Waldie

Black Monday, Sept. 15, will be remembered by a generation as the day the great recession that is now strangling the global economy became inevitable. On that day, the U.S. government made the fateful decision to allow Lehman Bros. to fail. But the catastrophe unleashed by Lehman's collapse has far-reaching roots.

NEW YORK/TORONTO—Richard Fuld sat still in his chair and stared straight ahead, facing his interrogators with a clenched jaw and the occasional flash of defiance.

He had been summoned to Washington on this chilly October morning to answer for the demise of Lehman Bros., a storied Wall Street firm that under his 15-year watch had staged a remarkable revival—and suffered an equally breathtaking collapse.

At least that was the ostensible reason. But now, as one congressman after another took turns grilling him over his lavish pay, and juxtaposing this with the financial plight of ordinary homeowners, it became clear that he had been brought here to answer for something much larger: the role of Wall Street in sparking the biggest economic meltdown in more than 80 years, a crisis that threatened not only long-lasting hardship, but a loss of faith in the very free-market system that had fashioned the country into a superpower.

"If you haven't discovered your role, you are the villain today," chided John Mica, the Republican representative from Florida. "So you have got to act like the villain here."

Mr. Fuld had been carefully chosen for the part. With his example, the lawmakers could provide angry Americans with a simple explanation of what went wrong, of how the reckless pursuit of self-interest among brokerage executives, traders, hedge funds and other financial types had fuelled the subprime mortgage binge and incited the biggest economic catastrophe since the Great Depression.

The hearing was a crash course in how the financial system has evolved in the postwar era. It showed, through the prism of Lehman, how banks had moved away from traditional services, like making loans and underwriting securities, to complex and risky forms of financial engineering.

This proved to be a momentous shift in the capital markets, one that accelerated over the past decade to create what is known, ominously, as the "shadow banking system"—an unsupervised, $10-trillion (U.S.) financial playground whose size now rivals the traditional banking industry.

This was a world populated by arcane instruments like credit default swaps, special investment vehicles, and collateralized debt obligations. These instruments were spread through every corner of the financial world, and their web of interconnections was so intricate that no one—not their creators, and certainly not the investors who lapped them up in search of higher returnscould forecast the damage they might wreak if the system came under stress.

They were, as billionaire investor Warren Buffett vainly warned, "weapons of mass financial destruction."

Black Monday, the day in September that Lehman declared the biggest bankruptcy in history, will be remembered by a generation for sounding the death knell for this shadow system.

And thanks to Congress, which was looking to provide an enraged country with a healthy dose of catharsis, that same generation will likely remember Mr. Fuld as the face of Wall Street avarice and treachery—perhaps even as the face of the crisis.

This might have been good theatre, but it was a woefully incomplete explanation of how a U.S. housing problem mushroomed into a global calamity—of why countries like Iceland nearly collapsed; why chastened auto makers have trudged to Washington, hats-in-hands; why pension funds from Norway to Australia find themselves in the grip of massive deficits; of why the commodities markets have withered, stunting the growth of developing economies.

Wall Street may have created the financial architecture that abetted the crisis, but it was by no means a lone actor. Indeed, when one takes a closer look at Lehman's participation in the housing market, and how this market eventually infected whole economies, all sorts of troubling questions emerge: questions that Congress quickly glossed over in its excoriation of Mr. Fuld.

For instance, why were investment banks allowed to borrow massive amounts of money to make risky bets? How could a shadow banking system, one ten times bigger than the Canadian economy, be allowed to flourish so quickly without any oversight from government regulators? Why were credit rating agencies stamping dubious products with their approval? And how could homeowners with poor credit histories or zero documentation, let alone jobs, qualify for mortgages?

In its haste to hand Americans a villain, Washington had failed to look to itself.

Home ownership has always been the most tangible embodiment of the American Dream. From the start, landless immigrants were drawn by the opportunity to own property. Later, as the country evolved from an agrarian society into a more urban one, the purchase of a home remained the key expression of upward mobility.

But home ownership wasn't merely about the collective aspirations of ordinary Americans: It was also viewed by government as an agent of social improvement and cohesion. In the 1920s, President Herbert Hoover said families who owned their own homes provided "a more wholesome, healthful and happy atmosphere in which to bring up children." His successor, Franklin D. Roosevelt, avowed that "a nation of homeowners is unconquerable."

During the Depression, millions of Americans defaulted on their mortgages, and thousands of banks collapsed. Mr. Roosevelt responded in 1934 by creating the Federal Housing Administration, an agency that provided government insurance on long-term mortgages and regulated their interest rates. These longer-amortization mortgages helped to ease down-payment amounts and made it easier for people to keep up with their monthly mortgage tabs.

The president also introduced what became known as Fannie Mae, a government agency that purchased the now federally insured mortgages from banks and other financial lenders, allowing them to issue more loans. Within the span of a couple of years, Washington had become the key player in several aspects of the mortgage market, and before long it was promising "a decent home and a suitable living environment for every American family."

The result wasn't merely an increase in home ownership levels, but a shift in expectations. With government making it an explicit policy goal, home ownership became less about aspiration and more about entitlement—regardless of whether people had the means to pay for a house or not.

It wasn't long before popular culture reflected this sentiment. Who can forget George Bailey, Jimmy Stewart's character in the 1946 film *It's a Wonderful Life*, upbraiding the slumlord Mr. Potter, who wanted to scrap home loans for the poor?

This dream of home ownership took root in the postwar years, and ownership levels rose steadily, buoyed in large part by the flowering of suburbs across the country. By the late 1970s, however, this policy of enfranchisement via property hit a snag.

In 1977, President Jimmy Carter moved to make housing more affordable by requiring banks to lend in low-income neighbourhoods. But before the decade was out, the scheme was stymied by record-high interest rates, courtesy of an inflation-fighting Federal Reserve Board.

Savings and loans institutions (or "thrifts"), which accounted for more than half of all mortgage lending, faced limits on the amount of interest they could charge on mortgages, as did conventional banks. When the Federal Reserve rate shot up to 10.3 per cent in 1979, almost double what it had been three years earlier, many lenders found themselves in a pinch. In some states, market interest rates were higher than the ceiling on mortgage rates, meaning banks and savings and loans institutions would actually lose money when they offered a loan. So in many cases they didn't.

The roadblock inspired a pair of policy responses that would ultimately lay the foundation for the ascendancy of subprime mortgages.

Congress responded first with the Depository Institutions Deregulation and Monetary Control Act, a sweeping piece of legislation passed in 1980. The most far-reaching part of the act concerned mortgages: DIDMCA would scrap state usury limits on mortgages, allowing lenders to charge whatever they wanted. Moreover, the act would wipe out these rate limits for any company—regardless of whether it accepted deposits—that lent more than $1-million a year.

"This ... is the statute that ultimately set the stage for the subprime home equity lending industry of today," Cathy Lesser Mansfield, a professor at Drake University, wrote in her 2000 examination of usury deregulation. There was virtually no discussion in Congress, she noted, of what sort of predatory lending tactics might take hold if mortgage rate ceilings were eliminated.

DIDMCA on its own didn't revive slumping house sales. With interest rates so high, and the country tipping into recession, fewer Americans were enticed to borrow. Once again, a desperate Congress sought to revive the market with deregulation. In 1982, shortly after Ronald Reagan came to power with his laissez-faire convictions, the U.S. government moved again, introducing the Alternative Mortgage Transaction Parity Act.

Congress noted that the rate environment was making it difficult for consumers to get long-term, fixed-rate mortgages, so it further loosened the rules, allowing lenders to promote a hodge-podge of "alternative" mortgage features. These included adjustable-rate mortgages, "negative amortization" loans (whereby borrowers don't pay off the principal), and "balloon" mortgages (which oblige borrowers to make a large payment at the end of the loan's maturity in exchange for lower monthly charges).

These "alternative" mortgages figure prominently in the current crisis, either through predatory lending, or poor risk controls, or hidden punitive charges that tipped people into foreclosure. Taken together, these two legislative overhauls opened the door wide for small consumer finance companies to pile into the mortgage business and begin peddling exotic, high-interest loans. Several of these upstart companies were already busy at work, waiting for just such a break.

Brian Chisick was always a salesman. Born in London, England, he moved to Vancouver with his parents at age 14, but dropped out of Kitsilano Secondary School after Grade 10 to start making money. Tanned and fit, with a jutting jaw and barrel chest, he turned his hand to peddling a variety of products.

By the late 1960s, Mr. Chisick and his wife, Sarah, had landed in Los Angeles, right in the middle of the postwar housing boom. They soon found something new to flog—loans.

Demand for loans was high, but regulations were tight and banks weren't interested in lending to people who didn't have a solid credit background.

Mr. Chisick gravitated to "hard money" lending: second mortgages and loans to people turned down by banks. Rates were slightly higher and the loans were secured by "hard" assets, such as cars or furniture.

After learning the ropes at a variety of hard-money outfits, in the late 1970s, Mr. Chisick and his wife co-founded First Alliance Corp.

His timing was perfect. The changes introduced by presidents Carter and Reagan in the early 1980s allowed Mr. Chisick to charge higher rates, and then use these to tempt investors into buying the loans he issued.

His pitch was a simple version of what he and other mortgage originators would later turn into the engine of the subprime machine. Investors would get the monthly payments from borrowers, whose loans carried a higher interest rate than bank mortgages. Mr. Chisick took the money from the resale of the loans, plus a fee, and then made more loans.

Finding borrowers wasn't hard. Mr. Chisick put dozens of ads in small papers and mailed out stacks of flyers. Finding investors proved more difficult. Mr. Chisick bought lists of potential investors, and then called them one by one to pitch the benefits of buying a loan.

Within a few years, First Alliance had half a dozen loan officers and a dozen investment counsellors—small-time, low-ranking salesmen. Later, as First Alliance and other originators grew, the salesman role would be assumed by high-powered Wall Street investment bankers, at Lehman and other blue-chip firms.

Mr. Chisick's model was so clever and that it wasn't long before others around Orange County began to take note. They helped start nearly a dozen subprime lenders, including eventual giants Option One Mortgage Co., New Century Financial Corp. and Ameriquest Mortgage Co. Over in another Los Angeles suburb, Countrywide Financial Corp. was launched.

But for the regulators that would later do battle with many of those companies, Mr. Chisick remains the godfather to the subprime lending world.

"We always say [the Chisicks] were the start of it all," says Chuck Cross, former director of the consumer services office in Washington state. "They were the first of the big bad predatory lenders. In many ways they were much worse than some of the big ones like Ameriquest to come along in subsequent years."

Mr. Chisick secured notoriety with regulators because of the savvy marketing techniques that he perfected. He also displayed an early knack for getting firms such as Prudential Securities and Lehman to help bankroll him.

To target borrowers, Mr. Chisick developed a profile of the most likely First Alliance customer: middle-class, preferably white, in his or her late 50s. The best candidates had been in their homes at least 10 years, and had built up about 30 per cent equity in their property. But most crucially, these people had other consumer loans or had fallen behind on tax payments and were therefore viewed as unattractive risks, or subprime borrowers, in the eyes of traditional lenders.

Mr. Chisick believed these borrowers would be the most receptive to his brand of high-priced second mortgages and loans. And if they ran into trouble, First Alliance would get a property with substantial equity.

Mr. Chisick spent up to $20-million annually to locate people who fit this profile. By the late 1980s, the company was sending 1.9 million pieces of mail every month to neighbourhoods carefully targeted from local tax records, real estate databases and credit records. He even bought lists of people who were delinquent on their taxes. "We would call them to see if we could give them some money," he said in a deposition in 2002.

A month's worth of mailings generated about 2,500 inquiries, which were fielded by a team of telemarketers. All promising prospects were referred to First Alliance's loan officers, who typically generated about 270 loans from each monthly mailing, according to documents filed in court.

The loan officers were the linchpin of the operation. Most were former car salesmen, well schooled in slick pitches. Each officer had to memorize a script, called the Track Manual, that outlined a 13-step presentation that was made to potential borrowers. To make sure they got it right, Mr. Chisick put new recruits through four weeks of videotaped rehearsals and role-playing with other officers.

The objective of the Track was to obfuscate the fees and terms of a First Alliance loan. For example, according to court filings, step 8 in the Track—dubbed "The Monster"—"tells the loan originator to divert the consumers' attention from the loan transaction that they are about to sign onto."

One judge later said the presentation "was so well performed that borrowers had no idea they were being charged points and other fees and costs averaging 11 per cent above the amount they thought they had agreed to borrow."

While most banks were lucky to make $4,000 in fees on a $100,000 loan, First Alliance pocketed as much as $20,000, according to state regulators.

By selling these second mortgages—essentially refinancings—Mr. Chisick had turned government policy on its head. He wasn't putting more people in homes, but encouraging homeowners who were already deemed at-risk by traditional lenders to take on additional debt.

This wasn't all that easy to do amid a depressed economy and soaring interest rates. But once again, luck intervened for Mr. Chisick in the form of Washington lawmakers. Until 1986, Americans could deduct interest payments on most types of consumer loans. But under President Reagan, the government wanted to simplify taxation and eliminate a range of shelters. Interest deductibility was no longer allowed, unless—and this was a big exception—it was the interest consumers were paying on their first or second homes.

Not surprisingly, people began to use their homes as piggybanks. Why take out a separate loan when you could borrow against your house, and be able to write off your interest payments?

Calculations by Ms. Mansfield of Drake University show that home equity loans grew from "virtually nothing" in 1983 to "about $40-billion" by the end of 1986, while second mortgage indebtedness more than doubled to a record high of about $150-billion in 1986. And by 1988, a scant two years after the tax code was changed, 68 per cent of home equity loans were used to fund things other than home improvements, compared with just 35 per cent in 1984, according to another study.

As companies like Mr. Chisick's grew exponentially thanks to the regulatory changes made during the 1980s, Wall Street reacted by devising new and more complicated ways to help them sell their loans to investors.

The most crucial innovation was the privately issued mortgage-backed security. In the old days of banking, a lender would issue a mortgage, and then hold it on its books until the loan was paid off. But now Wall Street saw a way to generate ever more lending revenue—it could pool these mortgages, turn them into tradable securities, and sell them to large investors.

Banks, thrifts, and mortgage originators like Mr. Chisick, meanwhile, could create a lending assembly line: By selling off their loans, they continually freed up room to issue more of them.

Securitization in itself was not a new phenomenon. Fannie Mae and Freddie Mac, the two quasi-governmental mortgage giants, had securitized mortgages and sold them to investors, but there was a big difference: These were mortgages backstopped by the U.S. government, thus viewed as safe for conservative investors such as life insurance companies, investment managers and pension funds.

In the mid-1980s, credit rating agencies began to rate the emerging, primitive form of mortgage-backed securities. This imprimatur encouraged large investors to begin dipping a toe in the market. Between 1984 and 1988, the percentage of home mortgages that were securitized jumped from 23 per cent to 52 per cent.

As the demand for these securities grew, lenders in turn sought more and more people to put in homes, a dangerous spiral that would inevitably force them to scavenge for loans among borrowers with dubious credit quality—the type Mr. Chisick's company targeted.

Suddenly, mortgage finance companies like First Alliance demonstrated massive growth. Regulatory sea-shifts had allowed them to waltz into the housing market and charge whatever they wanted for mortgages. The interest-deductibility change effectively turned homes into automated teller machines, and companies like First Alliance were only too happy to step up with the money for refinancing—again, at rates of their choice.

And Wall Street's securitization engine, though still in its infancy, began pumping out mortgage securities so quickly that lenders were scrambling to write more new mortgages to keep up with investors' demand.

In 1977, these little consumer finance companies owned a mere 0.5 per cent of the home equity loan market. But by the end of the 1980s, they had 32 per cent.

The Chisicks became multimillionaires. They bought a 5,000-square-foot mansion in Anaheim and had a $2-million house in Los Angeles and a condo in Hawaii. They became active in the Jewish community and made big donations, including one that put the Chisick name on a local auditorium.

Indeed, the real estate grab was so lucrative that pretty much everyone—brokers, lenders, investors and rating agencies—increasingly turned a blind eye to the risks. And why not? If banks were no longer holding onto these mortgages, and brokers were simply finding them for a fee, what did they care if borrowers eventually found themselves unable to pay the bills?

Although home ownership was reaching record levels, the government's series of rule changes had unwittingly charted a dangerous new course—one that, in the recent testimony of a former high-ranking mortgage executive, would transform the dream of owning a home into a nightmare of foreclosure.

Source: Sinclair Stewart and Paul Waldie, "How It All Began," *Globe and Mail*, December 19, 2008.

Recommended Reading

- Brisbois, Richard. 2004. "How Canada Stacks up: The Quality of Work: An International Perspective." Canadian Policy Research Networks (www.cprn.org). This paper compares workplaces in Canada, the U.S., and the member nations of the European Union in terms of four dimensions of job quality: work-life balance, health and well-being, skills development, and career and employment security. An additional indicator on overall satisfaction with working conditions is presented separately.
- Canadian Labour Congress. "Is Your Work Working for You?" This is an annually updated report on some key quality of work indicators (www.working4you.ca).
- Green, Francis. 2006. *Demanding Work: The Paradox of Job Quality in the Affluent Economy*. Princeton and Oxford: Princeton University Press. This book draws on extensive worker surveys as well as labour market data to chart trends in the quality of work and jobs, highlighting in particular the trend to work intensification.

- Lowe, Graham S. 2000. *The Quality of Work: A People Centred Agenda*. Toronto: Oxford University Press. As director of the Work Network at the Canadian Policy Research Networks, Canadian sociologist Graham Lowe was active in promoting a policy agenda for higher quality jobs, and quantitative indicators of job quality. Chapter 3 of this book summarizes evidence on what Canadians want from work, and Chapter 1 provides a broad overview and reflection on the future of work.
- Raphael, Dennis. 2007. *Poverty and Policy in Canada*. Toronto: Canadian Scholars' Press. This book provides a unique, interdisciplinary perspective on poverty and its importance to the health and quality of life of Canadians. Central issues include the definitions of poverty and means of measuring it in wealthy, industrialized nations such as Canada; the causes of poverty — both situational and societal; the health and social implications of poverty for individuals, communities, and society as a whole; and means of addressing its incidence and mitigating its effects.
- Shalla, Vivian. 2006. *Working in a Global Era: Canadian Perspectives*. Toronto: Canadian Scholars' Press. Divided into eight key parts with a total of 16 readings, this volume covers a great deal of ground: Fordist and post-Fordist methods of work organization; labour markets in transition; working in the Free Trade zones; migration, transnationalism, and domestic work; neo-liberalism and the dismantling of the welfare state; education, training, and skills in a knowledge-based economy; and the labour movement in transition. All major issues surrounding work in Canada are covered.
- Shalla, Vivian, and Wallace Clement (Eds.). 2007. *Work in Tumultuous Times: Critical Perspectives*. Montreal and Kingston: McGill-Queen's University Press. A wide-ranging set of essays that covers many aspects of today's labour market and workplaces from a critical, mainly sociological, perspective.

References

Clark, Andrew. 1999. *What Makes a Good Job?* Paris: Organisation for Economic Co-operation and Development (OECD).

Green, Francis. 2006. *Demanding Work: The Paradox of Job Quality in the Affluent Economy*. Princeton and Oxford: Princeton University Press.

Jencks, C., L. Perman, and L. Rainwater. 1998. "What Is a Good Job? A New Measure of Labor Market Success." *American Journal of Sociology* 93 (May): 1322–1357.

Maclean, Brian, and Lars Osberg (Eds.). 1996. *The Unemployment Crisis: All for Nought?* Montreal and Kingston: McGill-Queen's University Press.

Mishel, Larry, Jared Bernstein, and Heather Boushey. 2003. *The State of Working America 2002–03*. Washington: Economic Policy Institute and M.E. Sharpe.

Organisation for Economic Co-operation and Development (OECD). 2006. "Boosting Jobs and Incomes." *OECD Employment Outlook*.

Shalla, Vivian. 2007. "Theoretical Reflections on Work: A Quarter Century of Critical Thinking." In *Work in Tumultuous Times: Critical Perspectives*, ed. Vivian Shalla and Wallace Clement. Montreal and Kingston: McGill-Queen's University Press.

CHAPTER 2

Work, Wages, and the Living Standards of Canadian Working People

Introduction

This chapter surveys some of the most important developments in the Canadian job market and in the quality of jobs, particularly over the long period of economic growth from the mid-1990s through 2007. It looks at trends in wages and in the kinds of jobs that have been created, highlighting the significance and persistence of precarious (insecure and low-paid) forms of employment in a time of supposed prosperity, the stagnation of real (inflation-adjusted) earnings, and the sharp rise in earnings and income inequality among workers and working-age families. Links are drawn from how the job market works to rising income inequality and continued high levels of poverty.

Jobs, Jobs, Jobs: Trends in Employment and Unemployment

By some measures, Canada has done much better on the jobs front for the past 15 years than was the case over the 1980s and early 1990s. There were two major economic downturns, one in the early 1980s, and one in the early 1990s. The national unemployment rate peaked at 12% in 1983 and at 11.4% in 1993, and the periods 1982 through 1985, and 1991 through 1994, were all years of double-digit unemployment. Unemployment in the 1980s never fell below 7.5%. By contrast, the national unemployment rate fell steadily in the economic recovery, which began around 1993, to 6% in 2007, and the employment rate (the proportion of the population aged 15–64 holding jobs) has steadily increased. In fact, the national unemployment rate of 6% reached in 2007 was the lowest since the 1960s, and the national employment rate was at an all time high of 63.5%.

Table 2.1 provides some detailed data on changes in employment and unemployment rates over the past decade, 1997–2007. The national unemployment rate has fallen from 9.1%, to 6%, falling by about one-third for both women and men, and by slightly less for younger workers. (Chapters 5, 7, and 8 provide a detailed look at trends by gender and age.) Sustained economic growth has driven the national employment rate; the percentage of the working-age population aged 15–64 holding jobs is up very sharply, from 58.9% in 1997, to 63.5% in 2007. This is well above the previous peak of 62.2% reached in 1989, just before the recession of the early 1990s. The record high employment rate reflects a continuing increase in the employment rate of women—from 52.6% in 1997, to a record high of 59.1% in 2007. The employment rate for men rose, from 65.5% to 68%, 1997–2007, but was still below the peak of 73.1% in 1979, and 70.9% in 1988. This mainly reflects a trend to earlier retirement for men compared to the 1970s and 1980s, though, as shown, the proportion of persons aged 55 and over who are working has risen considerably over the past decade, from 22.5% in 1997, to a record high of 31.7% in 2007. The proportion of the Canadian population with jobs is now one of the highest in the advanced industrial world. Unemployment could and should be considered to be too high at 6%, but this still represents a very major step forward compared to the high unemployment levels of the mid-1970s through the mid-1990s. The rate of long-term unemployment is also very low, with the average length of a period of unemployment being about 20 weeks in 2007.

The major improvement in the availability of jobs has been shared by virtually all parts of the country. In 2007, the employment rate hit record highs in all provinces with the single exception of Ontario, where the employment rate has slipped slightly since 2003, as a result of major job losses in manufacturing and the forest industry, and is up only modestly from the 1997 level. The unemployment rate has fallen by at or near a third from 1997 levels to 2007 in almost all provinces, with the exception of New Brunswick, and particularly large declines were recorded in British Columbia and Alberta. While the picture has generally been one of an improving job market across the country over the past decade, significant regional differences remained very much in evidence in 2007. The employment rate stood at a national high of 71.5% in Alberta, well above the low of 51.2% in Newfoundland and Labrador. Much of Atlantic Canada experienced significant job gains and declines in unemployment

Table 2.1: Employment and Unemployment Trends over the Past Decade (percentage)

	1997	2007
Unemployment rate		
All	9.1	6.0
Men	9.3	6.4
Women	8.9	5.6
Age 15–24	16.2	11.2
Age 25–54	7.8	5.1
Age 55+	6.9	4.8
Newfoundland and Labrador	18.4	13.6
Prince Edward Island	15.4	10.3
Nova Scotia	12.2	8.0
New Brunswick	12.7	11.8
Quebec	11.4	7.2
Ontario	8.4	6.4
Manitoba	6.5	4.4
Saskatchewan	6.0	4.2
Alberta	5.9	3.5
British Columbia	8.4	4.2
Employment rate		
All	58.9	63.5
Men	65.5	68.0
Women	52.6	59.1
Age 15–24	51.5	59.5
Age 25–54	77.3	82.2
Age 55+	22.5	31.7
Newfoundland and Labrador	42.9	51.2
Prince Edward Island	55.9	61.2
Nova Scotia	52.5	58.6
New Brunswick	52.1	59.2
Quebec	55.0	61.0
Ontario	60.2	63.6
Manitoba	62.3	66.4
Saskatchewan	62.2	66.8
Alberta	67.8	71.5
British Columbia	60.0	63.5

Source: Statistics Canada Cat. 71F0004XCB. *Labour Force Historical Review.* 2007.

from 1997 to 2007, but the gap between the East and the very low unemployment provinces of the West remained evident. It is also notable that Quebec's job market performed much better than that of Ontario from 1997 to 2007, though Quebec still has a higher than average unemployment rate. Generally speaking, the incidence of low pay is also greatest in the higher unemployment provinces.

Another positive trend is that employment has increased somewhat faster than average in relatively highly skilled occupations. As detailed in Chapter 5, there was a modest shift to professional occupations in the decade 1996–2006, particularly among women, and a corresponding slight decline in the proportion of clerical jobs. However, the proportion of generally low-wage and often insecure sales and services jobs has remained almost constant, at 29% for women and 19% for men, and the proportion of men in blue-collar jobs has also remained almost constant at about one in three. The majority of women and men thus continue to work in blue-collar, clerical, and sales and service jobs, which generally require only modest levels of education, and generally do not lead to job ladders where earnings rise significantly over time.

Box 2.1: The *Labour Force Survey*

Every month, Statistics Canada releases the results of the *Labour Force Survey* based upon a large-scale survey of households. Results of the most recent release are available from www.statcan.gc.ca in *The Daily*. Each report provides up-to-date information on participation, employment, and unemployment for men and women and different age groups for Canada and the provinces, as well as changes in employment by industry. A comprehensive view of changes in the job market over long periods of time can be gained from the annual *Labour Force Historical Review*, released on a CD-ROM. The *Labour Force Survey* also provides data (since 1997) on hourly and weekly wages, and on unionization.

As defined by the *Labour Force Survey*, being unemployed means that a person is not working at all, and is actively seeking work. The headline unemployment rate is lower than alternative measures that count people who have recently worked but have given up looking for a job (known as discouraged workers), and count the lost hours of people working part-time who want to work full-time, but can't get the hours that they want.

Unemployment is generally a bit higher for men than for women. This reflects the fact that proportionately more men work in very seasonal industries, such as construction, and industries subject to frequent layoffs, like manufacturing. The rate of long-term unemployment is, overall, quite low, but highest among older men displaced by industrial restructuring. But, women are much more likely than men to be working involuntarily in part-time jobs, unable to find the hours of work that they want. The biggest gap in unemployment rates is between younger and older workers.

While unemployment in most of Canada has fallen very significantly, it has to be borne in mind that the average duration of an unemployment spell is fairly short, and that many workers cycle in and out of jobs over the year. Low unemployment is not the same thing as stable employment. Unemployment is experienced by a higher proportion of the total workforce over an entire year than the apparently low average monthly unemployment rate suggests. In recent years, about one in eight workers has been unemployed at least once in the year. Despite low unemployment and eligibility provisions that limit access to Employment Insurance (EI) to those who have worked a significant number of hours over the previous year, 1.3 million claims for regular EI benefits were still filed in 2005–2006, and about one-quarter of all regular EI claims are made by so-called frequent claimants (HRSDC 2006). Many workers, particularly younger workers and those working in seasonal industries, are in short-term jobs. About one in six full-time workers, aged 25–54 in 2007, had been in their current jobs for less than one year. In short, even excluding young people who may want short-term jobs, there is a lot of movement in and out of employment and unemployment in any given year. Moreover, a lot of jobs fail to offer very stable hours, and there is a lot of variation in annual hours worked by individuals from year to year.

Box 2.2: Is Canada Facing Acute Labour and Skills Shortages?

Starting from about 2003, falling unemployment, and very low unemployment levels in a few provinces, prompted complaints from many employers that Canada was facing a dire shortage of workers, especially skilled workers. This led to a major expansion of the Temporary Foreign Worker program, under which employers can bring migrant workers to Canada through temporary work permits. But the 10-year outlook for the Canadian labour market, released in 2006 by Human Resources and Social Development Canada, did not justify the alarmist view that Canada faces a serious shortage of workers, as opposed to a shortage of good jobs (HRSDC 2006b).

The report concluded that "no widespread labour shortages are expected to emerge over the next ten years," mainly because the Bank of Canada is expected to ensure that labour demand does not outstrip supply (p. 1). It is expected that there will be some shortages of skilled workers at a detailed occupational level, but no generalized problem, and no generalized shortage of lower skilled workers despite the pending retirement of many baby boomers. In fact, the report anticipated that the entry of large numbers of highly educated young Canadians and immigrants into the workforce will be more than sufficient to meet our needs for highly skilled workers. There is forecast to be a 1.6% annual growth to 2015 in the number of jobs requiring a university degree, which will be more than matched by a 2.2% annual growth in the number of workers with university qualifications.

The historical section of the report noted that, in recent years, "the strong rise in demand within high-skilled occupations has been adequately met by a rising supply of qualified workers. Real wages by broad skills level relative to the economy-wide average have been fairly constant since 1997 [suggesting] the absence of significant imbalances between the skills demanded by employers and the availability of qualified labour" (p. 4).

The report found that there has been some increase in the unemployment rate of university-educated workers compared to those with lower qualifications, and some

slippage in their relative earnings in recent years. "An increasing proportion of individuals with post-secondary education can be found in low-skilled occupations ... the
proportion of university-educated individuals in low skilled occupations [rose], from
12% in 1990, to about 17% in 2005, providing some evidence that there may be an
over-supply of university graduates" (p. 27).

The report undertook an evaluation of skills shortages at a detailed occupational
level in 2003–2005, using a methodology developed by the U.S. Bureau of Labor
Statistics, which looks at three factors within an occupation: employment growth,
the unemployment rate, and wage growth. To be considered an "occupation under
pressure," employment growth must be at least 50% greater than average; the unemployment rate must be at or near historically low levels, and wage growth must be at
least 30% greater than average.

Using this methodology, it was estimated that just 32 occupations representing
11.4% of overall employment in 2005 were showing signs of labour shortages. Almost
all of these occupations required post-secondary or apprenticeship training, and most
were in professional health and management occupations. Nine occupations, all low-
skilled, were found to be in a situation of excess supply of labour, with rising relative
unemployment rates, job losses, and falling wages.

The positive overall Canadian job picture of recent years is marred by some
very serious flaws. Most notably, working families have increased their incomes
mainly by continuing to work more weeks in the year as unemployment has fallen,
as opposed to increases in their real wages, and they have gone deeper into debt.
Most of the wage and wealth gains in a period of economic expansion have gone
to those at the very top of the earnings spectrum, rather than to the average worker
and average working family. The top 1% or so have pulled away from the rest of
the workforce. While jobs have been relatively easy to find in many regions of the
country, many workers still have very unstable and low-paid jobs, and the overall
quality of jobs in terms of forms of employment has not been improving. Canada has
relatively few workers who are unemployed for very long stretches of time, but we
have a significant proportion of workers who are regularly employed in a series of
low-wage and precarious jobs, and survive on low hourly and annual earnings. As
detailed in chapters 5 to 8, but not considered here in any detail, large inequalities
in the job market continue to exist between women and men, and between younger
and older workers, and have grown very sharply between recent immigrants and
racialized minorities, and other Canadians. The level of income inequality among
Canadian families and our rates of poverty are disturbingly high, particularly if we
compare ourselves to European countries rather than to the U.S. (Smeeding 2002).
Not only has earnings inequality significantly increased, re-distributive economic
transfers from government have been cut, and economic security and access to public
and social services have also been undermined by government policy changes. In
short, the labour market and jobs still fall far short of meeting the needs of many
working people.

Good Jobs, Bad Jobs—Forms of Employment

Compared to some Western European countries, Canada has long had a job market in which a high proportion of workers are employed in precarious jobs—that is, in jobs that are either insecure and/or low paid. Good jobs are often considered to be jobs that are full-time and permanent, involving an ongoing and stable relationship between a worker and a single employer (Vosko et al. 2003). While somewhat over-stated in that Canada has always had a layer of self-employed workers and a large seasonal workforce, the norm in the 1960s and 1970s was certainly that of full-time, permanent employment among men. Such jobs, whether held by men or by women, are often referred to as standard jobs as opposed to non-standard jobs, defined as those that are part-time, temporary, or come in the form of self-employment. As shown in Table 2.2, about two in every three Canadian male workers and 60% of Canadian female workers in 2007 were employed in full-time, permanent jobs, and one in three men and an even higher proportion of women were employed in more precarious jobs. While some part-time jobs are permanent and reasonably secure and well-paid, about one in five men and a bit more than one in 10 women are self-employed, and another 10% of men and 12% of women are temporary employees. Both of these forms of employment are generally not just more insecure, but also lower paid than permanent paid jobs.

Table 2.2: Trends in Forms of Employment (as percentage of total employment by gender)

	Men		Women	
	1997	**2007**	**1997**	**2007**
Employees				
Full-time permanent	65.4	65.4	57.6	60.2
Part-time permanent	5.5	5.5	19.0	16.4
Full-time temporary	6.2	6.8	5.1	6.3
Part-time temporary	2.6	3.2	5.0	5.7
Self-employed				
Employers	8.3	7.1	3.2	2.8
Own-account	11.9	12.0	9.3	8.4

Source: Statistics Canada. *Labour Force Survey.* 2007. Microdata extract.

The decline of standard, full-time, permanent jobs compared to the 1960s and 1970s has been closely associated with the entry of women into the workforce. As detailed in Chapter 5, women are much more likely to work part-time than men, partly out of choice, and partly because they find it harder to find full-time jobs. About one-third of adult women who work part-time say that they would prefer to work full-time, and this proportion would likely be higher if child care and elder care were more widely available and expanded their choices in balancing work and family. At the same time, part-time jobs allow employers to vary hours of work in line with changing business conditions, which might not at all match worker preferences. Many part-timers don't have much control of the hours that they work, and frequently work at nights and on weekends. The shift to temporary jobs has also been driven more by employers' increased desire to have a more flexible workforce, which can be increased or decreased in size on short notice, than by workers' desires for very short-term jobs. Similarly, increased self-employment can partly be explained by the desire of larger companies and governments to contract out work to outside suppliers of goods and, especially, services in order to reduce their costs.

The distinction between standard and non-standard jobs is not always one between good jobs and bad jobs. Entry-level, temporary, and part-time jobs for youth can be a good source of job experience. Many people, particularly students and some parents, want to work part-time. A layer of self-employed professionals and skilled workers—doctors, lawyers, accountants, architects, building contractors, artists, and so on—do very well. But, part-time and temporary jobs, on average, pay significantly less than comparable full-time jobs, are much less likely to provide health and pension benefits, and offer much more limited access to progressive career ladders. Most temporary workers other than students would rather have permanent jobs. And, a layer of self-employed workers—the so-called own-account self-employed who work by themselves and have no employees—tend to have very low annual earnings (Vosko 2006).

Ongoing restructuring in both the private and public sectors, driven by globalization, technological and organizational change, contracting out, and government spending cuts, has underpinned increased labour market segmentation. At one pole, we see a high level of insecure and/or low-paid precarious work among youth and young adults, recent immigrants, Aboriginal Canadians, persons with disabilities, and a layer of adults with limited education or in-demand skills. Women are more likely to be in precarious jobs than men, but the jobs of many men have become increasingly like the jobs traditionally held by women. Precarious work can be permanent, full-time employment that is low paid and/or frequently interrupted by unemployment; employment in temporary jobs; underemployment in involuntary part-time jobs, or employment in low-income, own-account self-employment. Precarious work also carries a high risk of not being developmental; not leading to the development of skills and capacities that increase workers' ability to access better jobs or to start and proceed on lifetime career ladders, and to better handle labour market risks, such as permanent layoffs due to economic change. Job experience and on-the-job training are sources of human capital that enable workers to make upward progression in the job market and better deal with economic uncertainty. Many low-wage and short-term jobs are traps rather than stepping stones to better jobs. Almost by definition, precarious workers are excluded from the internal labour markets of large companies and government organizations where the norm is for permanent workers to climb job ladders through promotion from within. Research shows that there was a significant widening of longer term or life-cycle earnings differentials and life chances in the 1990s, particularly among men (Beach et al. 2003). Being trapped in a low-wage job usually also means being unable to derive some meaning and fulfillment from work. Workers value jobs not only for purely economic reasons, but also to the extent that they provide interesting work and opportunities for self-development.

At the other end of the job spectrum, core jobs—reasonably secure, full-time, full-year jobs in larger workplaces—generally require higher levels of education and skills (particularly when routinized work can be contracted out to small firms employing peripheral workers). These jobs often involve the use of skills and discretion on the job, and provide access to lifetime career ladders. For professionals and skilled workers, work reorganization and new technology can produce more interesting and developmental jobs. But, there was also a lot of old-fashioned work intensification in the 1990s in the form of greater demands and longer hours. Surveys indicate high and rising levels of stress from very long hours, demands to do more with less in the wake of downsizing, the intrusion of paid work into the home, and reduced ability to balance the demands of paid work with those of family and community. Some of these issues are explored in Chapter 4.

Looking in more detail at the kinds of jobs held by Canadians, there was a significant shift to more precarious forms of employment in the recession and slow recovery of the 1990s, which has since only modestly reversed itself in a stronger job market. The recession of the early 1990s saw the loss of many permanent, full-time jobs, particularly for men in manufacturing. As the unemployment rate rose, the employment rate fell, and the proportion of part-timers, temporary workers, and self-employed increased. As the economic recovery gathered steam after 1993, job creation began to shift back to full-time jobs. The part-time rate (or the proportion of workers in part-time jobs) rose sharply from 1989 to the mid-1990s, but job growth has been mainly tilted to full-time jobs since that time. The part-time rate has fallen significantly for adult women, while remaining high for young workers. The proportion of own-account self-employed workers also increased in a slack job market, from 7.2% in 1989, to 9.8% in 2003, as did the proportion of temporary workers, which rose from 7% to 11% of the workforce (Vosko et al. 2003).

As shown in Table 2.2, the proportion of workers in the most precarious forms of employment has remained high over the past decade, 1997–2007. At one level, it is good news that the decline in the quality of jobs has stabilized. At another level, it is surprising that temporary work has actually further increased slightly, from 8.8% to 9% among men, and from 10.1% to 12% among women, since 1997. Temporary work has become entrenched as the norm for the entry of young workers into the full-time job market (Morissette and Johnson 2005). The proportion of own-account self-employed has remained about the same for men, while falling a bit among women. The proportion of all men who are in the most precarious forms of employment—temporary jobs and own-account self-employed—stood at a combined 22% in 2007, while the proportion of women in such jobs stood at 20%. Notwithstanding what was widely seen as a very strong job market, about one in five workers were thus in forms of employment that offered little security, and usually much lower pay and benefits than permanent paid jobs. Had there been serious and widespread labour and skills shortages, one would have expected employers to convert contract jobs to permanent jobs, but this has not been the case.

The Rising Corporate Share

From the mid-1990s, the Canadian economy grew quite rapidly and real (that is, inflation-adjusted) GDP (national income) per person rose by a cumulative total of 27% from 1996 to 2006. However, income in the hands of households failed to grow at anywhere near the same pace. Real personal income—the total of all before-tax wage, investment, small business, and government transfer income going to households, adjusted for increases in consumer prices—rose by only 17% over the same period. One reason for the shrinkage in households' share of national income has been that corporate pre-tax profits have grown rapidly as a share of the total economic pie. Labour's share of total national income (after taxes) has been on a declining trend ever since the late 1970s, while the corporate profit share has been trending upwards over the same period, and hit record highs almost every year after the recovery from the recession of the early 1990s.

While wages and household income used to rise more or less in lockstep with productivity growth—the rise in real business sector output per hour worked, which drives the rise in per-person national income—real wages have basically flatlined for much of the past 25 years, as detailed below. While returns from investments have boosted the incomes of very affluent households, wage stagnation in an expanding economy has meant that working family living standards have essentially stagnated despite reasonably strong economic growth (Russell and Dufour 2007). Reasonable people can differ about the right level of corporate profits, which are very important as a source of funds for private investment in the economy, and thus for creating more and better jobs. But, it is clear that the balance of bargaining power in the economy has tilted over time against Canadian workers. The same trend has been seen in most other advanced industrial countries since the late 1980s, and probably reflects the impacts of greater international trade and investment links with the rest of the world, which are explored in Chapter 11. Companies are generally free to shift investment and jobs to countries where profitability is higher, and this is certainly a factor when it comes to setting wages.

Stagnant Real Wages

A major study by Statistics Canada on changes in the structure of hourly wages between 1981 and 2004 found that most workers experienced very modest gains in their real (inflation-adjusted) wages over that extended period (Morissette and Johnson 2005). In fact, over this time period, the median male worker—one in the exact middle of the male earnings spectrum such that half earn more and half less—experienced a 2% fall in his real hourly wage. In other words, in 2004, the hourly wage of a median male worker was slightly less than that of a median male worker back in 1981. (Individual workers usually still see an increase in their own earnings over periods of their working lives as they enter the workforce and gain experience, but the normal path of real earnings for most men is no higher than a generation ago.) Over the same period, the median female worker experienced a real wage gain of 10.7%. While certainly doing better than men, a 10.7% cumulative real wage gain over 23 years is hardly a cause for celebration. This study further found that real wages had stagnated most in manufacturing (the sector that is the most heavily exposed to international competitive forces) and in the public sector, and had risen a bit more than average in high-skilled private service industries.

Looking at wage trends in the most recent decade, from 1997 to 2007, another Statistics Canada study found that there had been much higher real wage growth at the very high end of the wage distribution, that is, among very high income earners (Morissette 2008). Real wage gains were greatest for managers, professionals in business and finance, and computer and information system professionals over the entire decade, and averaged just 4.6% over the whole decade for employees in the private sector who were not managers, and even lower for public sector workers. The picture was a bit different in booming Western Canada. As noted in later chapters, stagnating real wages for most workers have been matched by cuts in benefits coverage, and by an erosion of the union wage and benefit advantage.

Table 2.3 provides data on real wage gains (in 2007 dollars) from 1997 to 2007, which averaged 5.9% over the entire decade. But higher paid employees, such as senior managers and professionals in business and finance, experienced much larger gains, while real wages were essentially flat for non-professionals, including blue-collar, clerical, and sales and service workers. Average real hourly wages began to increase a bit faster at the end of this period as unemployment fell to quite a low level, but averages can be misleading. Real wage gains have been very limited for the bottom 80% or so of Canadian workers despite a low unemployment rate and supposed labour and skills shortages. Wage gains have been a bit higher for ordinary workers in booming parts of the country, but even here it has to be taken into account that inflation, driven up above all by soaring housing costs, is also greatest in the provinces with the lowest unemployment rates.

Rising Wage Inequality—The Top Takes Off

Recent research has shown that Canada, like the U.S. and the U.K., has seen a very marked increase in the proportion of all income and, especially, wages going to very top income earners, such as senior corporate executives (Saez and Veall 2003). Between 1990 and 2000, the share of all income reported on annual income tax returns by the top 10% of individual Canadian taxpayers rose from 35.5% to 42.3% of the total. The top 10% in 2000 were those making more than $59,000 per year. Even within this top group, it was the very top that made the biggest gains. The top 1% of taxpayers increased their share of all income reported on tax return forms from 9.3% to 13.6% between 1990 and 2000. The average income of this elite group in 2000 was $171,728. The share of the top 1% was even higher in the 1920s and 1930s. It fell sharply in the 1940s, reaching a low of 7.5% in the mid to late 1970s, and began to rise again from the mid-1980s.

Murphy, Roberts, and Wolfson (2007) of Statistics Canada tracked the taxable incomes (i.e., earnings and investment income) of individual Canadians from 1992

Table 2.3: Change in Real Average Hourly Wage, 1997–2007 (constant 2007 dollars)

	1997	2007	Increase $	Increase %
All	19.28	20.41	1.13	5.9%
Men	21.13	22.17	1.04	4.9%
Women	17.24	18.62	1.38	8.0%
Age 15–24	10.50	11.14	0.64	6.1%
Full-time	20.45	21.73	1.28	6.3%
Part-time	14.08	14.33	0.25	1.7%
Selected occupations:				
Senior managers	34.25	38.92	4.67	13.6%
Professional occupations in business and finance	24.93	29.16	4.23	17.0%
Professional occupations in health	26.49	29.75	3.26	12.3%
Trades, transport, and equipment operators	19.71	20.38	0.67	3.4%
Machine operators/assemblers	18.03	18.37	0.34	1.9%
Clerical	16.62	17.10	0.48	2.9%
Sales and service	13.37	13.65	0.28	2.1%

Source: Statistics Canada Cat. 71F0004XCB. *Labour Force Historical Review.* 2007.

to 2004, and found that the share of the top 1% rose from 8.6% to 12.2% of all income, and that the real incomes of the top 1% grew by over 60% over this period, while stagnating for the bottom 40%, and barely increasing for the bottom 80%. The gains of the top 1% were, in turn, driven by very high income gains among the very, very affluent, such as the top one-tenth of 1% who earned an average of over $1.6 million (see Table 2.4).

In Canada, as in the U.S., rising wage inequality is partly explained by changes in labour market institutions. As stressed by noted U.S. economist and *New York Times* columnist Paul Krugman (2007), the "Great Compression" of wages from the 1940s through the mid-1970s was closely associated with the growth in the

Table 2.4: Level and Distribution of Individual Before-Tax Income

	1992	2004	Income gain	% Gain
Level ($ thousands, in 2004 dollars)				
Top 0.01%	$2,547	$5,920	$3,373	132.4%
Top 0.1%	$822	$1,641	$819	99.6%
Top 1%	$268	$429	$161	60.1%
Top 10%	$100	$128	$28	28.0%
Top 20%	$77	$93	$16	20.8%
60% to 80%	$37	$40	$3	8.1%
40% to 60%	$23	$25	$2	8.7%
20% to 40%	$14	$14	$0	0.0%
Bottom 20%	$5	$5	$0	0.0%
Income share				
Top 0.01%	0.8	1.7		
Top 0.1%	2.6	4.7		
Top 1%	8.6	12.2		
Top 10%	32.1	36.3		
80% to 90%	17.3	16.7		
50% to 80%	32.4	30.5		
Bottom 50%	18.2	16.5		

Source: Murphy, Brian, Paul Roberts, and Michael Wolfson. "A Profile of High Income Canadians, 1982 to 2004." Statistics Canada Cat. 75F0002MIE, No. 006, 2007

numbers and bargaining power of unions, and relatively high minimum wages and other worker-friendly legislation, which flowed from governments that were responsive to the demands and interests of labour. Changes in the economy and in politics have since placed labour, including unions, on the defensive. The most common explanation offered by economists for rising inequality—increased returns to skills due to globalization and new technologies—does not really explain why even the wages of highly educated workers are lagging well behind those at the very top.

A significant part of the increased share of very top income earners is likely explained by the very rapid growth of compensation of senior corporate executives, especially Chief Executive Officers (CEOs). Bebchuk and Grinstein (2007) found that the pay of the top five senior executives in U.S. public companies doubled from 5% to 10% of total company earnings from 1993 to 2003, driven mainly by the huge increase in low-priced stock options granted to senior managers. Here in Canada, the top 100 CEOs had average incomes of $8,528,304 in 2006, 218 times as much as the average worker who worked full-time for the full year. That is up from 104 times as much in 1998. Between 1998 and 2008, top CEO pay rose by 146% compared to 18% for all full-time, full-year workers and today CEOs earn about as much in one day as an average worker does in a year (Mackenzie 2007). Senior corporate executives have done very well, in part because they exercise a great deal of control over their own compensation, and their rising share cannot be justified by improved corporate performance (Bebchuk and Grinstein 2007; Gordon and Dew-Becker 2007). In the business world, there have also been huge increases of income among top bankers and investment professionals, such as those who run private equity funds and hedge funds.

The rising share of very high income earners in Canada in recent years is also probably explained, in part, by increased economic integration. Senior Canadian corporate executives, very highly educated, in-demand professionals in business and finance, law, medicine, and so on, and the sports stars and entertainers who top the earnings spectrum, can often move to the U.S. where the income share of the top 1% is the highest in the advanced industrial world. Saez and Veall (2003), and a report on trends in income inequality for the recent Report of the World Commission on the Social Dimension of Globalization (ILO), show that the share of the top 1% in national income varies a lot between countries, and has changed the most in the U.S., the U.K., and Canada. Leading British economist Tony Atkinson speculates that the high-income share is less driven by globalization, technological change, and big structural factors than by changes in norms and values. Once large income gaps emerge and become slowly accepted, a tipping point is reached, and very high incomes rapidly start to grow away from the rest.

Wealth and Debt

Parallel with the sharp increase in earnings and income inequality, wealth has become even more concentrated in the hands of the very rich (Morissette and Zhang 2006). Household assets consist mainly of financial assets (worth about one-half of all household assets) and housing, while about three-quarters of all debt consists of mortgage debt. Wealth is defined as assets minus debt, and is much more unequally distributed than income. In 2005, the richest 10% of Canadian households owned 58.2% of wealth, and had median assets of $1.2 million, reflecting the fact that ownership of financial assets in particular is highly concentrated in relatively few hands. The bottom 40% of households owned essentially no net wealth. The extreme concentration of wealth is somewhat less skewed if one takes into account that older households generally have more assets than younger ones, and if pension assets are taken into account. Still, it is clear that wealth is very unequally shared and has become significantly more concentrated.

The wealth share of the top 10% of households rose, from 51.8% in 1984, to 55.7% in 1999, to 58.2% in 2005 (the three years in which Statistics Canada conducted surveys). Within the top 10%, the share of the top 1% rose even faster, from 7.6% of all wealth in 1984, to 9.1% in 1999, to 9.6% in 2005. Between 1999 and 2005, the wealth of the bottom 40% stagnated or fell in dollar terms, and almost all of the increase in household wealth took place among the top 40%, especially the top 10%.

A study by the Vanier Institute of the Family (Sauve 2007) shows that household spending has been rising at a significantly faster rate than household income ever since 1990. Personal debt has jumped from 91% to 131% of personal after-tax income. Most of that is accounted for by increased mortgage debt. Canada's personal savings rate has steadily declined, from 10% in 1990, to just 1% in 2006, and some 100,000 households declare insolvency each year. It would seem that plenty of post-boomer households have taken on a lot of debt and increased their consumption by borrowing. High and rising levels of debt among ordinary working families represent the flip side of the increased concentration of income and wealth in the hands of the very affluent.

Low Pay

The Organisation for Economic Co-operation and Development (OECD) defines low pay as earning less than two-thirds of the national median hourly wage, which translates into making less than $12 per hour in Canada in 2007. As shown in Chapter 12, Canada stands out among advanced industrial countries in terms of having a high proportion of low-paid workers, and only the U.S. has a higher proportion of low-paid workers. What this tells us is that there is a significant group of Canadian workers who are paid well below the national norm. In recent years, about one in four Canadian workers has been low-paid by this definition, with the overall inci-dence of low pay standing at 27.2% in the first nine months of 2007 (Customized data from the *Labour Force Survey* supplied by Statistics Canada). The incidence of low wages is, not too surprisingly, very high among young workers aged 15–24 (70.4%) compared to workers aged 25–54 (17.6%). Among core-age workers aged 25–54, the inci-dence of low pay is much higher among women (24.4%) than men (11.4%). The incidence of low pay has changed little over time, meaning that a period of economic recovery has not brought up the wages of workers at the bottom compared to those in the middle of the earnings spectrum as one might have expected as unemployment fell (Morissette 2008). The incidence of low pay is, again unsurprisingly, much higher among clerical, sales, service, and labouring occupations where average pay is itself low, and generally quite low in occupations outside these clusters. The high incidence of low-paid work in North America helps explain why rates of poverty among the working-age population and after-tax income inequality are also much higher than in most European countries (Smeeding 2002). It is hard to maintain some rough equality of family incomes after taxes and transfers if there are large and growing earnings gaps among workers.

Growing Income Inequality among Families

As individual earnings inequality has increased, so has income inequality among working-age families. The period 1994–2004 saw a marked increase in inequality of earnings among families with children. Table 2.5 shows changes in earnings and in after-tax incomes for such families, ranked by decile, each representing 10% of the total. The share of all earnings of such families going to the top decile (the top 10%) rose from 26% to 30%, at the expense of the bottom 90% of families. By 2004, almost half of all the earnings of families with children were going to the top 20%, while the bottom 80% had to share the other half. This translates into major differences of opportunity between children based on the earnings of their parents.

Table 2.5: Changing Before- and After-Tax Income Shares of Families with Children, by Decile

	Earnings			After-tax income		
	1994	2004	Change	1994	2004	Change
Decile						
1	0.04	0.37	0.33	2.72	2.54	−0.18
2	2	2.34	0.34	4.76	4.38	−0.38
3	4.6	4.14	−0.46	6.32	5.65	−0.67
4	6.63	5.93	−0.70	7.59	6.87	−0.72
5	8.34	7.6	−0.74	8.73	8.10	−0.63
6	10.02	9.23	−0.79	9.85	9.37	−0.48
7	11.78	10.96	−0.82	11.09	10.7	−0.39
8	13.8	13.06	−0.74	12.63	12.4	−0.23
9	16.83	16.18	−0.65	14.84	14.88	0.04
10	25.96	30.2	4.24	21.46	25.12	3.66

Source: Yalnizyan, Armine. 2007. *The Rich and the Rest of Us.* Canadian Centre for Policy Alternatives.

How do we explain rising market income inequality among families? This is partly driven by changes in the way in which people form families. The rise of single-parent families from the 1980s meant that more families with children became dependent on just one person's earnings, usually those of the mother. Another change has been that higher income men and higher income women are more likely to live with each other than in the past. High-income men once often lived with spouses who worked at home or just on a part-time basis, but the norm is now for high-income female and male professionals and managers to live with each other. This compounds the impact of individual earnings inequality on inequality among families.

Box 2.3: "Fairness under Siege"
By Michael Valpy
When the University of British Columbia's David Green looks at just-released census data showing widening inequality in incomes, he sees a society on a path that he believes most Canadians don't want to take.

The award-winning economist, who has spent his academic lifetime analyzing wage structures around the world, said in an interview yesterday: "I think if you ask most

Canadians about fairness in their society, it's a value we hold dearly, and I think if we don't [address income inequality] we're moving away from it."

What Prof. Green and other economists underscore is that widening income inequality and the decline in the earnings of immigrants and young men is a product of profound economic and political change and not some transitory glitch that will be fixed once fat-cat baby boomers retire.

The census data show incomes at the bottom falling, in the middle level stagnant, and at the top breaking away from the pack.

Statistics Canada senior analyst René Morissette attributes the phenomenon to at least four factors: the decline of unionized jobs; the growing competition among employers to reduce expenses, including labour costs; changes in technology that have eliminated jobs, and what Mr. Morissette delicately calls shifts in trade patterns and employment markets, meaning the availability of offshore labour.

"But there are more than just those factors," he said. "And while it may be a boring answer, the truth is we don't really know what's causing it."

Just as Statistics Canada doesn't know precisely why most of the decline in young men's earnings took place from 1981 to 1986—other than that there was a change in how wages were set.

But what does seem clear is that there is unlikely to be some automatic labour market correction when baby boomers begin retiring.

Mr. Morissette pointed out that at one period during the past 25 years when young adult labour was scarce, its relative importance to the labour market still dropped substantially, with incomes for young men declining and for young women stagnating.

Theoretically, there will be another scarcity of young adult workers as the baby boomers retire. But that doesn't mean, that they'll suddenly be considered economically valuable. Moreover, no one can predict what the baby boomers will do, but one possibility is that they won't retire, but instead will come back on contracts, further weakening long-term work commitments.

Critics of Statistics Canada's Big Stagnation presentation earlier this week—the unveiling of data showing the median earnings for full-time Canadian workers had increased by just $53 between 1980 and 2005—argue that if family incomes rather than individual incomes are examined, the picture is rosier.

Which is true, in a way. Median family income rose to $68,341 in 2005 from $57,334 in 1980, an increase of 19.2 per cent.

But that is almost entirely due to increased full-time participation of women in the work force. When family incomes are broken down for gender, they show that the median income for males dropped to $44,150 from $46,652, while for females it rose to $20,025 from $3,633 (the figure reflects labour force participation as well as earnings).

Eventually, said Mr. Morissette, there will be a ceiling to women's participation rate. At which point, what will happen to family incomes?

As for the widening gap between rich and poor, Prof. Green said it was actually narrowing slightly until 1995, when governments began cutting income-support transfers to the poor and introducing tax cuts that favoured the well-off.

> Up until 1995, he said, Canadians seemed willing to accept the bargain of using tax-and-transfers to offset the growing inequality of market wages "but somehow along the line, that political will was lost."
>
> Source: Valpy, Michael. "Fairness under Siege," *Globe and Mail*, May 3, 2008, A7.

The main reason for rising inequality between families is increased inequality in the job market itself. Two big factors are at play. Families down the income scale are more likely to be made up of people in lower paid jobs, and they are less likely to be working full-time hours for the whole year if they are in temporary or own-account jobs. Families at the top end of the income scale now usually combine two well-paid, permanent jobs.

The way in which family income is distributed also reflects the impact of government action. Transfer payments from governments, such as child tax credits, Employment Insurance benefits, and social assistance benefits, go disproportionately to middle and lower income working-age families, while high-income individuals pay a higher proportion of their income in income taxes due to a progressive rate structure. As of 2007, the top federal tax rate was 29%, almost double the bottom rate of 16%. As shown in the second column of Table 2.5, family income after taxes and transfers is somewhat more equally distributed than earnings. In 2004, the top 10% of families with children received 30% of earnings, but 25% of after-tax income. The bottom 40% of families got about 20% of all after-tax income, much more than their share of earnings.

That said, the change in the distribution of after-tax family income between 1994 and 2004 was not very different from the change in the distribution of earnings. In other words, taxes and transfer payments have continued to offset earnings inequality, but they have not significantly blunted the big increase in income differences between the very top and the middle and the bottom. A similar conclusion was reached in a major Statistics Canada study by Heisz (2007). Looking at all households (not just working-age families) and carefully adjusting income figures for the size and composition of families, he found that between 1984 and 2004, the incomes of the top 20% of families after taxes and transfers rose, from 4.87 times as much as the bottom 20%, to 5.31 times as much. The incomes of the top 10% jumped, from 7.86 times as much as those of the bottom 10%, to 8.85 times as much. He found that the increase in market income inequality (that is, income from earnings and investments) was translated into after-tax and transfer income inequality. Taxes and transfers still make a big difference to income gaps, but the difference is not as large as it once was.

Box 2.4: Does Income Inequality Matter?
Some people argue that we should worry about poverty rather than income inequality, that we should not worry if some people have more than others so long as everyone gets the essentials of life. But, it is hard to argue that people don't care about their relative income, that is, where they sit along the income spectrum compared to others.

Consider the following thought experiments. Would you be happier with a job paying $10 per hour in a workplace where other people in the same job were paid $15 per hour, or with a job paying $9.50 per hour in a workplace where everybody gets the same wage? Would you be happier moving to the U.S. for a slightly higher income, even if you fell much lower down on the overall income ladder as a result? Would you be happier living in a neighbourhood of people at your level of income, or in a somewhat bigger house in a neighbourhood of large luxury homes owned by people making a lot more than you? The fact that people care about where they stand relative to others has led economists to link rising inequality to increased unhappiness and stress. One outcome is greatly increased hours of work and increased debt, as people spend more than they can really afford to match the lifestyles of those higher up on the income ladder.

It is hard to believe that there can be genuine equality of opportunity for individuals—something that most people think is a good thing—if there are very large differences in the economic circumstances of families. The life chances of a person are strongly determined by the family circumstances into which he or she is born in high-inequality countries. Thus, the chances of a person from a lower income family climbing the income ladder are lower in the U.S. than in Canada, and much lower in Canada than in Sweden (Fortin and Lefebvre 1998).

Research has shown that individual life expectancy and health are closely linked to relative and not just absolute income. It is not just that poor people are less healthy than people with average incomes; people in the middle of the income spectrum are also less healthy than those at the top. This seems to be mainly because of the adverse health impacts of high stress flowing from acute differences in status and power (Wilkinson 2005). In relatively equal countries like Sweden, the differences in life expectancy, health, literacy, education, and other key indicators of well-being between different sections of the population are much narrower than those in Canada, and gaps in Canada are narrower than in the U.S.

It is also often argued that earnings inequality is the necessary price we pay for providing incentives to work and to effort. No one argues that all jobs should pay the same. It is reasonable to pay people more if they take on extra responsibilities, or put in extra effort. But, it is far from clear that pay really reflects the demands of a job. Does a manager really have a more demanding and difficult job than a worker on an assembly line or in a high-volume call centre? And, how big should pay gaps be? Do senior corporate executives really need to make as much in a day as the average worker does in a year? It is striking that gaps between higher and lower paid workers vary a great deal between countries, and that high-equality countries like Sweden do not necessarily do worse in terms of economic growth and job creation than do high-inequality countries like the U.S. and Canada.

Perhaps most importantly, extreme polarization of income and wealth undermines the values of democratic citizenship. One might think that re-distributive government programs would be most developed where earnings inequality is high and many people have low-paid jobs, but in fact, they are least developed in high-inequality countries. Economic elites tend to wield political power as well, and to use the power of government to defend their own interests.

While economic growth has been quite strong and raised earnings from work as unemployment fell, the positive impact on the incomes of many working-age households was significantly offset by cuts to government social programs. These cuts were made partly to balance government budgets, but also to counter supposed rigidities and disincentives to work by increasing worker dependence on wages and jobs. Seniors' benefits were largely unaffected by policy changes, but government transfers to working-age households—mainly Employment Insurance and social assistance benefits—fell sharply. Both EI and welfare benefits fell in dollar terms because of falling unemployment, which is a good thing, but the cuts to EI benefits brought about through new legislation in the mid-1990s raised the number of hours of work needed to qualify for benefits, with a big negative impact on part-time and some seasonal workers. Also, the EI replacement rate (the proportion of insured earnings replaced by EI benefits) was cut from 60% to 55%, and the maximum benefit was frozen for a decade, cutting it in real terms by over 25%. From the early to mid-1990s, most provinces either froze or cut social assistance (welfare) benefits. In other words, even as many jobs continued to offer quite insecure hours and fluctuating earnings, and even as the incidence of low-wage work remained high, income supports for working families impacted by lost earnings were cut back quite seriously. By the late 1990s, this pattern reversed to a modest degree as child benefits, tilted to middle and lower income working families, were raised, and as a few provinces and finally the government began to increase some modest income benefits for the working poor (Novick 2007).

The Working Poor

Poverty can be defined in many ways, but the most usual measure in Canada is by using Statistics Canada Low Income Cut-Offs, which vary by the size of a family and the size of the community in which they live. Low income is basically defined as having to spend a much higher than average share of household income on food and shelter. The cut-off line in 2006 for a single person in a big city was $21,381 before tax and $17,568 after tax. For a two-person family, it rose to $21,202 and $26,396 respectively (Statistics Canada Cat. 75-202X. *Income in Canada*. 2006).

As shown in Table 2.6, the low-income rate (after tax) increased sharply between 1989 and 1996, the years of recession and slow recovery, and has since generally fallen back to/at/or near 1989 levels, at a bit above 10% for all Canadians. It is not at all surprising that the poverty rate should have fallen in a period of strong economic and job growth, as many persons and families found more hours and weeks of work over a year and moved from social assistance to paid work. What is more surprising is that a stronger job market in terms of high employment and low unemployment compared to the late 1980s has not reduced the poverty rate below 1989 levels. In fact, the poverty rate has fallen quite significantly for lone-parent families with children headed by women, and has fallen slightly for all children, perhaps reflecting modest increases in child benefits. But the poverty rate has increased for single men and women under age 65, to 31% and 37% respectively, and has increased among working-age persons, while falling very significantly among those over age 65.

Table 2.6: Percentage of Persons Living in Low Income

	(LICO-AT, 1992 base)		
	1989	1996	2006
All	10.2	15.7	10.5
Children	11.7	18.5	11.3
Age 18–64	9.4	15.7	11.3
Age 65+	11.3	9.8	5.4
Unattached under age 65:			
Men	25.0	38.2	31.2
Women	34.1	46.8	37.1
Female lone-parent families	46.1	55.8	32.3

Source: Statistics Canada. CANSIM 202-0802. Accessed 2007.

High rates of poverty among single, working-age people show how hard it is for people at the bottom end of the job market to get enough income from earnings. Low earnings are now by far the most significant factor in explaining poverty among working-age households. Families living on social assistance have incomes well below the poverty line, but, as Campaign 2000 has underlined in its annual Report Card on child poverty in Canada, the majority of poor children now live in working-poor families, and more than 40% live in families where at least one person is working full-time for the full year. A study by Human Resources and Social Development Canada (Fleury and Fortin 2004) notes that many people in low-wage jobs are not poor because they are cushioned from poverty by other earners in the family. But they still find that there were almost one million persons who had significant hours of work in 2001 and lived in low income. These working-poor adults made up almost 6% of the total workforce, and they had almost one million dependants.

Individuals and families move in and out of poverty for two main reasons. Changes in families due to the breakdown or establishment of relationships are important, especially for women with children who often fall into poverty after a divorce. The second major factor is the quality of jobs. A significant proportion of working families cycle in and out of poverty depending upon how many weeks of work they get in a year, and at what wage. The working poor tend to move from welfare to work, and back from work to welfare after a job ends, perhaps after a period of using up savings and drawing support from Employment Insurance. In round numbers, a single person had to be working more or less full-time in a full-year job and earning about $11 per hour to escape poverty in 2006. The threshold is obviously higher if a single earner has to support a child or a non-working spouse.

Minimum wages in 2003 were far too low in all provinces to put working families with even full-time jobs above the poverty line (Battle 2003), though they have since modestly increased in some provinces. Detailed calculations by the National Council of Welfare (2003) showed that even low-wage (below two-thirds of the median), full-time, full-year jobs, supplemented by government income supports, put most families in larger cities only very modestly above poverty lines. But, as noted above, among core-age workers aged 25–54, about one in 10 men and more than one in five women are in low-wage jobs, and two out of three young people (many of whom have left home) are in low-wage jobs. The chances of being out of work at sometime in the year are also high for low-wage workers in temporary and seasonal jobs, many of whom will fail to qualify for EI benefits during periods of no work due to insufficient qualifying hours. Low-wage workers also have difficulty accessing EI because many combine periods of paid (EI-insured) work with periods of own-account (uninsured) self-employment.

Most adult low-paid workers (particularly women and those with low levels of education) remain low paid, sometimes moving a bit above the poverty line, and sometimes falling below depending upon the state of the economy and their luck in finding a steady job. At least half of all adult low-wage workers seem to be more or less permanently trapped in low-wage jobs that would keep them barely above the poverty line (Beach et al. 2003; Drolet and Morissette 1998; Finnie 2000; Janz 2004). Vulnerability to poverty among adult low-wage workers is particularly great for single adults and single parents who must rely on one income and one wage, as opposed to two-person families, which can usually combine two wages. Vulnerability is also much greater than average for recent immigrants and racialized minorities, who tend to have low earnings despite higher-than-average levels of education and larger-than-average families to support.

Conclusion

Jobs clearly matter a lot to the well-being of Canadians. The record of the economic recovery since the mid-1990s has been good in many ways. The proportion of Canadians with jobs is at an all-time high, and many jobs are of reasonably high quality. Still, there are many very low-paid and insecure jobs; the proportion of such jobs has not been falling; the wages of most workers have been stagnant; and the earnings of high-paid workers and families have been pulling away. Canada has a major and growing problem of surging inequality, and a large underclass of working-poor families.

Recommended Reading

- Murphy, Brian, Paul Roberts, and Michael Wolfson. 2007. "A Profile of High Income Canadians, 1982 to 2004." Statistics Canada Cat. 75F0002MIE, No. 006. This highly credible technical report from Statistics Canada uses tax data to show the considerable extent to which wage growth in Canada has been concentrated among top earners, while the incomes of many individuals and families have stagnated.
- Novick, Marvyn. 2007. *Summoned to Stewardship: Make Poverty Reduction a Collective Legacy*. Campaign 2000. www.campaign2000.ca/res/dispapers/summoned_to_

stewardship.pdf. Campaign 2000 is the national coalition that was formed in 1990 to press for the implementation of the 1989 resolution of the House of Commons to eliminate child poverty by the year 2000. The website features annual report cards analyzing the level and determinants of child poverty. This major paper by Marvyn Novick, based on wide consultations, argues that a major part of the solution to child poverty, in tandem with increased child benefits, is raising the wages of the working poor above a poverty line threshold, such that a single person working full-time would get a living wage. Poverty trends in relation to job market trends are also regularly covered in papers and reports by the National Council of Welfare, the Canadian Council on Social Development, the Canadian Policy Research Networks, and the United Way of Greater Toronto.

- Vosko, Leah (Ed.). 2006. *Precarious Employment: Understanding Labour Market Insecurity in Canada*. Montreal and Kingston: McGill-Queen's University Press. This collection of papers comprehensively maps the different forms of precarious employment in Canada, with a focus on differences by gender, age, occupation, and industry. Canada is often placed in a comparative context. It also explores potential solutions to the growth of precarious work, including stronger unions and increased labour market regulation through employment standards.

- Wilkinson, Richard W. 2005. *The Impact of Inequality: How to Make Sick Societies Healthier*. New York and London: The New Press. Wilkinson is a leading population health researcher who famously found that health status among British public servants was strongly correlated to their position in the occupational hierarchy, and that these differences were not explained by poor health-related behaviour. This book closely explores the links from inequality to health and well-being, and advances a passionate and well-reasoned argument for more equal societies.

- Yalnizyan, Armine. 2007. *The Rich and the Rest of Us: The Changing Face of Canada's Growing Gap*. Ottawa: Canadian Centre for Policy Alternatives. This is the flagship report of the CCPA's Inequality Project, detailing trends in the distribution of earnings, hours of work, and after-tax incomes among families with children. Available from the project website www.growinggap.ca. The website also provides a series of short, accessible essays by senior Canadian scholars on the theme "Why Inequality Matters," and many other reports on inequality trends in Canada.

References

Battle, Ken. 2003. *Minimum Wages in Canada: A Statistical Portrait with Policy Implications*. Ottawa: Caledon Institute of Social Policy.

Beach, Charles, Ross Finnie, and David Gray. 2003. "Earnings Variability and Earnings Stability of Women and Men in Canada: How Do the 1990s Compare to the 1980s?" *Canadian Public Policy* XXIX, Supplement: 541–565.

Bebchuk, Lucian, and Yaniv Grinstein. 2005. "The Growth of Executive Pay." *Oxford Review of Economic Policy* 21 (2).

Drolet, Marie, and René Morissette. 1998. *The Upward Mobility of Low Paid Canadians, 1993–1995*. Ottawa: Statistics Canada. Cat. 75F0002M.

Finnie, Ross. 2000. *The Dynamics of Poverty in Canada*. Toronto: C.D. Howe Institute.

Fleury, D., and M. Fortin. 2004. "Canada's Working Poor." *Horizons* 7 (2). Government of Canada.

Fortin, Nicole, and Sophie Lefebvre. 1998. "Intergenerational Income Mobility in Canada." In *Labour Markets, Social Institutions and the Future of Canada's Children*, edited by Miles Corak, Cat. 89-553. Ottawa: Statistics Canada.

Gordon, Robert J., and Ian Dew-Becker. 2007. *Controversies about the Rise of American Inequality: A Survey.* www.people.fas.harvard.edu/~idew/papers/BPEA_final_ineq.pdf.

Heisz, Andrew. 2007. *Income Inequality and Redistribution in Canada, 1976 to 2004.* Ottawa: Statistics Canada. Cat. 11F0019 No. 298.

Human Resources and Skills Development Canada (HRSDC). 2006a. *Employment Insurance Monitoring and Assessment Report.* Ottawa: Government of Canada.

———. 2006b. *Looking Ahead: A 10-Year Outlook for the Canadian Labour Market (2006–2015).* www.hrsdc.gc.ca/en/publications_resources/research/categories/labour_market_e/sp_615_10_06/page00.shtml.

Janz, Teresa. 2004. *Low Paid Employment and Moving Up.* Statistics Canada Income Research Paper, Cat. 75F0002MIE2004009. Ottawa: Statistics Canada.

Krugman, Paul. 2007. *The Conscience of a Liberal.* New York and London: Norton.

Mackenzie, Hugh. 2007. *The Great CEO Pay Race: Over Before It Begins.* Ottawa: CCPA.

Morissette, René. 2008. "Earnings in the Last Decade." *Perspectives on Labour and Income* (February). Ottawa: Statistics Canada.

Morissette, René, and Anick Johnson. 2005. *Are Good Jobs Disappearing in Canada?* Ottawa: Statistics Canada. Cat. 11F0019 No. 239.

Morissette, René, and Xuelin Zhang. 2006. "Revisiting Wealth Inequality." *Perspectives on Labour and Income.* Ottawa: Statistics Canada. Cat. 75-001-XIE. December.

Murphy, Brian, Paul Roberts, and Michael Wolfson. 2007. *A Profile of High Income Canadians, 1982 to 2004.* Ottawa: Statistics Canada. Cat. 75F0002MIE, No. 006.

National Council of Welfare. 2003. *Income for Living?* www.ncwcnbes.net.

Russell, Ellen, and Mathieu Dufour. 2007. *Rising Profit Shares, Falling Wage Shares.* Ottawa: Canadian Centre for Policy Alternatives.

Saez, Emmanuel, and Michael Veall. 2003. *The Evolution of High Incomes in Canada, 1920 to 2000.* National Bureau of Economic Research Working Paper. www.nber.org/papers.

Sauve, Roger. 2007. *The Current State of Canadian Family Finances.* Ottawa: Vanier Institute of the Family. www.vifamily.ca/library/cft/famfin07.pdf.

Smeeding, Timothy. 2002. *Globalization, Inequality, and the Rich Countries of the G-20: Evidence from the Luxemburg Income Study.* Luxemburg Income Study Working Paper No. 320. www.lisproject.org.

Vosko, Leah (Ed.). 2006. *Precarious Employment: Understanding Labour Market Insecurity in Canada.* Montreal and Kingston: McGill-Queen's University Press.

Vosko, Leah, Nancy Zukewich, and Cynthia Cranford. 2003. "Precarious Jobs: A New Typology of Employment." *Perspectives on Labour and Income* (October): 16–26. Ottawa: Statistics Canada.

Wilkinson, Richard W. 2005. *The Impact of Inequality: How to Make Sick Societies Healthier.* New York and London: The New Press.

CHAPTER 3
Taking Lifelong Learning Seriously

Introduction

This chapter discusses the importance of lifelong learning to better jobs and higher living standards for Canadian workers. It draws attention to the importance of education and skills to individual workers as well as to the functioning of the economy as a whole. It highlights the critical problem of lack of access to workplace-based training for many workers, especially the great majority who are not managers and professionals, and argues that wider access to training could significantly improve the situation and prospects of lower paid workers.

Learning and Workplaces

It is now almost universally recognized that education and skills are the foundations for both a healthy society and a healthy economy, and that learning is an ongoing process that must take place over the whole life-course. Education, skills training, and lifelong learning (or what economists call investments in human capital) are seen as the key to success for individuals, firms, and countries in the new and rapidly changing global economy. The basic argument is that individuals with low skills will do badly in the job market, and that the Canadian economy will not thrive unless we raise the overall level of education and skills.

Ideally, people would participate in early childhood education programs and arrive at school ready to learn. They would receive a first-class school education that provides them with basic skills, such as literacy and numeracy, and the capacity to learn and work with others, as well as the knowledge needed to proceed to a post-secondary education appropriate to their particular skills and capacities. Post-secondary education is increasingly needed to acquire reasonably well-paid jobs that also provide career ladders to better jobs. It can span a wide range, from short-term vocational and technical training directly tied to entry-level requirements of jobs, to apprenticeship programs combining classroom and on-the-job instruction, to co-op and advanced technical and business education programs in college, to general and career-oriented professional programs in university.

Learning should be seen as a process that continues rather than ends with employment in a steady job, and the workplace should be seen as an important site for lifelong learning. In a fluid job market marked by constant industrial and firm restructuring, and by rapid technological and organizational change within workplaces, workers need to periodically upgrade their skills. Many will need training to switch jobs and careers. And, climbing up job ladders over a working lifetime almost always involves learning new skills.

The good news for Canadians is that our children do relatively well at school, scoring above average in internationally comparable tests of basic competencies, including math, science, and literacy and numeracy (OECD 2005). Moreover, the proportion of children and youth with very low scores is relatively low compared to many other countries, including the U.S. The proportion of Canadian youth who do not complete at least a high school education is still too high, at a bit under one in 10, but it is falling. Improving public education is obviously important, but this is an area where we have done reasonably well. The same is true to a degree of participation in post-secondary education. About one-quarter of 25- to 29-year-olds has graduated from university, and another quarter has graduated from college. By some measures, we have the most highly educated generation of young adults in the world, and one of the most well-educated workforces overall (OECD 2005).

The bad news for Canadians is that our workplace-based training system is relatively underdeveloped, and falls far short of producing the kind of results we get from public education (OECD 2002, 2003). Despite all of the rhetoric on the importance of skills and learning in the new knowledge-based economy, our performance leaves much to be desired. Many recent reports comprehensively document poor Canadian performance compared to other countries in terms of employer-provided training, especially for lower paid workers, and Canada has a very high proportion of adults with weak literacy and numeracy skills (Rubenson 2007; Myers and de Broucker 2006; Goldenberg 2006).

While adult workers can and do seek training, it is mainly employers who determine access. Unfortunately, employer-sponsored training is directed very disproportionately to already highly educated professional and managerial employees. Many
average employees with formal qualifications and the willingness to learn more do not
get access to the further training that they need to upgrade their skills and qualifications. Perhaps most importantly, if we take equality of opportunity seriously, there
is little in the way of a second chance for people who leave the educational system
with limited qualifications, or made early career choices that turned out to offer poor
job and career prospects.

Many working people are caught in a low skills trap. A little under one-half of even
young adults do not complete a post-secondary qualification and, like the many older
workers who left formal education early, are vulnerable to being trapped in low-
wage, dead-end jobs. An estimated four in 10 working-age Canadians have limited
literacy and numeracy skills, which makes it very difficult for them to take further
skills training (Myers and de Broucker 2006). Many new immigrants to Canada have
high formal qualifications, but often they also need further training to gain Canadian
equivalencies and credentials recognition. Most of these vulnerable workers are on
their own when it comes to the difficult task of upgrading their skills to find better
jobs and to deal with a changing job market. Employers are particularly unlikely
to invest in training in basic skills, such as literacy and numeracy, and most likely to
invest in skills training for those who already have good basic skills.

Box 3.1: What Are the Jobs of the Future?
Projecting what jobs will look like a decade or more from now is extremely difficult.
Past projections have often been wrong. After the mid-1990s, for example, many
more jobs were created in blue-collar jobs than had been expected, partly because
of a major boom in new housing construction.

Forecasts on the future Canadian job market can be found by looking at *Job Futures* at
www.jobfutures.ca. This provides information on wages by detailed occupations, together
with some idea of how strong demand will be for workers in each occupation.

Skills, the Economy, and a Changing Job Market

Investment in education and skills and the fostering of an advanced knowledge-based
economy are critical to maintaining and increasing the living standards of Canadian
workers. We live in a world of abundant cheap labour and cheap transportation costs,
and many good jobs producing goods and services that can be easily moved are being
transferred to countries that can combine relatively low wages with a reasonably high
level of skills. Labour-intensive industrial production has already decisively shifted to
developing countries like China and Brazil. Workers in developing countries employed
by transnational and domestic corporations with access to modern machinery and
equipment are quite capable of producing high-quality industrial goods, from clothes
and autos to planes and computers. New communications technologies also now

permit the outsourcing of a range of services jobs from data processing to software development. In the longer term, the jobs that will remain in the traded sectors of the advanced industrial countries—that is, in those sectors where production can be moved elsewhere—will have to be based on high productivity or on high value. Usually, this means jobs in operations that are very capital-intensive, or in enterprises that produce unique, sophisticated, or very high-quality products that can command a price premium in global markets to support decent wages. If Canadian-based companies are to successfully participate in very competitive global markets while maintaining good wages and working conditions, they must be highly productive and highly innovative. This, in turn, requires a highly educated and skilled workforce.

Technological change, especially change that is driven by the use of information and communications technologies, has been pervasive over the past 20 years and more. It has often been accompanied by major changes in the organization of production, such as automation, or the use of work teams and the devolution of more decision-making authority to front-line workers. Many routine clerical and blue-collar production jobs have been eliminated or radically changed, and many new occupations have appeared. There has long been a debate among social scientists as to whether these ongoing technological and organizational changes have fuelled a demand for higher worker skills, or have been introduced so as to deliberately de-skill the workers whose jobs survive automation and outsourcing. In practice, there has been change in all directions, depending upon the sector, the occupation, and the characteristics of individual companies. There are many very boring, routine, and stressful jobs working with new technology, such as work in many call centres, but also many interesting new jobs, such as running computer systems, or writing complex software, or running advanced diagnostic equipment in hospitals. The concept of skill is itself not neutral, and refers to a range of characteristics of jobs, from the need for vocational and educational credentials, to cognitive complexity, to the level of responsibility in the job.

The consensus among most researchers, supported by the Canadian evidence, is that the skill content of jobs has been slowly rising over time. There has been faster-than-average job growth in professional and technical occupations that usually require advanced qualifications and rising skill content in jobs within a wide range of other occupations (Applebaum et al. 2003; Betcherman et al. 1998). Change, however, is probably not much more rapid than was the case in earlier periods. Back in the 1950s and 1960s, there was a huge scare that automation would eliminate factory jobs. Since that time, but long before the computer revolution, there was indeed a big shift out of relatively unskilled but reasonably well-paid factory jobs into jobs in the service sector. The shift to services has produced many more skilled jobs in some sectors—such as health care, finance, and business services—but also many less skilled jobs in personal and consumer services, such as in restaurants and retail trade. Many low-wage, low-skill services jobs are not vulnerable to relocation to lower wage countries, and many are also not terribly subject to elimination through technological change. The shift of jobs to services, combined with technological and organizational change and greater international competition in manufacturing, and some high-end service industries, has helped divide the workforce between skilled workers with good jobs and relatively unskilled workers with poor jobs.

The major point is that there is a rising ante. It is getting harder and harder for workers with less than a post-secondary education to find a steady, well-paid job, and the skill requirements in good jobs in both the private and public sectors will probably continue to grow. The relatively uneducated and unskilled are increasingly consigned to precarious and marginal jobs that provide low levels of employment security, low pay, limited career progress, and a high risk of poverty. The increased premium upon education means that there is an increased risk of marginalization. Without broadly based, equitable access to education and skills training, many workers will be left behind. This is especially true of young people who leave school with limited education and skills, of women who leave the workforce for extended periods, of older workers who fall victim to industrial restructuring that devalues their existing skills, and of new immigrants whose skills and credentials are frequently not recognized.

Skills and Better Jobs

At the individual level, higher levels of education strongly influence earnings, and the evidence shows that less educated adults who return to school to gain a formal credential realize significant wage gains (Zhang and Palameta 2006). It is also very widely agreed that national investment in "human capital" is key to productivity growth and good national economic performance in a knowledge-based global economy. Investment in education and skills is central to innovation and, at a minimum, facilitates the introduction of productivity-enhancing new technology and new forms of work organization (OECD 2005). The OECD has found that increased educational attainment of the workforce raises the rate of real economic growth, and employer investment in training has been shown to have significant positive impacts on firm-level productivity (Bartel 2000).

Investment in worker training, in conjunction with changes in work organization that take full advantage of those higher skills, has been found in numerous Canadian and international studies to have positive, if hard to quantify, impacts on firm-level productivity and profitability (Arnal et al. 2001; Betcherman et al. 1998; Lowe 2000). While it is hard to separate out the impacts on productivity of new capital investments, technological change, changes in work organization, and investment in workers skills, it seems clear that the largest productivity payoff comes from a bundling together of all of these elements as part of a coherent, high value-added business strategy. Knowledge-based firms that adopt these kinds of strategies will tend to grow and expand, replacing good jobs eliminated in the process of technological and organizational change.

Beyond investment in public education at all levels, investments in the skills of employed workers through on-the-job training are particularly critical to the success of new forms of work organization based on employee involvement. However, there is strong evidence that companies, particularly Canadian companies, tend to underinvest in on-the-job training (Goldenberg 2006; Myers and de Broucker 2006). A comprehensive study of Canadian firms in the mid to late 1990s found that, at most, only about one in 10 firms had become serious learning organizations (Betcherman et al. 1998). Many firms do provide some training, particularly training for new employees, and occasional computer, marketing, and management training, but this is not the same thing as being systematically committed to constant upgrading of the skills of all employees as part of a comprehensive competitive strategy. According to a recent report aimed at employers, Canada's poor productivity record "is rooted in a chronic national blind spot—a lack of awareness that investing in the human capacity of Canada's workforce is paramount to success" (Bailey 2007, 4). The literature review in this report shows strong positive impacts of business investment in workforce training on business performance, and thus high returns to training investments, but this has not translated into increased investment in training.

There are many reasons why Canada lacks a strong workplace training culture. Traditionally, high levels of immigration of skilled workers kept down the need to train workers from within. High unemployment for much of the 1990s meant that firms could easily hire from outside for needed skills, rather than train and promote from within. And, there has been less of an expectation in Canada that firms will train and retrain workers than is the case in some other countries. In Germany and many other European countries, most companies accept that they have an obligation to provide apprenticeship training, and there is a highly formalized system of vocational training for young people who do not go on to an academic education. Canada lacks the works councils that are mandated by law in many European countries to help plan and deliver training. Restrictions on layoffs in many European countries have also encouraged companies to train during downtime when business is slow. Unions that often press employers for more training are weaker than in Europe.

There are more general factors that limit firm investment in skills. Training is costly, particularly for smaller firms, and the gains from training are uncertain and often unknown. It is often easier to pursue a cost-cutting strategy than it is to fundamentally rethink how production is organized. Many companies complain, perhaps with good reason, that too many of their employees lack the basic skills needed to learn. Perhaps most importantly, firms that do train risk losing the newly trained workers to other firms, thus losing out on their investment. Poaching skilled workers is particularly widespread in countries with no training culture, where free-riding firms can get away with behaviour that is damaging to the economy as a whole. Investment in training is thus likely to be greatest in large firms that provide steady employment at decent wages and, as a result, experience low worker turnover. Firms' widespread adoption of outsourcing strategies has driven the growth of more precarious employment relationships in smaller firms that are much less well equipped to invest in training.

The dominant focus of Canadian public policy toward "human capital" has been on public education, including post-secondary education, rather than on adult learning and workplace-based learning. However, widely cited recent research by Coulombe et al. (2004) suggests that raising the average level of skills (as measured by literacy and numeracy levels) actually has a stronger impact upon productivity than does raising the proportion of the workforce with very high levels of education and skills. This is, perhaps, unsurprising given that the majority of the workforce still has quite modest educational and skills attainments, and that many workers are employed in low productivity/low skilled jobs. They calculate that a 1% increase in mean literacy skills relative to the international average can raise labour productivity by 2%.

Most low-productivity/low-skilled/low-pay jobs are to be found in consumer ser-vices, such as retail trade and accommodation and food services, as well as in some business services (such as security and building cleaning). In combination, such services make up about one-fifth of the private sector economy. Rao et al. (2004) note that 85% of the widely lamented Canada–U.S. productivity difference is accounted for by services, with 30% of the gap accounted for by retail trade and "other services" largely outside of business services. Put simply, if we want to raise productivity, we have to think about how to improve low-pay/low-productivity jobs.

Skills, the Needs of Workers, and Human Development

In Canada today, employer support for training of employed workers on the job, or through paid courses and leaves, goes disproportionately to managers and profession-als with relatively high levels of formal education. Far from equalizing opportunities, the workplace training system increases inequality of income and opportunity based on class background and formal educational attainment. This lack of a good train-ing and adult education system thwarts the goal of human development. We may have the most highly educated generation of young adults in the world, but many Canadians are seriously underemployed (Livingstone 2004; Lowe 2000). At least one in five jobs requires education and skills far below those of the workers who hold these jobs. Underemployment in precarious jobs affects many young people as well as highly educated and skilled recent immigrants. There is evidence that skills gained in the educational system often atrophy and rot from lack of use in the workplace (Krahn and Lowe 1998).

Training is an essential ingredient in human development. Workers want to develop their individual capacities and capabilities, and work in jobs that allow them to exercise and develop their skills. The workforce has become more highly educated, and has justifiably higher expectations of what work will provide in terms of the ability to use an education and continued opportunities to learn. Higher levels of education and skills are generally associated with higher levels of autonomy at work, more varied and interesting jobs, and higher levels of job satisfaction. Investment in skills is also needed to promote the kinds of work reorganization that create more interesting and less stressful jobs, and give workers more control over the pace and content of work. Management and labour objectives are not always the same when it comes to work reorganization, which too often results in high levels of stress. But, investment in training is a major ingredient in jointly determined work reorganization processes that can satisfy the interests of both parties.

Education and training is about much more than meeting the skill needs of employ-ers alone. Workers will usually want to gain general rather than highly firm-specific skills, and skills that are recognized through formal certificates or credentials. These will give them much more leverage as individuals in the job market, and the option of either climbing a job ladder with their current employer, or looking around for a new job. Workers with a high level of general, certified skills are much less likely to experience prolonged unemployment or a deep pay cut if they lose their current jobs and are forced to seek another one.

Training programs are likely to be most developed and most likely to meet the different needs of workers and employers when they are developed jointly. This can take place through collective bargaining, European-style works councils established by law to deal with training and other issues, joint training committees, or similar institutions (ILO 2001). A major recent OECD study concludes that joint employer-employee approaches promote more equitable access to training, increase worker involvement in training activities, and increase the training intensity of firms (Arnal et al. 2001, 48). Close employee involvement in the design and delivery of training can facilitate the introduction of new technology and new work practices by ensuring that the current workforce is provided with the tools to adapt to, and benefit from, change.

New technologies and new forms of work organization can be introduced in very different ways, with very different implications for the skill content of jobs and the quality of work (Applebaum 1997). Joint approaches to workplace change and related training are much more likely to generate positive outcomes in terms of both higher employer productivity and worker well-being. Certainly, joint approaches to training are a key feature of the industrial and labour relations systems of some European countries with highly productive and innovative economies, notably Germany and the Scandinavian countries. Joint approaches are also common in unionized workplaces. In the U.S. and Canada, productivity gains from the introduction of new forms of work and new technologies have been greatest where there has been a comprehensive, negotiated process of workplace change (Black and Lynch 2000). The key reason for this outcome is, not surprisingly, that worker buy-in into work reorganization is far greater when workers have an independent voice, and when firms respond to their needs.

Joint approaches are also more likely to result in training programs that develop portable, as opposed to very narrow and firm-specific, skills. Such joint programs are often developed at the sectoral rather than firm level, raising the skill level of the workforce as a whole while spreading the costs across all employers in a sector. Recently, the advantages of a joint approach to training have been demonstrated in Canada through the successes of some sectoral skills councils, such as in the steel industry. Some unions and employers have negotiated access to training through collective agreements and joint training committees, as in the automotive assembly sector. Unions representing workers in the skilled trades have traditionally played a major independent role in the design and delivery of training, especially through apprenticeship programs. Many construction unions run their own training centres. In Canada, unionized workers enjoy greater access to employer-sponsored training because unions have pushed employers to take on the task of upgrading skills and providing current employees with better jobs, rather than just hiring from the outside to meet new needs (Sussman 2002; Livingstone and Raykov 2005).

Who Gets Access to Training?

Statistics Canada's *Adult Education and Training Survey* regularly gathers information on adult participants (aged 25–64) in formal job-related learning. Formal activities are defined as structured courses or programs leading to a certificate or qualification.

Courses are much shorter than programs, and include seminars and workshops. Overall, in 2002, just over one in three adults participated in formal, job-related training, up slightly from 1997. Participation is about the same for women and men, declines with increasing age, and rises with the person's level of education. The average amount of time spent in formal job-related training over the year was 25 days per participant, spent mainly in courses rather than programs (Peters 2004). A lot of this learning effort is undertaken by individuals without the support of employers. In addition, about one-third of all adults engage regularly in self-directed, job-related learning.

A major Canadian problem is the exclusion of roughly the bottom third of the workforce from workplace training and involvement in formal lifelong learning. While Canada scores about average in terms of literacy and numeracy scores among adults, based on data from the International Adult Literacy Survey (IALS), only about one in four adults functions at the highest levels (Levels 4/5) of prose literacy, document literacy, and numeracy, and about one in three adults scores at very low levels (Krahn and Lowe 1998). Literacy attainment in Canada is well below the OECD average for persons with low levels of formal education, and the situation has shown no signs of improvement (Coulombe et al. 2004).

Data from the IALS and Statistics Canada's *Adult Education and Training Survey* clearly show that, once in the workforce, those with advanced education are the most likely to receive employer-sponsored training. Participation in Canadian adult education is very heavily skewed to those with high literacy skills (60.5% of those at Level 4/5 vs. 17.2% at Level 1) (OECD 2002, 14). Just one in five workers in the private sector participates in formal employer-sponsored education, with much lower levels of participation by workers with low levels of formal education (one in 10 for those with no post-secondary qualification). Participation is even lower for the less educated in small firms, while the growing ranks of contract workers and solo self-employed are almost entirely excluded from workplace-based training. In short, and as is widely recognized, Canada does not have an effective adult education and training system in terms of reaching the bottom third of the workforce, and provides little in the way of a "second chance" for those who have not completed a post-secondary qualification (OECD 2002).

A recent survey shows that there was no increase at all in participation in adult education courses and programs in Canada between 1994 and 2003. The authors conclude that "despite concerns about skill shortages in an evolving knowledge-based economy, there has been very little expansion in organized forms of adult learning in Canada" (Rubenson et al. 2007, 76). Indeed, the situation had deteriorated among the unemployed and those not in the labour force due to cuts to government training programs. Those least likely to participate in formal and informal adult learning are those who are most in need of help in the job market: those with low literacy skills and low levels of formal education, the unemployed, and recent immigrants.

Table 3.1 and Figure 3.1 provide information on participation in formal, job-related training that is supported by employers. Either they directly provided the training, or they provided a paid leave, or, more minimally, they just provided some contribution of time or money. Employer-supported training obviously makes access for the

Table 3.1: Participation in Formal Employer-Supported Training, 2002, Adults (age 25–64)

	Employer-supported (%)	Mean annual hours
All	20.2	120
Men	20.2	132
Women	20.3	109
High school or less	9.5	86
Post-secondary, Non-university	23.5	115
University	31.8	145
Full-time	27.4	100
Part-time	17.2	189
Professional/Managerial	34.0	117
Other white-collar	18.9	99
Blue-collar	14.9	123

Source: Statistics Canada. *Adult Education and Training Survey.* 2003.

Figure 3.1: Participation in Formal Employer-Supported Training, 2002, Adults (age 24–26)

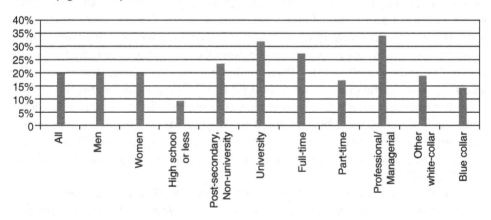

Source: Statistics Canada. *Adult Education and Training Survey.* 2003.

employee much easier, and is likely to be related to the current job and immediate career prospects of workers. As shown, just one in five adults participated in such training in 2002, about the same as in 1997. Participation rates are similar for women and men. Participation rises a lot with the level of education of the employee—from 9.5% for those with high school or less, to almost one-third for university graduates—and the participants with higher education also receive many more hours of training. In line with the pattern by level of education, professional/managerial workers are more than twice as likely to receive employer-supported training as are blue-collar workers.

Table 3.2 provides information from a different survey (*Workplace and Employee Survey*) on employer-supported training. Here, the definition of training is not restricted to formal activities leading to a certificate or diploma, but includes informal, on-the-job training. Participation rates of all employees in all forms of on-the-job learning are, as one would expect with this broader definition, quite high at 55%, though they are lower (at 37%) in formal classroom training. Again, participation increases with the level of education. Also, it is striking that employees in larger firms are much more likely to receive training, particularly classroom training, than are employees of small- and medium-sized firms. Employees in firms with more than 100 employees are almost twice as likely to get some classroom training as employees in firms with less than 20 employees. Unions make a difference, particularly in small firms.

Table 3.2: Proportion of Employees Participating in Employer-Supported Training, 1999

	Classroom or on-the-job	Classroom
All employees	55%	37%
Men	53%	37%
Women	56%	37%
Part-time	47%	25%
Union	58%	41%
Non-union	53%	35%
Education		
Less than high school	40%	21%
High school only	48%	28%
College diploma	57%	38%
University degree	64%	49%
Establishment size		
<20	44%	26%
20–49	51%	31%
50–99	59%	37%
100+	64%	48%

Source: Based on data from the Workplace and Employee Survey in a Study for Human Resources and Skills Development Canada. Turcotte, Leonard, and Montmarquette. Statistics Canada. Workplace and Employee Survey, 2003. http://www.hrsdc.gc.ca/eng/cs/sp/hrsd/prc/publications/research/2001-000075/page05.shtml

Note: Many persons receiving classroom training also receive on-the-job training.

In summary, employer-provided training is highly concentrated on the higher layers of the shrinking core workforce in larger firms and the public sector. The concentration of formal training on well-educated professionals and managers in large firms reflects the fact that such firms are not only more likely to be pursuing high productivity strategies that require skills, but are also still committed to promoting the skills of their core workers. Even blue-collar workers in large firms get more training than average. Also, larger firms are much more likely to be unionized, and the presence of unions makes a difference to training efforts.

Many workers clearly want more training than they are getting from the current system (Sussman 2002; Livingstone 2004). Training participation and desire for even more participation are both greatest among younger workers who want to embark on developmental job and career ladders. Often, older workers have low expectations of their employer, or have given up. Overall, 28% of all adults report that they want more job-related training, but face significant barriers in terms of either time and/or money (Peters 2004). "[R]eturning to school, whether to complete a high school diploma or to obtain a post-secondary credential, involves a tremendous commitment of time, money, and effort. Despite substantial rhetoric around the importance of lifelong learning, there are few programs and policies to support less educated adults who wish to upgrade their skills. Few workplaces offer skills upgrading opportunities to [them] and no province [except Alberta under certain circumstances] provides income support to adults who are already working, even if they are working in the low wage labour market. As a result, most adult learners must rely on family and friends and/or juggle work and school and/or incur significant financial debt" (Myers and de Broucker 2006, 66). It is testimony to the desire to learn that many adults who are excluded from formal adult education and workplace training programs actively seek out informal learning opportunities (Livingstone 2004).

The weaknesses of the employer-based adult training system have not been adequately compensated for through public policy. Governments do provide some support to adult learning for a small proportion of unemployed workers, mainly funded through the *Employment Insurance Act*. The fact that eligibility is restricted to current or recent EI recipients, however, means that many of the working poor, as well as recent immigrants, do not qualify. Classroom training for the unemployed was cut back over the 1990s. There are no programs in place to provide paid training leaves for adult workers who want to upgrade their skills or qualifications by returning to school, though some very modest support is provided through the tax system. Over the years, many reports have called for paid educational and training leaves to facilitate the goal of lifelong learning, but individuals are still pretty much on their own. Governments have also been very reluctant to intervene in employers' training decisions. Of the provinces, only Quebec mandates a minimum employer effort on worker training. Here, an employer who does not spend at least 1% of payroll on training must pay that amount to the provincial government. This has had some positive impacts on the overall level of employer-supported training, even though smaller firms are excluded (Peters 2004).

Canada in International Perspective

Countries differ greatly in terms of the extent to which they invest in active labour market policies to promote lifelong learning and labour adjustment, and Canada is a relatively poor performer. While it is hard to compare the training systems of different countries, the Organisation for Economic Co-operation and Development (OECD) finds that the Canadian annual participation rate in adult worker training is below the industrial country average, and that (at just over 1%) we also lag behind the average in terms of employer spending on training as a percentage of payroll costs (OECD 1999; Tuijnman and Boudard 2001). We lag behind not only European countries where there is a very strong emphasis on training, like Germany and the Scandinavian countries, but also the United States. Canada also lags well behind many European countries—but not the U.S.—when it comes to training programs for unemployed workers. As a share of the economy, we spend less than one-third as much as the Scandinavian countries, which are strongly committed to active labour market policies to get the unemployed into jobs. Research by the OECD suggests that it is particularly important for governments to invest in the basic skills of unemployed and low-wage workers, such as literacy and numeracy (Martin 2000).

Table 3.3: Canadian Job-Related Training in International Perspective

	Canada	U.S.	Denmark	OECD average
Employed (age 25+) participation in year (%)				
All	35.7	42.1	53.7	37.2
Men	36.4	41.8	51.5	36.6
Women	34.9	42.5	56.6	37.9
Mean number of hours per participant (firm size 100–499)	128	122	127	120

Source: Tuijnman, A., and Boudard, E. *Adult Education Participation in North America: International Perspectives*. Statistics Canada Cat. 89-574-XPE. 2001.

Investing in Skills to Raise the Quality of Low-Paid Jobs

The concept of lifelong learning figures prominently in major policy statements by Canadian governments as a key means to raise productivity and economic performance while also promoting more equal outcomes for individuals. In the economic jargon, investment in human capital is held to simultaneously promote economic efficiency and social equity. However, "supply-side" policies are only one part of the solution to low-wage/low-productivity/low-skill work and increasing wage and income inequality. While it is certainly true that better educated persons fare better as individuals in the job market, education credentials may act more as a sorting device in the job market than as a true indicator of skill demands. The fact that employers often demand higher levels of education and skills than they really need leads to underemployment. Krahn and Lowe (1998) and Livingstone (2004) provide overwhelming evidence that many low-wage workers are overeducated and/or overskilled in terms of literacy and numeracy levels relative to the very limited demands of the routinized jobs they hold. Some 20% to 30% of all jobs rarely, if ever, make use of literacy skills, and 40% rarely, if ever, draw on quantitative skills (Krahn and Lowe 1998, Table 2.5). About two-thirds of the jobs held by workers in relatively unskilled occupations involve little or no worker discretion or control. Adequate literacy and numeracy skills among younger workers who have recently left the education system often waste away due to lack of use in the workplace. In the Canadian context, there is also strong evidence that many recent immigrants are significantly underemployed relative to their education and skills. In short, the existence of skills does not mean that they are necessarily utilized by employers.

Part of the problem is that employers can and do adopt, consciously or unconsciously, a low-pay/low-skill strategy as opposed to a higher pay/higher skill strategy. "One of the most troubling aspects of Canada's economy is that the competitive human resource strategy of too many Canadian firms is based on a low cost/low added value approach ... [which] perpetuates a low skill/low wage equilibrium ... firms that gain their competitive edge from low cost, low skilled work have little incentive to invest in labour force development" (Myers and de Broucker 2006, v). Livingstone (2002) argues that there is no automatic translation of higher skills or education supply into higher employer demand for skills and that, while temporary skills shortages can and do exist, the dominant tendency in the job market is for the supply of worker skills to exceed employer demand. He argues for a supply/demand interaction theory in which employer demand for skills must be pushed up by bargaining and other external forces. For example, as noted above, unionized workers, holding all other factors constant, receive more training than do non-union workers (Livingstone and Raykov 2005). About half of all workers covered by collective agreements are covered by (usually permissive rather than mandatory) contract provisions on employer-provided training. While this partly reflects the fact that employers must raise productivity to pay higher union wages, it also reflects the fact that unions can and do push for access to training as a means to improve the quality of jobs and labour market opportunities for workers.

A key policy issue is how to change jobs so that employers develop and use the skills of workers in such a way as to make jobs more interesting and developmental, while also raising productivity and pay. One lever is to raise pay through higher minimum wages or higher unionization in low pay/low productivity sectors. Higher wages are likely to push employers to raise productivity by investing in skills. There is some evidence that skills investment and job redesign can indeed raise productivity in otherwise low pay/low productivity parts of the job market, such as consumer services.

The structure of hourly pay differs quite profoundly between advanced industrial countries. The Scandinavian countries have a much more equal wage distribution, mainly due to widespread collective bargaining even in private services, such as retail trade, and restaurants and hotels. Here, workers in the middle earn about 1.5 times as much per hour as those in the bottom 10% of the workforce compared to twice as much in Canada and the U.S. (data from OECD database). Retail trade workers in Sweden earn about 90% of the average manufacturing wage compared to about 60% in Canada.

When strong unions push up wages for those at the bottom, it seems that these higher wages do encourage employers to increase productivity by raising skills.

There are relatively fewer workers in sectors like retail trade in Scandinavia, and they are more skilled than in Canada. Data from the International Adult Literacy Survey show that the skills of the bottom third of the workforce (measured by literacy and numeracy) are significantly higher in Sweden and Denmark than those of the bottom third of the workforce in Canada (Schettkat 2002). The percentage of employees with low (Levels 1/2) literacy and numeracy scores is much lower in Sweden than in Canada (e.g., 20% vs. 34% for quantitative literacy, and 24% vs. 38% for prose literacy) (Willms 1999). Higher skills at the lower end of the Swedish workforce may partly reflect the impact of higher investment in early childhood learning and a more equal society generally, but workplace-based training jointly delivered by the "social partners" likely plays a major role as well. Levels of workplace training and labour market training for the temporarily unemployed are markedly higher in Sweden and the Scandinavian countries generally than the European, let alone the Canadian, norm. These higher skills appear to be utilized to a greater degree in the workplace according to data from the European Survey of Working Conditions.

In North America, training programs where they exist can have a big impact upon the working lives of people employed in traditionally low-wage sectors of the economy. Often, supposedly low-skill and low-wage jobs can be made into better jobs with greater responsibilities if training is provided. The employer often benefits from job enrichment through lower worker turnover. Usually, job ladders from lower to higher skilled jobs are few and far between in sectors like hotels, restaurants, building services, and support jobs in health care and social services. This is partly because the better jobs requiring higher skills, including supervisor positions, are filled by hiring people with higher skills or formal qualifications rather than by training current employees to take the better jobs when they open up. In hotels and hospital kitchens, for example, supervisors tend to be hired from college programs. But other approaches that lead lower skilled/lower paid workers to better jobs are possible. In some grocery stores in Ontario, employers and unions have agreed to training programs for cashiers that allow them to move into better paid jobs as meat-cutters. In Las Vegas, there is a large union-run training institute that now does almost all of the training for the huge hospitality industry in that city, allowing workers to gradually climb up the job ladder (Applebaum et al. 2003). Potential job ladders that can be climbed through language and skills training run from housekeeping, to food preparation, to food and beverage servers, to desk clerks, to supervisory and managerial positions, with pay and job quality improving at each step. Hotels that compete for customers design and deliver training with the union at a sectoral/community level, and recruit from the training centre. The commitment to training in Las Vegas is reported to lower worker turnover and improves service quality and productivity, in turn, supporting much higher pay than the hospitality industry norm (Wial and Richert 2002).

Conclusion

The importance of lifelong learning to better jobs and higher living standards has been widely recognized, but Canada falls well short of providing adequate access to training opportunities for most workers. This significantly harms national economic performance. The lack of a training culture is particularly harmful to precarious and low-paid workers. Investment in training can improve low-wage jobs when combined with strategies to convince employers to shift to a higher productivity/higher skill competitive strategy.

Recommended Reading

- Applebaum, Eileen, Annette Bernhardt, and Richard J. Murname. (Eds.) 2003. *Low Wage America*. New York: Russell Sage Foundation. This important book provides several case studies of low-wage industries in the U.S., and how low-wage jobs can be improved through a combination of work reorganization and training.
- Canadian Council on Learning. 2007. *Unlocking Canada's Potential: The State of Workplace and Adult Learning in Canada.* Available from www.ccl-cca.ca. The Canadian Council on Learning, especially its Work and Learning Knowledge Centre, has produced several studies of workplace learning in Canada as a basis for more informed policy-making and discussion among and between employers and unions.
- Livingstone, D.W. 2002. *Working and Learning in the Information Age: A Profile of Canadians*. Ottawa: Canadian Policy Research Networks. David Livingstone has long drawn attention to the efforts made by many Canadians to learn in the face of great obstacles, and the very real differences between the learning needs and strategies of working people and the resources that are available in workplaces.
- Myers, Karen, and Patrice de Broucker. 2006. *Too Many Left Behind: Canada's Adult Education and Training System*. Research Report W 34. Ottawa: Canadian Policy Research Networks. www.cprn.org. A rich, comprehensive overview of adult education in Canada today.
- Organisation for Economic Co-operation and Development (OECD). 2004. "Improving Skills for More and Better Jobs. Does Training Make a Difference?" *OECD Employment Outlook*, 183–222. Paris: OECD. This article summarizes the most recent research, which shows that greater employer and public investment in skills is indeed a major factor in creating more and better jobs.

References

Applebaum, Eileen. 1997. *The Impact of New Forms of Work Organization on Workers*. Washington, DC: Economic Policy Institute.

Applebaum, Eileen, Annette Bernhardt, and Richard J. Murname (Eds.). 2003. *Low Wage America*. New York: Russell Sage Foundation.

Arnal, Elena, Wooseok Ok, and Raymond Torres. 2001. *Knowledge, Work Organization, and Economic Growth*. Labour Market and Social Policy Occasional Paper No. 50. Paris: OECD.

Bailey, Allan. 2007. *Connecting the Dots: Linking Training Investment to Business Outcomes and the Economy*. Ottawa: Canadian Council on Learning.

Bartel, A. 2000. "Measuring the Employer's Return on Investments in Training: Evidence from the Literature." *Industrial Relations* 39: 502–524.

Betcherman, Gordon, Kathryn McMullen, and Katie Davidman. 1998. *Training for the New Economy: A Synthesis Report*. Ottawa: Canadian Policy Research Networks.

Black, Sandra, and Lisa Lynch. 2000. *What's Driving the New Economy: The Benefits of Workplace Innovation*. National Bureau of Economic Research Working Paper No. 7479.

Coulombe, S., J.F. Tremblay, and S. Marchand. 2004. *Literacy Scores, Human Capital, and Growth across Fourteen OECD Countries*. Statistics Canada Cat. No. 89-552-MIE, No. 11.

Goldenberg, Mark. 2006. *Employer Investment in Workplace Learning in Canada*. Ottawa: Canadian Policy Research Networks.

International Labour Organization (ILO). 2001. *World Employment Report*. Geneva: ILO.

Kapsalis, Constantine. 1997. *Employee Training: An International Perspective*. Statistics Canada Cat. 89-552-MPE, No. 2.

Krahn, Harvey, and Graham Lowe. 1998. *Literacy Utilization in Canadian Workplaces*. Statistics Canada Cat. 89-552-MIE, No 4.

Livingstone, D.W. 2002. *Working and Learning in the Information Age: A Profile of Canadians*. Ottawa: Canadian Policy Research Networks.

Livingstone, D.W. 2004. *The Education-Jobs Gap: Underemployment or Economic Democracy?* Toronto: Garamond.

Livingstone, D.W., and M. Raykov. 2005. "Union Influence in Worker Education and Training in Canada." *Just Labour* 5 (Winter).

Lowe, Graham. 2000. *The Quality of Work: A People Centred Agenda*. Toronto: Oxford University Press.

Martin, John P. 2000. *What Works among Active Labour Market Policies: Evidence from OECD Countries*. OECD Economic Studies No. 30. Paris: OECD.

Myers, Karen, and Patrice de Broucker. 2006. *Too Many Left Behind: Canada's Adult Education and Training System*. Research Report W 34. Ottawa: Canadian Policy Research Networks.

Organisation for Economic Co-operation and Development (OECD). 1999. "Training of Adult Workers in OECD Countries." *OECD Employment Outlook*: 133–175.

———. 2002. *Thematic Review on Adult Learning: Canada*. Paris: OECD.

———. 2003. *Beyond Rhetoric: Adult Learning Policies and Practices*. Paris: OECD.

———. 2005. *Education at a Glance 2005*. Paris: OECD.

Peters, Valerie. 2004. *Working and Training: First Results of the 2003 Adult Education and Training Survey*. Ottawa: Statistics Canada.

Rao, Someshwar, Jianmin Tang, and Weimin Wang. 2004. "Measuring the Canada–U.S. Productivity Gap: Industry Dimensions." *International Productivity Monitor* 9 (Fall).

Rubenson, Kjell, Richard Desjardins, and Ee-Seul Yoon. 2007. *Adult Learning in Canada: A Comparative Perspective*. Statistics Canada Cat. 89-552-MIE, No. 17.

Schettkat, Ronald. 2002. *Regulation in the Dutch and German Economies at the Root of Unemployment?* Center for Economic Policy Analysis, New School University. Working Paper 2002-05.

Sussman, Deborah. 2002. "Barriers to Job-Related Training." *Perspectives on Labour and Income* (Summer): 5–12.

Tuijnman, A., and E. Boudard. 2001. *Adult Education Participation in North America: International Perspectives*, Statistics Canada Cat. 89-574-XPE. Ottawa: Statistics Canada and Human Resources Development Canada.

Wial, Howard, and Jeff Rickert. 2002. *U.S. Hotels and Their Workers: Room for Improvement*. Washington, DC: Working for America Institute.

Willms, J. Douglas. 1999. *Inequalities in Literacy Skills among Youth in Canada and the United States*. Statistics Canada Cat. 89-552 MIE, No. 6.

Zhang, Xuelin, and Boris Palameta. 2006. *Participation in Adult Schooling and Its Earnings Impact in Canada*. Statistics Canada Analytical Studies Branch Research Paper No. 276.

CHAPTER 4
The Unhealthy Canadian Workplace

Introduction

The purpose of this chapter is to provide a broad overview of the impact of employment, working conditions, and the work environment on health. The focus is on the quality of work as opposed to wider conditions in the labour market.

Health researchers have demonstrated a clear link between income and socioeconomic status and health outcomes, such that longevity and state of health rise with position on the income scale (Raphael 2004). Very little of this relationship is explained by important lifestyle differences between income groups, or by differential access to health care in countries like Canada which provide universal health care. The fact that higher income people are in better health and live longer than middle income people suggests that the health gradient is linked to relative position on the income scale, rather than to absolute deprivation or poverty.

Given the simple fact that the experience of work dominates the lives of most working-age people, it seems plausible that the close link between socioeconomic status and health runs in significant part through different workplace experiences. Those at the lower end of the income spectrum are most likely to experience stress from job insecurity and from stress in the workplace itself, and they are also most likely to face hazards to physical health at work.

Research has established strong links from unemployment and precarious employment to poor health outcomes, and from poor working conditions to poor physical and mental health. Poor employment conditions include: dirty and dangerous jobs, including exposures to harmful substances that pose risks to physical health in terms of injuries and occupational disease; jobs that are stressful by virtue of the pace, demands, or repetitive content of the labour process; jobs that are stressful because of the exercise of arbitrary power in the workplace and lack of social supports; jobs that are stressful because they do not meet human developmental needs; and jobs that are stressful because they conflict with the lives of workers in the home and in the community.

Work and Health

In recent years, health researchers have increasingly emphasized the links between work stress and physical and mental health. Stress can arise from many sources, including job insecurity, the physical demands of work, the extent of support from supervisors and co-workers, work-life conflict, and job strain (Wilkins and Beaudet 1998). High job strain—a combination of high psychological demands at work combined with a low degree of control of the work process—has been linked to an increased risk of physical injuries at work, high blood pressure, cardiovascular disease, depression and other mental health conditions, and increased lifestyle risks to health.

Work poses physical risks, and is clearly a major source of psychosocial stress, which has been identified as one major cause of increased morbidity and mortality. As the leading population health researcher Brian Wilkinson puts it, "to feel depressed, bitter, cheated, vulnerable, frightened about debts or job or housing insecurity; to feel devalued, useless, helpless, uncared for, hopeless, isolated, anxious. These feelings can dominate people's whole experience of life, colouring their experience of everything else. It is the chronic stress arising from feelings like these which does the damage" (cited in Dunn 2002, 26).

It is ironic, not to say tragic, that the shift to a post-industrial society with an increasingly well-educated and skilled workforce is associated with rising levels of stress rather than increased well-being at work. Research has shown some negative consequences for health to date, but the full impact of current conditions is likely to be slow to appear. Many of today's older workers and retirees were workers in the Golden Age of postwar capitalism when working conditions were more closely regulated and conditions were improving. The health impacts of 21st-century work may just be appearing.

This chapter seeks to provide a general overview of current conditions and the overall direction of change, to look at some important cleavages among workers in terms of access to good jobs, and to place the situation in Canada in a comparative context. Comparisons are made with the European Union because better working conditions in the E.U. along some dimensions do suggest that improvement of the quality of the Canadian work environment is not incompatible with having a highly productive economy.

What Is a Good Job?

An appropriate starting point is to consider what constitutes a good job from the perspective of workers. For all of the emphasis (rightly) placed on the fundamental importance of waged employment as the critical source of income, other dimensions of employment are at least as important to workers. On the economic front, non-wage benefits, job security, and opportunities for advancement are as important as wages. The content of work and the nature of the labour process are less tangible and measurable, but count for a lot as well. The EKOS/CPRN survey of changing employment relationships in Canada (www.jobquality.ca) confirmed that a large majority of workers place a high value on having interesting and personally rewarding work, enjoying some autonomy on the job, and having the ability to exercise and develop their skills and capacities. Lowe (2007, 56) found that the most important criterion of job quality, cited by 72% of workers as being "very important," is being in a healthy and safe workplace, followed closely by work-life balance, which 63% cited as "very important." Jencks et al. (1988) found that there is much more unequal distribution of quality jobs along valued dimensions other than pay, indicating that even large pay differences are an imperfect proxy for large class differences in the quality of employment.

The statement that quality of employment involves much more than pay will come as a surprise only to economists who have been trained to view work as a "disutility" endured in order to gain income. Work is better seen as a potential sphere for the development of individual human capacities and potentials. Production is also a social process. Good workplaces are those in which there are valued relationships with co-workers and some degree of active participation and democratic control of the work process. Bad workplaces, by contrast, are alienating and authoritarian.

For the purposes of this chapter, seven key dimensions of employment with relevance to well-being and health are considered:

- Job and employment security
- Physical conditions of work

- Work pace and stress
- Working time
- Opportunities for self-expression and individual development at work
- Participation at work
- Work-life balance

Before these dimensions are considered in detail, it is useful to briefly summarize some of the wider economic and social forces impacting upon Canadian workplaces.

Forces Shaping Workplace Change in Canada

The terms of employment—wages and benefits, hours, working conditions—reflect the relative bargaining power of workers and employers, and the related willingness of governments to establish minimum rights and standards. Over the 1980s and 1990s, the context was one of high unemployment and underemployment, increased employer ability to shift production and new investments to lower cost regions and countries, and an ideologically driven retreat from state intervention on behalf of workers.

There has been a pervasive and ongoing restructuring of employment relationships intended to promote productivity and competitiveness, as opposed to promotion of a worker-centred agenda of good jobs (Lowe 2000). The basic direction of change is best understood as a simultaneous intensification and casualization of work by employers. The most common forms of organizational change have been downsizing, contracting out of non-core functions, and securing greater flexibility of time worked through a combination of increased overtime and increased part-time and contract work.

The restructuring of work has been driven by employers. Governments have been, at best, mainly passive bystanders. But countervailing forces do continue to exist in workplaces in the form of unions and regulation of some working conditions.

Dimensions of Job Quality

Job Security
In considering the linkages from labour market conditions to health, researchers have studied both the availability of work and the nature of work. It is well established from studies of laid-off workers in the high unemployment 1980s and 1990s that the state of unemployment is bad for health for both material and psychological reasons. However, the relatively well-studied transition from stable employment to long-term unemployment that followed rapid deindustrialization and major layoffs in response to shocks like the Canada–U.S. Free Trade Agreement in the late 1980s and early 1990s is less frequent today than alternation between short-term unemployment and precarious employment. Frequent short-term unemployment is a source of stress and anxiety due to lack of income, uncertain prospects for the future, and its potential to undermine social support networks (World Health Organization 1999). Workers who must often move between short-term jobs are also likely to derive less satisfaction and meaning from their paid work.

Most Canadians are familiar with the national unemployment rate, which is reported monthly and stood at about 6% in 2007. Taken at face value, this number considerably understates the true extent of employment insecurity. To be counted as employed, one need only have worked for a few hours in a week, so employment includes temporary employees, part-time workers who want more hours, and people working in low-wage survival jobs while looking for regular jobs matching their skills. To be counted as unemployed, a person has to have been unable to find any work at all, and to have been actively seeking work even if they knew that no suitable jobs were available. Moreover, there is continual turnover in the ranks of those who are counted as unemployed over a year. While well down from levels in the early 1990s, a 6% average monthly unemployment rate combined with an average unemployment spell of about 20 weeks still means that up to 15% of the workforce were unemployed at some point in 2007.

Long-term unemployment in Canada is much lower than in other advanced industrial countries. In 2005, just 17% of unemployed workers had been out of work for more than six months compared to a 47% average in Organisation for Economic Co-operation and Development (OECD) countries, and 64% in the European Union (OECD *Employment Outlook 2006*, Table G). The Canadian job market is marked less by chronic long-term unemployment than by frequent transitions for many workers, especially women, recent immigrants, and racialized minorities, between low-paid precarious jobs and relatively short periods of unemployment. Precariously employed workers also tend to be trapped in low-wage jobs. Layoffs from relatively good jobs also began to rise from 2005 because of large manufacturing job losses in Ontario and Quebec.

Box 4.1: Fear of Job Loss

As one would expect from the unemployment data, many working Canadians worry about losing their jobs. The Personal Security Index (PSI) of the Canadian Council on Social Development (CCSD) was used to track the proportion of people who think there is a good chance they could lose their jobs over the next two years. This stood at 37% in 1998, but fell to just 21% in 2006. Fear of job loss is slightly higher among men than women, and much higher in lower income households. The PSI also tracked the proportion of workers who are confident they could find an equivalent job within six months if they lost their current job. Thirty-three percent were not confident in 2006, down from 38% in 1998. This suggests that while risk of job loss has been falling, many workers still fear they would be unable to find as good a job as their current one if they were to be laid off.

Precarious work in Canada is not only widespread, it is much more precarious than in many other countries. In the European Union, there are often job security laws and regulations that limit the power of employers to lay off long-tenure workers. A binding policy directive establishes that there should be limits on renewals of temporary contracts. Minimum pay laws and widespread collective bargaining provide a wage and benefit floor to the job market. As a result, there are far larger pay gaps between precarious and core workers in Canada than in most E.U. countries.

Job insecurity in the precarious labour market is heightened by lack of supports and services to promote access to better employment. The dominant ethos is that heavy sticks are needed to drive the unemployed into available low-wage jobs. Our minimal and deeply punitive social welfare system is designed to make even poverty-line wages look attractive, and qualifying hours requirements for Employment Insurance (as high as 700 hours or 20 weeks of full-time work) effectively cut off many precariously employed workers who need income support between jobs the most. Employment Insurance rules effectively disqualify many who survive by patching together sequences of paid employment with self-employment.

Canadian analysts of linkages from work to ill health have developed the concept of "employment strain" (Lewchuk et al. 2006). Lewchuk et al. argue that, in addition to stress arising from specific job characteristics (such as high job demands, fast speed of work, and low degree of control), stress with adverse implications for health arises from the precarious nature of many employment relationships in today's job market. Precarious work—such as temporary and contract work—is stressful in its own right, and also carries a high risk of exclusion from the protections and support networks found in more secure and stable jobs in larger workplaces. Studies have found a higher risk of injury and illness, greater workload, and greater exposure to dangerous substances among the self-employed and those who work for small contractors, and higher risk of self-reported ill health and a greater incidence of working in pain among precarious workers compared to workers in similar jobs who are in more secure forms of employment.

Another key difference between relatively secure and more precarious employment with direct implications for health is access to employer-sponsored health benefits. The most important benefit for the working-age population is prescription drug coverage. Drug benefits are typically provided by governments only to seniors, social assistance recipients, and, sometimes, people leaving welfare for work. Having a low-wage job with no health benefits can mean an inability to buy medically necessary prescription drugs, as well as needed dental and other health services not provided by physicians and hospitals whose costs are covered by Medicare. In 2000, just 50% of employees had extended medical, dental, and life/disability coverage, usually provided as a package. While 70% of union members were covered, only 40% of non-union members were so fortunate, and coverage was very low in firms with less than 20 employees (27%), part-time jobs (14%), and temporary jobs (17%) (Marshall 2003, Table 2). Lowe (2007) considers the best data to show that health benefits coverage has been falling. Moreover, the rising cost of employer health plans, especially drug costs, has led to reduced coverage for many workers, imposing heavier co-pays and more limitations on allowable prescriptions. In a better world, all citizens would be covered by a comprehensive public health care plan, but the large gaps in our current system mean that there is a tight link between having a good job and having good health-related benefits, and between having a more unhealthy job and having no or very limited benefits. There are also large gaps between secure and more precarious workers in terms of access to paid sick leave, though here there is at least entitlement to a modest floor through the Employment Insurance program. Many precariously employed workers thus face directly higher risks to health because of the quality of their employment.

Lack of employer-sponsored pension coverage for many precarious workers combined with a relatively ungenerous public pension system implies longer working lifetimes. Many low-wage, older workers are significantly better off after they retire at 65 and qualify for the combined Old Age Security pension and Guaranteed Income Supplement, which at least provides an income close to the poverty line.

To summarize, a large minority of workers experience continuing precarious employment and a significant risk of periodic unemployment. The risks to health of precarious employment caused by stress and anxiety are compounded by lack of access to benefits.

Physical Conditions of Work

One might have thought that dirty and dangerous work was a thing of the past, banished along with the dark satanic mills of the Industrial Revolution. But deaths, occupational diseases, and injuries rooted in the physical conditions of work are still very much a feature of the contemporary workplace.

Box 4.2: Five Deaths a Day: Workplace Fatalities in Canada

According to data collected by the Association of Workers' Compensation Boards of Canada, 1,097 workplace fatalities were recorded in Canada in 2005, up 45% from 758 in 1993, and up 8% from 958 in 2004. As Canadians work on average 230 days per year, this means that there were nearly five work-related deaths per working day.

The chances of a worker dying from a workplace-related accident or disease in Canada vary greatly by industry, occupation, gender, and age group. The most dangerous industry in which to work over the 1996–2005 period was mining, quarrying and oil wells (49.9 deaths per 100,000 workers or one out of 2,000), followed by logging and forestry (42.9 per 100,000 workers or one out of 2,300), fishing and trapping (35.6 fatalities per 100,000 workers or one out of every 2,800 workers), agriculture (28.1 fatalities per 100,000 workers or one out of every 3,600 workers), and construction (20.6 per 100,000 workers or one out of 4,900). Finance and insurance was the least dangerous industry, with only 0.2 fatalities per 100,000 workers or one death for every 500,000 workers.

Men are much more likely to die on the job than women. In 2005, the incidence of workplace death was 30 times higher among men than women: 12.4 deaths per 100,000 workers versus 0.4 deaths.

Workplace fatalities arise from both accidents and occupational diseases. In 2005, out of the 1,097 workplace fatalities, 491 (44.8%) were from accidents, and 557 (50.8%) were from occupational diseases. Asbestos-related deaths alone accounted for about 340 deaths in 2005.

The ILO Workplace Fatality database shows that, in 2003, Canada had the fifth highest incidence of workplace fatalities out of 29 OECD countries. Only Korea,

Mexico, Portugal, and Turkey had higher workplace fatality rates, and all four countries are at a much lower level of development than Canada. Unfortunately, definitions of workplace fatalities differ from country to country, and the ILO makes no attempt to standardize the data. Nevertheless, even if one fully adjusted for definitional differences, it is very unlikely that Canada would emerge as a low workplace fatality country relative to its peers.

Source: The above is an abbreviated version of the Executive Summary of a report by Andrew Sharpe and Jill Hardt, *Five Deaths a Day: Workplace Fatalities in Canada, 1993–2005*. Centre for the Study of Living Standards, Research Paper 2006-04. December 2006. Available at www.csls. ca/reports/csls2006-04.pdf.

Unlike workplace fatalities, the incidence of work-related accidents and injuries appears to be falling. Reported injuries are those that are made known to provincial workers' compensation boards since they involve time lost from work and payment while off the job. In British Columbia, reported lost time claims fell from 8.8 to 5.4 per 100 full-time equivalent male workers between 1990 and 2001, and fell from 6.1 to 2.8 reported workplace injuries per 100 male workers in Ontario. Lost time claim rates are much lower among women, but have fallen more modestly. For example, claims for women in Ontario fell from 3.3 to 2 per 100 workers over the same time period (Breslin et al. 2006). As one might expect, workplace injuries—like work-time fatalities—are heavily concentrated among men in blue-collar industrial jobs. These kinds of jobs shrank over much of the 1990s, but have recently grown as a result of the resource boom in Western Canada and a strong housing construction market.

The release of the CSLS report on growing workplace fatalities in 2006 (see Box 4.2) sparked a major public debate on the real trend in workplace injuries. It is generally recognized that workplace fatalities are at the tip of an iceberg, standing above workplace injuries and "near misses," so a decline in injuries combined with an increase in fatalities is curious. The CBC Radio program *The Current* ran a program on this issue as part of a series on health and safety in the workplace (www.cbc.ca/thecurrent/2007/200701/20070108.html). Focusing on the situation in Alberta, some argued that workplace accidents are seriously underreported. Troy Ophus, whose hand was crushed against an I-beam by a falling trolley, said that "a lot of injuries don't get reported" because workers feel they will be fired or treated as troublemakers. Dr. Louis Francescutti, an Alberta emergency room physician and university teacher, said that there is "not a shortage of injuries; it's just not being reported."

Part of the problem is that provincial workers' compensation systems have shifted toward experience-rating the premiums paid by employers, so that higher accident rates result in higher costs to them (Lippel 2006). The laudable aim has been to increase the incentive for employers to take workplace health and safety seriously, but, at the same time, it also now makes sense for employers to contract out the most dangerous jobs, and to try and persuade their own workers not to report injuries. Some employers provide awards for days worked without injuries, increasing pressure on workers not to report an injury.

Workplace health and safety issues are usually taken most seriously in larger work-places, which are often unionized, where formal procedures and rules are in place, where safety training is most frequently provided, and where government inspections of health and safety conditions in response to worker or union complaints are most likely to take place. The shift of jobs to smaller, usually non-union workplaces, and the growth of more precarious forms of employment—such as own-account self-employment and employment with small subcontractors—has thus worked to undermine physical safety on the job. Self-employed workers are generally not covered by government health and safety legislation or by workers' compensation legislation and programs, even though they may be working for large employers, so work-related accidents among them will not be reported (Lippel 2006). Contract employees—who are covered in theory—may not know that they are protected by legislation and workers' compensation programs. These kinds of arm's-length employment are quite common in some high-risk industries, such as construction. Also, some quite dangerous jobs—such as farm jobs—are often not covered by health and safety legislation at all. Seasonal agricultural workers who come to Canada from other countries under special temporary work permits are especially vulnerable.

The nature of workplace injuries and conditions is also changing. There has been a disturbing upward trend in repetitive strain and other soft tissue injuries associated with highly repetitive machine and keyboard work. These account for an upward trend in the proportion of workplace injuries reported by women. As one would expect, physical injuries—sprains and strains to backs and hands, cuts, punctures, lacerations, fractures, and contusions—are associated with physically demanding jobs. Manufacturing and construction account for 20% of employment but about 40% of injuries, explaining the gap between injury rates among men and women. But injury rates are also high in sectors such as retail trade and health and social services, which involve repetitive physical work.

Sullivan (2000) argues that workers' compensation practices, which were designed to address physical trauma in a world of manual, blue-collar, male work, have not changed to sufficiently recognize the growing reality of less visible physical injuries that develop over a period of time. Soft tissue injuries, such as repetitive strain injuries affecting women clerical and service workers, are under-reported and under-compensated.

Musculoskeletal pain and chronic back pain are on the increase, especially with an aging workforce in physically demanding jobs, and are a major cause of work absence and disability (Shainblum et al. 2000). Many of these conditions have no specific causal event, are slow in onset, and develop progressively over time, and it is hard to separate out the specific job-related factors that may be involved. There is a clear link to the poor ergonomic conditions of work in specific kinds of jobs involving heavy work and repetitive tasks, but few workers are able to make successful worker compensation claims. Often, workers will have moved between jobs and even occupations while a condition has been developing, so a condition cannot be attributed to a specific work experience with a specific employer. Similarly, Canada is experiencing a rapidly rising rate of chronic stress-related disability, which often has workplace roots but cannot be identified as solely work-related or solely attributable to a specific job and employer. Many critics of the current workers' compensation system feel that it is inadequate in terms of measuring, let alone compensating for, work-related risks to health in a post-industrial environment.

Occupational diseases are, of course, also related to workplace risks and exposures. Lung diseases and cancers are linked to physical risks, including inhalation of toxic fumes, handling of hazardous chemicals, and exposure to carcinogens. In a very limited number of cases, there is a very clear causal linkage between occupational exposure and disease onset, which has been recognized by workers' compensation boards. For example, boards recognize that occupational exposure causes asbestosis among asbestos mine workers, and a range of lung diseases among other miners. A handful of highly specific cancers have been demonstrably linked to exposure to specific carcinogens at work. But, the overall incidence of occupational disease compared to workplace injuries is extremely low, if we go by the official data.

The workers' compensation system demands high standards of scientific proof of cause and effect in order to keep down costs and many carcinogens are present in the general environment as well as in the workplace. Experts estimate that anywhere from 10% to 40% of cancers may be caused primarily by workplace exposures, but only a tiny proportion of cancer victims qualify for workers' compensation. Similarly, workplace stress and heavy physical exertion are associated with heart conditions, but only a tiny proportion of heart attack victims (e.g., firefighters) qualify. The key point is that occupational diseases due to the physical hazards of work are prevalent, but largely unrecognized. Somewhat ironically, employers end up bearing a large share of the costs anyway through employer-funded, long-term disability plans.

An official European Union institution, the European Foundation for the Improvement of Living and Working Conditions, regularly conducts surveys on European working conditions. The third survey in 2000 followed surveys for 1990 and 1995. It found that "[e]xposure to physical hazards at the workplace and conditions such as musculoskeletal disorders and fatigue caused by intensification of work and flexible employment practises are on the increase" (European Foundation for the Improvement of Living and Working Conditions 2000, 10).

In 2000—defining significant exposure as exposure at least one-quarter of the time—29% of European workers were exposed to noise; 22% to inhalation of vapours, fumes, and dust; 37% reported having to move or carry heavy loads; and no less than 47% reported having to work in painful or tiring positions. In each case, a little under half of those reporting the hazard were exposed all of the time. Fortunately, given increasing rather than declining exposure to all of these risks (except inhalation exposure), 76% of European workers reported that they had been well-informed of hazards. As one would expect, exposure is greatest in occupations such as machine operators, but the E.U. data also indicate quite widespread exposure to physical hazards.

The European survey also provides data on the incidence of repetitive work, for which no general Canadian information is available. In the E.U., 31% of workers report continuous, repetitive hand/arm movements, and 23% report working at short, repetitive tasks with cycle times of less than one minute. One in four (24%) workers report continuously working at high speed, with the level being highest among machine operators (35%), but still high among clerical workers (20%) and service workers

(23%). The incidence of high-speed work due to tight deadlines has been modestly increasing, though there is variation between countries and between different categories of workers. The survey found that those working at high speed were much more likely to report negative health effects, such as muscular pain, stress, and anxiety.

The 2005 survey found that intensity of work in the European Union has continued to increase, with a steadily rising proportion of workers expected to work at very high speed and/or working to tight deadlines. Between 1991 and 2005, those working at very high speed at least three-quarters of the time rose from just over one in five to about one-third, and the proportion working to tight deadlines at least three-quarters of the time rose from about one-quarter to more than one-third. There has also been a modest decrease in the proportion of employees who can exercise autonomy at work, though a majority still report an ability to change the order of tasks, the speed of work, and the methods of work. Reported job satisfaction has been declining, with 22.8% of workers reporting being not very or not at all satisfied with working conditions in 2005, up from 15.2% in 1991. These trends are rather disturbing given the priority that the European Union has accorded to measuring, monitoring, and improving working conditions. On a more positive note, however, only about one in four E.U. workers feel their health and safety is threatened at work, down from about one in three in 1991, and there has been some increase in working-time flexibility and a decline in very long working hours (European Foundation for the Improvement of Living and Working Conditions 2007).

Comparable data on the physical demands of work are simply unavailable for Canada, though one recent Canadian survey suggests that the incidence of high-speed work in Canada and the U.S. is well above the average of all advanced industrial countries (Brisbois 2003). There is little reason to believe that the situation here is any better than in the E.U.

To summarize, despite the transition to a post-industrial society, the risks of occupational injury and disease are still high. One-third of Canadian workers (31.3%) feel that their employment puts their health and safety at risk—a bit above the average for advanced industrial countries (Brisbois 2003). Regrettably, little hard data are available on the physical hazards of work in Canada. One aspect of work reorganization likely has been the intensification of physical demands on some groups of workers. Highly repetitive work with short cycle times is likely just as prevalent as in the E.U., explaining the sharply rising incidence of repetitive strain injuries among clerical and industrial workers.

Workplace Control and Stress

Sources of stress at work include the pace and demands of work, and the degree of control that workers have over the labour process. Karasek (1990) and others have emphasized that jobs are particularly stressful if high demands on workers are combined with a low level of decision latitude with respect to the use of skills and discretion on how to do the job. Stress from high-strain jobs (high demands, low control) is greater among women than men, primarily because of lower levels of job control (Wilkins and Beaudet 1998). High-strain jobs are most prevalent among lower income sales and services workers (Park 2007).

High-stress jobs have been found to be a significant contributing factor to high blood pressure, cardiovascular diseases, mental illness, and long onset disability. Workers in high-strain jobs are about twice as likely to experience depression as other workers of the same age and socioeconomic status with the same social supports (Shields 2006). There is a link from low levels of control over working conditions not only to stress, but also to higher rates of work injuries. Even where work is physically demanding, there is less risk of injury if workers can vary the pace of work, take breaks when needed, and have some say in the design of work stations.

While there have been case studies pointing to high levels of stressful work in many Canadian workplaces (Lewchuk and Robertson 1996), general data are again limited. Statistics Canada's *General Social Survey* provides some information. In 2000, 35% of workers reported experiencing stress at work from "too many demands or too many hours," up slightly from 33% in 1994, and up from 27.5% in 1991. Stress from this source is highest among professionals and managers, at 49% and 48% respectively, but is still high among blue-collar workers (28%) and sales and service workers (29%). By industry, the incidence of stress from "too many demands or hours" is highest in education, health, and social services at over 40% (see data at www.jobquality.ca). As one would expect, there is a strong relationship between working long hours and working in jobs that impose high demands. A 2005 survey with a somewhat different question found that one in three workers (32.4%) find most days "quite a bit or extremely stressful," with self-reported work stress being well above average in finance and insurance, and in health care (Lowe 2007, 47).

Women are more likely than men to report high levels of stress from "too many hours or too many demands"—37% compared to 32%. This partly reflects work-life balance issues considered below. But, it also reflects the high proportion of women working in the high-stress educational, health, and social services sectors, as well as in clerical positions that involve highly routinized, fast-paced work.

With respect to job control, data from the *General Social Survey* indicate that, in 1994, just 40% of Canadian workers reported that they had "a lot of freedom over how to work," down sharply from 54% in 1989. Data from a 2002 survey suggest there was a very slight increase in decision latitude in jobs between 1994–1995 and 2002 (Lowe 2007, 49). It should, however, be taken into account that the education level of the workforce increased significantly over this period. Men generally exercise more control than women (43% compared to 38% in 1994). Professionals and managers predictably report that they exercise much more control than skilled workers who, in turn, have more freedom than unskilled workers (51% vs. 35% vs. 31%, respectively). The same survey indicates that about half of all working Canadians believe that their jobs involve a high degree of skill, with self-reported levels of exercising a high level of skill being a bit higher among women than men.

Data from the *National Population Health Survey* for 1994–1995 have been used to construct a measure of decision latitude based on responses to two questions: "I have a lot to say about what happens in my job" and "My job allows me the freedom to decide how I do my job." This response is now being used as an official population health indicator. In 1994–1995, 48.8% of all respondents (52.3% of men and 44.5% of women) reported high decision latitude, while 36.6% (30.7% of men and a full 44% of women) reported low or medium decision latitude (Statistics Canada 2001).

To summarize, while we lack detailed information on changes in the overall incidence of work involving high demands and low worker control, high-stress work is common and likely on the increase.

Opportunities for Self-Development

As noted, a valued characteristic of work is the opportunity it provides for the exercise and development of skills and capacities. Most of us welcome the chance to work in interesting, challenging jobs, and the opportunity to learn new things. The data presented above suggest that skilled workers, particularly professionals, are usually able to utilize their skills on the job, and enjoy a fair degree of control over the labour process. Educational credentials are increasingly the major requirement to enter these kinds of good jobs. Access to training on the job is also an important determinant of well-being over the course of a working lifetime, since it provides opportunities for further skills development, and for advancement to more challenging and rewarding work. However, there are major barriers to training for those who lack time, resources, and employer support.

There is abundant evidence that many jobs are structured to minimize the need for skills rather than to further develop the capacities of workers, and that overqualification is a serious problem (Livingstone 2002). More than one in four Canadian men and women — and 40% of young people under 25 — feel overqualified for their current job according to a survey by Canadian Policy Research Networks (www.jobquality. ca). The skills and credentials of many new immigrants are routinely overlooked by employers with the result that they are sidelined into low-paying, dead-end jobs.

Working Time

A historic goal of the organized labour movement has been to expand free time. Important breakthroughs were: the ten- and then the eight-hour working day; the five-day working week and the advent of the weekend; the negotiation of paid days off, and pensioned retirement at progressively earlier ages. By the 1950s, the healthy norm of the standard, five-day, 40-hour workweek with paid annual vacation, and retirement with a decent pension was firmly entrenched.

While progress was made through the 1970s and into the 1980s in terms of reduction of weekly hours, annual hours, and the length of a working lifetime, the 1990s saw an increase in daily, weekly, and annual hours for many core workers in full-time jobs. Long hours are most prevalent among salaried professional and managerial workers, and among skilled blue-collar workers who frequently work paid overtime. From an employer perspective, overtime helps adjust production to changing market demand, and provides a particularly high cost-saving if the extra hours are not paid for. Even overtime pay premiums are often cheaper than the costs of hiring, training, and providing non-wage benefits to additional workers. Unpaid overtime is increasingly required not just of managers and professionals, but also of public and social services workers attempting to cope with increased workloads. Self-employed workers also tend to work very long hours.

While some workers want to work overtime for higher pay or out of commitment to the job or a career, most have limited ability to refuse demands for longer hours under employment standards legislation and under collective agreements. In most provinces, overtime well in excess of 40 hours can be required up to varying maximum levels of 50 hours or even more for some workers under special exemptions, sometimes provided an overtime premium is paid. Only 25% of unionized workers have some right (usually conditional) to refuse overtime. Today, about one in four workers work overtime in any given week, averaging 8.5 hours or the equivalent of an extra day's work. About half of this overtime, usually that worked by salaried managers and professionals, is unpaid, suggesting that a large share is the result of too many demands compared to a normal workweek (Lowe 2007, 56).

The Statistics Canada *Workplace and Employee Survey* found that 9% of all workers and 12% of workers in firms of more than 500 in 1999 would have preferred to work fewer hours for less pay. This can be considered an underestimate of involuntary long hours to the extent that many other workers would choose to take part of a compensation increase in the form of reduced hours. Reduced work time has recently been emphasized by several major industrial unions. For example, the Communications, Energy and Paperworkers Union (CEP) have limited overtime in pulp and paper mills, and the CAW have increased paid days off in the auto assembly sector.[1]

There was a strong trend to long (and short) working hours for both men and women in the 1980s and 1990s at the expense of the 40-hour workweek norm.[2] The proportion of core-age men aged 25–54 working more than 40 hours per week in their main job rose steadily from 15% in the early 1980s to about 20% in 1994, and has continued at that level through 2006. Over the same period, the proportion of core-age women working more than 40 hours per week rose from 5% to about 7%.[3] About one in three core-age men and one in eight core-age women in paid jobs—those most likely to face work-family time conflicts—now work more than 41 hours per week. Moreover, work is increasingly taken home, especially with the rise of laptops and BlackBerries, which make electronic work easily portable. About one in five workers now work from home in addition to their normal work hours, with this being most prevalent among professionals in both the public sector and working for large private sector employers (Lowe 2007, 19). So-called "good" jobs today make major demands on unpaid time outside of the workplace.

As noted above, working long hours is closely associated with working in high-demand jobs. While these jobs may be interesting and challenging, and give rise to opportunities for advancement, long hours and high demands can be harmful to both physical and mental health. Studies suggest that very long hours are linked to high blood pressure and cardiovascular disease. Statistics Canada has found that moving to longer working hours has some negative impacts on health risks, such as smoking, drinking, and poor diet.[4] Long hours also create a high risk of stress in terms of balancing work with domestic and community life.

The shift of core workers to long daily and weekly hours of work is much more characteristic of the U.S. and Canada than the more regulated job markets of continental

Box 4.3: "Increase in Shift Work Takes Heavy Toll"
By Virginia Galt

Almost 30 per cent of Canadians now work irregular shifts, which can mess with their sleep cycles and cut into family time, Statistics Canada reported yesterday.

And, not surprisingly, shift workers are more inclined to be unhappy with their work-life balance than employees who work regular day jobs, Statscan found in analyzing the results of a general social survey conducted in 2005.

Analyst Cara Williams wrote that working 9 to 5 may be what many consider a normal full-time job.

However, "in an economy that often demands 24/7 activity," shift work has become increasingly common.

The survey found that, in 2005, 28 per cent of 14.6 million employed Canadians worked something other than a regular day shift.

Certain occupations, such as policing and health care, have long been associated with shift work because of the nature of the jobs. In addition, more manufacturers and shippers operate round the clock now to meet demands for just-in-time delivery. Call centres and information-technology help desks are also populated 24/7.

Public transit drivers are among those being called upon to work more irregular hours—to transport growing ranks of other shift workers to and from their jobs, said transit union president Bob Kinnear, who represents employees of the Toronto Transit Commission.

"As for providing bus service and subway service, we recognize that the vehicles have to be out there," Mr. Kinnear said.

However, the Amalgamated Transit Union has long pushed for more consistent shifts, he said, because rotating schedules—where employees shift from nights to days to afternoons—are particularly disruptive.

"It's not a healthy lifestyle. Your body is not sure when to eat, when to sleep."

There is plenty of evidence that fatigued employees become ill more frequently, Mr. Kinnear added.

The majority of shift workers—55 per cent—say they work irregular hours because of the nature of their jobs, according to the Statscan report, Work-Life Balance of Shift Workers.

"However, for some, shift work was preferred because of family or child care (8 per cent), school (3 per cent), better pay (7 per cent), or personal preference (11 per cent). For another 8 per cent, it was the only type of job that [they] could get."

Ms. Williams wrote that work-life balance "is a self-defined, self-determined state reached by a person able to effectively manage multiple responsibilities at work, at home, and in the community."

This state is difficult for full-time workers to reach at the best of times, she wrote.

"Role overload—too much to do and not enough time to do it—provides another measure of wellbeing," Ms. Williams wrote.

"For example, often feeling that not enough is accomplished in the day, worrying about not spending enough time with family, constantly feeling under stress, trying to accomplish more than can be handled and cutting back on sleep are all indicators of role overload."

Cutting back on sleep is one of the most common tactics used by full-time workers to accomplish more in a day, but shift-workers are more likely than nine-to-fivers to resort to this.

"For example, just over half of all day workers cut back on sleep compared with 70 per cent of evening shift workers and 63 per cent of rotating shift workers," Ms. Williams wrote.

"This may be particularly problematic for shift workers, since they may already be having difficulty with sleep time."

Source: Galt, Virginia, Workplace Reporter. "Increase in Shift Work Takes Heavy Toll," *Globe and Mail*, August 28, 2008, B7.

Europe. The usual weekly hours of full-time paid workers in the E.U. are below 40, and falling (European Industrial Relations Observatory 2006). Some countries, notably France, the Netherlands, and Germany, are now close to a 35-hour norm. The proportion of men working weekly hours much in excess of 40 hours is generally very low.

Weekend working appears to be increasing rapidly. The incidence has gone from 11% in 1991, to 15% in 1995, to 25% in 2000, and 27% in 2003.[5] Women are more likely to work on weekends than men (28% compared to 21%), reflecting high employment rates in retail and health services. More than one in three production workers works on weekends, reflecting the rising incidence of continuous industrial production.

As noted, regular hours are shorter and jobs are less precarious in most European countries. These countries also provide much more generous paid time off work. In Canada, the minimum vacation entitlement under provincial employment standards is two weeks after a minimum length of service of about one year. (As of 2007, only Saskatchewan provided a minimum of three weeks.) Most provinces—but not Ontario as of 2007—provide for three weeks for workers with a lot of seniority, between five and fifteen years. In collective agreements, the norm is three weeks of paid vacation, rising to four weeks after 10 years. (Seventy percent of unionized workers qualify for four weeks after 10 years, and 28% qualify after five years.) By contrast, in the E.U., the minimum statutory entitlement to paid vacation leave is 20 days or four weeks, and the average provided in collective agreements is 25.7 days, or more than five weeks. German, Danish, and Dutch workers get six weeks of paid vacation per year (EIRO 2006). Statutory paid holidays on top of paid vacation entitlements are comparable between Canada and European countries.

The average age of retirement in Canada has been steadily falling, but there is generally very limited provision for a phased-in retirement process, which would allow older workers to voluntarily reduce their hours of work. Indeed, most defined pension plans create an incentive to maximize earnings (and, therefore, hours) just before retirement. By contrast, most European countries rely more heavily on public than on private pensions, and the tendency in many continental European countries has been to provide more flexible options for older workers.

To summarize, there is a strong trend toward longer hours for core workers, as well as to more unsocial hours and more variable hours. Vacation entitlements and phased-in retirement provisions in Canada are quite limited compared to many European countries. These conditions all have direct implications for stress, and for physical and mental health.

Work-Life Balance

Longer and more unpredictable hours combined with high and rising job demands are particularly likely to cause stress and anxiety in families where both partners work, and for single-parent families. In both cases, women bear the brunt of the burden (Duxbury and Higgins 2002).

Increased family working time has been a critical factor in maintaining real incomes in a labour market marked by more precarious employment and stagnating wages. Family work hours obviously determine both income and the time potentially available to spend with family, children, and in the community. While long hours may result in higher incomes, work-family time conflict may affect the physical and mental health of parents, and also influence the well-being of children. Much of the burden of caring for elderly parents as well as children is borne by working families. These pressures in terms of balancing work and family are greater in Canada than in many other countries because of the relative underdevelopment of publicly financed and delivered early childhood, elder, and home care programs.

Box 4.4: Working Families

There has been a very large increase in the total working hours of two-person families with children since the mid-1970s. This has come through increased work hours for many men, the increased entry of women into the workforce, and the shift of women into full-time jobs. About one in four (73%) of two-person families with children have two earners today compared to one in three in 1975, and three in four (73%) of working women in two-parent families work full-time. Thus, the majority of women in two-person families with children now work full-time. Six in 10 women single parents (63%) with children work, 77% of whom work full-time. Full-time employment rates for women are only slightly lower for those with pre-school age children, reflecting maternity and parental leaves taken after the birth of a child.[6]

Time pressures are steadily increasing. Between 1992 and 1998, 25- to 44-year-old parents employed full-time put in an average of two hours more per week in paid work activities. In 1998, fathers averaged 48.3 hours and mothers averaged 38.5 hours per week of paid work and related activities—up 5% for fathers and 4% for mothers from 1992. Lone-parent mothers increased their time in paid work even more than married mothers.

Work-family conflicts arise not just from longer and longer hours, but also from the frequent incompatibility of work schedules with the schedules and needs of children.

While a minority of employers do offer flex-time arrangements that are responsive to the needs of employees, the great majority of part-time jobs do not offer comparable pay, benefits, and career opportunities.

Box 4.5: "'Role Overload' Makes Workers Sick"
By Wallace Immen

A decade of increasing demands from employers combined with conflicts between home and office has created a generation of frazzled Canadians who are booking more time off for mental and physical fatigue, according to a study done for Health Canada.

The effects of "role overload" are costing Canadian businesses as much as $10-billion a year in overtime and contracting out required to complete the work of absent employees, estimated Linda Duxbury, a business professor at Carleton University in Ottawa.

"We should all be concerned about this," Prof. Duxbury said. "We knew there was a problem a decade ago. Organizations throughout the '90s talked about the importance of people, but then treated them like any other commodity. It is clear we've left the decade in far worse shape in terms of the work force, in terms of their health, and in terms of how they feel about their employer."

Prof. Duxbury and Chris Higgins of the University of Western Ontario assessed the cost of absenteeism as reported by 31,500 Canadians who work in public, private, and non-profit organizations. About 55 per cent of those who responded were women, many of them in their 40s facing mid-career pressures and a "full nest" at home, with the need to care for children and elderly parents.

The study is the fourth of seven the authors are doing on aspects of work comparing the results of the 2001 National Work-Life Conflict Study to a similar poll of workers at private, public, and non-profit organizations done in 1991. The survey found 25 per cent of Canadians worked at least 50 hours a week in 2001, which was up substantially from a decade earlier, when only 10 per cent of workers reported such long hours.

The biggest pressure, what Prof. Duxbury termed "role overload," is the feeling there is not enough time available to meet the demands in the job and their personal life.

Professional women in the survey reported working as hard as the men at work but also working harder than men at home. "It's the 'super-mom' thing," Prof. Duxbury said.

The survey found 60 per cent of all respondents said they have trouble balancing their work and family demands and 28 per cent had missed at least three days of work in the previous six months because of illness. One in 10 reported taking "mental health days" because of emotional or mental fatigue.

"Elder care is going to be the next big thing," said Prof. Duxbury. A decade ago, only one in 12 reported having to deal with the care of elderly parents or relatives, but in the 2001 survey, 60 per cent said they had some form of elder care. In the survey, 10 per cent said it was causing them stress and physical fatigue every day, and another 15 per cent said it was causing stressful situations at least once a week. "That's because of the aging of the boomers. I think the point to make is: For years employers have talked about working families and really dismissed it."

While the survey found women still have primary responsibility for child care, one in three men reported having primary responsibility for elder care. "The reality is, if it's your parent you take the active role," Prof. Duxbury said.

The widespread use of cellphones, e-mail, and laptop computers have also added the expectation of instant response to work outside of office hours.

"Some organizations now expect people will be available 24/7 and that is also contributing to stress," she added.

The strain was most obvious among people in management roles. "A decade ago, people believed to be a manager was the best job to have in Canada. You got paid more, you had more status and had more flexibility."

But many organizations have seen the downsizing of middle management. "Now we enter the new decade with a group that is absolutely critical to our ability to change within the organization. And that is the group that reports it has the most workload and the heaviest demands, and that they find their jobs less interesting and increasingly demanding," Prof. Duxbury said.

Commitment among managers has declined the most precipitously in the decade, the study found. While 62 per cent of employees reported being highly satisfied with their jobs and 66 per cent felt committed to their organization in 1991, the satisfaction level dropped to 46 per cent in 2001 and commitment was down to 53 per cent.

"That is an appalling decline," Prof. Duxbury said.

For employers, the message is: "You're not going into this as an accommodation or to be nice to people, you're doing this because it makes business sense. If you can reduce work-life conflicts you can reduce absenteeism by at least a quarter, if not more." Benefits costs will also be reduced.

"And if you don't focus on balance in work-life conflicts, good luck in recruiting and retaining employees in the next decade as we move into a sellers' market because you're not going to get loyalty.

"You can pay for their presence but you can't buy their passion. The only way you can motivate this work force and get creative work and great customer service out of them is to actually focus on work-life balance."

The study suggests employers should:

- Identify ways of reducing workloads, particularly of managers and professionals.
- Start recording the total costs of understaffing and overwork.
- Hire more staff in areas overly reliant on overtime work.
- Give employees the right to turn down overtime. Saying "no" should not be a career limiting move.
- Allow time off in lieu of overtime pay.
- Offer both child care and elder care referral services.

For employees, the study recommends:

- Say "no" to overtime hours if work expectations are unreasonable.
- Limit the amount of work they take home.

- Try to reduce the amount of time spent in job-related travel.
- Take advantage of available flexible work arrangements.

Source: Immen, Wallace. "'Role Overload' Makes Workers Sick," *Globe and Mail*, October 22, 2003, C3.

Levels of time stress and work-family stress among parents with children are extremely high. More than one-third of 25- to 44-year-old women who work full-time and have children at home report that they are severely time stressed, and the same is true for about one in four men. Twenty-six percent of married fathers, 38% of married mothers, and 38% of single mothers report severe time stress, with levels of severe stress rising by about one-fifth between 1992 and 1998. About two-thirds of full-time employed parents with children also report that they are dissatisfied with the balance between their job and home life. Fathers and mothers alike blamed their dissatisfaction on not having enough time for family, which tends to lose out in the event of conflict.[7] Work-family conflict is driven by mounting demands from work, the still largely unchanged division of domestic labour between men and women, and the failure of governments to provide caring services like child care and elder care on a sufficient scale.

A major 2004 report for Health Canada explored the links between work-life conflict and Canada's health care system (Higgins and Duxbury 2004). The prem-ise was that an employee's ability or inability to balance work and life demands would be associated with key outcomes such as absenteeism, job satisfaction, job stress, family life satisfaction, level of overall stress in life, and that these outcomes would, in turn, be linked to mental and physical health outcomes. The majority (58%) of workers in their sample of employees of medium to large organizations experienced high levels of "role overload," or having too much to do in a given amount of time. They found that compared to their counterparts with low levels of role overload, employees with high role overload were almost 2.9 times more likely to say their health was just fair or poor, 2.6 times more likely to have sought care from a mental health professional, and about twice as likely to have made frequent visits to a physician. As a result, work-life stress results in high public and private health care costs that could be avoided through better work organization, more family-friendly workplaces, and more supports for working families. The authors concluded that current workloads are not sustainable over the long term. Indeed, in a subsequent study they found that lack of serious progress toward creating more family-friendly workplaces has been a key reason why today's younger workers are putting off having children for many years, if at all. Those who get ahead today are those who put work first.

Social Relations and Participation at Work

Work is a social process, and the social relations of production are an important aspect of the quality of jobs and of working life. But, little hard information is avail-able on this relatively intangible dimension. In 2000, 15% of workers reported stress in the workplace from "poor interpersonal relations," down slightly from 18.5% in 1994, but up from 13% in 1991.[8] Women report higher levels of stress from this cause than do men. Less than one-half of employees feel that they have much influence on their jobs. A survey by Canadian Policy Research Networks found that only 10% of workers feel that they can strongly influence employer decisions that affect their job, and 45% feel that they have no influence at all. There are few significant differences by age or gender.[9]

Unionized workers do have some influence through the process of collective bargaining. About one in three paid workers in Canada is covered by the provisions of a collective agreement. Coverage is highest by far in the public sector and in large private-sector firms, particularly in primary industries, manufacturing, transportation, and utilities. By definition, collective agreements give access to a formal statement of conditions of employment, such as hours and working conditions, and access to a formal grievance and arbitration process. A formal grievance system militates against the exercise of arbitrary managerial authority, and against harassment by co-workers. Collective agreements also often provide for joint processes to govern working conditions over the life of a contract, such as labour management, training, and health and safety committees. While the great majority of agreements contain a management rights clause clarifying the power of management to assign and direct work, the majority also provide for some advance notification of, and consultation over, technological and organizational change. Many collective agreements also feature detailed job descriptions, meaning that changes in tasks are subject to joint agreement.

Most Canadian unions have adopted formal policies relating to workplace health and safety, work-family balance, work reorganization, and access to training, and have paid some attention to all of these quality of work-life issues in bargaining. Improvement of the work environment has been on the agenda, and some unions have made gains. However, there are also continuous pressures to increase productivity so as to maintain employment and wages, which tend to militate against an agenda of humanizing work and creating more healthy workplaces.

While some non-union workers also enjoy access to formalized (if non-binding) processes of dispute resolution and collective consultation, worker "voice" in the Canadian workplace is much weaker than in countries where unionization rates are much higher. Moreover, many European countries have legislation providing for joint works councils with powers to at least discuss working conditions. The E.U. survey shows that 78% of workers believe they have the possibility to discuss working conditions, and 71% the possibility to discuss organizational change, most frequently on a formal basis.

John O'Grady (Sullivan 2000) shows that effective workplace health and safety committees effectively reduce rates of injuries and disability, but are largely absent from the precarious labour market.

To summarize, institutions of collective representation are relatively weakly implanted in Canadian workplaces, undercutting the ability of workers to shape working conditions.

Conclusion

This overview suggests many grounds for concern over the potential health impacts of trends in Canadian workplaces. Workplace threats to physical health in the form of fatalities, injuries, and occupational disease remain significant for many workers. Pervasive job insecurity is a source of stress. In core workplaces, the pace and intensity of work are on the rise, and many are working very long hours in very demanding jobs. The incidence of high-strain jobs that combine high demands and limited control is quite high, particularly among women. The best available evidence suggests that the quality of work along most dimensions valued by workers is deteriorating. Summarizing the most recent trends, Lowe (2007, vii) concludes that "economic prosperity has not brought commensurate gains to workers in terms of job quality since the millennium." These negative trends exist across the skills and income spectrum, with well-paid professionals enduring high levels of stress from overwork, while the less skilled and less well paid endure stress from unstable work, physical risks, poor working conditions, and high job demands combined with low levels of control.

We need more information about the level and trends of workplace determinants of health. We lack systematic evidence of the kind collected in Europe. This could be remedied if Statistics Canada conducted regular surveys on the quality of the work environment and working conditions. The now discontinued *Workplace and Employee Survey* (WES) provided only very limited information in this area, and the *National Population Health Survey* provides only very limited information on working conditions.

Governments must intervene to help shape and improve workplace conditions. A wide range of relevant recommendations have been made over the years, most recently in the 1990s by two major Human Resources Development Canada initiated consultations. These were the Donner Task Force (the *Report of the Advisory Group on Working Time and the Distribution of Work)* and the *Collective Reflection on the Changing Workplace*, the Report of the Advisory Committee on the Changing Workplace. The thrust of the first was to regulate working time by limiting long hours and by making precarious work more secure. The thrust of the second—which included a very wide range of options—was to propose changes to employment standards and forms of collective representation. A more recent milestone report was the report of a federal task force on employment standards, *Fairness at Work: Federal Labour Standards for the 21st Century*. Commissioner Arthurs in 2006 again called for limits on long working time and arbitrary work schedules, more paid time off the job, and measures to secure respect for human rights in the workplace. He set out a "decency principle" which stated in part that "no worker should be subject to coercion, discrimination, indignity or unwarranted danger in the workplace, or be required to work so many hours that he or she is effectively denied a personal life" (Government of Canada 2006). At the end of the day, it is unlikely that there will be significant positive changes in the workplace if everything is left to employers, and if governments do not help equalize bargaining power between workers and employers.

Recommended Reading

- Duxbury, Linda, and Chris Higgins. 2002. *The 2001 National Work-Life Conflict Study*. Health Canada. www.hc-sc.gc.ca. Duxbury and Higgins have conducted several major studies of conflicts between work, family, and community life over the past several years, sparking increased interest in work-related stress as a key determinant of health.
- European Foundation for the Improvement of Living and Working Conditions. 2000 and 2007. *Report on the European Survey on Working Conditions*. www.eurofound.ie. Reports based on this regular European Union-wide survey provide a much more detailed picture of working conditions than is available for Canada.
- Human Resources and Skills Development Canada. 2006. *Fairness at Work: Federal Labour Standards for the 21st Century*. Written by a noted labour lawyer and academic, Harry Arthurs, this sets out a detailed account of what is wrong in Canadian workplaces, and how governments should intervene to promote positive change.
- Karasek, Robert, and Tores Theorell. 1990. *Healthy Work: Stress, Productivity, and the Reconstruction of Working Life*. New York: Basic Books. The is a classic study of the impacts of workplace stress on health. Stress is seen as the result of high job demands combined with low levels of control.
- Raphael, Dennis. 2008. *Social Determinants of Health: Canadian Perspectives*. Second Edition. Toronto: Canadian Scholars' Press. The social determinants of health are the socioeconomic conditions that shape the health of individuals, communities, and jurisdictions as a whole. They establish the extent to which Canadians possess the resources to identify and achieve personal aspirations, satisfy needs, and cope with the environment. This contributed volume unites top academics and high-profile experts from across the country.
- Sullivan, Terrence (Ed.). 2000. *Injury and the New World of Work*. Vancouver and Toronto: University of British Columbia Press. Contains recent studies of trends in workplace injuries, showing how "soft tissue" injuries attributable to fast-paced work have grown compared to traditional workplace accidents.

Notes

1. On working time issues, see Human Resources Development Canada, *Report of the Advisory Group on Working Time and Distribution of Work*, 1997.
2. Statistics Canada, "The Changing Work Week: Trends in Weekly Hours of Work," *Canadian Economic Observer* (September 1996).
3. *Labour Force Survey* data, available at www.jobquality.ca.
4. Statistics Canada, "Longer Working Hours and Health," *The Daily*, November 16, 1999.
5. 1991 and 1995 data from the *Survey of Work Arrangements*; 2000 data from the *Workplace and Employee Survey* (WES).
6. Statistics Canada, *Work Arrangements in the 1990s*, Cat. 71-535 MPB, No. 8, Tables 3.1, 3.2.

7. Statistics Canada, *The Daily*, November 9, 1999.
8. www.jobquality.ca
9. www.jobquality.ca.

References

Breslin, F. Curtis, Pete Smith, Mike Koehoorn, and Hyunmi Lee. 2006. "Is the Workplace Becoming Safer?" *Perspectives on Labour and Income* (December). Statistics Canada Cat. 75-001-XIE.

Brisbois, Richard. 2003. *How Canada Stacks Up: The Quality of Work—An International Perspective*. Ottawa: Canadian Policy Research Networks.

Dunn, James R. 2002. *A Population Health Approach to Housing*. Ottawa: Canadian Mortgage and Housing Corporation.

Duxbury, Linda, and Chris Higgins. 2002. *The 2001 National Work-Life Conflict Study*. Ottawa: Health Canada. www.hc-sc.gc.ca.

Duxbury, Linda, Chris Higgins, and Sean Lyons. 2007. *Reducing Work-Life Conflict: What Works? What Doesn't?* Ottawa: Health Canada. www.hc-sc.gc.ca/ewh-semt/alt_formats/hecs-sesc/pdf/pubs/occup-travail/work-travail/balancing-equilibre/report-rapport_e.pdf.

European Foundation for the Improvement of Living and Working Conditions. 2000 and 2007. *European Working Conditions Survey*. www.eurofound.europa.eu.

European Industrial Relations Observatory (EIRO). 2006. *Working Time Developments: Annual Update 2*. www.eiro.eurofound.eu.int.

Higgins, Chris, Linda Duxbury, and Karen Johnson. 2004. *Exploring the Link between Work-Life Conflict and Demands on Canada's Health Care System*. Ottawa: Health Canada. www.phac-aspc.gc.ca/publicat/work-travail/report3/index.html.

Jencks, C., L. Perlman, and L. Rainwater. 1988. "What Is a Good Job? A New Measure of Labour Market Success." *American Journal of Sociology* (May): 1322–1357.

Karasek, Robert, and Tores Theorell. 1990. *Healthy Work: Stress, Productivity and the Reconstruction of Working Life*. New York: Basic Books.

Lewchuk, Wayne, and David Robertson. 1996. "Working Conditions under Lean Production: A Worker-Based Benchmarking Study." *Asia Pacific Business Review* (Summer): 60–81.

Lewchuk, Wayne, Alice de Wolff, Andrew King, and Michael Polanyi. 2006. "The Hidden Costs of Precarious Employment: Health and the Employment Relationship." In *Precarious Employment: Understanding Labour Market Insecurity in Canada*, ed. Leah Vosko. Montreal and Kingston: McGill-Queen's University Press.

Lippel, Katherine. 2006. "Precarious Employment and Occupational Health and Safety Legislation in Quebec." In *Precarious Employment: Understanding Labour Market Insecurity in Canada*, ed. Leah Vosko. Montreal and Kingston: McGill-Queen's University Press.

Lowe, Graham. 2000. *The Quality of Work: A People Centred Agenda*. Oxford: Oxford University Press.

———. 2007. *21st Century Job Quality. Achieving What Canadians Want*. Canadian Policy Research Networks (September).

Marshall, Katherine. 2003. "Benefits of the Job." *Perspectives on Labour and Income* (May). Statistics Canada Cat. 75-001-XIE.

Park, Jungwee. 2007. "Work Stress and Job Performance." *Perspectives on Labour and Income* (December). Statistics Canada Cat. 75-001-XIE.

Raphael, Dennis (Ed.). 2004. *Social Determinants of Health: Canadian Perspectives.* Toronto: Canadian Scholars' Press Inc.

Shainblum, Esther, Terrence Sullivan, and John W. Frank. 2000. "Multicausality, Non Traditional Injury and the Future of Workers' Compensation." In *Workers' Compensation: Foundations for Reform*, ed. Morley Gunderson and Doughlas Hyatt. Toronto: University of Toronto Press.

Shields, M. 2006. "Stress and Depression in the Employed Population." *Health Reports* 17 (4). Statistics Canada.

Sullivan, Terrence (Ed.). 2000. *Injury and the New World of Work.* Vancouver and Toronto: UBC Press.

Wilkins, Kathryn, and Marie P. Beaudet. 1998. "Work Stress and Health." *Health Reports* 10, no. 3 (Winter).

World Health Organization. 1999. *Labour Market Changes and Job Insecurity.* Regional Publications/European Series No. 81.

PART II

Inequalities and Differences: Gender, Race, Ability, Age

This part of the book takes an in-depth look at the labour market and work experiences associated with specific groups: women, minorities, and older workers. The job market is marked by deep inequalities and differences along lines of gender, race, ability, and age, all of which intersect with differences in wages and the quality of employment.

Chapter 5, "Women in the Workforce," compares and contrasts the occupational distribution, forms of employment, and earnings of women and men, and shows that there are deep and systematic differences based upon gender. Women are more likely than men to be in lower paid and precarious jobs, and the pay gap between women and men remains well entrenched. That said, it is important to emphasize that there are significant differences among the labour force experiences of different groups of women, as well as among men.

Chapter 6, "Seeking Equality in the Workforce," examines the experiences of workers of colour, Aboriginal Canadians, and persons with disabilities. Despite huge differences, what these groups have in common is vulnerability to discrimination in the job market, which also means a failure by employers to accommodate differences.

This chapter summarizes evidence of significant pay, employment, and opportunity gaps between racialized workers (a large proportion of whom are recent immigrants) and other Canadians. These differences are disturbing in that they cannot be explained away with reference to education and ability. It is not just new immigrants, but also workers of colour born and educated in Canada who operate at a disadvantage. This poses a real challenge to the goal of social inclusion of all Canadians.

While a layer of new immigrants and racialized workers do very well in the job market, the same cannot be said of many Aboriginal Canadians. The very low level of economic well-being of many Aboriginal people and communities reflects the fact that their pay levels are very low compared to the Canadian norm, and that their jobs are often very unstable.

Persons with disabilities face a different problem—great difficulty gaining access to any kind of employment. While one would expect employment rates for persons with disabilities to be lower than average, the large gap also reflects a collective failure to accommodate people with different needs in the workplace.

Chapter 7, "Older Workers, Pensions, and the Transition to Retirement," looks at paths from work to retirement, the changing fortunes of older Canadian workers, and older people who are still active in the job market. Chapter 8, "Troubled Transitions," looks at the barriers to entry into good jobs faced by many younger workers. These chapters highlight the different experiences of different age groups and what has come to be known as the changing life-course.

Related Websites

All of the websites listed in Part I are also relevant to many of the issues faced by women, minorities, and older workers.

- The Assembly of First Nations (www.afn.ca/article.asp?id=3). The AFN is a major national voice for First Nations peoples and provides regular reports on work and living conditions.
- Canadian Council on Social Development (CCSD) (www.ccsd.ca). A leading social research organization, the CCSD has produced a number of studies on the labour market experiences of visible minorities and new immigrants, and reports for the United Way of Greater Toronto that cover issues facing recent immigrants. The Disability Research Information Page on the CCSD website provides access to all CCSD research on disability issues, plus links to major disability research sites.
- Changing the Canvas (www.changingthecanvas.org/). This innovative website provides the stories of many racialized workers facing barriers to inclusion in the job market.
- Council of Canadians with Disabilities (www.ccdonline.ca). As the lead advocacy organization for persons with disabilities, the council has published a wide range of position papers covering human rights, income supports, and other issues.
- The Gender and Work Database (www.genderwork.ca). This portal housed at York University provides a library, interactive statistical database, and thesaurus built around issues of gender inequality in the labour market and at work.
- Organisation for Economic Co-operation and Development (www.oecd.org). The Paris-based OECD is supported by member governments and covers many economic and social policy issues. The Directorate of Labour and Social Affairs (DELSA) publishes an annual report, the *OECD Employment Outlook*, which focuses on labour market issues and summarizes more technical research. The OECD has undertaken major comparative studies of older workers, retirement, an aging society, and the fortunes of young workers, immigrants, and persons with disabilities.

CHAPTER 5

Women in the Workforce: Still a Long Way from Equality

Introduction

Some people see the issue of economic equality for women as rather outdated and out of tune with a supposed new world of opportunity that has opened up with higher education for women and a more equal division of work between women and men. Yet, the fact of the matter is that, after many years of progress through the 1970s and 1980s, the gender wage gap in Canada has remained stuck since the mid-1990s at one of the highest levels in the advanced industrial world.

The pay gap is one key indicator of the wider issue of economic equality for women. Strikingly, the gap has grown rather than narrowed even as women have become more educated than men, and even as most women have decided to have fewer children later in life. Women are participating in the paid labour force at higher levels than ever before, and very few women now drop out of paid work for very extended periods of time. But the gap persists and grows.

One key reason for continued economic inequality is that women without high levels of education (or whose credentials are unrecognized in Canada) are much more likely than men to be employed in very low-paid and insecure part-time and temporary jobs, especially in private sector sales and service jobs.

When it comes to better paid jobs, women are still largely excluded from blue-collar jobs, especially in the skilled trades. But a large and growing layer of women have indeed moved into professional and skilled technical jobs in education, health care, and other community and public services. But these women are still paid less than comparable men, and are significantly under-represented in very well-paid jobs.

One of the key causes of continuing inequality between women and men is that our workplaces and our social and labour market policies fail to reflect the realities of women's lives. Today, the great majority of women, including mothers of young children and women with elderly parents, participate in the paid workforce. But working women still take on most of the responsibility for care and for work in the home.

Many employers demand very long hours of full-time workers, fail to provide reasonable and stable work schedules that match family needs, and will penalize women who take temporary leaves. As a result, many women are forced to work in lower paid and more unstable part-time jobs, or pay a big price for dropping out of the workforce for a year or two, or decide to work very long hours and not to have children at all.

While this chapter makes a lot of comparisons between the experiences of women and men, it is also important to emphasize that there are major and growing differences in labour market experiences among women. The progress of some women has not been experienced by all. There are also large differences in the quality of jobs between women of colour and other women, and between women who belong to unions and other women. These issues are considered separately in chapters 6 and 9.

Women Continue to Enter the Workforce

Women continued to enter the Canadian workforce in increasing numbers in the 1990s and over this decade, though at a slower rate than in the past. The labour force participation rate of women aged 15–64, which was just over one-half in the mid-1970s, had reached two-thirds by the late 1980s, and stood at an all-time high of almost three-quarters (73.5%) in 2006. This is still appreciably below the participation rate of 82.2% for men, though the rate for men has been stable or even falling because of a trend to earlier retirement over most of the 1980s and 1990s. While short periods of time outside the paid workforce remain common, the past few years have seen a big increase in the participation rate of older women. For women aged 55–59, the participation rate has jumped from just under one-half in the mid-1990s to 62.3% in 2006. Almost half of women aged 60 to 65 are now still in the paid workforce, up from just one-third a decade or so ago. Unlike earlier generations, most of today's older women have worked for all or most of their lives.

In almost all advanced industrial countries, the participation rate of women in the workforce has steadily climbed since the 1960s, and the gender gap in employment rates has narrowed considerably. The participation rate of women in Canada is now one of the very highest among the advanced industrial (OECD) countries. As noted, in 2006, 73.5% of women aged 15–64 were participating in the paid workforce, either working or actively seeking work. This compares to an OECD average of just 60.8%. For women aged 25–54, the participation rate in Canada was a very high 86.2% in 2006 compared to an OECD average of 76.5% (OECD 2007, Table C). Labour force participation in Canada by women only lags (very slightly) behind the Scandinavian countries.

Women Still Juggle Work and Family Responsibilities

In all countries, participation rates and employment in full-time jobs tend to be lower for women because women still bear the primary responsibility for child care, as well as elder care, and work in the home generally. Almost everywhere, the gap between the employment rates of women and men increases with the presence and number of children in a family. The especially low participation rates of women in some European countries, such as Germany, Italy, and Spain, reflects the survival of a traditional male breadwinner family model in which men are still the main source of family income, and many married women with children do not participate in paid work at all. This model is eroding as more women have sought economic equality with men, and as cultural norms, including the division of domestic work, have changed. But it is still a significant influence on the job market. It is interesting to note that the number of children born per woman has plummeted most in countries where women have made progress in the educational system and job market, but are still expected to bear a highly unequal share of caring work and work in the home (Beaujot and Kerr 2007).

The very high participation rates of women in the Scandinavian countries (and, likely, the narrow gender pay gap in these countries) reflect the fact that many of the caring needs of households that were traditionally taken care of by women in the home have now been assumed by the whole society through the public and not-for-profit sector. Child care and care for the elderly are readily available at low cost, which has helped women to work outside the home, and also to pursue career paths and climb job ladders without major interruptions in their work experience. The OECD judges that the cost to women of having children in terms of reduced lifetime earnings is lowest in France and the Scandinavian countries, which have public child care programs (OECD 2007, 61). Public investment in caring services outside the home has also directly created many good jobs for women.

Canada's very high rate of labour force participation by women does not reflect a well-developed system of government-supported child care. Even in Quebec, a comprehensive system is relatively new. Outside Quebec, quality care is hard to find, and is expensive. There is now some evidence that the Quebec program has, as might be expected, helped boost labour force participation by women, while lack of formal child care has held participation back in other provinces like Alberta (Roy

2006). It would seem that the major impact in Canada of a lack of organized, quality child care and elder care services is not low labour force participation by women, but rather a heavy tilt toward part-time work, as detailed below. The burden of care does not stop women from working, but it pushes them into lower paid and more insecure jobs.

Very high rates of participation by Canadian women in paid work undoubtedly reflect the fact that most women want to work to pursue a career, and to enjoy some measure of economic independence, rather than be full-time caregivers at home for extended periods of time, or completely dependent on the earnings of a spouse. Cultural norms have shifted much further away from the male breadwinner model of the 1950s than in many European countries, but high participation in paid work by Canadian women also reflects some new and more disturbing economic realities. As the real wages of men have stagnated, and for many declined, ever since the mid-1970s, women have entered the labour force to maintain and increase real family incomes. There would have been no real income growth for the great majority of Canadian working families over the past 30 years if it had not been for the rising incomes of working women. Incomes of women have increased as more women have worked, as their hours of work have risen, and because the wage gap between women and men narrowed until the mid-1990s.

The dual-earner family is now very much the Canadian norm, and the earnings of women currently make up one-third of the income of dual-earner families. This proportion has remained steady since the late 1990s after trending up from 25% in the late 1960s (Statistics Canada 2006, Chapter 5). About one in four women in dual-earner families now earns more than their male spouse, and the earnings of women are, of course, the main source of income for most single-parent families and for the many women who live alone. Low earnings of many women are a major part of the explanation for very high poverty rates among single-parent families headed by women. Low earnings for many women are also a big factor behind low family incomes, since high-earning men now tend to live with higher earning women. Of course, a layer of well-paid men can, and do, support spouses who do not work, or work only part-time, but this is much less common than a generation ago. The key point is that the earnings of women are hugely important to economic well-being, and are now rarely just an add-on to male earnings. This makes the low earnings of many women and the gender pay gap highly problematic for both economic and equality reasons.

Three in four (73%) of Canadian two-parent families with children are now two-earner families. While many women (and a few men) with children work part-time, half of all two-parent families with children have two full-time earners. And, more than six in 10 (63%) of single-parent families with children are headed by someone in the workforce. Employment rates are a bit lower for women with very young children. The domestic responsibilities of women, and the fact that many women with young children still take some time out of the paid workforce, still make a difference. In 2006, one in three women (33.6%) with a child under age six and about the same proportion with a child under age three (35.7%) were not in paid employment (Statistics Canada 2006, Table 5), and very few men take extended parental leaves to care for a young child. The participation rates of women who have given birth to a child in the last three years are about 10 percentage points below those of other women in the same age group. The length of maternity and parental leaves has recently increased partly because of expanded rights to maternity/parental benefits under the Employment Insurance program (Zhang 2007). While more than twice as likely to be in the workforce as 30 years ago, lower than average labour force participation rates for women with very young children reflect the choice and opportunity of many women to take short-term or somewhat longer maternity and parental leaves, a choice that has been facilitated by improved maternity/parental benefits, and perhaps influenced by problems of access to quality affordable child care. Very long working hours for some men are also likely a factor why some couples with children decide to live on one income, at least for a period of time.

Regardless of the reasons, the evidence suggests that giving birth to a child lowers the future earnings of a Canadian mother compared to a comparable woman without children by between 5% and 13% (Drolet 2002; Zhang 2007). The OECD points out that those mothers have significantly lower lifetime earnings than do women who have no children, with the price being lowest in countries with public child care services. In today's job market, periods spent outside of paid work to care for children may be taken voluntarily, but nonetheless come at a price.

Many women, especially those working in part-time jobs, must deal with unstable and unpredictable work schedules. There was an increase in unsocial working hours in the 1990s, with more women working at night and on weekends. More women are also now working very long hours. About one in seven women now work more than 41 hours per week. Unpredictable or long hours combined with high and rising job demands cause acute stress for many women, because women still bear the major responsibility for domestic labour (child care, elder care, household maintenance, etc.). While more men are doing some household work, women in dual-earner families in 2005 undertook 62% of the total hours spent by the household in domestic work, or almost one hour more per day than men (Marshall 2006). Working women are typically more likely than men to be responsible for dropping off and picking up children at child care, and for shopping. As a result, levels of time stress and work-family stress among women with children are extremely high. More than one-third of 25- to 44-year-old women who work full-time and have children at home, and 38% of single mothers, report that they are severely time stressed, with levels of reported severe stress rising by about one-fifth over the 1990s. About two-thirds of full-time employed parents with children also report that they are dissatisfied with the balance between their job and home life (Statistics Canada, *The Daily*, November 9, 1999). This acute time conflict for many women likely leads many to "balance" work and family by opting out of jobs with very long hours and/or very heavy work demands, and this is likely a key factor behind the continuing wage gap.

The Persistent Gender Wage Gap

One striking development in Canada over the past decade or so has been that the gender pay gap has, after many years of gradual progress toward equality, remained more or less stuck. Continued economic inequality between women and men, despite the fact that formal educational qualifications of at least younger women now exceed those of men, tells us that women still face discrimination and barriers, and that real equality of opportunity does not yet exist. This in turn means that many women remain, to a significant degree, economically dependent upon the earnings of men to sustain a decent family income, and that many women experience or are especially vulnerable to low income and poverty. This is especially true in an age of unstable families where about four in 10 of all marital unions end in divorce. Wage gaps and low income over the course of a working lifetime condemn many women to low income in old age, with the low income rate of single elderly women significantly exceeding that of men (8.4% compared to 3.2% in 2005).

The most commonly cited indicator of the gender wage gap is annual earnings of full-time, full-year workers. This indicator used to be prominently reported upon each year. By this measure, women earned just 70.5% as much as men in 2005, or $39,200 compared to $55,700. If we look at all workers—including part-time and part-year workers, the gap is even greater, with women earning just 64% as much as men. These annual earnings indicators combine the impact of lower hourly wages with fewer weeks and hours worked over the year. What is striking, as illustrated

Table 5.1: The Pay Gap: Earnings of Women vs. Men

	2000	2001	2002	2003	2004	2005
Average annual earnings of men (full-year, full-time)	$53,300	$54,400	$54,500	$54,300	$56,300	$55,700
Average annual earnings of women (full-year, full-time)	$37,700	$38,000	$38,300	$38,100	$39,300	$39,200
Pay gap	$15,600	$16,400	$16,200	$16,200	$17,000	$16,500
Average annual earnings of women as % of men:						
All	61.7%	62.1%	62.8%	62.9%	63.4%	64.0%
Full-year, Full-time	70.6%	69.9%	70.2%	70.2%	69.9%	70.5%
Full-year, Full-time with university degree	68.6%	65.5%	69.0%	69.0%	65.6%	67.9%

Source: Statistics Canada. *Income Trends in Canada*, 2007. Cat. 13F002XIE, Tables 2020102 and 2020104.

Note: Income data are in constant 2005 dollars.

Figure 5.1: Female/Male Earnings Ratio (%), 1980–2006, Full-Time, Full-Year

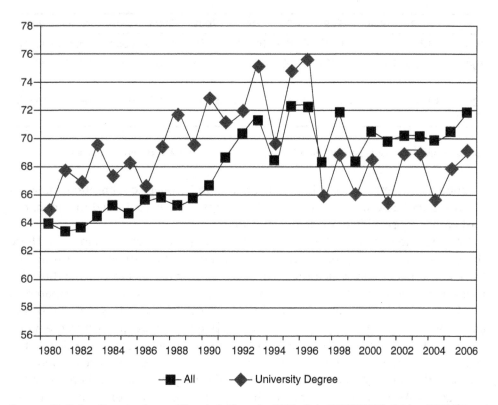

Source: Statistics Canada. *Income Trends in Canada*, 2006. Cat. 13F0022XIE, Tables 2020102 and 2020104. Note: Income data are in constant 2006 dollars.

in Figure 5.1, is that the gender wage gap for full-time, full-year workers closed steadily through the 1980s until the mid-1990s. Over that period, women's annual earnings rose from about two-thirds to about 70% that of men, but the wage gap has since stagnated at that level. As further shown in the chart, the gender wage gap for workers with a university degree also closed steadily until the mid-1990s, and then suddenly rose again in 1997. It has remained stuck at between 66% and 68% since that time. In short, the long trend toward greater economic equality of women and men has drawn to a close over the past decade or so. Data for 2000 to 2005 are provided in Table 5.1.

As shown in Table 5.2, the hourly wage gap between women and men has narrowed only slightly over the past decade, and has increased slightly among young people. The failure of the gender wage gap to continue to close is particularly surprising in view of the fact that the educational attainment of women, especially younger women, has continued to improve compared to that of men. As of 2001, only 26% of women aged 20–24 did not have some education beyond high school compared to 36% of young adult men. By age 25–44, 44.5% of women in 2001 had a post-secondary qualification compared to just 40.1% of men, with women accounting for the majority of university

Table 5.2: Average Hourly Wage of Women as Percentage of Men

	1997	1998	1999	2000	2001	2002	2003	2004	2005	2006
All	81.6%	81.4%	81.1%	80.6%	80.9%	81.8%	82.3%	83.2%	83.8%	83.8%
Age 15–24	91.2%	91.0%	91.0%	89.3%	89.5%	90.0%	90.6%	90.4%	91.1%	90.5%
Age 25–54	81.3%	81.2%	80.7%	80.4%	80.6%	81.9%	82.5%	83.4%	84.2%	84.0%

Source: Statistics Canada. *Labour Force Survey*. 2006. Cat. 71F0004XCB, Table cd3t01an.

graduates, and almost 60% of those with a community college qualification (Statistics Canada 2006, Table 4.2). Yet, the annual earnings gap has continued to widen, not least among those with a university education.

Table 5.3 shows average hourly wages for a range of occupations in 2006. These show a pure gender gap per hour worked, as opposed to larger pay gaps for the week and for the year, which reflect not just lower pay rates for women but also fewer hours worked. Women earned an average of $17.96 per hour compared to $21.43 for men in 2006, meaning that women earned, on average, 83.8% of the male hourly wage. As indicated, the wage gap tended to be greatest in the male-dominated, blue-collar occupations, and in the low-paid sales and service sector. Overall, women earned significantly less than men in lower paid occupations. By contrast, the wage gap is smaller in better paid occupations, especially in health occupations. As will be detailed below, the impact of these wage differences between occupations and wage gaps within occupations is amplified by the fact that women

Table 5.3: Average Hourly Wages by Occupation, 2006

	Men	Women	Women as % of men
All	$21.43	$17.96	83.8%
Management	$33.33	$27.68	83.0%
Business, finance, administrative	$20.97	$17.95	85.6%
Natural and applied sciences	$28.70	$24.60	85.7%
Health occupations	$23.68	$23.02	97.2%
Social science, education, government services	$28.69	$24.22	84.4%
Art, culture, recreation, sport	$20.69	$18.96	91.6%
Sales and service	$14.91	$11.74	87.7%
Trades, transport, equipment operators	$19.86	$14.67	73.9%
Processing, manufacturing, utilities	$18.79	$13.57	72.2%

Source: Statistics Canada. *Labour Force Historical Review*. 2006. Cat. 71F0004XCB, Table cd3t01an.

are disproportionately over-represented in low-wage occupations. Data for hourly wages are consistently available only from 1997, and show a slight decrease in the gender wage gap, suggesting that hours of work play a major role in the annual earnings gap.

Table 5.4 and Figure 5.2 indicate that there are a higher proportion of women than men in all earnings brackets until income levels of $35,000 to $40,000 are reached. At an annual earnings level of $60,000 and more, men predominate in a proportion of about 2.5 to one. Almost one in five men earned more than $60,000 in 2005 compared to well under one in 10 women.

At the very top of the income spectrum, men overwhelmingly dominate. In 2004, the top 5% of Canadian tax-filers earned $89,000 or more. Of this top group, 76% were men, rising to 79% in the elite top 1% group earning more than $181,000. The highly disproportionate representation of men in the very highest income groups helps explain the failure of the gender wage gap to continue to close since the mid-1990s, since the proportion of all income going to the male-dominated high-income group has been steadily rising. The top 5% of individual taxpayers declared 25.3% of all income in 2004, up from 20.9% in 1992 (Murphy, Roberts, and Wolfson 2007).

The gender wage gap exists in all OECD countries, with the median hourly pay of women full-time workers averaging 18% less than that of men (OECD 2006, Table

Table 5.4: Distribution of Annual Earnings of Women vs. Men, 2005

All earners	Women	Men
<$5k	17.2	13.1
$5–10k	13.0	8.2
$10–15k	10.0	7.1
$15–20k	8.9	6.0
$20–25k	8.0	5.6
$25–30k	7.4	5.9
$30–35k	6.9	6.7
$35–40k	5.8	6.1
$40–45k	4.7	5.4
$45–50k	3.8	4.9
$50–60k	5.4	8.3
$60k>	8.8	22.9
Median	$20,200	$32,700
Average	$26,800	$41,900

Source: Statistics Canada. *Income Trends in Canada*, 2007. Cat. 13F0022XIE, Table 2020101. Note: Income data are in constant 2005 dollars.

Figure 5.2: Distribution of Annual Earnings of Men and Women (%), 2006 (all earners)

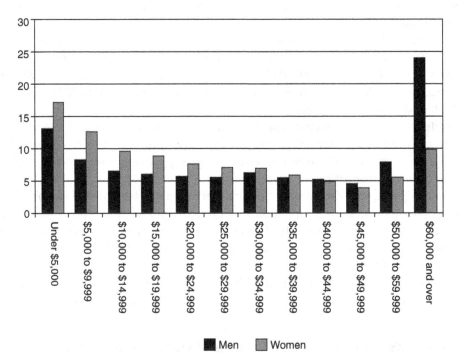

Source: Statistics Canada. *Income Trends in Canada*, 2006. Cat. 13F0022XIE, Table 2020101.

Note: Income data are in constant 2006 dollars.

EQ3.3). The gender pay gap in Canada measured by this key international indicator is, however, well above average, with women earning 23% less than men in full-time jobs. The gender pay gap in Canada is now the fifth greatest among 22 OECD countries, and somewhat greater than in the United States.

The Changing Generational Fortunes of Young Women and the Pay Gap

The past 30 years or so have seen a huge shift in the life experiences of younger adults. A generation and more ago, young people left home, entered into marital unions, found stable jobs, and had children at a much earlier age than is now the case. Today, it is not until their mid-twenties that the majority of young people are working full-time. Before that age, the majority are still at school. More than 40% of people in their twenties still live at home, up from just one in four in 1981. At age 25–29, close to half of all young women are still single compared to just one-quarter a generation ago. The average age at which a woman has a first child has risen by four years to age 28, and single-child families are increasingly the norm (Beaujot 2004). Adding to all of these changes, families have become much more unstable.

Key changes in the job market help explain this delayed transition to the adult norm of a generation ago. Good jobs require higher levels of education, and there has been a significant deterioration in the quality of jobs available to young people who do not have a post-secondary education. In the 1990s, wage gaps and differences in employment and unemployment rates between young people with and without post-secondary qualifications greatly increased. As a result, post-secondary enrolment in Canada has soared to one of the highest levels in the world.

On balance, young women have made progress. Compared to earlier generations, families have been prepared to invest in the education of all children, and most young women now expect and want to pursue an education and a career. As noted, the education gap between the sexes no longer exists and indeed has reversed. Partly as a result, compared to earlier generations, the earnings of young women have fallen less than those of young men (Jackson 2006). However, the pay gap between young women and young men remains surprisingly intact.

Box 5.1: "Workers 'Cut' Family for Jobs: Study"
Researchers find half of Canadians put off or don't have children to cope with stress
By Kathryn May

Half of Canadians are coping with the growing stress and workload of their jobs by delaying or not having children, a strategy a new study concludes works better than the family-friendly policies offered by their employers.

The federally-funded study, to be released today, found employers in all sectors are shifting the burden of balancing work-life on to workers, forcing them to make sacrifices such as sleeping less, working harder, giving up social lives and having fewer children.

In fact, the study concluded that "family-friendly" policies such as unpaid leave, job-sharing and flexible work arrangements not only force workers to deal with the upheaval in their lives with their own time and money, but they increase stress and workload because workers who take advantage of them don't get ahead.

"When work and family becomes too much, we cut the family and just work. That's what we're doing," Said Linda Duxbury, who co-authored the study, the fifth in a series of reports into how Canadians handle the work-life balance.

"And the strategy works because their overload and balance is better, but people are making those decisions when their careers are going up, they're doing well and they feel they can't handle any more. Then, they hit their late 40s and there's nothing they can do."

Ms. Duxbury, a professor at Carleton University's Sprott School of Business, co-wrote the series of reports based on a survey of nearly 33,000 workers. The survey was commissioned by Health Canada to examine how Canadians are coping with the demands of their work and family lives. It was conducted by Ms. Duxbury and Chris Higgins of the University of Western Ontario and surveyed workers in 100 major organizations in the private, public and not-for-profit sectors. The findings are considered accurate within 1.5 percentage points, 19 times out of 20.

Today's study analyzed four types of work-life conflict—role overload; work interferes with family; family interferes with work and caregiver strain; defined as the stress of taking care of children and elderly parents.

Role overload, that frazzled feeling of never having enough time to get things done, and work interfering with family were at the root of most conflict for workers, their families and the companies they work for.

Ironically, the study shows that the most overworked and stressed-out employees work in government, education and health, the public sector employers who offer the most support policies.

Ms. Duxbury has long argued Canada's employers get off easy by offering support policies that "aren't worth a hill of beans." They typically shift all cost to workers, who take less pay with part-time jobs, unpaid leave and time off without pay or turn to counseling and hire extra help.

The study showed the few who decide to put family first and copy by prioritizing, delegating work to others, saying no to extra work and seek support from friends and family have less stress, but they typically don't get ahead. The majority "try to do it all" and turn to "self-sacrifice" tactics. And having fewer or no children proves effective in easing stress because the smaller families reduce obligations at home.

One in four respondents said they coped by having fewer children, while 28 per cent said they delayed having children or opted to have none at all. It's most dramatic among educated women. Two-thirds of the female professionals and managers opted for fewer or no children so they could better juggle their work and home lives.

But Ms. Duxbury said it's high time employers realize that work and family lives are no longer "separate worlds" and Canada's productivity depends on helping employees manage them together.

Off Balance

Canadians are finding it increasingly difficult to balance the demands of work and family. Here are some of the findings from a survey of 33,000 Canadians who work for companies with 500 or more employees. A similar survey was done in 1991.

- One in four Canadians work more than 50 hours a week, compared to one in 10 who put in those kinds of hours in 1991.
- 60 per cent of Canadians complain of "role overload," the inability to find the time to manage their jobs and family. That's an 11-per-cent increase over the past decade.
- One in four says their work gets in the way of their family responsibilities. Only 10 per cent say family obligations interfere with work.
- Three times as many Canadians say they put work before family as those who put family before work. At the same time, the percentage of working Canadians who put family over work doubled in the past decade and is expected to increase as the population ages and more people have to care for elderly parents.

- The mental health of workers is declining. Half reported high stress; one in three said they were burned out and depressed. About 40 per cent said they were satisfied with their lives and one in five was dissatisfied. One in five described their physical health as fair to poor.
- The number of employees who complain of high stress is three times higher than it was in 1991. The proportion of employees who say they are committed to their jobs and enjoy high job satisfaction fell significantly.
- The culture of an organization and the workload are the two biggest predictors of "role overload" and work is getting in the way of family.

A culture of working long hours to get ahead is the unwritten rule in most organizations. It bred a generation of women who think family, not work culture, is the problem. Employers respond, she said, with support policies that spell the kiss of death for the careers of those who use them.

She argued policymakers have to recognize workload is a key reason for Canada's declining birth rate and labour force.

"Most employers have the attitude, 'you decided to have kids, so you figure out how to balance your lives," said Ms. Duxbury. "So, people had fewer children and now we're paying the price with dropping fertility. And we're not going to get fertility rates up by (the government) paying us $100 a month to have kids. It's not going to happen. That won't buy the day care and support you need to have a career and family."

Ms. Duxbury predicts that "moralizing" attitude is coming back to haunt employers because the next generation of workers won't tolerate it. In a sellers market for talent, their skills are in big demand and they can pick up and move to employers who will given them the flexibility to have both family and work lives.

What makes a big difference is not flexible work arrangements policies, but whether employees feel they have the freedom to use them. Only one-third of the respondents working for companies with such policies felt that they had any "real" flexibility in juggling the demands of work and home.

Ms. Duxbury argues workers want to feel free to come in late or leave early of necessary; work at home to care for a sick child and slip out of the office for a couple of hours to see a child's Christmas concert or to take an elderly parent to the doctor. One in three respondents, for example, said they can't take vacation when they want.

The challenge for employers will be even bigger because young workers have a completely different view of balance from the workaholic baby boomers who have dominated the labour market.

Take Generation X. They're the managers of tomorrow, between the ages of 30 and 42, who find themselves sandwiched with young children and aging parents. Most companies didn't hire in the 1990s and as people retire, this generation will have the pick of the jobs. Unlike the boomers, they put family, not work, first. The younger workers hitting the job market now, the so-called millennial generation, see balance as "having time for hobbies, fun and pleasure outside of work."

"So either companies take control and see what they can do with work-life balance, or they will lose control and employees will take control in their own hands and they'll say no. 'No extra work, I'm leaving on time and if you want me to work overtime, you pay me.' Workers couldn't do it before, but they can do it now."

Ms. Duxbury argues the most effective action companies can take is grooming better managers. The biggest indicators of stress for most workers was their managers because "who you work for is a key predictor of how much flexibility an employee perceives they have with respect to their hours and work schedule."

Managers are the more overworked, stressed-out and among the unhappiest workers in the country. The downsizing of the 1990s, coupled with technologies such as cellphones and e-mail, made management a 24-hour-a-day job. More than half of respondents said they worked for "inconsistent" or "non-supportive" managers who had little time for their people.

Ms. Duxbury said one big problem is that many work-life policies are designed to manage the office "abusers or jerks," the 10 per cent of workers who take advantage of any flexibility. As a result, workers don't feel trusted and, in a tight labour market, the top performers "will walk" and the solid, steady workers who are the backbone of any operation will disengage.

"The fact is organizations drive this and their actions have the most impact on families and workers. Most companies tell their employees 'go ahead, say no to more work, and take control,' but those who buck the system are the ones who get nowhere in their careers," said Ms. Duxbury.

"Well, expect more buckers in a sellers market for labour. I tell you that means organizations have to change. I hope they can take these lessons to heart because the companies who will be able to recruit and retain people will be the ones who don't force them to choose between a life and a job."

Source: May, Kathryn. "Workers 'Cut' Family for Jobs: Study," *Ottawa Citizen*, October 3, 2007, A1, A4.

A Statistics Canada research paper looks at employment and earnings for young men and women aged 25–29 in each of 1981, 1991, and 2001 (Frenette and Coulombe 2007). Over those years, the educational gap between young women and men continued to widen as the proportion of women in that age group with a university degree rose from 16.2%, to 19.1%, to 31.3%, while the proportion of university-educated young male adults rose at a slower pace, from 15.5%, to 16.1%, to 26.1%. The employment gap between university-educated young adult men and women also shrank as the proportion of women graduates working full-time rose.

Despite progress in terms of educational attainment and obtaining full-time jobs, the pay gap between university-educated young women and young men exploded in the period from 1991 to 2001 (after narrowing between 1981 and 1991). In 2001, university-educated young adult women earned an average of $36,782 or 18.4% less than the average earnings of $45,054 for comparable men. This compares to a gap of 12.2% in 1991. Between 1991 and 2001, average earnings of university-educated young women actually fell, from $37,066, while rising among comparable men, from $42,219 in 2001. (These are real or inflation-adjusted earnings, in year 2000 dollars.)

Meanwhile, the earnings gap remained constant for college-educated and high school-educated young adults.

The authors attribute much of this gap to the fact that university-educated women suffered pay cuts as a result of disproportionate employment in public sector health and education jobs, while men gained due to disproportionate employment in private sector jobs in engineering, computer science, and commerce. The fact remains that it is young adult men university graduates who have had access to the best paid jobs due to continued occupational segregation, as detailed below.

Pay Discrimination and Pay Equity

Economic research has consistently shown that the greatest part of the gender wage gap in Canada, as in other industrial countries, cannot be explained by supposedly objective factors such as the educational level and job experience of women, but is created by gender itself (Drolet 2002; OECD 2002). In other words, there is an unexplained differential by gender when analysts control for other measurable factors (some of which themselves are influenced by gender). Pay gaps can and do result from cultural preconceptions of the value of particular jobs, reinforced by comparisons with other employers operating on the same assumptions, rather than from an objective analysis of job characteristics as a guide to pay levels. Male blue-collar workers are still often paid more than women clerical workers, even though their jobs are neither more highly skilled, nor involve greater responsibility, nor are necessarily more demanding. Well into the 1970s, nursing and elementary school teaching were low-paid jobs mainly because these were professions dominated by women, rather than because the skill level and responsibility of the work were low. Traditionally, male workers were more highly unionized than women, and greater bargaining power helped raise their relative wages. (Low unionization for women compared to men is still a big factor in the private sector.) Until at least the 1960s and 1970s, the cultural norm was that men should be paid a family-supporting wage, and women were viewed as secondary income earners.

Pay gaps can arise from the fact that women are discriminated against when it comes to accessing better jobs and promotions. Such discrimination can be overt—protection of male job monopolies or more systemic—a failure to recognize and accommodate differences between women and men. While differences in total work experience are not necessarily very large, the perception that a career comes second seems to be a major factor behind the glass ceiling that continues to exist in some workplaces and professions.

The struggle for legislated pay equity for women goes back a long way. The demand for laws requiring equal pay for women and men doing the same job dates back to the nineteenth century and, by the 1950s, most Canadian provinces had legislated against pay discrimination in the sense of forbidding employers from paying women less than men performing the same job. However, expressed in this way, the principle of equality is problematic for the simple reason that women and men mainly work in different jobs, rather than side-by-side, for different pay in the same job. Pay discrimination by gender is less discrimination against individuals than systemic, in that the kinds of jobs held by women are undervalued compared to the jobs of men, and pay lesser wages (Armstrong, Cornish, and Millar 2003).

From the mid-1970s, the federal government and some provinces began to legally require some employers to pay women equal pay for work of equal value, that is, to equalize pay between comparable job groups or classifications within the same establishment. Usually, such legislation has applied to public sector employers, and application to even large private sector employers has been much more limited and episodic. Small employers have almost invariably been excluded.

Proactive pay equity laws covering only the public sector have been introduced in Manitoba, New Brunswick, Prince Edward Island, and Nova Scotia. However, Newfoundland and Labrador, Alberta, British Columbia, and Saskatchewan still have no legislation at all governing equal pay for work of equal value. Only Ontario (1998) and Quebec (1996) have proactive pay equity laws covering both the public and private sectors. Preliminary reports on the tenth anniversary of the Quebec *Pay Equity Act* indicated that one-third of the completed pay equity exercises had resulted in salary adjustments of between 3.9% and 8.1%. The federal legislation, which requires filing a complaint, is embedded in the *Canadian Human Rights Act*. Similar human rights provisions also cover Yukon, the Northwest Territories, and Nunavut.

The federal legislation is much less effective. Equal pay for work of equal value can only result from a complaint by employees. When a complaint has been made, employers and unions have had to undertake complex comparisons of job classifications to determine if female-dominated jobs have been undervalued and if so, to calculate any pay differential that should be eliminated. And employers have used lack of clarity in the legislation to challenge the positive results of pay equity studies, and to tie up the process for years by resorting to the courts.

There have been some significant pay gains for some groups of women under the federal law, as in landmark legal settlements for women clerical and support workers in the federal public service, and women workers at Bell Canada. (Men in female-dominated classifications also benefited.) However, these victories came only after years of protracted negotiations and extremely expensive legal struggles. In practice, the legal struggle for pay equity has only benefited women working for large employers, mainly where a union has been prepared to actively press the case.

The principle of equal pay for work of equal value has not been effectively applied outside a few parts of the job market, and has been undercut by the restructuring of work in such a way as to undermine large workplaces where systematic comparisons can readily be made between the jobs of women and men (Armstrong, Cornish, and Millar 2003). Pay equity legislation would be much more effective if all employers were required to proactively ensure that their pay classification systems were gender neutral.

Precarious Work

The fact that more women are working is positive from the point of view of the economic independence of women and the incomes of families, but tells us nothing about the quality of the jobs that women are finding. A significant and disproportionate number of women workers are employed in precarious jobs—that is, in insecure jobs that carry a high risk of unemployment and/or low pay, and provide limited access to benefits, such as pensions and drug and dental plans. Precarious jobs also involve limited control of working hours and conditions, and offer limited prospects for advancement in the job market.

Table 5.5: Employment of Women and Men by Form of Employment, 2006

	Men (%)	Women (%)
Full-time	89.2	73.9
Part-time	10.8	26.1
Employees	81.4	88.7
% of Employees in public sector	17.3	28.6
% of Employees in temporary jobs	12.3	13.7
Self-employed	18.6	11.3
Self-employed (of which are unincorporated or have no employees)	43.4	58.1

Source: Statistics Canada. *Labour Force Historical Review.* 2006. Cat. 71F0004XCB, Tables cd1t07,08,44an.

The incidence of precarious and insecure forms of work rose significantly in the 1990s, and is higher for women than men (Vosko et al. 2003). Table 5.5 shows the major differences in the kinds of jobs—or "forms of employment"—held by women and men. The biggest difference by far, explored in more detail below, is that women are much more likely to work in part-time jobs. More than one in four women (26.1%) works part-time compared to just over one in 10 men (10.8%), and the gap is even greater when young workers are excluded. Men are more likely to be self-employed, but women have been catching up fast and are more likely to be in the most insecure form of self-employment, working by oneself in an unincorporated business. Women are modestly more likely to work in temporary jobs, which can be contract or seasonal jobs.

Another key dimension of precarious employment is the incidence of low pay. Even steady full-time jobs can provide little or no economic security if they are in low-paid businesses and sectors. In 2007, 31.4% of all women were in low-paid jobs compared to 20.9% of men, and, while the incidence of low pay is highest among young workers, fully 21.6% of women aged 25 to 54 were low paid compared to just 11.5% of men in the same age group. Low paid is defined as earning less than two-thirds of the median wage, which translated to under $12 per hour in 2007. (Custom data supplied by Statistics Canada Labour Force Survey Division. This definition of low pay is used by the OECD to make international comparisons above.)

If we understand precariousness as a combination of unstable work and low-paid work, it is clear that women are much more precariously employed than men. This translates into a high risk of poverty for single women, especially those with children. In 2005, 33.4% of all single-parent families headed by women fell below Statistics Canada's Low Income Cut-off Line (after tax), as did 37.1% of unattached (single) women under 65 compared to 32.1% of unattached non-elderly men.[1] Low wages also imply a significant degree of economic dependence upon men for many women in dual-earner families.

Women of colour are especially likely to have low earnings. Data from the 2001 Census showed that, while women had average annual earnings of $24,390, visible minority women earned an average of $22,301, and women immigrants who had come to Canada in the previous five years had average annual earnings of just $18,113. Low earnings of women are clearly one major factor behind very high poverty rates among recent immigrant families. Women from most immigrant groups participate at high levels in the paid workforce, but are often only able to find low-paid and precarious jobs. Many such women have high levels of education, but face difficulty in having international credentials recognized, and also face racial discrimination. Women with disabilities also had below average earnings ($20,821). These women, like Aboriginal women, experience not just low pay, but also much higher than average rates of unemployment, and low levels of employment. Among all equality-seeking groups, women earn significantly less than their male counterparts.

Unemployment

The unemployment rate of women is usually a bit lower than that of men. In 2006, the unemployment rate for women aged 15–64 was 6.1% compared to 6.6% for men, and for core working-age women aged 25–54, it was 5.2% compared to 5.4% for men. For both women and men, these were the lowest annual average unemployment rates for more than 30 years. Women also tend to be unemployed for a slightly shorter period of time than men—an average of 15.8 weeks compared to 17.4 weeks in 2006. Lower unemployment rates for women mainly result from the fact that a higher proportion of men are employed in seasonal jobs like construction and primary industries, while relatively more women are employed in steadier public and social services jobs. Also, women who lose a job are a bit more likely than men to spend a period of time outside the workforce rather than to actively look for another job right away. That said, many women have experienced unemployment in recent years. The unemployment rate for women topped 10% in both 1992 and 1993 before slowly falling over the rest of the decade. Even at a superficially low unemployment rate of 6%, it has to be borne in mind that a much higher proportion of workers, about 10%, will experience at least one spell of unemployment over the course of a year. Younger women have experienced and continue to experience very high rates of unemployment. In 2006, the unemployment rate for young women aged 15–24 was 10.4%, still below the 12.8% rate for young men.

While women are unemployed a bit less often than men, they are also less likely to have very stable employment. The average woman worker aged 25–54 has been in her job for 94 months or a bit under eight years, almost one year less than a man in the same age group. Among workers aged 25–54, about one in five of both women and men have been in their current job for less than one year. Shorter job tenure is one indicator of more precarious employment, and also reflects periods spent out of the workforce caring for children. There continues to be a significant gap between the proportion of women and men who work full-time hours for a full year—that is, who are steadily employed. In 2005, 55.2% of men worked full-time hours for the full year compared to 45.8% of women (Statistics Canada. *Income in Canada*. 2006. Table 202013).

Box 5.2: Women and the Employment Insurance (EI) Program

Despite deep cuts in the mid-1990s affecting who is eligible and the amount of benefits that are paid, EI remains critical to the well-being of workers and working families. In 2005–2006, even with a low overall unemployment rate, the program provided about $8 billion in benefits to provide income support to workers between jobs, about $3 billion in maternity/parental benefits to parents (almost all to mothers), and $1 billion in sickness benefits. Some two million claims were filed in that year. In 2006, the maximum weekly benefit was $423, representing 55% of maximum insurable earnings of $40,000 per year (Human Resources and Skills Development Canada 2006).

EI income support during periods of unemployment, maternity/parental leave, and periods of sickness is obviously important in terms of stabilizing and supporting family incomes, and also supports the economic independence of women since benefits are not based on family income (with the exception of a small supplement for low-income families), but rather on insured individual earnings. However, key EI program rules exclude or unfairly penalize women because they fail to take into account the different working patterns of women compared to men. While the great majority of adult women now engage in paid work, the hours they work exclude many from EI benefits, as do periods of time spent away from work caring for children or others.

As Monica Townson and Kevin Hayes document in a study originally conducted for Status of Women Canada (whose research program was eliminated in 2006), only 32% of unemployed women qualify for regular EI benefits compared to 40% of men who are unemployed. Over 70% of women and 80% of men qualified for benefits before major cuts were imposed in the early 1990s. The key reason for the gender gap is that to qualify, a person must have worked in the previous year, and must have put in between 420 and 700 hours of work, depending on the local unemployment rate. Workers in most large urban areas now have to put in 700 hours, roughly the equivalent of 40 weeks of full-time work (Townson and Hayes 2007).

Fewer unemployed women qualify than do men because many women take extended leaves from work to care for children or others. After a two-year absence from paid work, the entrance requirement jumps to 910 hours, or more than six months of full-time work. And, when they work, women are much more likely than men to be employed in part-time and/or temporary jobs as opposed to full-time, permanent jobs providing steady hours. Because they lack enough qualifying hours, only about half of part-time workers who lose their jobs actually qualify for unemployment benefits.

Even when they do qualify, the lower pay of women combined with more unstable work patterns means that they usually qualify for lower benefits (an average of $291 per week compared to $351 for men in 2005–2006). Only about one-third of the total dollar amount of regular EI (unemployment) benefits are paid to women, even though women now participate in the paid workforce at almost the same rate as men.

The EI program now provides up to 15 weeks of maternity benefits and 35 weeks of parental benefits, 90% of which are taken by women. Expansion of maternity/parental leaves stands as a major gain for working women in recent years, especially the 2001 increase in parental benefits from 10 to 35 weeks. To qualify, a woman must have worked 600 hours in the previous year. About three-quarters of all women giving birth to a child do qualify, and about 60% claim a benefit. But a full year of leave is much more likely to be taken by women who qualify for a reasonable benefit, or whose employer supplements the EI benefit. Quebec has recently begun its own EI maternity/parental program, which offers much higher benefits (covered through higher premiums), and also covers self-employed workers for the first time.

The key reforms to the EI program, which have been advocated by labour and anti-poverty groups, are a reduction in the number of qualifying hours for regular benefits to 360 in all regions, a longer duration of up to 50 weeks of regular benefits, and an increase to at least 60% in the percentage of insured earnings replaced by EI benefits.

Part-Time Work

The paradox of part-time work is that this is a form of employment that can help women balance work and family roles, but one that usually comes at a high cost in terms of job quality (Duffy and Pupo 1992). Certainly women are much more likely to work part-time than men, and part-time jobs are usually much less desirable than full-time jobs. Some part-time jobs — usually in unionized workplaces, public services, and with some larger companies — can offer good pay and benefits, stable hours and regular shift times, and decent career development prospects. In such contexts, the flexibility of part-time work is welcomed by many, mainly women, workers who may choose to work part-time for a few months or even a few years before returning to full-time work.

However, most part-time jobs are low paid, and some employers deliberately create part-time jobs to keep labour costs to a minimum. In 2006, part-time jobs paid an average hourly wage of just $13.80 compared to $20.99 in full-time jobs. Adult female part-timers actually make more on average than male part-timers, but the fact remains that there is a huge hourly wage gap between the two kinds of work. In part, this reflects the fact that many part-time jobs are to be found in relatively low-wage industries, such as retail trade and the hospitality industries, but studies have also shown that part-time jobs tend to be paid less than comparable full-time jobs. Typically, part-time jobs are also only about one-half as likely to provide benefits as full-time jobs. Thus, in 1999, just one in five part-timers (18.9%) was covered by an employer pension plan compared to 41.6% of full-timers, and 19.8% of part-timers were covered by a supplementary medical insurance plan compared to 59.5% of full-timers (data from Statistics Canada *Workplace and Employee Survey*).

Work schedules are often extremely variable with part-time work. Four in 10 (37.9%) non-union part-timers work irregular hours or are on call compared to one in four unionized part-timers (data from Statistics Canada *Survey of Work Arrangements* 1993). Irregular part-time hours make it extremely difficult to balance work and family, and work and education. In many stores and restaurants, part-time workers have little or no control of their work schedule. Hours can be posted with little advance notice to meet the fluctuating demands on a business for goods and services, or to fill holes in the work roster. Part-time schedules are usually much more variable than those of full-time workers who are promised 35 to 40 hours of work per week. It is not uncommon for part-time and casual workers to be obliged to sit at home and wait to be called into work, depending on whether business is good or slow. This practice of varying the hours of part-timers may make business sense, but makes a mockery of the common idea that part-time work gives women workers the ability to work the hours that they want. Employment standards legislation in most provinces is all but silent on the right of part-timers to advance notice of hours, and on equal wages and pro-rated benefits between full- and part-time workers (Broad and Hagin 2002).

Table 5.6: Part-Time Workers in 2006 among Core-Age Workers (age 25–54)

	Men (%)	Women (%)
% of All workers in age group working part-time due to:		
Caring for children, personal and family responsibilities	0.3%	6.2%
Lack of availability of full-time jobs	2.2%	5.6%
Personal preference, voluntary, other	2.1%	7.6%
Total (for all reasons)	4.6%	19.4%

Source: Statistics Canada. *Labour Force Historical Review*. 2006. Cat. 71F0004XCB, Table cd1t08an.

Someone is considered by Statistics Canada to be a part-time worker if he or she works in a main job for less than 30 hours per week. More than one in four women work part-time compared to only about one in 10 men (26.1% compared to 10.8% in 2006). Most male part-timers are students. In the core working-age group (age 25–54), just 4.6% of men worked part-time in 2006 compared to 19.4% of women. These proportions have been stable or somewhat declining in recent years. Women with children, especially two or more children, are much more likely to work part-time than other women. As shown in Table 5.6, 6.2% of all core-age women are working part-time for reasons related to caring responsibilities, more than 30 times the proportion of men in the same age group. Women are also twice as likely as men to be working part-time because of problems finding a full-time job.

Significantly more women than men also express a preference for part-time work. Working part-time can, in principle, be desirable, allowing women, and potentially men, to better balance the demands of work and family, and participate actively in community life. However, this choice must be seen, in part, as socially constructed. Some women "choosing" to work part-time would likely choose to work full-time if they could find high-quality, affordable child care or elder care, or if their spouses took on a greater share of work in the home. The incidence of part-time work for women tends to be much lower in countries like Sweden and Denmark, which offer organized child and elder care arrangements, and the gap between women and men working part-time are more modest in the Netherlands, where it is common for both partners to work part-time and to share child care responsibilities.

Box 5.3: Improving Part-Time Work

Innovative amendments to the *Saskatchewan Labour Standards Act* in 1994 required employers to post part-time work schedules one week in advance, to provide rest and meal breaks to part-timers, and to provide pro-rated benefits to part-time workers (in establishments with more than 10 employees). Some provinces have enacted similar limits on the ability of employers to treat part-timers as "just-in-time" workers.

Very strong opposition from the business community meant that the Saskatchewan government failed to implement, and ultimately repealed, the most innovative section of the new Act, which would have required employers to offer available hours of work to their current part-time workforce before hiring new part-timers. This would have allowed part-timers to gradually turn themselves into full-time workers, and undercut the ability of employers to create a mainly part-time workforce. Employers did not want to lose the control of total hours worked, which comes with maintaining a predominantly part-time workforce.

For details, see studies by Dave Broad and colleagues from the Social Policy Research Unit of the University of Regina, posted at www.uregina.ca/spr.

Temporary Jobs and Self-Employment

Both corporate and public sector employers have tried to limit hiring of more costly full-time, permanent employees with guaranteed hours, and usually benefit by hiring temporary workers to meet spikes in demand and by outsourcing or contracting out some tasks to outside suppliers. Many of these contractors in turn contract out work to sub-contractors and to individuals, with the quality of employment generally declining at each link in the chain. As a result, there has been a steady increase in contract or temporary workers, and also in the number of self-employed workers over the past decade and more. This has come on top of a traditional layer of self-employed workers who run their own businesses.

Contract and temporary work can lead to a permanent job, and a few workers enjoy moving from contract to contract or want to work only in a seasonal job. But, such employment is rarely a first choice for adult workers, since temporary workers are typically excluded from benefit plans, training programs, and career ladders, and are paid less than comparable permanent employees.

As noted, in 2006, 13.7% of all female employees compared to 12.3% of male employees were in temporary jobs, which are defined as jobs that are casual, seasonal, or most often have a defined end date. The incidence of temporary employment for women has about doubled since the late 1980s, and has been inching up even in the low unemployment period since the late 1990s. Female temporary workers are much more likely to work part-time than temporary male workers.

Another form of precarious employment is self-employment. A layer of self-employed workers are high-earning professionals—such as doctors, lawyers, architects, engineers, and accountants—who usually work with professional colleagues and employ support workers. Others are owners of small- and medium-sized businesses that employ workers. These people are mainly self-employed by choice, and can earn high and stable incomes. However, a large and growing layer of self-employed workers are running tiny businesses of their own mainly because they cannot find stable, permanent employment. Unincorporated microenterprises with no employees run the whole range from home and building cleaning, to household maintenance, to child and elder care, to making clothes, to working as freelance writers and editors and artists. Many of these solo self-employed workers have just a few clients and can, in many cases, be considered to be hidden employees.

The rapid growth of self-employment in the first half of the 1990s was mainly driven by the increasing numbers of so-called own-account workers—that is, self-employed workers who are unincorporated and employ no paid help. About one-half of all own-account workers reported in the mid-1990s that they would rather have regular jobs (data from Statistics Canada's *Survey of Self-Employment*). A lot of people are self-employed for short periods and many low-paid precariously employed workers frequently alternate between solo self-employment and temporary jobs. The legal distinction between self-employed and contract workers is not clear-cut, and can even differ from one legal statute to another (Fudge et al. 2002). As the Arthurs Report on federal labour standards (see Chapter 4) made clear, many disguised employees are covered by minimum labour standards in theory, but are often not aware of that fact. Arthurs recommended that all workers should be given formal notice of their employment status and their legal rights as employees (*Federal Labour Standards Review* 2006).

Self-employment among women rose in the first half of the 1990s, from 9.9% of total women's employment in 1990, to 11.6% in 1997, but fell slightly to 11.3% by 2006. While self-employment is more prevalent among men, accounting for fully 18.6% of all men's jobs in 2006, self-employed women are much more likely to be own-account workers, running their own microenterprises with no employees. Women self-employed workers are also much more likely to have very low earnings than are self-employed men. In 2000, almost half (45%) of all self-employed women made less than $20,000 from their businesses compared to 19% of self-employed men. Less than one-fifth of self-employed workers making more than $60,000 per year were women.

The Restructuring of Women's Work: Two Examples

1. Clerical Work
Traditional "pink-collar" clerical or office support work performed by women has been dramatically changed by new information and communications technologies, changed management strategies, and by the outsourcing of work once performed in-house to contractors and sub-contractors. One theme that emerges from recent Canadian studies is the increased precariousness of clerical work. In their study of the customer payments centre in a large telecommunications company, Fox and Sugiman (2004) detail a shift from full-time and permanent to part-time and temporary jobs among a predominantly female workforce, and the erosion of already limited prospects for mobility to better jobs. Similarly, Good and McFarland (2004) show how mainly women workers in a New Brunswick call centre must be prepared to work very flexible hours, and to change shift schedules so that the number of operators always just matches the volume of inbound calls. In both cases, the work is intensive, mainly consists of quite narrowly defined tasks, and is closely monitored by management. However, it is not unskilled, often requires some degree of discretion and judgment to deal with customer problems, and pays better than minimum wage. Also, in both cases, management has experimented with new forms of work organization, such as teams and rotation between jobs.

2. Public-Sector Employment
As the welfare state expanded in the 1960s and 1970s, so too did opportunities for women to enter relatively good public sector jobs. Since public sector jobs tend to be better paid and more secure than average, the major expansion of employment of women in public and social services helped close the overall pay gap. Comparative studies of OECD countries show that women have benefited greatly from the growth of public sector employment, and that the pay gap is lowest in countries with higher levels of employment in public and social services (Fuller 2005, 409–412).

In the public sector, women are employed in jobs that share many of the characteristics of the best jobs held by men in the private sector. Many public sector jobs require high levels of education, and many public sector employers are large employers. As in the private sector, large employers are more likely to offer decent wages, benefits, and working conditions. The public sector is also highly unionized and wages are more equal between different categories of workers, not least men and women, when workers bargain collectively with employers. Public sector women workers have also benefited from struggles to make governments "model employers" in important areas, such as pay equity and access to maternity and parental leaves. Public services employment also tends to be more stable than in the private sector. Last but not least, when controlling for occupational differences, men are paid more or less the same whether they work in the public or private sector. Women, however, are better paid if employed in the public sector while holding other objective factors that govern pay constant. This suggests that outright pay discrimination against women while certainly still present, is less significant than in the private sector.

It has not gone unnoticed among private sector employers that the public sector provides better jobs for women, resulting in pressures on them to pay higher wages. For example, the Canadian Federation of Independent Business (CFIB) argues that decent wages in public services "distort" the labour market and make it harder for them to recruit and retain workers at the wages they want to pay (CFIB 2006). While reflecting other factors, the drive by governments at all levels to contract out and privatize public services reflects demands from business employers to reduce cost pressures on them. Privatization and contracting out are also driven by the intent to lower public sector wage costs to (more discriminatory) private sector levels, at the expense of mainly women workers.

A large number of women are employed in so-called "ancillary" jobs in health care—everything from clerical support work, to food preparation, to cooking and cleaning, to provision of personal care, such as washing and bathing. This is heavily gendered and frequently devalued work, often dismissively referred to as "hotel work," even though it is actually very important to good health outcomes for patients. In both hospitals and long-term care homes, the quality of care is critically bound up with the quality of ancillary jobs, since it is these kinds of workers with whom most patients and residents come into contact, and since good food and clean facilities are critical to the health of both patients and professional health care workers (Armstrong and Laxer 2006). Nonetheless, in recent years, there have been ongoing attempts by some governments and health care institutions to cut health care costs by contracting out ancillary health care work, shifting it from predominantly unionized hospitals and often unionized long-term care homes to non-union private contractors who pay much lower wages and benefits.

In British Columbia, the provincial government passed legislation in 2002 removing job security and no contracting out clauses from the collective agreements of health care and social service workers. Bill 29 permitted regional health authorities and long-term care facilities to lay off support staff and conclude new agreements with global firms such as Sodexho, Aramark, and Compass. Housekeeping services, as well as dietary, security, and laundry services, were contracted out. As a result, more than 8,500 workers who were members of the Hospital Employees' Union (HEU) lost their jobs in less than a year (Stinson, Pollack, and Cohen 2005, 10). Almost immediately, the unions representing the health care workers launched a court case to challenge the legality of Bill 29—the *Health and Social Services Delivery Improvement Act*— which had resulted in the largest mass firing of women workers in Canadian history.

In that year, women who worked in the private sector earned 64% of what women in the public sector earned, while men employed in the private sector earned 77% of their public sector counterparts (Fuller 2005, 419). The great majority of HEU members are women, many of whom are workers of colour. As unionized public sector health care workers, they were much less vulnerable to pay discrimination and low wages than in the private sector. When their jobs were contracted out, these workers experienced large pay cuts. At $10.25 per hour, the newly contracted out wages were 79% lower than the HEU Health Support wage of $18.32 per hour. These workers immediately joined the ranks of the working poor and began to face unsafe working conditions, inadequate training, and planned overwork. The quality of caring services began to rapidly deteriorate due to disruption of teamwork, higher staff turnover, reduced capacity to provide quality cleaning services, and a reduced capacity to respond quickly to urgent requests from doctors, nurses, and unit clerks (Stinson, Pollack, and Cohen 2005; HEU 2007).

Before the major cuts in British Columbia, 19.3% of women were employed by the B.C. government, and 71.3% of workers in the broader provincial public sector were women (Fuller 2005, 408). In addition to Bill 29, the B.C. government committed itself to large cuts to public spending and downsizing, and public sector employment fell by about 10% from 2002 to 2005. Fuller (2005) found that this drop in public sector employment resulted in significant downward pressure on wages, which was more pronounced for women than men. As a result of public sector downsizing, there was a 3.4% increase in the gender wage gap in B.C. over these years (Fuller 2005, 436).

Five years after the fact, the Supreme Court of Canada ruled (in June 2007) that key sections of Bill 29 were unconstitutional and violated the *Canadian Charter of Rights and Freedoms*. This decision found, for the first time, that rights to collective bargaining are protected to some degree by the Charter's right to freedom of association. At the beginning of 2008, the affected unions and the B.C. government and health employers were discussing a plan to implement the Supreme Court's decision.

Occupational Segregation of Women and Men

In Canada, as in all advanced industrial countries, there is still very marked occupational segregation between women and men. In other words, men and women hold very different kinds of jobs, working in almost parallel occupational worlds. This is an important part of the reason for the gender wage gap, because jobs where women predominate still tend to be lower paid than jobs where men predominate, even though the educational and skill requirements may differ very little. Traditionally, men were relatively concentrated in blue-collar industrial occupations, as well as in white-collar management jobs and in the professions, while women were relatively concentrated in low-level, pink-collar clerical and administrative jobs in offices, and in sales and services occupations. This division has broken down over time as women have entered professional and managerial jobs in increasing numbers. But, women in better paid occupations are still mainly to be found in only a relatively few occupational groups, notably working in health, education, and social services jobs in the broader public sector. Women are much more likely than men to work in the public sector, defined as working directly for government or in almost entirely government-funded bodies, such as schools, universities, and hospitals. One in four women (28.6%) worked in public services in 2006 compared to just less than one in five men (17.3%). The better paid professional and managerial jobs in the business sector of the economy and, indeed, many of the higher jobs in the public sector are still held mainly by men.

Table 5.7 provides a fairly detailed picture of employment of women and men by broad occupational groups in 1996 and 2006. Looking first at 2006, it is striking that

Table 5.7: Distribution of Employment of Women and Men by Occupation (%)

	1996		2006		Women as %
	Women	Men	Women	Men	Employment within occupa- tion in 2006
Managers	8.2	11.6	7.1	11.0	36.3
Professionals	28.8	20.3	32.5	22.9	55.9
Clerical, administra- tive	25.6	7.2	24.1	7.1	75.0
Sales and service	28.6	19.2	28.6	19.3	56.8
Primary	2.1	6.5	1.5	5.3	20.5
Trades, transport, construction	2.1	26.4	2.1	26.3	6.5
Processing, manufac- turing, utilities	4.7	8.8	4.1	8.1	31.1

Source: Statistics Canada. *Women in Canada. Work Chapter Updates.* 2006. Cat. 89F0133XIE, Table 11.

four in 10 men (39.7%) are still to be found in blue-collar jobs—the total of the share of all men's jobs to be found in primary industries (5.3%); trades, transportation, and construction occupations (26.3%); and processing, manufacturing, and utilities jobs (8.1%). These kinds of jobs include blue-collar jobs in manufacturing, utilities, trucking, and other transportation industries, as well as in construction. Many of these jobs are in the skilled trades and require an apprenticeship or college-level education, while others are relatively unskilled. While by no means all well-paid, these kinds of jobs do tend to command about average pay and are often unionized. In 2006, by contrast, just 7.7% of women were employed in these blue-collar jobs, one-fifth the proportion of men, and this small minority of women are mainly to be found in relatively low-paid manufacturing jobs in sectors like clothing rather than in the well-paid skilled trades, which women have barely penetrated.

By contrast, one-quarter of women (24.1%) are still to be found in non-professional office jobs—that is, in clerical, administrative, and secretarial jobs—compared to just 7.1% of men. Many of these jobs are quite skilled, certainly involving computer skills, but they tend to pay less than skilled blue-collar jobs. (See Table 5.3 for average wages by occupational group.)

A lot of men and women work in usually low-paid, often part-time, sales and service jobs, a big occupational category that includes salespersons, chefs and cooks, security guards, and child care and home support workers. But more women are employed in these lower end jobs than are men, explaining why women are much more likely to be low paid than men. More than one in four women (28.6%) worked in these occupations in 2006 compared to one in five men (19.3%), and the men who work in these kinds of jobs tends to be teens and young adults.

Table 5.8: A Closer Look at Professionals, 2006

	%		Women as %
	Women	Men	Employment within occupa- tion
Business and finance	3.3	2.8	51.6
Natural sciences, engineer- ing, mathematics	3.2	10.1	22.0
Social sciences, religion	6.7	2.4	71.3
Teaching	5.6	2.8	63.9
Doctors, dentists, other health-related	1.4	1.0	55.3
Nursing, therapy, other health-related	8.9	1.1	87.4
Artistic, literary, recreational	3.4	2.6	54.1
Total	32.5	22.9	55.9

Source: Statistics Canada. *Women in Canada. Work Chapter Updates.* 2006. Cat. 89F0133XIE, Table 11.

Turning to professional occupations, which usually require formal post-secondary education and qualifications, women now hold a significant edge over men. Almost one in three women (32.5%) works in these kinds of jobs, a much higher proportion than for men (22.9%). But women are significantly more likely than men to work in professional jobs to be found in public and social services: in health care occupations; in social services and government jobs; and in teaching. As shown in Table 5.8, in 2006, women accounted for 55.9% of all professional jobs, but 87.4% of jobs in nursing, therapy, and other health-related professional jobs (not including doctors and dentists, where the majority of workers are still men); 71.3% of professional social sciences and religion jobs (most of them in public and not-for-profit social services); and 63.9% of teaching jobs. Of the 32.5% of all women who are professionals, two in three are employed in these predominantly public-sector, female-dominated occupations. Clearly, issues of privatization and contracting out of public services work are of particular importance to working women.

By contrast, men still overwhelmingly predominate in natural sciences, engineering, and mathematics professional jobs (where women account for just 22% of employment), and still account for about half of all professional jobs in business and finance. That said, it is notable that the proportion of women in professional business and finance occupations has increased rapidly, from 38.3% in 1987, to 46.9% in 1996, to 51.6% in 2006 (Statistics Canada 2006, Table 11).

Men also still hold a big lead in management jobs. More than one in 10 men (11%) are in management jobs compared to 7.1% of women. Moreover, men hold double the proportion of senior management jobs, which makes up 0.8% of all men's jobs compared to just 0.3% of all women's jobs. These are the kinds of positions that predominate in the top 1% of the workforce whose share of all earnings exploded in the 1990s.

To summarize, the majority of women still work in the traditional and relatively badly paid clerical, sales, and services categories, and very few women work in the blue-collar occupations. A high and rising proportion of women work in professional occupations requiring higher levels of education and providing better levels of pay, but these women are still relatively concentrated in public and social services.

The report of the federal government's Pay Equity Task Force (Government of Canada 2004) further details the fact that women are still highly concentrated in a small number of traditionally female occupational categories—health care, teaching, clerical, administrative, and sales and services jobs, and overwhelmingly predomi-nate in the very lowest paid occupations, such as child care workers, cashiers, and food services workers. Women are still greatly under-represented in most of the very highest paying professions, from specialist physicians, to senior private sec-tor managers, to corporate lawyers, and security dealers. Even in the public sector where women predominate, men are much more likely to hold senior management jobs. In the federal public service, men are more than twice as likely to be senior managers. These differences persist despite employment equity policies that were intended to increase the proportion of women in management jobs (as in the federal public service).

All that said, there has clearly been some continued progress made by a layer of women who have moved into professional and managerial jobs. Since 1987, the pro-portion of women in management jobs has risen from 6% to 7.1%. Most importantly, the proportion of women in professional occupations has risen from 24.1% in 1987, to 28.8% in 1996, to 32.5% in 2006 (Statistics Canada 2006-b, Table 11). This occupational shift has been much more pronounced than for men. (The proportion of men employed in professional jobs rose from 18% in 1987, to 20.3% in 1996, to 22.9% in 2006.) The shift of women into professional jobs has been led by the growth of employment for women in health, social sciences, and government jobs, but it has also taken place in professional occupations in business and finance, and in the natural sciences. In short, a small group of women are moving into higher end jobs in the private as well as the public sector. Paralleling this upward shift, the proportion of women in non-professional office jobs, such as clerical workers and administrative workers, fell from 29.7% to 24.1% of all women's jobs (1987 to 2006), while the proportion of women in low-paid sales and services jobs decreased only slightly, from 30% to 28.6%, over the same period.

Conclusion

This chapter has shown that the economic inequality between women and men remains very significant, and that it has failed to close in recent years despite the fact that the education gap between women and men has closed and reversed itself. The gender gap remains large and persistent even among younger, well-educated women workers.

There are many important explanations for the continuing wage gap. Perhaps the most important is that women still bear the greatest burden of work in the home, and pay a price for dropping out of the workforce or for working shorter hours in part-time jobs in order to care for children or others. This price seems to exist even if the actual difference in work experience is not all that great, since the great majority of women with young children now exit the paid workforce for only brief periods. International experience—as recently summarized by the OECD in its major *Babies and Bosses* report—shows that the availability of high-quality, affordable child care is associated with greater economic equality between women and men, as is the availability of work schedules that help women workers balance the demands of paid work and caring work (OECD 2007).

There is still very marked occupational and industrial sector segregation between women and men, with women being much more likely than men to be employed in low-wage private services jobs, and much less likely than men to be employed in average pay blue-collar jobs. While a significant layer of women now work in better paid professional jobs, these women are relatively concentrated in public and social services. Men still predominate in highly paid and senior management jobs, especially in the private sector.

Public policies that could help close the economic opportunity gap between working women and men span a wide range, from child care programs and pay equity laws, to Employment Insurance and public pension reforms, to improved minimum employment standards. The recent proposals of the Arthurs Report on federal employment standards included rights to unpaid leaves from work, rights to vary hours to meet family needs, equal treatment for part-time workers, new rights for temporary workers, and higher minimum wages. A very wide range of policies should be reviewed for their impact on economic equality between women and men.

Recommended Reading

- Armstrong, Pat, and Hugh Armstrong. 1994. *The Double Ghetto: Canadian Women and Their Segregated Work*. Toronto: McClelland & Stewart. Now dated in terms of data, but a groundbreaking treatment of the key differences between the jobs of women and men and of the relationship between paid work and domestic work.
- Drolet, Marie. 2002. "The Male-Female Wage Gap." *Perspectives on Labour and Income* (Spring), 29–37. A Statistics Canada summary of trends in, and causes of, the pay gap between women and men.
- Organisation for Economic Co-operation and Development (OECD). 2002. "Women at Work: Who Are They and How Are They Doing?" *OECD Employment Outlook*, 61–125; and 2007, *Babies and Bosses: Reconciling Work and Family Life*. Paris. These studies provide a wealth of information that show how Canadian women are faring in the job market compared to women in other countries, and how public policies and workplace practices can and do make a real difference.

- Vosko, Leah F. (Ed.) 2006. *Precarious Employment: Understanding Labour Market Insecurity in Canada*. Kingston and Montreal: McGill-Queen's University Press. An excellent collection of papers on the issue of precarious work that shows how work insecurity and low pay are systematically linked to gender.
- Wallis, Maria, and Siu-ming Kwok. 2008. *Daily Struggles: The Deepening Racialization and Feminization of Poverty in Canada*. Toronto: Canadian Scholars' Press. This volume offers a critical perspective on poverty by highlighting gender and race analyses simultaneously. This book connects human rights, political economy perspectives, and citizenship issues to other areas of social exclusion, such as class, sexuality, and disability.

Notes

1. Statistics Canada. http://www40.statcan.ca/l01/cst01/famil19a.htm?sdi=low%20i ncomehttp, accessed December 20, 2007.

References

Armstrong, Pat, Mary Cornish, and Elizabeth Millar. 2003, "Pay Equity: Complexity and Contradiction in Legal Rights and Social Processes." In *Changing Canada: Political Economy as Transformation*, ed. Leah Vosko and Wallace Clement. Kingston and Montreal: McGill-Queen's University Press.

Armstrong, Pat, and Kate Laxer. 2006. "Precarious Work, Privatization and the Health Care Industry: The Case of Ancillary Workers." In *Precarious Employment: Understanding Labour Market Insecurity in Canada*, ed. Leah F. Vosko. Kingston and Montreal: McGill-Queen's University Press.

Beaujot, Roderic. 2004. *Delayed Life Transitions: Trends and Implications*. Ottawa: The Vanier Institute of the Family. www.vifamily.ca.

Beaujot, Roderic, and Don Kerr. 2007. "Emerging Youth Transition Patterns in Canada." Ottawa: Government of Canada Policy Research Initiative.

Broad, Dave, and Fern Hagin. 2002. *Women, Part-Time Work and Labour Standards: The Case of Saskatchewan*. Regina: Social Policy Research Unit, University of Regina.

Canadian Federation of Independent Business. 2006. *Capitalizing on Canada's Entrepreneurial Spirit: Business Outlook & Budget Priorities for 2006*. February 20, 2006. www.cfib.ca/legis/national/pdf/5304.pdf.

Drolet, Marie. 2002. "The Male-Female Wage Gap." *Perspectives on Labour and Income* (Spring): 29–37.

Duffy, Ann, and Norene Pupo. 1992. *Part-Time Paradox: Connecting Gender, Work, and Family*. Toronto: McClelland & Stewart.

Fox, Bonnie, and Pamela Sugiman. 2006. "Flexible Work, Flexible Workers: The Restructuring of Clerical Work in a Large Telecommunications Company." In *Working in a Global Era*, ed. Vivian Shalla. Toronto: Canadian Scholars' Press Inc.

Frenette, Marc, and Simon Coulombe. 2007. "Has Higher Education among Young Women Substantially Reduced the Gender Gap in Employment and Earnings?" Statistics Canada Analytical Research Paper 11F0019MIE2007301. Ottawa.

Fudge, Judy, Eric Tucker, and Leah Vosko. 2002. *The Legal Concept of Employment: Marginalizing Workers*. Report for the Law Commission of Canada. Ottawa.

Fuller, Sylvia. 2005. "Public Sector Employment and Gender Wage Inequalities in British Columbia: Assessing the Effects of a Shrinking Public Sector." *Canadian Journal of Sociology* 30, no. 4 (Autumn): 405–439.

Good, Tom, and Joan McFarland. 2004. "Technology, Gender, and Regulation: Call Centres in New Brunswick." In *Challenging the Market: The Struggle to Regulate Work and Income*, ed. Jim Stanford and Leah F. Vosko. Montreal and Kingston: McGill-Queen's University Press.

Government of Canada. 2004. Pay Equity Task Force Final Report. *Pay Equity: A New Approach to a Fundamental Right*. Ottawa.

Hospital Employees' Union Newsletter. September 14, 2007. www.heu.org.

Human Resources and Skills Development Canada. 2006. *Employment Insurance Monitoring and Assessment Report*. Ottawa.

Human Resources and Skills Development Canada. 2006. *Fairness at Work: Federal Labour Standards for the 21st Century*. Ottawa: Government of Canada.

Jackson, Andrew. 2004. "Gender Inequality and Precarious Work: Exploring the Impact of Unions." Ottawa: Canadian Labour Congress. www.canadianlabour.ca/index. php/Andrew_Jackson_Paper/389.

———. 2006. "A Statistical Portrait of Young Workers in Canada." Ottawa: Canadian Labour Congress.

Lochead, Clarence. 2000. "The Trend to Delayed First Childbirth." *ISUMA: Canadian Journal of Policy Research* (Autumn): 41–44.

Marshall, K. 2006. "Converging Gender Roles." *Canadian Economic Observer* (August). Statistics Canada Cat. 11-010.

Murphy, Brian, Michael Wolfson, and Paul Roberts. 2007. "A Profile of High Income Canadians: 1982 to 2004." Statistics Canada Cat. 75F0002MIE2007006. Ottawa.

Organisation for Economic Co-operation and Development (OECD). 2002. "Women at Work: Who Are They and How Are They Doing?" OECD *Employment Outlook*: 61–125. Paris: OECD.

———. 2004. *Developing Highly Skilled Workers: Review of Canada*. Directorate for Science, Technology, and Industry. Paris: OECD.

———. 2007a. *Babies and Bosses: Reconciling Work and Family Life*. Paris: OECD.

———. 2007b. *Employment Outlook*. Paris: OECD.

Roy, Francine. 2006. "From She to He: Changing Patterns of Women in the Canadian Labour Force." *Canadian Economic Observer* (June). Statistics Canada Cat. 11-010.

Statistics Canada. 2006a. *Women in Canada: Fifth Edition*. Cat. 89-503XIE.

———. 2006b. *Women in Canada. Work Chapter Updates*. Cat. 89F0133XIE, Table 11.

Stinson, Jane, Nancy Pollak, and Marcy Cohen. 2005. *The Pains of Privatization: How Contracting Out Hurts Health Support Workers, Their Families, and Health Care*. Vancouver: Canadian Centre for Policy Alternatives. www.policyalternatives. ca/index.cfm?act=news&call=1087&do=article&pA=BB736455.

Townson, Monica, and Kevin Hayes. 2007. *Women and the Employment Insurance Program*. Ottawa: Canadian Centre for Policy Alternatives.

Vosko, Leah, Nancy Zukewich, and Cynthia Cranford. 2003. "Precarious Jobs: A New Typology of Employment." *Perspectives on Labour and Income*: 16–26. Ottawa: Statistics Canada.

Zhang, Xuelin. 2007. "Returning to Work after Childbirth." *Perspectives on Labour and Income* (December). Statistics Canada Cat. 75-011XIE.

CHAPTER 6

Seeking Equality in the Workforce: Recent Immigrants and Racialized Workers, Aboriginal Canadians, and Persons with Disabilities

Introduction

This chapter looks at the quality of jobs, earnings, and the incidence of poverty for equality-seeking groups. Under the federal *Employment Equity Act*, four major groups are designated as likely to experience discrimination in employment: women, visible minorities (defined as non-Aboriginal persons who are non-white in colour

133

and non-Caucasian in race), Aboriginal people, and persons with disabilities. These are, of course, very different groups, and each in turn is composed of a very diverse range of individuals. But, on average, all experience poor labour market conditions and outcomes compared to the Canadian norm, and employment or lack of it is one of the major factors at play behind lower incomes and higher rates of poverty. While not explaining everything, discrimination in the job market is one of the key factors at play in structuring inequality and poverty in Canada today.

In her groundbreaking Royal Commission on Equality Report, which first drew the attention of Canadians to the reality of discrimination, Judge Rosalie Abella stated that:

> Discrimination ... means practices or attitudes that have, whether by design or impact, the effect of limiting an individual or group's right to the opportunities generally available because of attributable rather than actual characteristics. What is impeding the full development of potential is not the individual's capacity but an external barrier.

These barriers can be intentional, as in overt racism in hiring and promotion deci-sions, or they can be the by-product of discriminatory systems and procedures. The failure to properly appraise foreign skills and credentials or the job experiences of new immigrants is one example. The failure to see beyond a disability to the talents of an individual job applicant is also a barrier to equal opportunity. Barriers include a failure to accommodate differences, as in lack of provision for employment supports such as special devices for persons with disabilities, or a refusal to recognize possible conflicts between religious beliefs and workplace practices. Disadvantage in the job market also flows from the frequent but more subtle practice of giving preference in hiring and promotions to job applicants from the same gender, social background, and social networks as the person doing the hiring. This is particularly the case in periods of high unemployment when many qualified applicants are available to fill vacant jobs. Employers may assert that they are without prejudice, but rationalize discriminatory hiring by saying that some new hires might not "fit in." Discrimination is at work not just in hiring, but also in pay structures and career paths based on job ladders and promotions to better jobs.

Commonly, employment equity laws and practices to remedy discrimination simply require a formalized and transparent hiring and promotion process so that individual applicants are truly judged on their individual merits. In the case of Canada, employ-ment equity laws are limited in scope, mainly covering only public-sector and some very large private-sector employers in a few jurisdictions. Pay equity laws, requiring equal pay for work of equal value, cover many more workers, but are almost always limited to differences of pay between full-time men and women workers, and do not apply to workers from other disadvantaged groups.

Chapter 9 details the impacts of unions on the pay and employment of minorities, which are positive and significant. In a more general way, equality-seeking groups probably benefit from being employed in public services and in larger private-sector workplaces and enterprises that have relatively formalized pay grids, hiring processes, and job ladders. Once hired into stable, full-time, permanent jobs, minority workers probably experience much less discrimination moving up the job ladder than in the job market as a whole. This underlines the fact that one of the key problems is that such workers are more likely to be employed in unstable and precarious jobs.

Racialized Workers and New Immigrants in the Workforce

The term "visible minority persons" is used in statistical surveys and legislation. The terms "person of colour" and "worker of colour" are often used interchangeably, and are preferable in the sense that so-called minorities constitute the vast majority of the world's peoples and are already almost the majority in at least two of our biggest cities: Vancouver and Toronto. Many prefer the term "racialized workers" to signal that race is not an objective biological fact or a valid scientific concept, but is rather a social and cultural construct.

Immigration from non-traditional source countries over the past 25 years and more has dramatically changed the face of Canada and the Canadian labour force. Data from the 2006 Census, the main source of information for this chapter, show that one in five Canadians (19.8%) is now foreign born, up from one in seven in the 1950s (Statistics Canada 2007a, 2007b). Between the 2001 and 2006 Censuses, the foreign-born population grew four times as fast as the population as a whole and immigration now accounts for about two-thirds of overall population growth and almost all net labour force growth. (This does not mean that new immigrants are the only people entering the job market, but rather that the large numbers of echo baby boomers entering the job market just about matches the large numbers of retiring baby boomers.)

Since the mid-1990s, the proportion of immigrants coming from what used to be called non-traditional countries (i.e., mainly non-white countries outside the U.S. and Western Europe) has been well above 80%, with six in 10 immigrants coming to Canada between 2001 and 2006 arriving from Asia, especially China, and another one in 10 coming from each of Africa and the Americas outside of the U.S. The largest source countries for Canadian immigrants are now China, India, the Philippines, and Pakistan, with rising levels from Eastern European countries in recent years. While Canada as a whole is increasingly diverse, about two-thirds of all immigrants settle in the Toronto, Vancouver, and Montreal greater urban areas.

Since the late 1970s, the proportion of immigrants who are also counted as visible minorities rose from 55% to above 80%, and, as of 2006, visible minority persons made up one in six of the population (16.2%) compared to 11.2% in 1996. The largest racialized groups are South Asians from India and Pakistan, Chinese, Southeast Asians from countries like Vietnam, Blacks, Filipinos, Arabs, and Latin Americans.

An ever-rising proportion of racialized Canadians are not immigrants but born in Canada, the second generation of families who settled in Canada in the 1980s and 1990s and earlier. One-third of all visible minority persons in 2006 were born in Canada, and many more are counted as part of the first generation even though they arrived in Canada as young children, grew up in Canadian communities, and were educated in Canadian schools. Over time, the proportion of racialized Canadians consisting of both recent immigrants and the Canadian-born has grown particularly rapidly among young adults and younger workers. Close to one-half of all racialized Canadian youth were born in Canada, and about one in four young Canadians in their twenties are racialized persons.

The category of racialized workers is, of course, enormously diverse. Quite aside from distinctions between, say, Chinese and Blacks, Chinese communities in Canada include many descendants of nineteenth-century immigrants, as well as recent immigrants from both Hong Kong and different areas of mainland China. The Black community includes descendants of persons who escaped slavery in the U.S. 150 years ago, many West Indian immigrants from the 1950s and 1960s and, more recently, new immigrants from Africa. Studies show that Blacks and South Asians are most vulnerable to racial discrimination (Reitz and Banerjee 2007).

If it were not for new arrivals to Canada, we would see a more rapidly aging workforce and fewer labour force entrants than retirees. New immigrants help fill some shortages of skilled workers, though, as noted in earlier chapters, such shortages have been subject to a great deal of exaggeration. Clearly, our economic future as a country depends on continuing immigration. Even more important, our future depends upon successfully integrating newcomers into the Canadian labour market. More successful inclusion of recent immigrants into the workforce could give a very significant boost to economic growth through higher productivity and higher earnings (Conference Board of Canada 2004). Ignoring international skills and experience is very costly. A study by the Conference Board of Canada found that 540,000 Canadian workers lose between $8,000 and $12,000 per year in potential earnings because of unrecognized learning credentials, and that the annual cost of the learning recognition gap is between $4 and $6 billion (Bloom and Grant 2001). The study shows that half (47%) of unrecognized learners belong to visible minority groups, and that 340,000 Canadians have unrecognized foreign post-secondary degrees and diplomas. They provide a striking example: only 56% of engineers who settled in Canada in the first half of the 1990s found work as engineers.

Box 6.1: "We Are Capable People"
By Marina Jimenez

It is a great irony to many in the immigration field, and to newcomers themselves, a bitter joke. Canada has a shortage of skilled professionals, and yet thousands of internationally trained doctors, engineers, teachers, and nurses are forced to deliver pizzas and drive taxis.

Some immigrants believe that this is intentional, that Canada wants them only for their genetic potential. They may sweep floors and clean offices, but their offspring will be intelligent and creative. Why else would the government accept them and then make it so very difficult to have their credentials recognized?

Citizenship and Immigration Canada bristles at such a suggestion, and advises immigrants to check the ministry's Website, which clearly warns newcomers there is no guarantee they will find work in their chosen profession.

Still, frustration is mounting: This week, a British-trained accountant and his bookkeeper wife launched a lawsuit against the federal government, alleging that they were misled by immigration officials who assured them they would find good jobs here. Instead, the couple—he is originally from Sri Lanka and she from Malaysia—have spent five years in Edmonton shovelling snow, cleaning toilets, and borrowing money to support their teenaged son.

"What angers me is we are capable people. We have the credentials. We just can't get the jobs," complained Selladurai Premakumaran, who feels the government has shattered his hopes and dreams.

Last year, when Canada changed the way it selects immigrants, many were happy to see the end of the old system, which matched newcomers with worker shortages.

Critics had long complained that, by the time the physiotherapists and teachers arrived, those jobs had been filled and the labour shortages were in other fields.

Now, Canada chooses immigrants based not on their occupation, but on their education, skills, and language abilities. Applicants must score 67 of a possible 100 points to be accepted. Ostensibly, being talented and smart should make them more employable.

But it isn't working out that way. Canada is recruiting the right kind of people, but they are stuck in a bottleneck, as the agencies and bodies that regulate the fields of medicine, engineering, teaching, and nursing struggle to assess their qualifications.

"We have a disaster on our hands," says Joan Atlin, executive director of the Association of International Physicians and Surgeons of Ontario.

"There are thousands of un- and under-employed foreign professionals across the country. At the same time, we have a shortage of skilled professionals, especially in the health-care field. We don't so much have a doctor shortage as an assessment and licensing bottleneck."

About 1,300 doctors from more than 80 countries have joined the association she heads, but she estimates there are many more out there. Ontario alone may have as many as 4,000, most of them still trying to get their medical licences.

At the same time, there is a shortage of as many as 3,000 physicians across the country, especially in smaller communities in Alberta, British Columbia, Saskatchewan, and Ontario (provinces that have been forced to recruit doctors from South Africa, whose medical training Canada considers acceptable).

A recent Statistics Canada study of 164,200 immigrants who arrived in 2000 and 2001 found that 70 per cent had problems entering the labour force. Six in every 10 were forced to take jobs other than those they were trained to do. The two most common occupational groups for men were science (natural and applied) and management, but most wound up working in sales and service or processing and manufacturing.

Patrick Coady, with the British Columbia Internationally Trained Professionals Network, believes that far too many engineers are coming—as many as 60 per cent of all those accepted each year. (In Ontario, from 1997 to 2001, nearly 40,000 immigrants listed engineering as their occupation.)

"When they arrive, the Engineering Council for Canada evaluates their credentials, which sets up the engineer to think there are opportunities here," Mr. Coady says. "Then they discover that each province has a body that regulates the industry. They need up to 18 months of Canadian work experience before they will get professional engineering status. And, there isn't a great need for consulting engineers. A lot of the infrastructure has already been built in this country."

Michael Wu, a geotechnical engineer from China, is a classic example of what's happening. Accepted as a landed immigrant last spring, he came here with his wife and child, leaving behind a relatively prosperous life in Beijing, and now works for $7 an hour in a Vancouver chocolate factory.

Back in Beijing, "I had a three-bedroom apartment and took taxis everywhere—the Chinese government sent me to build a stadium in St Lucia," says Mr. Wu, who has a PhD. "Here, no-one will hire me. Many engineering companies think engineers make false documents. They are suspicious of my qualifications. I never imagined I'd end up working in a factory. But I will keep trying. Every month I go to the Vancouver Geotechnical Society lecture."

Susan Scarlett of the Immigration Department points out that regulating the professions is a provincial, not federal, responsibility. "We advise people who are thinking of coming to Canada to prepare by really researching how their credentials will be assessed."

Ms. Atlin says that "Canada has been very slow to change. Our regulatory systems have not caught up with our immigration policies."

But some relief may be on the horizon because the issue has become such a political flashpoint.

A national task force is about to report to the deputy minister of health on the licensing of international medical graduates. And this month Denis Coderre, the federal Immigration Minister, announced that he wants to streamline the process of recognizing foreign credentials, and have provinces announce their inventory of needs so Ottawa can work to fill the shortages.

Source: Jimenez, Marina. "We Are Capable People," *Globe and Mail*, October 25, 2003, F9.

The Changing Fortunes of Immigrant Workers

It might be expected that it would take newcomers to Canada some time to catch up to the Canadian-born and, indeed, there has always been at least a modest earnings gap between recent immigrants and the Canadian-born. However, many studies show that this gap has grown significantly over the past 25 years (Aydemir and Skuterud 2004; Picot 2008). In 1980, male immigrants earned just 13% less than the native-born one year after arrival, but the gap is now more than one-third. The trend is similar for women. Immigrants who arrived in Canada in the 1970s caught up to the Canadian average after 15 years, but newcomers who arrived in the 1980s are still well below the average (Frenette and Morissette 2003). The gap has grown even though a higher proportion of earlier immigrants came under the family class provisions of the *Immigration Act*, meaning that they were not selected by immigration officials for their ability to quickly integrate into the Canadian job market and often had limited language ability in English or French. More than one-half of immigrants entering the labour force in recent years, by contrast, have been economic immigrants selected for their educational credentials and language ability. While the gap between economic immigrants and the rest of the workforce is smaller than for all immigrants, it is still significant and growing. The earnings gap has widened and the period of catch-up has grown longer, even though the educational gap between immigrants and the Canadian-born has widened in favour of immigrants. Today, about one-half of all new immigrants have a university-level qualification (Frenette and Morissette 2003).

Table 6.1 shows the median (midpoint) annual earnings of native born, immigrant, and recent immigrants aged 25–54 for 1995 and 2005 in constant (or inflation-adjusted) dollars. Looking first at the data for 2005, it is apparent that there is a significant earnings disadvantage for immigrants, especially recent immigrants compared to the Canadian-born. This is especially the case for those with university degrees. What is striking is that there were modest earnings gains between 1995 and 2005 — years of reasonably strong economic growth and falling unemployment — among the Canadian-born, especially women with university degrees. By contrast, annual earnings stagnated in real terms over the decade for immigrants, and actually fell among university-educated immigrants. The same was broadly true, though rather less so, for

Table 6.1: Median Earnings of Immigrants and Non-immigrants (age 25–54, in constant 2005 dollars)

	Canadian-born		Immigrants		Recent immigrants	
	1995	2005	1995	2005	1995	2005
All						
With university degree	$48,805	$51,656	$40,394	$36,451	$24,368	$24,636
Without university degree	$30,256	$32,499	$27,115	$27,698	$18,347	$18,572
Men						
With university degree	$58,784	$62,566	$48,733	$42,998	$29,337	$30,332
Without university degree	$37,434	$40,235	$33,542	$33,814	$21,963	$24,470
Women						
With university degree	$40,444	$44,545	$32,964	$30,633	$19,491	$18,969
Without university degree	$23,682	$25,590	$21,972	$22,382	$14,714	$14,233

Source: Statistics Canada. *Census of Canada*. 2006. Income and Earnings, Topic-based Tabulations, Table 44.

the most recent immigrants. In short, immigrants did not catch up with the Canadian-born over the past decade, and indeed fell even further behind.

Sociologist Jeffrey Reitz (e.g., Reitz and Banerjee 2007) has written extensively on the growing gap between immigrants and other Canadians in terms of employment success and incomes. The extensive research he summarizes shows that employers tend to undervalue both foreign (i.e., international) educational credentials and foreign work experience, particularly the latter, placing immigrants at a clear disadvantage in the job market. While it is true that credentials from non-traditional countries are not necessarily equivalent to Canadian credentials, there are relatively few formal channels through which formal equivalencies can be determined. Even partial recognition would be of value if twinned to bridging programs that led to credentials recognition. As it is, many foreign-trained professionals have to start again in Canada from scratch. It is even more difficult for employers to assess the value of international work experience, and research shows that it is given virtually no recognition by Canadian employers (Aydemir and Skuterud 2004). Non-minority immigrants from traditional source countries do gain a small wage premium for their work experience, but this premium does not exist at all for immigrants from non-traditional source countries. Also, the wage premium for higher education is lower for immigrants from non-traditional source countries compared to traditional source countries. Thus, a new immigrant doctor or engineer or architect from India or China fares much worse than a similarly qualified immigrant professional from the U.S., Britain, or France. This is a key factor behind the growth of earnings gaps between immigrant and Canadian-born workers with university qualifications. Also worth noting is the fact that the many immigrants with professional qualifications who do find work in their field are paid less than their Canadian-born colleagues, and also tend to find it very difficult to move beyond skilled technical and professional jobs into management occupations.

While educational levels among recent immigrants are high, and while recent immigrants are, on average, much more highly educated than the Canadian-born, it is also the case that educational levels have been rising at an even faster pace among the younger Canadian-born population, the echo baby boomers, who have been entering the labour force in large numbers. The relative educational advantage of recent immigrants then has been falling. It also has to be taken into account that both recent immigrants and younger workers have been entering a job market that, as shown in other chapters, has been generating more precarious jobs and greater earnings and economic security gaps between peripheral and core workers. In other words, recent immigrants must enter the new kinds of jobs being created, which are often inferior to the shrinking pool of good jobs held disproportionately by older Canadian-born workers and members of earlier immigrant groups.

Also worth noting is the fact that many immigrants were permanently affected by coming to Canada in the serious and prolonged economic downturn of the early to mid-1990s. Failing to find decent work in the period after entry, they often became and remain trapped in jobs that do not match their credentials and work experience. Immigrant information technology and engineering professionals were also a major part of the workforce in the high-tech sectors that collapsed in the wake of the collapse of the high-tech boom in 2000. Even high levels of skills were not easily transferable to other jobs since they were so specialized.

Immigration policy is, in a sense, partly to blame for poor outcomes for many highly qualified immigrants. The most important criterion by far for selecting economic migrants—who now make up the majority of recent arrivals—is formal educational qualifications. However, as noted, Canadian employers heavily discount foreign credentials as well as work experience acquired in non-English- (and French-) speaking countries. Highly educated economic migrants to Australia, by contrast, have done significantly better than in Canada since the government there tests language skills intensively before migration, and gives great weight in the selection of immigrants to labour market demand by detailed occupation and skill area. The government thus screens out immigrants who would likely face difficulties finding good jobs, given the perspectives of employers (Hawthorne 2008).

Partly in response to the Australian practice of directly tying immigration to labour market demands, the Canadian government has attempted to bypass the long queue of approved economic and family class applicants by giving work permits to temporary foreign workers recruited by employers. As many as half of migrant workers coming to Canada in 2007 and 2008 entered with temporary work permits. Skilled workers have been given a path to citizenship based on successful work experience in Canada. As critics have pointed out, this has given birth to a growing layer of unskilled migrant workers in Canada, such as farm workers, who lack any rights to residence if they lose their job and have no such route to citizenship. This is a recipe for abuse, and reduces immigration policy to a narrow job-matching exercise driven by employers.

Barriers to the successful integration of immigrants into the Canadian job market, particularly in the first year or two after settlement, could and should be more systematically addressed by Canadian governments. As of 2009, despite many promises, the federal government had still not set up an office to assess formal foreign credentials and only referred new immigrants to a patchwork of agencies, some of which are effective and others are not. Some professional associations have done a good job of fairly evaluating and recognizing international credentials and work experience, but governments have often been reluctant to break down barriers imposed by professional organizations to keep out qualified newcomers.

Another key barrier to inclusion is lack of English or French language skills appropriate to specific occupations. It is often the case that immigrants have good basic language skills, but not language skills at the level needed to work in a specific occupation, be it a trade, nursing, engineering, or accounting. Government and settlement agency language programs tend to be very short and focused on basic skills, rather than longer and more specialized. Mentoring programs, which give to newcomers the skills needed to navigate the particularities of Canadian workplaces, have proved effective, but funding for settlement agencies running such programs is very limited.

The continuing deterioration of immigrant outcomes has generated very high rates of poverty among families who have recently arrived in Canada (Picot and Hou 2003; Picot, Hou, and Coulombe 2008). Between one-third and one-half of new immigrants experience poverty in the first year after arrival, and two-thirds experience poverty at least once in their first 10 years in Canada. The poverty rate among recent immigrants has risen steadily, from one in four in 1980, to 36% in 2002, which is 2.5 times the (falling) poverty rate of the Canadian-born. While most who enter poverty shortly after arrival do escape, about one in five remain trapped in low income over many years, and the poverty rate for immigrants even after 10 years in Canada remains very high at almost one in three. The exceptionally low pay and incomes of many recent immigrants help explain the growing earnings gap between immigrants and non-immigrants.

Over the 1990s, there has been an increased concentration of low-income households in low-income neighbourhoods in our big cities, and many very low-income neighbourhoods have a very high proportion of new immigrant and minority residents (Hou and Picot 2003). In the case of Toronto, this trend to high concentrations of racialized poverty has been well-documented in reports by the United Way. Concentrated poverty worsens the already negative impacts of family poverty on individuals, particularly children, and can create very disadvantaged communities, such as inner city ghettos in the U.S. Low income still remains quite widely dispersed in Canadian cities, as many immigrants live in high-income ethnic communities as well as in middle-income and diverse communities, and many low-income minority workers move up the income ladder over time. Still, Canada runs a very serious risk of creating more and more very low-income communities that are also highly racialized if the labour market disadvantages of visible minorities and new immigrants are not seriously addressed.

The Role of Race and Racial Discrimination

While earnings and employment gaps between recent immigrants and non-immigrants are, as noted above, based on factors other than narrowly defined racial discrimination, it is hard to escape the conclusion that the growing and now acute settlement problems of recent immigrants are closely connected to the changing racial profile of the immigrant population. The evidence of deteriorating outcomes rising in lockstep with the increasing proportion of racialized immigrants suggests that discrimination, overt or systemic, helps explain rising income and opportunity gaps.

The significant income and employment gaps that exist between new immigrants and other Canadians are clearly greatest among the recent immigrants who belong to racialized groups (Galabuzi 2006; Canadian Race Relations Foundation 2000). The role of racial discrimination is often glossed over or ignored in economic studies, which tend to argue that pay and employment gaps based on race do not reflect discrimination, but rather hidden differences in job qualifications, the inferior quality of education in developing countries, and differences in language skills between immigrants and the Canadian-born. "The broader Canadian population remains skeptical of the significance of racial discrimination and there is a prevailing view that racism is marginal in Canada" (Reitz and Banerjee 2007, 11).

However, the existence of racial barriers to employment has been well-documented in hundreds if not thousands of complaints to human rights tribunals and in public opinion surveys. Aside from the empirical evidence of earnings and employment gaps, surveys—notably Statistics Canada's *Ethnic Diversity Survey*—show that many (36% in 2002) racialized Canadians report personal experience of racial discrimination, with that figure rising to 50% among Blacks. The percentage is even higher among second-generation racialized Canadians (42%). Experiments have shown that job applicants with identical qualifications are treated differently by employers based on racial status. As Galabuzi (2006) has eloquently and convincingly argued, racism is systemic, institutional, and cultural, and the evidence demands that Canadians should stop denying its reality and take concrete actions to counter exclusion and marginalization.

The degree of equitable integration of second-generation visible minority immigrants into the Canadian labour market and wider society is a key litmus test of whether Canada is truly an inclusive society where genuine equality of individual opportunity exists. The children of visible minority immigrants—as well as the "1.5" generation of immigrants who came to Canada as children—have grown up as part of, if not necessarily fully included in, Canada, and have been educated in Canadian institutions. Differences in outcomes for them compared to non-racialized Canadians can be reasonably suspected to indicate major barriers to inclusion based on racial status. The issue has been widely recognized as a critical one for social stability and the test of equality, since many immigrants did not necessarily expect to catch up to the Canadian norm rapidly, but have had high hopes that their children would do well, especially if highly educated in Canada.

Boyd (2008) and Corak (2008) find—looking at 2001 Census data—that rates of high school and university graduation for visible minority second-generation Canadians are generally higher than the average for white native-born Canadians of the same age, and are significantly higher than average for Asians. However, Blacks and Latin Americans have graduation rates well below the average. The same pattern is found in terms of earnings and entry into highly skilled, well-paid occupations. While most of the second generation do relatively well in terms of education, this educational advantage may not be fully reflected in economic outcomes.

Kobayashi (2008) and Brooks (2008) argue that many second-generation racialized Canadians do not see themselves as fully belonging to the dominant white society, and that many see racism as a very serious issue. In fact, the second generation are actually less likely to report that they feel they belong to Canada than their parents. Conceptions of identity are quite fluid, with many second-generation racialized minorities feeling themselves to be less "visible minorities" than part of a hidden majority experiencing various forms of racial exclusion, some overt and some very subtle. Discrimination on the basis of race is experienced most by those with very visible racial characteristics, notably skin colour.

It is particularly significant that racialized workers who were born in Canada and educated in Canada still have poorer economic outcomes than otherwise comparable white Canadian workers. The most recent Census data (for 2005) show that the unemployment rate was much higher among visible minority non-immigrants than white non-immigrants (9.8% vs. 6.3%). The gaps are greater for men than for women. Cheung (2006) finds that unemployment rates for Canadian-born racialized workers are usually somewhat lower than for first-generation immigrant racialized workers,

Table 6.2: Unemployment Rate in 2005 (%)

	All	Men	Women
All	6.6	6.5	6.6
Not a visible minority	6.2	6.3	6.1
Visible minority	8.6	7.8	9.3
Immigrants	6.9	6.1	7.8
Non-immigrants	6.4	6.6	6.2
Chinese	7.5	7.2	7.9
South Asian	8.6	7.0	10.8
Southeast Asian	8.5	7.4	9.6
Black	10.7	10.3	11.1
Non-immigrants			
Visible minority	9.8	10.3	9.3
Not a visible minority	6.3	6.5	6.1

Source: Statistics Canada. *2006 Census of Population*. Cat. 97-562-XCB2006013.

but are still much higher than the average. Canadian-born Blacks, Southeast Asians, and South Asians all do much worse than the average. Similarly, the proportion of Canadian-born racialized workers employed in full-time permanent jobs lags well behind the average.

Reflecting more precarious jobs, higher unemployment, and concentration in lower paying occupations, there are large gaps between the median annual incomes of racialized and white Canadians, with visible minority men earning median annual incomes of $22,670—which is $11,228 or 33% less than non-visible minorities in 2005,

Table 6.3: Median Annual Income of All Visible Minority Persons in 2005

	All	Men	Women	As % median income of all workers All	Men	Women
All	$25,615	$32,224	$20,460	100.0%	125.8%	79.9%
Not a visible minority	$26,863	$33,898	$21,164	104.9%	132.3%	82.6%
Visible minority	$19,115	$22,670	$16,638	74.6%	88.5%	65.0%

Source: Statistics Canada. *2006 Census of Population*. Cat. 97-563-XCB2006007.

and women visible minority workers having median incomes of $16,638—which is $4,526 or 21% less than non-visible minority women. Some of these gaps can be explained by the fact that racialized non-immigrant workers are younger than average, but gaps remain.

Table 6.4: Median Annual Income in 2005 (persons aged 25–44) with a University Degree

	All	Men	Women	As % all in this age and education group		
				All	Men	Women
All	$41,814	$49,699	$37,184	100.0%	118.9%	88.9%
Not visible minority	$46,172	$55,515	$40,741	110.4%	132.8%	97.4%
Visible minority						
All	$29,717	$34,803	$25,232	71.1%	83.2%	60.3%
First-generation immigrant	$27,241	$32,842	$22,479	65.1%	78.5%	53.8%
Second-generation immigrant	$41,675	$45,885	$39,527	99.7%	109.7%	94.5%
Second-generation immigrant						
Chinese	$47,012	$50,773	$43,301	112.4%	121.4%	103.6%
South Asian	$41,259	$44,952	$41,213	98.7%	107.5%	98.6%
Southeast Asian	$36,648	$42,379	$36,985	87.6%	101.4%	88.5%
Black	$37,914	$41,415	$36,203	90.7%	99.0%	86.6%

Source: Statistics Canada. *Census of Canada*. 2006. Income and Earnings, Topic-based Tabulations, Table 45.

Table 6.4 shows the median annual income in 2005 of persons aged 25–44 with a university degree. In other words, age and education are more or less held constant as an explanatory factor. As shown, visible minority workers in this age and educational category earn 74.6% of the median for the group as a whole, while non-visible minority workers earn 105% of the median. The racial income gap is greater for men than for women, though visible minority women have the lowest median annual income.

As further shown in the table, second-generation visible minority persons in this age and educational group earned less than non-visible minorities ($41,675 compared to $46,172). This is almost entirely accounted for by the gap between second-generation visible minority men and non-visible minority (white) men—$45,885 compared to $55,515. The gap for women is much smaller, just over $1,000, but still exists. Further, the gap is different for different racialized communities, with Chinese and South Asian second-generation women actually earning a bit more than the median for white women. For the four categories shown in Table 6.4, however, all second-generation racialized men fall well short of the earnings of non-visible minority (white) men, with the income gap being largest among Blacks.

In sum, the most recent Census data show that there are significant and troubling income gaps between racialized and non-racialized Canadian-born university graduates. Some of this may be accounted for by a somewhat lower average age and thus less work experience in the racialized group, and some might, perhaps, be explained by different choices of fields of study. Still, the evidence very strongly suggests the existence of a major economic gap based on race among the second generation. The intersection of race and economic disadvantage is surely a recipe for increased racial tensions in an increasingly diverse and also more unequal Canadian society.

Canadian population growth and patterns of urban growth have been enormously influenced by new immigration, which now greatly eclipses both natural population growth and internal migration as sources of population change. As urban geographer Larry Bourne notes, "the combination of declining rates of natural increase and highly focused immigration flows has divided the country into declining and growing places more sharply than in the past, and into communities that are increasingly homogeneous or increasingly heterogeneous in social characteristics" (Bourne 2004). New racialized immigrants and second-generation racialized workers are highly concentrated in our "majority minority" three largest cities, and are also increasingly concentrated in low-income neighbourhoods in these cities. This gives rise to the disturbing prospect that Canada may be moving in the direction of U.S.-style concentrated urban poverty among racialized communities.

Aboriginal Persons in the Workforce

Self-identified Aboriginal people make up about 4% of the Canadian population and the Canadian workforce, or more than 1.1 million people in 2006 (Statistics Canada 2007-c). (Unfortunately, as of the date of writing, not all Census data for 2006 were available, so some earlier Census data are drawn upon in this section.) While this sounds low, the Aboriginal population is much younger than average and grew very rapidly, by 45%, from 1996 to 2006. Aboriginal workers will make up a much greater proportion of new entrants to the workforce over the next 20 years, particularly in Western Canada.

The category of Aboriginal persons is quite mixed and includes treaty status Indians on reserves, Métis people, the Inuit, and treaty and non-treaty status Indians living off reserves. Just 40% of the First Nations peoples—who make up 70% of all persons who self-identify as Aboriginal persons—live on reserves, with most of the population living in urban centres. There is a major ongoing movement to larger cities, and there are large Aboriginal identity populations in Winnipeg, Edmonton, Vancouver, Saskatoon, and Regina. That said, other big cities such as Toronto and Montreal also contain significant numbers of Aboriginal residents. Many people move back and forth between cities and reserves.

The situation of Aboriginal people is incredibly diverse. There are many reserves, especially in rural and remote areas, where the economic base is very limited, very few people have paid work, and incomes are extremely low. In 2001, the labour force participation rate of the on-reserve population was just 52% compared to 65% for the off-reserve population. The median income per adult on reserves (half have more and half have less) was just $15,000 in 2001, and the data for the on-reserve population are not very reliable (some bands refuse to participate in the Census and other surveys). Social conditions on many reserves are appalling, helping account for a massive difference in life expectancy (seven years for men and five years for women) between Aboriginal people and all Canadians. At the other end of the spectrum, there is a small but growing well-educated, urban Aboriginal middle class.

Generalizations are difficult, but Aboriginal people are at a big disadvantage in the job market because many live at a distance from job opportunities, and because average education levels are low. Half (48%) of the Aboriginal population in 2001 had less than a high school education compared to less than one-third of all Canadians, and just 4% had completed university compared to 15% of all Canadians. In addition, Aboriginal people often confront discrimination in accessing good jobs, even in resource industries near where they live. The Royal Commission on Aboriginal Peoples of 1996 identified lack of jobs and discrimination as the main barriers to employment. Good jobs, where they exist, tend to be in public services, in Aboriginal enterprises, and in resource industries that have been prepared to hire and train Aboriginal people.

Data from the 2006 Census show that the employment rate of Aboriginal persons was 53.7% compared to 62.4% for the population as a whole, and the unemployment rate was a very high 14.8% (16.1% for men and 13.5% for women) compared to just 6.6% for the population as a whole. The unemployment rate among Aboriginal youth age 20–24 was a very high 20.8%. Clearly, many were left behind even in a growing economy.

As shown in Table 6.5, Aboriginal persons had median earnings of $18,982 in 2005 or 29% less than the non-Aboriginal workforce. There was, however, a small closing of the earnings gap between 2000 and 2006, with the median earnings of Aboriginal women rising quite significantly, though from very low levels.

Due to high unemployment and low earnings for many, the low income or poverty rate for Aboriginal families was one in three (31.2%) in 2001, or 2.4 times the Canadian average. Aboriginal people were significantly less likely to work full-time for a full year in 2001 than the general population (40.5% compared to 53.9%).

In sum, Aboriginal people do very badly in the job market, not so much because they do not work, as because they have great difficulty finding permanent, reasonably well-paid jobs. There is some evidence that gaps may be closing with rising educational levels and as a result of economic development efforts driven by or including Aboriginal peoples. To a large degree, the job issues facing Aboriginal peoples are inseparable from the wider economic and social problems facing Aboriginal communities. Community economic development efforts can make a big difference. For example, new mining and resource developments in the North now commonly make efforts to hire Native people, and economic development benefits are sometimes negotiated with Native communities. The federal government supports some

Table 6.5: Median Employment Income of Aboriginal Identity Persons

	2000	2005
All	$28,123.00	$26,852.00
Aboriginal identity	$17,991.00	$18,982.00
Men		
All	$34,103.00	$32,867.00
Aboriginal identity	$22,407.00	$22,452.00
Women		
All	$22,447.00	$21,545.00
Aboriginal identity	$15,154.00	$16,089.00

Source: Statistics Canada. *Census of Canada*. 2006. Income and Earnings, Topic-based Tabulations, Table 46.

Aboriginal-led labour market initiatives, such as the Aboriginal Human Resource Council, which was established in 1998.

Box 6.2: What's the Situation for Equality-Seeking Groups in My Community?

Statistics Canada have made available on their website a wealth of detail from the 2006 Census on employment and incomes of visible minorities, new immigrants, and Aboriginal Canadians on a city-by-city basis, as well as by such variables as age, gender, and level of education. Go to www.statcan.gc.ca and follow the links from "Census" to "Data" to "Topic-based Tabulations" to "Income and Earnings."

Note that you can change the active dimension in these tables to look at differences, but you have to click "refresh" to get the desired variables. Table 44 provides data on immigrants, Table 45 provides earnings data for racialized workers, and Tables 27 and 46 provide data on Aboriginal Canadians. As of early 2009, data for persons with disabilities were still not available.

Source: www12.statcan.ca/english/census06/data/topics/ListProducts.cfm?Temporal=2006&APATH=3&THEME=81&FREE=0&GRP=1

Workers with Disabilities

People are considered to have a disability or activity limitation if they have a physical or mental condition or a health problem that restricts their ability to perform activities that are normal for their age. Exclusion due to disability is now generally considered to be the result of a failure by society and employers to accommodate different levels of ability through the provision of appropriate supports and accommodations, and elimination of discrimination rather than a medical condition of individuals. Canadian disability rights groups have put forward an action agenda for an inclusive and accessible Canada, noting that, while progress has been made, many Canadians with disabilities and their families continue to experience major barriers to their full and equal participation in Canadian society.

While many of these barriers exist in the community, lack of access to and supports in the workplace are increasingly recognized as a key aspect of exclusion and marginalization of many persons with disabilities (OECD 2003). While it is certainly true that many people with disabilities are unable to participate in the paid workforce, it is also true that many others could work, and would like to work, but are prevented from doing so because of discrimination and barriers. The goal should be to facilitate inclusion into the job market consistent with people's desires and abilities.

While the situation of persons with disabilities in the job market is very poor, there is increasing support for positive changes. The federal and provincial governments have begun to advance a more positive agenda, and funding for community and employment supports is slowly increasing (Human Resources and Social Development Canada 2006). Due to a series of far-reaching legal decisions, employers are also increasingly obliged to accommodate the special needs of workers with disabilities, which is of particular importance to workers who have stable employment and then become ill or are injured. Disability rights organizations are extremely active in pushing an inclusion agenda that includes workplace inclusion. There would be many more opportunities in the workforce for persons with disabilities if adequate supports and services were to be provided, and if differences were to be properly accommodated. This requires changes in the workplace itself as well as supportive changes to public policies, such as income support programs.

Box 6.3: Defining Disability

Statistics Canada's *Participation and Activity Limitation Survey* (PALS) tracks persons whose activities are limited because of a physical or mental health-related condition or problem. By this definition, which covers a very broad range of limitations in terms of both type and severity, the total disability rate in 2006 was 11.5% for the total Canadian working-age population (aged 15–64)—or 2.5 million people—rising to 15.1% for those aged 45–54, and 22.8% for those aged 55–64 (Statistics Canada 2006). None of us can be certain that we will never experience a major activity limitation over the course of our working lives.

Disability rates rise significantly with age, partly because of health risks due to increasing age alone, and partly due to injuries or an accumulated lifetime exposure to unhealthy working conditions. Many older workers experience chronic pain arising from repetitive or heavy work or from injuries, and mental illness is increasingly prevalent due to the stresses of the contemporary workplace. Disability rates are slightly higher among women than men and much higher—two to three times the national average—among Aboriginal Canadians mainly because of high rates of poverty and deprivation.

About four in 10 adults with a disability report a severe or very severe disability, and most persons with activity limitations report multiple conditions. In fact, 65% report three or more disabilities. Many conditions are time-limited or episodic. Roughly one-half of all persons with disabilities experience a continuing, long-term disability, while many more working-age Canadians experience a temporary disability at some time, often as the result of workplace injuries, an accident, or a disease that eventually responds to treatment.

The most common forms of disability among adults are those related to mobility, agility, or pain, followed by difficulties in hearing and seeing, all of which are more common as workers age.

The evidence shows, not surprisingly, that working-age persons with disabilities, particularly long-term and severe disabilities, are much less likely to hold paid jobs than are other Canadians (Statistics Canada 2008). This may reflect an inability to work at all or, in many other cases, discrimination and/or a lack of appropriate supports and accommodations. In 2006, just over one-half (51%) of persons with disabilities were employed compared to three in four persons without disabilities. This employment rate is a bit higher than in most other industrial countries, though definitions vary. Canada, however, spends considerably less as a share of the economy on both disability supports and services and on disability-related income supports than do many European countries (OECD 2003). The gap in employment rates in Canada between persons with and without disabilities is even higher among older age groups, and is a bit higher among women than among men.

Employment rates are especially low for persons with severe disabilities. While this reflects the fact that some of these people are simply unable to engage in paid work, government support programs also tend to focus on younger persons and on low-cost interventions. Employment rates are lowest (under 40%) for those with developmental and communication disabilities, whereas employment rates are closer to average for those with hearing problems and problems with pain, mobility, and agility. Likely the latter are barriers to employment in a narrower range of jobs. Persons with mental disabilities are also more likely to experience discrimination. Unemployment rates are also significantly higher for persons with disabilities—10% compared to 6% in 2006—showing that exclusion from jobs is partly due to barriers to finding work, and not just due to inability to work. Despite lower rates of participation in the paid workforce and higher unemployment, there were still well over one million workers with disabilities in Canada in 2006, almost evenly divided between women and men. While such workers are to be found in virtually all industries and occupations, they are significantly under-represented in managerial, supervisory, and professional occupations. Interestingly, the unionization rates of workers with and without disabilities are about the same.

While some disabilities preclude regular paid employment, even if community and workplace supports were in place, lack of employment is most often due to a failure by society and by employers to address barriers to employment and to accommodate differences (OECD 2003; Fawcett 1996). Many persons with disabilities need some help in the home or the community, and/or assistive aids and devices, or have special travel needs, or need flexible hours, or specially designed and configured work stations. If these supports and services were in place, rates of employment would be much higher.

Participation in the labour market is an important part of life for Canadians seeking personal independence and long-term financial security, and should be promoted as a viable choice for people with activity limitations. In addition to finding employment, a person with a disability may be limited in the amount or kind of work they can do; they may require workplace accommodations, such as modified hours or duties or structural modifications. In 2006, about two in three Canadians aged 15–64 with an activity limitation who were not in the labour force reported that they were completely prevented from working. These non-participants in the paid workforce were much more likely to report a severe or very severe disability. In contrast to people who were completely prevented from working, the 2006 *Participation and Activity Limitation Survey* (PALS) explored whether people felt that their condition limited the amount or kind of work they could do as opposed to completely preventing work. In 2006, more than four out of 10 persons with an activity limitation who were employed reported that they were indeed limited. In other words, the problem is not just exclusion from

Table 6.6: Types of Modifications Required in Order to Be Able to Work, by Severity, Canada, 2006

Type of workplace accommodation	Mild or moderate (%)	Severe or very severe (%)
Modified hours or days	14.0	41.1
Special chair or back support	12.4	30.3
Job redesign	9.6	30.3
Modified or ergonomic workstation	8.8	17.1
Other equipment, help, or work arrangement	3.2	5.1
Accessible elevator	2.0	6.9
Appropriate parking	2.0	10.3
Accessible washrooms	1.9	9.7
Accessible transportation	1.6	6.4
Human support	1.6	6.6
Technical aids	1.0	3.5
Computer modifications	0.6	5.2
Handrails or ramps	0.5	7.3
Communication aids	0.3	n/a

Source: Statistics Canada. *Participation and Activity Limitation Survey.* 2006.

jobs, but also lack of accommodations and supports that would allow those who are working to work with less difficulty, and also to work at their full potential.

Workplace accommodations are defined by Statistics Canada as modifications to the job or work environment that can enable a person with an activity limitation to participate fully in the work environment. These modifications can include many things ranging from modified hours or duties and software or hardware modifications, to structural items such as handrails or accessible washrooms.

Statistics Canada reports that the most common workplace accommodation required for employed people with activity limitations is modified hours or days, or reduced work hours, reported by about one in five workers. Approximately one in six workers with an activity limitation requires a special chair or back support (16.5%) or a job redesign (14.2%), while about one in 10 requires a modified or ergonomic workstation (10.7%). The need for supports is generally greater for older workers. On average, two-thirds (65%) of workers with disabilities report that their need for a workplace modification has been met, but this rate is higher for those with less severe activity limitations. Unfortunately, the rate of satisfaction with workplace modifications seems to have been falling.

Persons with activity limitations who are not in the labour force or who are unemployed tend to have more severe limitations, and thus have even greater requirements for workplace accommodations in order to be able to work. For women with disabilities who are not in the workforce, the most common cited and needed workplace accommodations are modified hours or days (30%), job redesign (24%), and special chair or back support (21%). Modified hours or days and job redesign are the most common needed accommodations cited by men with disabilities who are not working or are unemployed (28% for both).

The Canadian Council on Social Development has closely studied the problem of workplace exclusion. They report as follows: "Our findings ... indicate that there is a fairly high requirement for some type of workplace accommodation among those with disabilities, but these requirements are often for things that do not seem difficult to provide. Since modified workstations and accessible parking are the most commonly required structures, and modified work hours and job redesign are the most commonly required aids, one might think that these items would be relatively simple to provide. Instead, however, a fairly high number of individuals have unmet needs for these items, and these unmet needs can act as major barriers to their labour force participation and economic security."

In a recent report by the Canadian Abilities Foundation (CAF) using data gathered specifically for their study, similar conclusions are drawn. While the requirement for workplace accommodations is fairly high, these accommodations are usually not terribly costly. They estimated that "annual workplace accommodation costs are under $1,500 for almost all workers who have a disability." According to their study, for just over half of those requiring some type of accommodation, the estimated cost would be less than $500 per person per year; for one-third, the cost would be $500 to $1,500 per year; and for 16%, the cost was estimated at over $1,500. These costs are probably much lower than many employers realize. For many persons with disabilities, an employer's reluctance to provide accommodation on the job can be extremely disheartening and frustrating: "Employers are still ignorant about what it takes to hire and accommodate a person with a disability" (CCSD 2005).

Discrimination through discouragement or even exclusion can be a difficult obstacle for people with disabilities. Data from the *Participation and Activity Limitation Survey* show that, in 2006, one in four unemployed persons with a disability and one in eight persons with a disability who were not in the labour force believed that, in the past five years, they had been refused a job because of their disability. One in 12 employed persons with a disability also reported that they had experienced discrimination, with the proportion reporting discrimination increasing with the severity of activity limitations.

Many disabled adults are supported by a working spouse or partner, and some collect reasonable disability benefits from private insurance. But for many others, exclusion from the job market often means having to live in poverty. Approximately one in three persons with a disability receive some kind of (low) government income benefit—with 10% receiving social assistance, 10% receiving disability benefits under the Canada or Quebec Pension Plan, 5% receiving workers' compensation for a work-related accident or injury, and 6% receiving a veterans' benefit (Prince 2008). By contrast, just 6% are collecting disability benefits from a private insurance company. Such benefits typically replace a high share of previous wages, but only about one-half of the workforce has such coverage.

Canada provides very modest disability benefits under the Canada/Quebec Pension Plan to some persons with disabilities, but many disabled persons, particularly those without a long work history, rely on social assistance benefits. These persons almost invariably fall below the poverty line, even though some provinces provide somewhat higher benefits to those who can prove that they are unable to work. The poverty rate for persons with disabilities aged 16–64 is about one in four, or 2.5 times as high as the general population, and persons with disabilities are more than four times as likely to experience long-term poverty (Human Resources Development Canada 2001).

A key problem with CPP/QPP disability benefits, and most disability benefits paid by provinces as part of their social assistance programs, is that they require recipients to demonstrate a severe and ongoing disability that precludes paid work. While this may seem reasonable on the surface, it means that persons with activity limitations who could work part-time or part-year are placed in a catch-22 situation, forced to choose between giving up their benefits (and, often, access to prescription drugs and supported housing) and very insecure and low incomes from employment. If they choose the latter, it is very difficult to re-qualify for disability-related benefits. A better solution would be to supplement the wages of persons with disabilities who want to work, but, for various reasons, can work for only limited hours or periods of time (Prince 2008; Priest 2008).

The OECD has set as a policy goal the maximum feasible participation of people with disabilities in the job market, and contrasted this with the general reality of marginalization and exclusion from the job market on low benefits, which results from the current structure of income support programs combined with the lack of appropriate supports and services for individuals (OECD 2003). For the OECD, best practice would involve providing both income supplements and individualized supports to people with disabilities who choose to work. While Canada does provide some tax credits to workers with disabilities, these are very modest and often only cover, at best, additional costs of working and living. By contrast with other countries, both disability income supports and investments in home, community, and workplace supports are very low.

Even when they find jobs, persons with disabilities are significantly less likely to work full-time for the full year than other workers, and have lower hourly wages. Research by the Canadian Council on Social Development (CCSD) shows that the median hourly wage of male workers with disabilities is about 95% of the median wage of workers without a disability, while women with a disability earn just 86% per hour as much as other women (CCSD 2002). As a result, of both time worked and lower hourly wages, annual earnings of workers with disabilities are much lower than for the rest of the population.

This pay gap partly reflects lower levels of education. Less than one-half of persons with disabilities aged 25–54 (46%) have completed some kind of post-secondary education compared to 57% of people of the same age without disabilities. This partly reflects barriers to education for children and youth with disabilities. However, workers with disabilities are also older and more experienced, and those who surmount barriers to gain jobs might be expected to be paid better than average. A number of submissions to the recent federal government Pay Equity Task Force found evidence of discrimination in pay after controlling for differences between workers with and without disabilities, and argued that persons with disabilities should be covered by pay equity laws. Lower wages may reflect employer preconceptions about the capacity of workers with disabilities to perform at higher levels, and it is striking that relatively few workers with disabilities are in professional, supervisory, and management positions.

Exclusion from the workplace and lack of proper accommodation within the workplace are both major problems for Canadians with disabilities. The major solutions include changes to income support programs to remove the catch-22 choice, which too often has to be made between low benefits and working in a poverty-wage job, employer and government support for accommodations, and supports and services in the workplace as well as in the home and the community.

Conclusion

While equality-seeking groups are very different, there is a pervasive pattern of labour market disadvantage for new immigrants, racialized workers, Aboriginal Canadians, and persons with disabilities. Persons from these groups have greater difficulty finding and keeping steady jobs, receive below-average pay, and are most exposed to poverty. Specific factors come into play with each of these groups, but discrimination is a common factor. In all cases, interventions in terms of public policy and workplace practices are needed to promote greater inclusion and better outcomes.

Recommended Reading

- Changing the Canvas (www.changingthecanvas.org) is a remarkable website that provides written and visual media portraits of individual struggles against racism. The site highlights the experiences of immigrants of colour in the workforce, reminding us that real people live behind the statistics about racism, barriers to employment, chronic poverty, and failures in how Canada recognizes international credentials and work experience.
- Galabuzi, Grace-Edward. 2006. *Canada's Creeping Economic Apartheid*. Toronto: Canadian Scholars' Press Inc. This book calls attention to the growing racialization of the gap between rich and poor, which, despite the dire implications for Canadian society, is proceeding with minimal public and policy attention. The author challenges some common myths about the economic performance of Canada's racialized communities and points to the role of historical patterns of systemic racial discrimination as essential to understanding the persistent over-representation of racialized groups in low-paid and insecure jobs.
- Priest, Alicia et al. 2008. *Removing Barriers to Work: Flexible Employment Options for People with Disabilities in BC*. Vancouver: Canadian Centre for Policy Alternatives. Provides many examples of policies and programs that can break down barriers to employment among persons with disabilities, especially those trying to escape poverty and reliance on social assistance.
- The Report of the Royal Commission on Aboriginal Peoples. 1996. www.ainc-inac.gc.ca. Draws on a wealth of research to describe and analyze the historical origins of the many economic and social problems facing Aboriginal peoples.

References

Aydemir, Abdurrahman, and Mikal Skuterud. 2004. "Explaining the Deteriorating Entry Earnings of Canada's Immigrant Cohorts, 1966–2000." Ottawa: Statistics Canada, Analytical Studies Branch.

Bloom, Michael, and Michael Grant. 2001. *Brain Gain: The Economic Benefits of Recognizing Learning and Learning Credentials in Canada*. Conference Board of Canada. www.conferenceboard.ca.

Bourne, Larry S. 2004. "Beyond the New Deal for Cities: Confronting the Challenges of Uneven Economic Growth." Research Bulletin 21 (March). Toronto: Centre for Urban and Community Studies, University of Toronto.

Boyd, Monica. 2008. "Variations in Socioeconomic Outcomes of Second Generation Young Adults." In *The Experiences of Second Generation Canadians*, ed. Audrey Kobayashi. Special Issue of *Canadian Diversity* 6 (2). Association of Canadian Studies: pp. 20–25.

Brooks, Meghan. 2008. "Imagining Canada, Negotiating Belonging: Understanding the Experiences of Racism of Second Generation Canadians of Colour." In *The Experiences of Second Generation Canadians*, ed. Audrey Kobayashi. Special Issue of *Canadian Diversity* 6 (2). Association of Canadian Studies: pp. 75–79.

Canadian Council on Social Development (CCSD). 2002. Disability Research Information Sheet No. 4. Ottawa.

————. 2005. Disability Research Information Sheet No. 18. Ottawa.

Canadian Race Relations Foundation. 2000. *Unequal Access: A Canadian Profile of Racial Differences in Education, Employment, and Income.* www.crr.ca.

Cheung, Leslie. 2006. "Racial Status and Employment Outcomes." Canadian Labour Congress Research Paper No. 34.

Conference Board of Canada. 2004. "Making a Visible Difference: The Contribution of Visible Minorities to Canadian Economic Growth."

Corak, Miles. 2008. "Immigration in the Long Run." IRPP *Choices* 4, no. 3 (October). Institute for Research on Public Policy.

Fawcett, Gail. 1996. *Living with Disability in Canada: An Economic Portrait.* Ottawa: Human Resources Development Canada.

Frenette, Marc, and René Morissette. 2003. "Will They Ever Converge? Earnings of Immigrant and Canadian Born Workers over the Last Two Decades." Ottawa: Statistics Canada, Analytical Studies Branch.

Galabuzi, Grace-Edward. 2006. *Canada's Economic Apartheid.* Toronto: Canadian Scholars' Press Inc.

Hawthorne, Lesleyanne. 2008. "The Impact of Economic Selection Policy on Labour Market Outcomes for Degree Qualified Migrants in Canada and Australia." IRPP *Choices* 4, no. 5 (May).

Hou, Feng, and Garnett Picot. 2003. "Visible Minority Neighbourhood Enclaves and Labour Market Outcomes of Immigrants." Ottawa: Statistics Canada.

Human Resources Development Canada. 2001. *Disability in Canada: A 2001 Profile.* Ottawa.

————. 2006. *Advancing the Inclusion of People with Disabilities.* Ottawa.

Kobayashi, Audrey (Ed.). 2008. *The Experiences of Second Generation Canadians.* Special Issue of *Canadian Diversity* 6 (2). Association of Canadian Studies.

Organisation for Economic Co-operation and Development (OECD). 2003. *Transforming Disability Into Ability: Policies to Promote Work and Income Security for Disabled People.* Paris: OECD.

Ostrovsky, Yuri. 2007. "Earnings Inequality and Earnings Instability of Immigrants to Canada." Statistics Canada Analytical Studies Research Paper No. 309.

Picot, Garnett. 2008. "Immigrant Economic and Social Outcomes in Canada: Research and Data Development at Statistics Canada." Analytical Studies Research Paper No. 319.

Picot, Garnett, and F. Hou. 2003. "The Rise in Low Income among Recent Immigrants to Canada." Ottawa: Statistics Canada.

Picot, Garnett, Feng Hou, and Simon Coulombe. 2008. "Poverty Dynamics among Recent Immigrants to Canada." *International Migration Review* 42 (2): 393–424.

Priest, Alicia et al. 2008. *Removing Barriers to Work: Flexible Employment Options for People with Disabilities in BC.* Vancouver: Canadian Centre for Policy Alternatives.

Prince, Michael. 2008. *Canadians Need a Medium-Term Sickness/Disability Income Benefit.* Ottawa: Caledon Institute of Social Policy.

Reitz, Jeffrey G., and Rupa Banerjee. 2007. "Racial Inequality, Social Cohesion, and Policy Issues in Canada." Montreal: Institute for Research on Public Policy.

Statistics Canada. 2006. *Participation and Activity Limitations Survey 2006: Analytical Report.* Cat. 89-628-XIE, No. 002.

———. 2007a. "Immigration in Canada: A Portrait of the Foreign Born Population." 2006 Census.

———. 2007b. "Canada's Ethnocultural Mosaic." 2006 Census.

———. 2007c. "Aboriginal Peoples of Canada." 2006 Census.

———. 2008. *Participation and Activity Limitations Survey 2006: Labour Force Experiences of Persons with Disabilities*. Cat. 89-628-X, No. 007.

CHAPTER 7

Older Workers, Pensions, and the Transition to Retirement

Introduction[1]

One of the key transitions in life is that from paid work to retirement. This chapter discusses Canada's retirement income system, the incomes of seniors (which are heavily influenced by their work history), older workers in the job market, and debates over pensions and changing transitions to retirement.

Until relatively late in the 20th century, the period of retirement was short because most workers died at a much younger age than today's elderly, and had to work until late in life because of the inadequacy of public and private pensions. Old age was very often spent in poverty. That changed greatly in the latter part of the century as public and private pension systems matured. Today's elderly frequently enjoy long and reasonably secure periods of retirement, and poverty rates among the elderly are very low compared to rates among Canadian working-age adults and compared to seniors in other OECD countries (Myles 2000). Until quite recently, Canadian workers were retiring at much earlier ages than was the norm even in the 1960s and 1970s, typically at about age 60, and most people seem to have been retiring voluntarily and enjoying reasonable income security.

However, many older workers did not fare well in the economic restructuring of the 1980s and 1990s and enjoy only modest incomes, and private pension coverage is slipping fast among those now approaching retirement. Perhaps relatedly, older workers are staying in the paid workforce much longer than was the case as recently as 2000. There has been increasing advocacy for policies that would push older workers to work longer (Townson 2006). It is then far from clear that the relatively favourable patterns of the recent past in terms of a secure retirement will continue. Indeed, we are likely to see much greater inequality among older workers moving forward, and much greater gaps between the retirement incomes of some and their previous earnings.

Canada has a rapidly aging population. The proportion of all Canadians aged 55 and over will rise from about one in five in 2000, to one-quarter in 2011, to an expected one-third by 2021. The so-called old age dependency ratio—persons aged 65 and over as a proportion of the population aged 15–65—will increase from 20% in 2000, to 30% by 2025, to an expected 40% by 2050 (PRI 2005, 7). If people retire at age 65, they will be outside the working population for a good 20 years in the case of men, and 25 years in the case of women. The prospect of an aging society enjoying early retirement has caused great concern among many policy-makers. It has been feared that current pension arrangements will become unaffordable, that government expenditures, especially on health care, will surge, and that we will face serious labour shortages, especially shortages of skilled workers. Some commentators have seen it as undesirable that the proportion of a person's total working life spent in the paid workforce should slip so far, from about 74% in the 1960s (for men) to below 50% (Hicks 2003). However, proposals to raise the age of eligibility for public pensions have been dropped, mainly because the idea of retirement remains very popular. That said, there is widespread support for the idea of facilitating and supporting more choices for older workers, and increased recognition that desirable paths to retirement can be quite different. Many older workers continue in the workforce even as they begin to draw pension income and, as will be shown below, labour force participation rates for older workers have recently been rising rapidly.

Box 7.1: "Canada Faces Challenge to Keep Aging Economic Engine in Tune"
By Simon Avery

The engine of the nation's work force faces a dramatic overhaul in the coming years as the baby boomers begin to retire.

Traditionally, the government has relied on workers in their 30s to drive the economy. With the graying of the work force, new drivers must be found, said Andre Ramlo, a demographer and director of the Vancouver-based Urban Futures Institute.

"If we want to have that economic growth in the future, we're going to have to rely on other things, such as higher productivity."

In the past two decades, companies have boosted productivity by investing in a plethora of new technologies. Faster computers and more powerful software may mitigate the challenges of an aging labour force, but Mr. Ramlo says they won't be a panacea.

"You can only throw so much technology at problems. There is a point of diminishing returns with technology. What we're going to need is workers to be more flexible, [with] higher education and skills, and the economy needs to focus on higher value production."

New census data shows that between 2001 and 2006, the median age of the labour force increased to 41.2 years from 39.5 years, and workers 55 and over accounted for 15.3 per cent of the total labour force, up from 11.7 per cent.

Industry employment – Median Age
46.3 Median age – agriculture
45.7 Median age – real estate
44.6 Median age – transportation
42.7 Median age, industry – goods
41.5 Median age of Canadian industrial worker
41.1 Median age, industry – services
Source: Statscan.

Statistics Canada pointed to at least half a dozen occupations where the median age of employment was at least 50 in 2006. These include farmers, real estate agents, property administrators, transit operators, and senior managers in health care and education.

The numbers reflect the baby boomers approaching retirement and a growing trend among older workers to stay in the labour force, said Danielle Zietsma, a labour force economist at Statscan.

"The notion of retirement is starting to change. It's becoming an active retirement," Mr. Ramlo said.

He sees a limited window for organizations to take advantage of older workers while they stick around. "There is an opportunity to quickly download a lot of the information and experience from the older body of employment," he said.

The over-55 crowd showed the biggest increase in participation in the work force between 2001 and 2006. While the overall participation rate dipped a fraction for men and increased just 1.8 per cent for women, in the 55-plus category, it jumped 13 per cent for women and 26 per cent for men, Statscan said.

One of the largest real estate firms in the country says it is using mentorship programs to help bring younger blood into the ranks.

Christine Martysiewicz, a spokeswoman for RE/MAX Ontario-Atlantic Canada, said the company has attracted an influx of recent university graduates over the last 18 to 24 months. The booming real estate market has a lot to do with the trend, but she also credits mentoring and the opportunity for younger agents to now do a lot of their training and development through online courses.

Occupations with a relatively old work force include university professors and physicians. For every ten specialized doctors aged 55 or older, there are only eight between the ages of 20 and 34. For every 10 professors in the older category, there are only four n the younger group.

Occupations with a relatively youthful composition include software engineers, computer programmers, oil and gas drillers and occupational therapists, Statscan says.

Source: Avery, Simon. "Canada Faces Challenge to Keep Aging Economic Engine in Tune," *Globe and Mail*, March 5, 2008, B6.

Retirement patterns for the baby boomers, who are now mostly in their mid to late fifties, may be quite different than those of their parents and people now in their seventies. Most significantly, women now entering their fifties and sixties are much more likely than their mothers to have spent all or most of their lives in the paid workforce, and many will continue to work as they grow older. The gradual shift of employment away from very physically demanding jobs may also lead some workers to want to remain in the paid workforce until a later age than in even the recent past. Many of today's older workers are well educated, and such workers tend to retire early from their career jobs, but are also much more likely than average to pursue second careers.

The economic circumstances of people in and approaching retirement vary greatly. Some were victims of economic restructuring, while others have been in steady full-time jobs with good pensions for most of their working lives. Another factor at play is investment returns. Such returns are quite variable over time, and the sharp decline in share prices in 2000 with the end of the dot-com boom, together with low interest rates, hit the retirement savings of some older workers, and had negative impacts on the assets of many pension plans. One can expect even more individualized paths to retirement, perhaps including a steady rise in the age of retirement after many years of decline, as well as a rise in the proportion of older people who combine pension and employment incomes. Looking further forward, it seems likely that today's young adults will have to work much longer than their parents and grandparents because of declining private pension plan coverage and because other life transitions, notably that from education to work and to independent family formation are taking place so much later in life.

Canada's Retirement Income System

Canadian workers gain income in retirement from three main sources: public pensions—the Old Age Security (OAS) program, the Guaranteed Income Supplement (GIS), and the Canada/Quebec Pension Plan (CPP/QPP); private, employer-sponsored pensions; and private savings, including RRSPs. Two of the main sources of income for retirees—CPP/QPP and private pensions—are provided on the basis of earnings and work experience, and are explicitly intended to replace earnings, while the OAS program provides a flat benefit of just in excess of $6,000 in 2008 to all Canadians over age 65 (though higher income taxpayers making more than about $65,000 per year now have some or all of their OAS clawed back). As a very rough rule of thumb, pension experts and policy-makers believe that individuals should be able to obtain 50% to 70% of their previous earnings in retirement. Public pensions are intended to replace only 30% to 40% of median earnings, so it follows that employer pensions and private savings must make up a significant share of retirement income, particularly for higher income earners (Ambachtsheer 2008).

Public Pensions

The GIS, linked to the OAS, is an income-tested benefit. In combination, these two programs provide a minimum income floor for older Canadians. For the single elderly (who are overwhelmingly women), the floor currently (2008) amounts to a guaranteed minimum income of about $15,000 per year, and $20,000 for couples. This is still below the low-income line in a large urban centre as established by Statistics Canada. Even so, many working poor individuals and families experience a substantial income gain when they reach age 65 and qualify for OAS/GIS, and the vast majority of senior households have sufficient income from all sources combined to push them above the poverty line.

The Canada/Quebec Pension Plan (CPP/QPP) is a compulsory, earnings-related program, financed from employer and employee contributions, which provides retirement (and disability and death) benefits to the employed and the self-employed and their survivors. The retirement benefit provides 25% of pre-retirement earnings, but only for those earning up to the rough equivalent of average wages and salaries with a steady history of employment. Those earning more than average will get a lower benefit as a proportion of their pre-retirement income, and those with short work histories will get less than 25%. The average CPP/QPP benefit is only half of the maximum benefit of $10,615 (in 2008). A notable feature of the CPP/QPP is that allowance is made for periods of time spent by women outside the workforce to care for children. Benefits are indexed to inflation, while pensionable earnings track average wages. The normal age of entitlement to CPP/QPP retirement benefits is age 65, though reduced benefits are available at age 60, and higher benefits can be obtained by delaying retirement up to age 70. The CPP/QPP is explicitly designed to contribute to the goal of replacing pre-retirement earnings, and is not just an anti-poverty program. It is worth noting that CPP/QPP benefits were once entirely financed from current premiums (a pay-go system), but a significant investment fund has now been built up to cover most of the extra costs associated with an aging workforce.

In combination, the OAS and CPP/QPP provide a maximum of almost $17,000 per year and a minimum of about $15,000 to persons over age 65, and replace approximately 40% of previous wages for an average worker. Because of the offsetting influences of the GIS and the CPP/QPP, the distribution of public pension benefits among the elderly is actually quite close to a flat amount (Myles 2000; OECD 2001). Compared to many European countries, Canada's public pension programs are modest in scale, and the labour movement, anti-poverty groups, women's organizations, and others have long advocated significant improvements to public pensions (Townson 2006). Few would see an income replacement rate of 40% for an average worker as adequate to secure a comfortable retirement. This is, however, deliberate. In the mid-1960s, when the basic structure of our pension system was put in place, and again after a decade-long debate on pension reform that ended in the mid-1980s, the Canadian government was quite emphatic that it wanted to leave significant room for privately administered retirement income arrangements (Department of Finance 1994; LaMarsh 1968). The expectation has been that Canadians should finance part of their own retirement from savings through pension plans or RRSPs, which in turn are an important source of savings in the economy and a key pillar of the financial sector. Financial interests have traditionally favoured private savings over public pensions since this is a significant source of revenues and profits.

Workplace Pensions

Employers in the private sector are not legally obliged to establish a workplace pension plan, though pensions for government employees are often established by statute. Private plans are often created to recruit and retain employees. Generally speaking, employers have seen value in such plans since they foster employee loyalty and discourage workers from quitting to take another job. Pension plans have also been established as a result of pressure from unions. Workplace pensions are undoubtedly of benefit to workers, usually generating a significant and secure pension as a proportion of previous earnings. It is not uncommon for workers with long years of service to draw a good pension well before age 65. Just under one-half of all workplace pension plans, covering approximately 80% of all plan members, are of the defined benefit variety, providing benefits based on prior earnings and years of service. Defined contribution-type plans, by contrast, provide much more uncertain benefits based on investment returns. The share of such plans has risen from about 8% in the mid-1980s to 20% in 2005 (Informetrica 2007). The post-retirement benefits provided by workplace pension plans vary greatly. A very good but not untypical plan would provide a benefit of 2% of earnings multiplied by years of service, indexed to inflation, thus replacing the majority of earnings at retirement for those who have worked for 25 years. Other plans deliver a fixed benefit or lower benefit, and only a minority of pension plans provide even partial adjustments for inflation (Statistics Canada 2000). In combination with public pension benefits, most workplace plans provide an adequate replacement income, and help account for the fact that the great majority of Canadian retirees currently enjoy retirement incomes exceeding 60% or more of their pre-retirement earnings.

That said, very few new defined benefit plans have been established since the 1980s, and many consider them to be a legacy of the more stable economic conditions of the 1960s and 1970s. Employers often complain about the costs and the risks that they bear in sponsoring a pension plan that delivers a defined retirement benefit irrespective of the actual investment returns of the plan. Pension liabilities can indeed loom large in the finances of even large employers, particularly those like the Big Three North American auto companies, who have radically downsized over time and have a large proportion of retirees to current workers. However, pension plans have also often earned large surpluses, which have been used to deliver some combination of reduced contributions or increased benefits. Where they do exist, workers must usually help pay for any deficits, most often in the form of lower wage increases. Defined benefit pension plans are best suited to employers who want to maintain a stable, core workforce, and to workers who stay for many years with one employer. They have thus been undercut by a shift to more precarious and unstable work, and have tended to shortchange members who leave their employer before reaching retirement age, whether by choice or because of an involuntary layoff. Employer-sponsored pension plans have delivered income security and a decent retirement to workers consistent with the goals of many employers, and will likely remain a significant, but smaller, feature of the landscape moving forward.

It is clear that employer pension coverage of the workforce is slipping, and that the relative role of employer plans will likely continue to diminish. In 2001, 43.5% of paid employees belonged to workplace pensions, down from 48.5% in 1991. Just one in three employees in the private sector is now covered. Traditionally, women workers were less likely to be covered than men, but the gender difference has now virtually disappeared. The chances of being covered by a workplace pension plan increase with income, level of educational attainment, and the size of employer (Statistics Canada 2000). These numbers exclude self-employed workers, and also include group RRSPs, which offer very variable and uncertain returns.

As shown in Table 7.1, the proportion of all tax filers showing a contribution to a registered pension plan is now down to about one in three persons aged 35–54, and is even lower for those aged 25–34 (Morrissette and Ostrovsky 2006). Coverage has declined markedly among men since the mid-1980s. Only about 20% of private-sector workers are now members of a defined benefit pension plan, and coverage is minimal in enterprises with less than 100 workers (Ambachtsheer 2008, 6). A detailed study undertaken by Informetrica (2008) confirms the slow erosion of employer pension plan coverage, which has been concentrated entirely in the private sector. Statistics Canada recently looked at workplace pension coverage for couples and found that more than half of all couples with husbands aged 35–54 have no workplace pension coverage at all, while a lucky 14% are covered by two pensions. Almost half of all couples in the top 20% of earners have two pension plans, while three-quarters of all couples in the bottom 20% have no workplace pension plan coverage at all (Morissette and Ostrovsky 2006, Tables 5, 6).

Table 7.1: Tax Filers with Contributions to a Registered Pension Plan (%)

	Men		Women	
	25–34	**35–54**	**25–34**	**35–54**
1986	27.7	41.5	28.4	33.4
1995	22.7	37.5	27.4	38.9
2003	21.1	32.8	28.3	38.1

Sources: Morrissette, René, and Yuri Ostrovsky. 2006. *Pension Coverage and Retirement Savings of Canadian Families, 1986 to 2003*; Statistics Canada. Cat. 11F0019MIE, No. 286.

Aside from working in the public sector, where about 80% of workers belong to a pension plan, the factor that is most decisive is union membership. Overall, 80% of union members belong to workplace pensions compared to just 27% of non-union members. In workplaces of 20 employees or less, 70% of union members still belong to workplace pensions compared to just 13% of non-union members (Akyeampong 2002; Informetrica 2008). Since the end of World War II, the negotiation and improvement of workplace pensions has been an important union bargaining priority and remains so to this day. The launching of Canada's modest public pensions in the 1950s and 1960s allowed some shift in emphasis in collective bargaining from the negotiation of benefits starting at age 65 or later to the negotiation of early retirement programs.

The third major source of retirement income is private savings, notably through tax-supported registered retirement savings plans (RRSPs). Contributions to RRSPs are tax deductible, and investment returns in them accumulate tax free, which means there is a large subsidy to savings. While of use to the self-employed and those with no or an inadequate pension plan, RRSPs provide most benefits to higher income earners who are in the best position to save significant amounts, and very few people use all of their available RRSP contribution room. RRSP contributions are, unlike workplace pension plan contributions, voluntary, and many people postpone saving until it is too late to generate a decent income in retirement. As a very rough rule of thumb, a person needs about 20 times as much in savings at age 65 to provide a given amount of annual retirement income to last until death, matching inflation. Thus, one would need about $300,000 in savings to guarantee a continuing real annual income of $15,000 (with the amount varying by life expectancy and real interest rates). Tal (2007) reports that total unused RRSP contribution room—the amount people could have contributed and received a tax deduction, minus the amount actually contributed—stood at a staggering $491 billion in 2006 and 90% of tax filers had contribution room. Just 38% of Canadians aged 25–64 made a contribution in the most recent year, and the average was just over $2,000 per household. Contributions have not been keeping pace with either inflation or income growth. As of 2005, the median amount in RRSPs (half have more and half have less) was just $60,000 for those nearing retirement (aged 55–65). The average is higher because RRSP contributions are heavily concentrated among a small number of the relatively well off. While some people do save enough for a decent retirement and invest funds well, others do not save nearly enough and do not invest well. A key problem with RRSPs is that investment returns are far from certain and that equity values in particular, while rising over the long term, are subject to large fluctuations in the short term and can stagnate over long periods. Even if people do save a lot, RRSPs are a very costly savings instrument. Management and sales-related fees eat up 2% to 4% of assets every year, eating deeply into investment returns. Large pension plans and the CPP Investment Fund achieve much higher rates of return on investments than individual investors (Ambachtsheer 2008, 3). Effectively, the decline of workplace pensions has shifted the risk of income insecurity in old age to individuals at significant cost to most (Townson 2006).

The Canadian Institute of Actuaries finds that only about one-third of households above low-income levels are currently saving at sufficient levels on top of public pensions to replace pre-retirement income, mainly because of the decline of defined benefit pension plans and insufficient investments in RRSPs. Statistics Canada (2001) has also calculated that one-third of households approaching retirement (household head aged over 45) have not saved enough to either replace two-thirds of their income, or to have an income above the poverty line. Pension experts now generally agree that Canada's three-pillar pension system is unlikely to work nearly as well moving forward as it has in the past (Ambachtsheer 2008). Middle and higher income Canadians in particular are at high risk of facing steep declines in their incomes in retirement—or long working lives—due to the fact that public pensions provide only a very modest replacement income, while workplace pensions do not cover the majority and are in decline.

Incomes of Canada's Elderly

The last quarter of the 20th century was a period of very rapid improvement in the incomes of older Canadians. The real incomes of elderly households increased by 50% over the period from 1973 to 1996, and by even more for lower income seniors. Poverty rates among the elderly fell dramatically. Not only did the incomes of the elderly increase in purchasing power, but the incomes of the elderly compared to younger age groups increased as well. From 1973 to 1996, the average income of elderly households increased from 47% to 80% of that of non-elderly households, when the numbers are adjusted for differences in household size (Baldwin and Laliberté 1999; Myles 2000). Over this period, two sources of income of the elderly grew particularly rapidly—income from the Canada and Quebec Pension Plans, and income from workplace pensions. The CPP/QPP share of total income of the elderly grew from 2.8% in 1973 to 17.8% in 1996. Workplace pension income increased from 10.4% to 22.3% over the period. By 1996, almost all elderly households received income from OAS/GIS, and 86.5% received income from the CPP/QPP, up from only 28.4% only 23 years earlier. Just over one-half (53.2%) received workplace pension income, 57.9% received some investment income (often in very small amounts), and 20.3% received some employment income.

Among lower income senior households, income from public pension programs is of decisive importance. If we divide households into 10 equally sized groups ranked by income, we find that income from OAS/GIS and CPP/QPP accounts for more than half of all income for all households in the bottom 60%, while only the top 10% receive less than 30% of their income from public pensions. Income from workplace pensions is particularly important for those with above-average incomes, with the exception of those at the very top. Public pensions address the poverty issue, while workplace pensions are the key lever for comfortable retirement incomes and sustained economic well-being in the transition from work to retirement.

There is still a substantial and persistent income gap between older men and women. And, there are striking differences in terms of sources of income of men and women. OAS/GIS and investment income are more important for women and CPP/QPP and workplace pensions for men. This reflects the working patterns by gender of previous years, and differences may shrink in the future to some degree.

A retirement income system could be judged to be successful if poverty among the elderly is low, and if retirees do not experience a large decline in income compared to their working years. Canada stands out among advanced industrial countries in terms of now having a very low level of poverty among the elderly, though there are still major problems for single elderly women (OECD 2001). In fact, using a common definition of poverty (household income of less than one-half the median), the poverty rate of Canadian seniors is just 2.5% compared to 20% in the U.S., and about 10% in most Western European countries. Deep poverty has been all but abolished by public pensions, but it is important to note that a high proportion of elderly households are still living on incomes that are quite close to the Canadian low-income line, and that single elderly women in particular are vulnerable to poverty.

Turning to income replacement, a recent Statistics Canada study (LaRochelle-Côté, Myles, and Picot 2008) looked at the incomes of individuals and their families as they moved from age 55 in the mid-1980s through their retirement years. For the average family, income falls after retirement, but by age 68, it stabilizes at about 80% of the income that had been earned at age 55. The fall in income compared to prior earnings is less for lower income families because public pensions replace quite a high share of earned income. Indeed, the majority of the incomes of the bottom 20% of retired persons in their late sixties come from public pensions. By contrast, the decline in income in retirement is greater for the more affluent earners at age 55, the majority of whose income in retirement comes from private pensions and investments.

There is a lot of variation in the extent to which persons and families experience a decline in their incomes in retirement. Among middle and upper income individuals and families, high income replacement rates in retirement are closely associated with earning employment income into the early retirement years and having a private pension income. Table 7.2 shows the incomes and income replacement rate for individuals aged 71–73 in the year 2000. As shown, incomes were much higher for the top 20%. Over one-third of the income of the highest income group came from private pensions and RRSPs, with just 16.6% coming from public pensions. By contrast, public pensions provided 57% of the income of the bottom 20% of retirees, and an average of 31.9% of income for all persons aged 71–73.

Table 7.2: Incomes of Persons Aged 71–73, 2000

	Pre-tax income	% from Public pensions	% from Private pensions/ RRSPs	% from Earnings	% from Investments
All	$46,100	31.9%	34.7%	12.6%	20.4%
Bottom 20%	$24,400	57.0%	17.6%	13.9%	9.5%
Top 20%	$89,700	16.6%	36.5%	14.9%	31.9%

Source: LaRochelle-Côté, Sebastien, John Myles, and Garnett Picot. 2008. *Income Security and Stability During Retirement in Canada*. Statistics Canada Analytical Studies Research Paper No. 306.

The authors of this study found that about one in five persons in this age group had inadequate replacement incomes, defined as 60% or less of previous earnings. However, more than one-third (36.2%) of those in the top 20% did not meet this income replacement threshold.

Pension Debates

In the 1970s, there was a major pension debate in Canada in which the major concern was the incomes of the elderly. It resulted in major pension improvements. In the 1990s, the main issue was seen to be the affordability of pensions in an aging society in which workers will live much longer lives after retirement. The debate was initiated by the World Bank and the OECD who have favoured later retirement and more individualized pensions based on personal savings (OECD 2000; World Bank 1994). Despite the success of the pension arrangements put in place in Canada, many voices here also called for a return to reliance on individual savings. There was a vigorous campaign by conservative think-tanks in the mid-1990s to abolish the CPP/QPP in favour of individual retirement accounts (Lam and Walker 1997; Robson 1996).

The federal government forecast in 1993 that expenditures on Old Age Security and the Canada and Quebec Pension Plans would increase from 5.3% of national income in 1993 to more than 8% in 2030. While this caused great anxiety to some, it is striking that OAS and CPP/QPP expenditures were projected to increase as a share of GDP by only 50% over a period in which the over-65 population was expected to double as a share of the population. One way or another, the costs of aging would have to be borne. The government claimed that if no changes were made to the CPP/QPP, those who came after the baby boomers would be asked to pay two to three times more for the same pensions as those who came before them. While true to a degree, this appeal to fairness between generations tended to ignore the fact that there had been a very large income transfer to the first generation to benefit from the CPP/QPP.

Ultimately, increases in the retirement age and a radical shift to individual accounts were ruled out. Instead, benefits were modestly trimmed and contribution rates were raised from 5.6% to 9.9% of earnings below the maximum amount, with the aim of building up an investment fund to spread some of the cost of future pensions over a longer period. It is now generally agreed that only minor adjustments will have to be made to ensure that the CPP/QPP is financially sustainable. The federal government eventually abandoned a proposal to replace the OAS/GIS program with a single seniors' benefit, which would have been based on family rather than individual income. Opposition arose because this proposal would have deprived many older women of an individual old age pension, would have resulted in lower benefits for higher income families, and also would, some feared, erode incentives to save for retirement.

Over the period since 1998, there has been little impetus for fundamental change in Canada's pension system. The costs of an aging society to public pensions—if not to health care—now seem quite manageable. It will be possible to keep up transfers to a growing elderly population with no reduction in the standard of living of the working-age population if we continue to have steady economic growth. However, there are some potential sources of disturbance to the current system. On top of declining workplace pension plan coverage, some plans, particularly in the private sector, could face serious financial difficulties as workforces shrink while the numbers of retirees grow. Plans are required to accumulate assets to match future liabilities, allowing for short-term fluctuations in financial markets. However, many plans are not fully funded which could result in reduced benefits. We may see more pension plan windups and/or conversions of defined benefit plans to defined contribution plans.

The limited nature of the first pillar—public pensions—combined with growing problems for workplace pensions have prompted some recent thinking about alternatives. The labour movement has long advocated a doubling of CPP/QPP benefits to replace a higher share of previous earnings, and thus reduce reliance on often inadequate and usually costly and unstable private savings. Neutral pension experts have also begun to advocate for new pension alternatives, such as large new quasi-public plans to parallel the CPP/QPP (Ambachtsheer 2008). However, these proposals have yet to become central to political and policy debates.

Older Workers in the Canadian Job Market

Table 7.1 and figures 7.1 and 7.2 summarize trends in the participation rate of older workers—that is, the proportion of people in the age group who were working or seeking jobs in the year. The overall pattern is that the participation rate of older men—especially those aged 60–64 and aged 65–69—declined very significantly until 2000 as the age of retirement fell. Since about 2000, however, the trend has sharply reversed. Labour force participation rates for older women were steadier—and increased for women aged 55–59—until 2000, reflecting the fact that women entering older age groups were increasingly likely to have been working at younger ages rather than caring for children. Like men, participation rates for women aged 60–64 and 65–69 have jumped sharply since about 2000.

As of 2000, just 16% of men aged 65–69 were still active in the paid workforce, down from 21.4% in 1980. The participation rate of men aged 60–64 fell steadily from the mid-1970s to 2000, from about two-thirds to under one-half, and by 2000, more than one in four men aged 55–59 had dropped out of the workforce. This sustained decline in older men's workforce participation mainly reflected decisions to retire earlier than in the past, at an average age of just above 60. This would have been facilitated by the contribution of the pension arrangements described above. However, it also reflected the fact that many older workers lost their jobs in the economic restructuring of the 1980s and the first half of the 1990s. In short, both push and pull factors were at play.

The pattern for women is different. From the mid-1970s to 2000, the participation rate of women aged 55–59 rose steadily from about one-third to more than half, while that of women aged 60–64 and 65–69 was quite stable, at about one in four and about one in 12 respectively. The difference in the trends between women and men basically reflects the fact that the older women of the mid-1990s had been more likely to spend most of their lives in the paid workforce than were women of the same age in the mid-1970s. In fact, there is a clear break, with women born after the mid-1950s being

Figure 7.1: Participation Rate of Older Men, 1976–2007

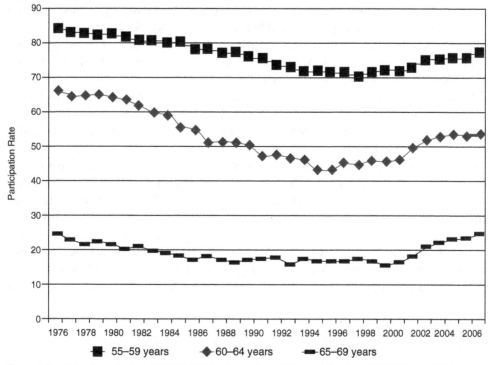

Source: Statistics Canada Cat. 71F0004XCB Labour Force Historical Review 2007. Table cd1t01

Figure 7.2: Participation Rate of Older Women, 1976–2007

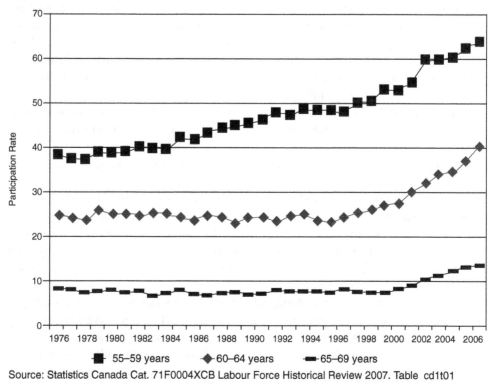

Source: Statistics Canada Cat. 71F0004XCB Labour Force Historical Review 2007. Table cd1t01

much more likely to work than those born before. Women do tend to retire earlier than men, since couples often retire at the same time, and married women are typically younger than their spouses, and because family considerations also influence the work decisions of older women. Retirement from paid work is often determined by the need to care for family members. Such pressures to retire are likely to intensify as publicly provided social services are cut.

While the median age of retirement has remained about age 61, there has been a very pronounced increase in the participation rate of older workers since about 2000. As shown in the table and figures, participation rates of both men and, especially, women aged 55–59 have risen significantly, and they have also jumped sharply for those in the older age groups. These increases probably represent, in part, the previous work histories of the current near elderly women compared to previous generations, and an increase in individual choices to remain at work. More older workers today are in good health and well educated, and many such workers want to continue to work in some capacity—perhaps in a new job—and jobs have been much more readily available after 2000 than was the case in the 1990s. Delayed withdrawal from the workforce may also reflect losses to savings following the stock market collapse of 2000. It is difficult to judge how much of the change is voluntary and how much is involuntary.

Displaced Older Workers and Involuntary Retirement

For many laid-off older workers in the recession and slow recovery of the late 1980s to the mid-1990s, early retirement was an unplanned consequence of a layoff (Pyper and Giles 2002; Schellenberg 1994). Planned retirements may, in fact, account for only a modest proportion of all supposed "retirements" in times of severe economic downturn (Rowe and Nugyen 2003). While many older workers were pushed out by layoffs in the 1990s, companies that were downsizing also often introduced early retirement incentives funded from then quite healthy pension plan surpluses to maintain jobs for younger workers.

Workers aged 55–65 have, on average, held their current job for a considerable period of time (17 years for men and 12 years for women). Many will move from that job into retirement. However, those who lose their job before a planned retirement often experience great difficulty in finding new employment. As a group, displaced older workers are less well educated than average, less likely to have up-to-date skills matching those demanded in new jobs, and are less willing and able to move to new jobs. Geographical mobility is not a desirable or realistic option for many such workers, and the potential for moving into a different occupation is often limited by formal education and skill levels. Many employers are unwilling to hire displaced older workers, and governments have, unfortunately, not often been prepared to invest significantly in retraining.

While both unemployment and long-term unemployment rates today are markedly lower than was the case for most of the past 20 years, workers aged 55 and over today still experience significantly longer average unemployment spells than do all workers (19.9 weeks compared to 14.6 weeks, in 2006). Adjustment difficulties are obviously most serious for those with very firm-specific or dated skills, who live in areas with few alternative job opportunities. Long-term unemployment among older workers is most serious in Quebec and Atlantic Canada. Further, displaced older workers who do find new jobs often experience a significant loss of income. High seniority, displaced workers generally experience wage losses of between one-fifth and one-third (Morissette, Zhang, and Frenette 2007).

The Current Debate on Older Workers and Retirement

As discussed above, concerns about the affordability of pensions and future labour shortages has led to an interest in increasing the age of retirement, and in more complete utilization of the labour force in the "near retirement" years. The catalogue of policy responses put forward by the OECD and others includes raising the age of eligibility for public pension benefits, removing early retirement incentives in pension plans, and ending mandatory retirement.

It is quite true that good workplace pension plans do create strong incentives to retire at or often before age 65. Few workers will choose to work for a fraction of their former income if this means deferring a decent pension for very long. When early retirement programs are being valued for actuarial purposes, it is common practice to assume that the actual age of retirement will fall halfway between the normal retirement age and the date when the right to early retirement without actuarial reduction is established. Access to good pensions is a major reason why public-sector workers tend to retire at an earlier age than private-sector workers, and why the self-employed tend to work longer than employees. In fact, early retirement is, not surprisingly, concentrated in sectors that tend to have good pension plans, such as public administration, utilities, and education (Kiernan 2001). Moreover, Canadian tax rules make it difficult if not impossible for workers to phase into retirement by combining part-time employment and pension income from the same employer. Thus, the mainstream policy prescription to decrease incentives to early retirement to get workers to stay in the paid workforce longer has some elements of truth. It is also true that increasing the labour force participation of older workers could make a potentially important, once-and-for-all contribution to increasing national income.

All that said, the mainstream view completely ignores what we know about workers' preferences. Given access to a decent pension income at age 60 or 65, the great majority of healthy workers will choose to retire. (Retirement due to ill health or disability is quite common, but not considered here.) Public opinion polling suggests that proposals to delay public pension eligibility are very unpopular. Focus groups conducted by the federal government's Policy Research Initiative found that most Canadians wanted to retire relatively early and were not very supportive of government efforts to encourage them to work longer (not least when many participants pointed out that they were still financially supporting underemployed young adults still living at home). Huge protests have greeted proposals to raise the retirement age or to cut pensions in many European countries. The short shrift given to the possibility of increasing the age of eligibility for Canada Pension Plan benefits in the mid-1990s likely reflected a fair reading by politicians of the public mood. Looking beyond the results of public opinion polls, it is a fair generalization that as societies have grown more affluent, working people have shown a strong desire to take advantage in the form of shorter working hours and pensions. Worker preferences for paid time off may well continue in the face of population aging (Burtless and Quinn 2002).

The preoccupation with early retirement effects of pensions also oversimplifies individuals' retirement decisions, and the fact that a wide range of factors influence decisions to work or not to work in the older years. There are significant variations in both the trends and levels of labour force participation of older workers from country to country and within countries. Countries with high levels of older worker participation vary a great deal in terms of other labour market characteristics, including their apparent preference for paid time off as opposed to higher incomes over the entire course of working life (Hayden 2003). One key factor at play is the overall strength of employer demand for workers and the level of unemployment. Germany, with a relatively high unemployment rate, has a very low participation rate for older workers. Sweden and the U.S. have very different labour markets, but both have low unemployment and relatively high participation rates for older workers. It is striking in the case of Canada that provinces with low unemployment rates tend to have higher rates of older worker participation in the labour force, while older people tend not to work in provinces with relatively high unemployment rates. As well, as noted, labour force participation rates have jumped significantly as the national unemployment rate has fallen since 2000. The increase in labour force participation rates of older workers since 2000 provides a reminder of the importance of the overall demand for workers. In short, if jobs are available, many older workers will continue to work. This may be because they are no longer pushed out of work, because they choose to work longer, or because employers actively seek to have them stay at work.

The preoccupation with pensions' supposed disincentives to work also tends to lead people to ignore negative push factors in the workplace that may play at least as great a role as the pull factor of pensions. As shown in other chapters of this book, for many people, work can involve high levels of stress, long hours of work, discrimination and harassment, poor physical working conditions, lack of training, and lack of control over the work process itself. And, high job demands are indeed associated with decisions to take early retirement (Turcotte and Schellenberg 2005). It is little wonder that many people choose to retire as soon as they are able to do so. However, working conditions could be modified to make work more attractive. To take a concrete example, great concern is currently being expressed about a potential shortage of registered nurses in Canada, given that few new nurses have been hired in recent years while a large share of the current nursing workforce is nearing an age at which pensions can be drawn upon. Nurses tend to retire well before age 65, in part because of pensions, but also in significant part because many nursing jobs can be very physically demanding as well as stressful, and involve unsocial working hours. Today, many nurses work very variable shifts due to a shortage of permanent, full-time jobs. Many in the nursing profession say that some nurses might choose to work longer if these negative aspects of the job were modified. It is also probable that some people would choose to shift from full-time to part-time work later in life, especially if they could combine pension and part-time income from the same employer.

Many employers do not necessarily wish to retain and use the skills of older workers. Until very recently, the common practice of mandatory retirement in workplaces with pension plans generally reflected union/employer agreement on the desirability of a known path to retirement. From an employer perspective, retirement means that the employment relationship can be ended amicably, and that normal job ladders for younger workers can continue to operate. As of 2005, older worker retention was not a major issue for the great majority of Canadian employers, and very few had implemented active programs to retain older workers for all of the talk of growing skills shortages (PRI 2005; Conference Board 2005; Lowe 2005). Lowe (2005) reports on the basis of a large sample survey of workers that some older workers, perhaps as many as one-third, would choose to continue to work at least somewhat longer if they were given attractive options to consider. But very, very few employers have offered options such as extended vacations and flexible hours, which might allow workers to phase in to retirement.

Box 7.2: The Debate on Mandatory Retirement

During the period of high unemployment that gripped Canada and the U.S. at the end of the 1950s and the beginning of the 1960s, there was a great deal of concern that laid-off older workers faced discrimination based on age. Many jurisdictions adopted human rights legislation that banned employment discrimination on the basis of age, up to age 65. This is specified as the age of retirement in many private pension plan arrangements and employment contracts. While these are private arrangements, they used to be permitted in most provinces by making them an exception to the general principle of non-discrimination in employment on the basis of age. Contractual mandatory retirement had, however, been eliminated in most jurisdictions as of 2008.

The key argument against mandatory retirement was that it is discriminatory, and that discrimination in employment on the basis of age is not warranted. It is noted that most workers over age 65 are in good physical and mental health. Some opponents of mandatory retirement wanted older workers to stay in the workforce to reduce pension costs and to meet future skill needs, while some supporters of mandatory retirement feared that its abolition could be the "thin end of the wedge," leading to changes in public pensions and longer working lives for all. However, changes to human rights legislation are meant to facilitate an individual choice to stay on at work rather than to modify pension entitlements or the normal age of retirement for all workers.

Supporters of contractual mandatory retirement argued that these are private arrangements that suited the needs of most employers and most workers, and that governments should have left them alone. It is often argued that a fixed age of retirement protects the job security and working conditions of older workers, since employers may be forgiving of lower productivity and poorer performance if they know that an older employee will leave at a fixed date. Getting rid of mandatory retirement could, it is feared, lead to more intense monitoring of work and, perhaps, to disputes over the work performance of older workers. In many unionized workplaces, older, high-seniority workers tend to hold the most desirable jobs, and it is often seen as unfair if they remain past age 65. It has also been argued that mandatory retirement opens up jobs for younger workers.

   Studies have found that getting rid of mandatory retirement has, in fact, had only a limited impact on the age at which most workers will retire, with a few exceptions, such as university professors. If good pension arrangements are in place, most workers will choose to retire well before the mandatory age of retirement. Exceptions may include some individuals who began their career with a particular employer relatively late in life, and thus do not have a good pension at age 65, as well as individuals who have particularly pressing financial needs or derive a great deal of personal satisfaction from a job.

In the context of declining defined benefit pension coverage, wealth and the returns from financial markets will increasingly influence retirement decisions, and it seems very probable that the recent rise in employment rates for older workers partly reflects the fact that some people who were dreaming of "Freedom 55" have decided to work longer simply because they cannot afford not to work. A shift to individual retirement savings will make it more difficult to forecast retirement decisions since financial returns are so unpredictable. Adding to the affordability issue, older workers are more likely than in even the recent past to still be supporting children in the post-secondary education system.

   The debate over the age of retirement as influenced by pension incentives tends to ignore the complexity of paths out of the paid workforce, and the fact that many older workers combine pension and employment income. Hidden within the overall participation rate numbers for older workers are many transitions from career jobs to second careers. One in five older workers whose career jobs (defined as a job that had been held for more than eight years) ended voluntarily in the mid-1990s continued working in a different full-time job over the next two years (Pyper and Giles 2002). People who continue working after 65, and many aged 60–65, seem to be engaged in second careers. They are much more likely to be working part-time than pre-retirement-age workers (Schellenberg, Turcotte, and Ram 2005). Rates of self-employment are also much higher than among core-age workers—24% for workers aged 55–64 compared to 15% for workers aged 25–54 (Marshall and Ferrao 2007, Table 2). In fact, a very high proportion is self-employed. They are also likely to be well educated. Employment rates of university-educated seniors over age 65 are double those of people with only a high school education (Duchesne 2004). During the period of rapid economic expansion following the recession of the early 1990s, there was a striking increase in the number of people combining employment and retirement income.

   There could be broad support for a later average age of retirement if this arose not from the erosion of income security for older workers, but through policies to expand choices, such as more effective labour adjustment programs for older workers, improvements to social services that reduce the pressure on older women workers to leave paid work to care for family members, and, more generally, improvements in the quality of work that make it less burdensome. Participation rates of older workers could be raised in a positive way not just by recognizing their special needs, but also through more advice and support. Older workers sometimes have difficulty recognizing how their personal work histories might relate to prospects for future employment and training. In some European countries, governments have begun to promote longer working lives more through the use of these kinds of measures than the stick of reduced pensions (Foden and Jespen 2002).

Conclusion

In the current discussion on the situation of older workers, the most hotly contested issue is the appropriate age of exit from the labour force. The issue should be approached in a manner that recognizes workers' legitimate needs and desires for a financially secure retirement. Looking beyond the concerns associated with pension financing, and bearing in mind that the overall state of the job market will play a vital role in determining the actual age of retirement, there are clearly some contrary pushes and pulls on the age of retirement. Unsafe, unhealthy, and unsatisfying work are likely to drive people to look for a safe haven in retirement. Downsizing of large public and private employers will likely have the same effect. Clearly, though, if work remains attractive to employees, and employers want to pay for them to remain and to accommodate special needs and circumstances, there will be a growing supply of healthy older workers to draw upon.

Conflicting views about the appropriate age of retirement will continue to fuel political debate in the years ahead. The range of possible outcomes will be framed, in part, by economic circumstances. Will labour productivity increase at a pace that will allow a growing number of pensioners to receive relative incomes at or above their current level, while also permitting real income growth among the non-elderly? And, how will people evaluate the choice of using productivity gains to increase incomes today rather than taking paid time off in retirement tomorrow?

No matter how the age of retirement issue is resolved, there are groups of older workers whose work situation should be a matter of public concern, such as the older unemployed and people who have faced discrimination in employment. The situation of older adult immigrants bears particular scrutiny given low earnings, and many older women still have very low retirement incomes. It is also important that the age of exit issue gets resolved in a manner that creates employment opportunities for older workers who want employment and, at the same time, does minimal damage to the employment prospects of younger workers.

Recommended Reading

- Duchesne, Doreen. 2004. "More Seniors at Work." *Perspectives on Labour and Income* (Spring): 55–67. A statistical overview of seniors in the workforce today.
- Hicks, Peter. 2003. "The Policy Implications of Aging." *Horizons* 6 (2). www.policyresearch.gc.ca. This paper looks at some of the implications for public policy regarding aging and the changed life-course of younger Canadians compared to

previous generations, and favours more varied and later paths to retirement.

- Kiernan, Patrick. 2001. "Early Retirement Trends." *Perspectives on Labour and Income* (Winter).
- Organisation for Economic Co-operation and Development. Country reports on the employment of seniors, including in Canada, are available from the OECD website at www.oecd.org. See under "Employment" on the sub-site "Ageing Society."
- Townson, Monica. 2006. *Growing Older, Working Longer: The New Face of Retirement.* Ottawa: Canadian Centre for Policy Alternatives. This book provides an interesting and well-documented overview of pension issues and the search for policies and practices that improve the lives of older workers.

Note

1. This chapter draws from Canadian Labour Congress (CLC) research papers written by Bob Baldwin.

References

Akyeampong, Ernest. 2002. "Unionization and Fringe Benefits." *Perspectives on Labour and Income* (Autumn): 5–9.

Ambachtsheer, Keith. 2008. *The Canada Supplementary Pension Plan: Towards an Adequate, Affordable Pension for All Canadians.* Toronto: C.D. Howe Institute.

Baldwin, Bob, and Pierre Laliberté. 1999. *Incomes of Older Canadians: Amounts and Sources, 1973–1996.* Research Paper No. 15. Ottawa: Canadian Labour Congress.

Burtless, Gary, and Joseph Quinn. 2002. *Is Working Longer the Answer for an Ageing Workforce?* Boston: Centre for Research on Retirement, Boston College.

Conference Board of Canada. 2005. *Work to Retirement Transition: An Emerging Business Challenge.* Ottawa.

Department of Finance. 1994. *Action Plan on Pension Reform: Building Better Pensions for Canadians.* Ottawa: Department of Finance.

Duchesne, Doreen. 2004. "More Seniors at Work." *Perspectives on Labour and Income* (Spring): 55–67.

Foden, David, and Maria Jepsen. 2002. "Active Strategies for Older Workers in the European Union: A Comparative Analysis of Recent Experiences." In *Active Strategies for Older Workers in the European Union*, ed. David Foden et al. Brussels: European Trade Union Institute.

Foursly, Michel, and Marc Gervais. 2002. *Collective Agreements and Older Workers in Canada.* Ottawa: Labour Program, Human Resources Development Canada.

Hayden, Anders. 2003. "International Work-Time Trends: The Emerging Gap in Hours." *Just Labour* (Spring). www.justlabour.yorku.ca.

Hicks, Peter. 2003. "The Policy Implications of Aging." *Horizons* 6 (2).

Informetrica Ltd. 2007. *Occupational Pension Plan Coverage in Ontario Statistical Report.* Prepared for Ontario Expert Commission on Pensions.

Kiernan, Patrick. 2001. "Early Retirement Trends," *Perspectives on Labour and Income* (Winter): 7–13.

Lam, Karen, and Michael Walker. 1997. "The Next Step in Changing the Canada Pension Plan." *Fraser Forum*. www.fraserinstitute.ca.

LaMarsh, Judy. 1968. *Memoirs of a Bird in a Gilded Cage*. Toronto: McClelland & Stewart.

LaRochelle-Côté, Sébastien, John Myles, and Garnett Picot. 2008. *Income Security and Stability during Retirement in Canada.* Statistics Canada Analytical Studies Research Paper No. 306.

Lipsett, Brenda, and Mark Reesor. 1997. *Employer-Sponsored Pension Plans — Who Benefits?* Ottawa: Human Resources Development Canada.

Lowe, Graham. 2005. *Work Retirement Decisions: A Synthesis Report.* Prepared for Human Resources and Skills Development Canada.

Marshall, Katherine, and Vincent Ferrao. 2007. "Participation of Older Workers." *Perspectives on Labour and Income* (Autumn).

Morissette, René, and Yuri Ostrovsky. 2006. *Pension Coverage and Retirement Savings of Canadian Families, 1986 to 2003.* Statistics Canada Cat. 11F0019MIE, No. 286.

Morissette, René, Xuelin Zhang, and Marc Frenette. 2007. *Earnings Losses of Displaced Workers: Canadian Evidence from a Large Administrative Database on Firm Closures and Mass Layoffs.* Statistics Canada Analytical Research Paper.

Myles, John. 2000. *The Maturation of Canada's Retirement Income System: Income Levels, Income Inequality, and Low Income among the Elderly.* Ottawa: Statistics Canada.

Organisation for Economic Co-operation and Development (OECD). 2000. *Reforms for an Ageing Society.* Paris: OECD.

———. 2001. *Ageing and Income: Financial Resources and Retirement in 9 OECD Countries.* Paris: OECD.

Policy Research Initiative. 2005. *Encouraging Choice in Work and Retirement Project Report.* Ottawa: Government of Canada.

Pyper, Wendy, and Philip Giles. 2002. "Approaching Retirement." *Perspectives on Labour and Income* (Spring): 5–12.

Robson, William. 1996. *Putting Some Gold in the Golden Years: Fixing the Canada Pension Plan.* Toronto: C.D. Howe Institute.

Rowe, Geoff, and Huan Nugyen. 2003. "Older Workers and the Labour Market." *Perspectives on Labour and Income* 15, no. 1. (Spring): 23–26.

Schellenberg, Grant. 1994. *The Road to Retirement: Demographic and Economic Changes in the '90s.* Ottawa: Canadian Council on Social Development.

Schellenberg, Grant, Martin Turcotte, and Bali Ram. 2005. "Post Retirement Employment." *Perspectives on Labour and Income* (Winter).

Statistics Canada. 2000. *Pension Plans in Canada, 1999.* Ottawa: Statistics Canada.

Tal, Benjamin. 2007. *Retirement: Ready or Not?* CIBC World Markets Special Report. www.cibc.com/research.

Townson, Monica. 2006. *Growing Older, Working Longer: The New Face of Retirement.* Ottawa: Canadian Centre for Policy Alternatives.

Turcotte, Martin, and Grant Schellenberg. 2005. "Job Strain and Retirement," *Perspectives on Labour and Income* (Autumn).

World Bank. 1994. *Averting the Old Age Crisis: Policies to Protect the Old and Promote Growth.* Washington: World Bank.

CHAPTER 8

Troubled Transitions: A Note on Young Workers

Introduction: Work, School, and Economic Independence

Youth—conventionally defined as persons aged 15–24—generally participate in the job market on a part-time and/or part-year basis as they transition from high school to—for most—some form of post-secondary education, to full-time paid work. For teens, an entry-level part-time job is usually all that they want, but the level and stability of earnings become increasingly important to young people as they have to finance full- or part-time post-secondary studies, and are even more important as young adults enter the labour force full-time and seek economic independence from their parents. The fact that many jobs held by young workers are low paid, part-time, and insecure should be of concern, even though most young people do eventually move into full-time, permanent work by their mid to late twenties. The quality of jobs in what can be a decade-long transition from age 15 to age 25, and from high school to a permanent job, is important not just in terms of earnings, but also in terms of gaining useful work experience.

The proportion of youth in Canada's workforce has been falling for much of our recent history for the basic demographic reason that birth rates have been falling. However, the "echo baby boom" generation now moving into the job market is still a large group. In 2007, over four million people aged 15–24 accounted for one in six people in the working-age population. The fact that all net labour force growth is now coming from immigration still means that many younger workers will be replacing the retiring baby boomers. This younger workforce is itself increasingly diverse as it includes many second-generation immigrants and those who came to Canada as young children.

Box 8.1: "A Generation of Failure"
For a while, it looked like young workers had finally caught a break. It didn't last long.
By Jason Kirby

Finally things were looking up. For years Joe Martin had found himself stuck in a series of lousy jobs. As a teenager he served time at McDonald's. In the wake of the 1990s recession he toiled at a golf course for low wages alongside disgruntled university grads. Later, he installed garage doors, working for years to earn meagre raises with zero benefits. Then, three years ago, Martin finally caught a break. He landed a coveted spot on the assembly line at Cami Automotive in Ingersoll, Ont.—and everything began to fall into place. At $33 an hour the pay was good. The full benefits package was even better. He met Kate Fisher, another employee, and with a sense of confidence born of their joint paycheques, they bought a small home together in nearby Dorchester and prepared to have a child. "We were able to actually have a plan that we could move forward on," says Martin, who's now 36. "Things were looking good and the company said if there was ever any trouble, they'd just reduce production and rotate layoffs." After a pause, he adds, "It didn't work out that way."

Last spring the couple both received pink slips, making them front-line victims of the unemployment storm to come. In June, Fisher gave birth to a baby girl. And Martin, already a father of three, now finds himself right back where he started. He's working with garage doors again, earning $11 an hour while his fiancée struggles to raise their young family. "I'm starting all over," he says. "We have no idea what we're going to do to get by. It's the same thing for everyone we know. My generation is in serious trouble."

Canada's economy is built on a simple but deeply entrenched belief: that every new generation will do better than the one before it. But now, as we slide into what is expected to be a long and painful recession, there's a very real feeling the cycle of generational one-upmanship has come to an end. Mounting evidence suggests today's 18- to 40-year-olds are struggling just to keep up with the lifestyle their parents once enjoyed, let alone pull ahead. It's all the more frustrating because before the recession hit, workers such as Martin were just starting to gain some traction—for the first time in their lives, they really felt like they were getting ahead. Then they slammed into the recession. It's left experts asking some uncomfortable questions. Will younger workers ever dig themselves out of the hole they're in? And could this be the first generation in decades to do worse than their parents?

Many Canadians certainly seem to believe younger workers are at risk of being left behind. In an Environics Research Group survey published last year on behalf of the federal government, the majority of people in Canada said they felt they were better off financially than their parents were at the same age. Yet when asked about the prospects of the next generation, only three in 10 thought younger people will pull off the same feat. They have good reason to be pessimistic. When you look at the most crucial yardstick of our financial well-being—our paycheques—you find that young workers are indeed falling behind. In 1976 the median income for families in the 25-to-34 age group was $56,300 (after adjusting for the effects of inflation). Three decades later that figure has actually dropped to $50,100. And with the economy backsliding, economists warn incomes could take an even bigger hit.

There's more to the gloomy outlook facing the under-40 set than just dwindling pay. Students preparing to enter the job market today are already shouldering a huge burden. Many are staying in school much longer to chase higher degrees, in the belief that an alphabet of credentials after their names will guarantee a higher paying job. It was drilled into the head of Kate Fisher, Martin's fiancée, as she was growing up. "Parents push you to go to university so you can do all these great and wonderful things," says Fisher, who graduated from the University of Guelph in 2004 with a degree in geography and minors in biology and environmental studies. "But not everyone is going to get those super-high-paying jobs that we got our degrees for. I'm not a doctor, or a lawyer, or a teacher. I'm just a regular middle-class person trying to make a living."

Even when students do land a position in their field, chances are they'll still lag those who came before them. Extra degrees do boost incomes. But with so many master's and Ph.D.s floating around, that framed piece of paper on the wall now offers less bang for the buck than it used to. Numerous studies have found that to earn what a regular university graduate made 30 years ago, one must now obtain an additional M.A., or even a Ph.D., which entails an extra five to nine years of schooling. Put another way, says Richard Shearmur, a research professor at the University of Quebec, after inflation, a 25-year-old who graduated this decade can expect to earn just 85 to 90 per cent of what the same graduate would have pulled down in 1980.

The lower income is bad enough, but all that extra schooling comes with a hefty price tag too. In 2006, the average graduate left school with about $24,000 in debt, up dramatically from $8,300 in 1990, according to the latest report from the Canada Millennium Scholarship Foundation. (All figures are in 2006 dollars.) What's more, over the same period, the number of university students in hock when they graduated jumped from 45 per cent to nearly 60 per cent. More debt, more degrees and more time spent in school. "It all adds up to most people below the age of 40 having a harder time settling down and acquiring the lifestyle their parents thought was normal when they were under 40," says Shearmur.

Not that older Canadians typically have much sympathy for those toiling away in school. With more thirtysomethings boomeranging back to mom and dad's place, there's a suspicion that young people are choosing university life as a way to avoid the harsh realities of the working world. Yet there's no denying that the world is far more complex and competitive than it used to be. Today, goods flow across borders with ease, as do jobs. Trade has helped lower the price of flat-screen TVs and the grocery bill, but many believe globalization has also put downward pressure on what Western countries can pay for skilled labour, since it can often be done cheaper overseas. "When I was young, Canadians didn't have to compete with people all over the world for jobs, but now to a greater extent they do," says Malcolm Hamilton, of Mercer Human Resource Consulting in Toronto. More and more, it looks like the days of landing a decent-paying job fresh out of high school are over.

But despite all that, after a full quarter-century of spinning their wheels, there were indications earlier this decade that young workers were finally making up for lost ground. It wasn't just Martin who had seen his fortunes improve. After decades of lagging previous generations, younger workers were pulling ahead, at last. Between 1997 and 2007, hourly wages for workers under the age of 35 outpaced those for all other age groups, according to a Statistics Canada report released last year. Suddenly, with unemployment at a 30-year low and companies struggling to find workers, the new generation finally seemed to have the upper hand. "At last those groups that had been left behind were becoming more valuable as a source of labour," says Roger Sauvé, president of People Patterns Consulting. On top of that, the younger generation was told they could expect an employment windfall as Canada's 10 million baby boomers, fully one-third of the population, began to retire.

Then, with almost no warning, young workers ran headfirst into what may be the worst recession in decades. The economic collapse has already claimed 274,000 jobs in Canada over the past four months. Economists believe that figure could easily rise by another 200,000 by year-end, and even that could prove to be optimistic. With each round of layoffs, any hope young workers had of negotiating higher salaries is slipping away. "This generation has been screwed by demography," says Linda Duxbury, a professor at Carleton University's Sprott School of Business. "They've been through a recession, a jobless recovery and stagflation, while the baby boomers got in there and clogged up all the jobs in the hierarchy," she says. "Finally, they thought, this was going to be their time. And now we have another recession."

Duxbury hopes that the situation for young workers will improve somewhat when the economy finally rights itself. "We had a profound labour force crisis before the recession, and when we come out of this recession, we're still going to have a labour force crisis," she says. Because of that, she thinks employers are being incredibly shortsighted by focusing on younger workers when it comes to layoffs. "I'm warning employers, if you treat them badly now, it's going to come back and haunt you." Still, depending on how long and deep this recession goes, it could certainly wipe out the meagre gains of the past few years. And if it does, then today's young workers will have the dubious distinction of going down in history as the first Canadian generation ever to do worse than their parents.

Even if things do improve for young workers down the road, it's cold comfort to couples such as Martin and Fisher. They're still trying to figure out how they'll cope with the mortgage payments and other costs of raising a family over the next few years. After catching a tantalizing glimpse of the lifestyle their parents enjoyed, now it's back to square one. "I can't get out of the bucket," says Martin. "I don't know how I'm supposed to get out when there's no work."

Source: Kirby, Jason. "A Generation of Failure," *Maclean's*, February 12, 2009, 41–44.

The current youth cohort will, on average, take far longer to leave the educational system than did their parents, and will likely face greater difficulties in finding reasonably well-paid and secure jobs. Perhaps the most dramatic change of the past 20 years and more has been the greatly increased rate of young adult participation in full-time education (OECD 2008). Between the mid-1980s and today, the proportion of teens who are full-time students rose from 75% to over 80% as high school dropout rates fell. More dramatically, the proportion of young adults aged 20–24 studying full-time (usually attending college or university) rose from one in five to more than one in three (Gunderson et al. 2000). Increased post-secondary enrolment rates reflect several factors: good jobs not requiring such qualifications have become increasingly difficult to find; and the fact that young women now have career aspirations at least equal to those of men underpins even higher enrolment rates than for young men.

The transition from full-time school to full-time work and economic independence has been pushed back for a significant proportion of youth compared to previous generations (Beaujot and Kerr 2007). About half of all young people now enter some form of post-secondary education more or less immediately after high school, and many do not seek a full-time job until their mid-twenties or even later. Many young people also move back and forth between work and education for an extended period. At the same time, more and more young adults bear a heavy burden of student debt. While increased educational attainment is a good thing and strengthens eventual prospects for stable employment at decent wages—and young Canadians are probably the best educated in the world—the transition to work is taking longer and longer, and has been becoming more difficult for those without good educational qualifications.

Statistics Canada's *Youth in Transition Survey* has followed groups of young people by age. They have found that many youth who drop out of high school in their late teens eventually complete their studies, and that many young adults move back and forth between work and post-secondary studies. A survey of 22-year-olds at the end of 2001 found that just 11% of the group (14% of men and 8% of women) had not completed high school, and about one-third of these dropouts had nonetheless participated in some form of post-secondary education. At age 22, 76% of young people had participated in some kind of post-secondary education at some time, and almost half of the group (40% of men and 48% of women) was still in school. Just 34% of young people were out of school and working full-time (about the same proportion of women and men), and another 7% were not in school and working part-time. Thus, at age 22, about the same proportion of young people are in school as are in work and not studying. About one in seven 22-year-olds (14% of women and 15% of men) were not working and not studying (Statistics Canada. *The Daily*, June 16, 2004).

A slightly later snapshot of 22- to 24-year-olds in 2003 found that just under one-half had completed some form of post-secondary education, of which more than one in three were "gappers" who had taken a break at some time between school and work, most commonly after finishing high school (OECD 2008, 56), and 15% of the group had dropped out of post-secondary education. By their mid-twenties, the majority of young adults have completed some form of post-secondary education (including apprenticeships), very few have still not completed high school, and many of the remainder have participated in, but not yet completed, post-secondary education. An Alberta study of persons aged 25 in 2003 found similar patterns, with 60% of the group having a post-secondary qualification, and a very high proportion of 88% having been in post-secondary education at some point, including some who were still studying. This group of 25-year-olds had held an average of 5.6 jobs since age 18 (cited OECD 2008, 61).

The increasingly common pattern of combining paid work and participation in post-secondary education over extended periods, rather than moving quickly from school to a permanent job, is likely explained by a wide range of factors, including the continued difficulty of finding steady, well-paid work; the cost of maintaining steady enrolment in full-time studies; and experimentation with different educational and work options. The good news is that a high proportion of Canadian young adults do eventually acquire qualifications and make a transition to steady employment, and that relatively few end up with no qualifications and/or experience unemployment for very extended periods. Canada has one of the lowest rates of long-term young adult unemployment among industrial countries, and relatively few young people are neither studying nor working (OECD 2008).

Increasingly, young people are also delaying marriage and cohabitation, opting to live with their parents through much of their twenties. Census figures for 2005 show that 44% of young people aged 20–29 were still living at home, including 60% of those aged 20–24, and one-quarter of those aged 25–29. Young men are even more likely than young women to stay at home. Following in lockstep, young people are also delaying having children and choosing to have fewer children when they do start families. Delayed economic independence likely results from high levels of student debt for many; high housing costs, especially in large urban centres; and difficulties finding the stable, well-paid employment needed to establish independence. Parents may also be quite willing to share households for longer periods of time than was the case a generation ago (Beaujot and Kerr 2007).

Most students seek paid work of some kind. Many full-time students want part-time work during the school year, and most want full-time summer jobs to finance their studies, maintain some economic independence, and gain relevant work experience. At the same time, post-secondary education has become more and more important as a means to access reasonably well-paid and secure jobs that provide ladders to better opportunities. Young workers who are high school dropouts or who have only a high school education are at increasing risk of being able to find only insecure, low-paid, no future jobs. Data from the 2006 Census show that male university graduates aged 25–34 earned an average of $46,373 compared to $34,460 for male non-graduates, and women graduates earned an average of $35,970 compared to $23,617 for women non-graduates. (See Chapter 5 for an exploration of these earnings differences between men and women.)

There is a very significant wage premium for a university education, and a more modest premium for college graduates and those who complete trade apprenticeships. Unemployment is also lower for those with higher educational credentials.

The Declining Fortunes of Young Workers

Research by economists has documented a major decline in the fortunes of young workers as compared to other workers (often their parents) who were of the same age in the mid to late 1970s (Beaudry, Lemieux, and Parent 2000; Gunderson, Sharpe, and Wald 2000; Picot, Heisz, and Nakamura 2001). Much of that decline was concentrated in the period of recession and slow recovery from 1989 through the 1990s. In slack labour markets, much of the burden of unemployment falls on new entrants to the job market, who lack experience, even though they may have good credentials. Also, there was very little new hiring into larger workplaces offering better jobs over this period, which left younger workers chasing lower paid and often temporary and insecure positions. As noted below, somewhat surprisingly, the major gap that opened up between the earnings of younger and other workers has failed to close significantly in recent years even as the youth unemployment rate has fallen, as the educational credentials of young adults have continued to rise, and as the size of the youth cohort has fallen.

Figure 8.1: Employment Rates for Young Adults Age 20–24 (1989–2007)

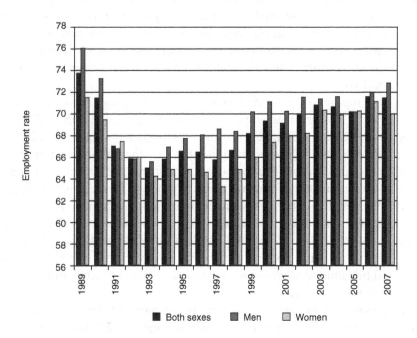

Source: Statistics Canada. Cat. 71F0004XCB Labour Force Historical Review 2007. Table cd1t01

Figure 8.2: Unemployment Rates for Young Adults Age 20–24 (1989–2007)

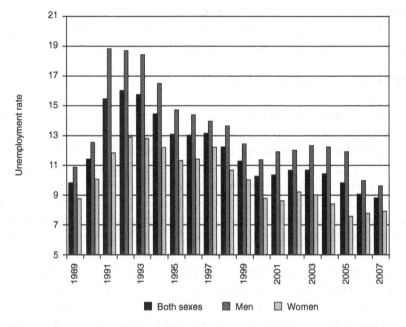

Source: Statistics Canada. Cat. 71F0004XCB Labour Force Historical Review 2007. Table cd1t01

The proportion of all young workers with jobs fell sharply, from 63.4% in 1989, to a low of 51.5% in 1997, before recovering to 59.5% in 2007. As shown in Figure 8.1, the employment rate for those aged 20–24 fell sharply from 1989 (the peak before the recession) to the mid-1990s, but has since almost recovered. Employment rates for this age group are a bit higher for young men than for young women, likely because women are spending more time on average in post-secondary education, and some are having children.

The youth unemployment rate has been persistently very high since the mid-1970s, never falling below 10%, and reaching a recent high of 17.2% in 1992. In 2007, the youth unemployment rate was still 11.2%, but was much higher among teens (14.8%) than those aged 20–24 (8.7%). As shown in Figure 8.2, the unemployment rate for those aged 20–24 fell sharply from 1992 to the late 1990s, and has recently dipped even lower. The unemployment rate for men in this age group has been significantly greater than that for women, likely because women are more likely to have post-secondary qualifications. Students today continue to experience quite high unemployment rates. During the school months of 2007, student unemployment (usually meaning they were seeking but could not find a part-time job) averaged over 11%, increasing to over 13% in July among students who planned to return to work in the fall (Data from the *Labour Force Survey*).

Unemployment may be lower among young women, but they continue to earn significantly less than young men. In 2007, women aged 15–24 earned an average of $11.14 per hour and an average of $306.68 per week compared to $12.46 per hour and

$412.44 per week for men in the same age group (Statistics Canada Cat. 71F0004XCB, *Labour Force Historical Review,* CD3, Table 01). The 2006 Census showed that women aged 15–24 earned an average of $9,899 in 2005 compared to $12,892 for young men. These large wage gaps persist despite the rising relative educational attainment of young women compared to men, for reasons explored in Chapter 5.

Table 8.1: Average Hourly Earnings (in 2007 dollars)

	1997	2007
Age 15–24	11.07	11.81
Age 25–54	20.98	22.28
Relative youth wage (%)	52.80	53.00
Men:		
Age 15–24	11.56	12.46
Age 25–54	23.05	24.21
Relative youth wage (%)	50.20	51.50
Women:		
Age 15–24	10.54	11.14
Age 25–54	18.73	20.33
Relative youth wage (%)	56.30	54.80

Source: Calculated from Statistics Canada, *Labour Force Historical Review.* 2007. Cat. 71F0004XCB, Table CD 3T03.

On top of continuing significant gaps between unemployment rates for younger and older workers, there are large differences in wages between age groups. The other major dimension of the declining fortunes of young workers compared to earlier gen-erations has been in terms of real wages. Today, young men aged 15–24 earn only about 75% as much as did the young men in the same age group in the mid-1970s in terms of "real" or inflation-adjusted hourly earnings (Picot, Heisz, and Nakamura 2001). Young women have done slightly better, but they still earn only about 80% as much as did the young women of the mid-1970s. The pay gap between young women and young men has narrowed slightly, but the gap between youth and adults has greatly increased. By some measures, Canada now has the most highly educated generation of young workers in the world, but young adults have not regained the ground that was lost in the 1990s.

As shown in Table 8.1, in 2007, young workers aged 15–24 earned an average of $11.81 per hour compared to $22.28 per hour for core-age workers aged 25–54, or 53% as much. This proportion has been essentially unchanged since 1997, showing that the somewhat improved employment situation for young people has had no impact on their relative hourly earnings. The average hourly earnings of young women compared to women core-aged workers has actually fallen slightly since 1997—from 56% to 55%. Young men earn relatively less than core-age men—51.5% as much in 2007, but the gap has narrowed slightly from just 50% in 1997 (Statistics Canada Cat. 71F0004XCB, *Labour Force Historical Review*, CD3 Table 01). Data from the 2006 Census similarly show that the pay gap between younger and older workers has not been narrowing, and indeed has grown somewhat. In 2005, young workers aged 15–24 earned just 25% as much as workers aged 45–54 ($11,427 compared to $48,582 in inflation-adjusted dollars), which represented a small increase from the 24.5% gap in 2000 ($11,358 compared to $46,273). Annual earnings gaps are far larger than hourly earnings gaps since so many young workers are employed only part-time or part-year. It is notable that the annual earnings of young workers were essentially unchanged between the two censuses, while they increased for older workers.

As detailed elsewhere in this book, one of the dark sides of the post-industrial economy has been the expansion of low-wage, low-skill jobs in private services. These jobs typically provide "ports of entry" to the labour market for young adults, but rather than moving quickly to the bottom rungs of what turn out to be "career jobs," many youth, including well-educated youth, spend several years in a series of low-wage, low-skill jobs in sectors like fast food and retail. Most young people are working in parts of the job market that typically provide low wages, limited, if any, pension or health benefits, and part-time or unstable hours. The majority of young women aged 15–24 work in the two lowest paid, broad industrial sectors—retail trade, and accommodation and food services (i.e., in stores, restaurants, and hotels)—as do four in 10 young men. One in four young men work in construction or manufacturing jobs—which are more likely than private services to provide full-time hours at decent wages—while one in 10 young women work in health and social services.

In looking at falling unemployment rates for youth, it has to be borne in mind that to be unemployed means that a person has been unable to find any kind of job, even a low-paid, temporary or part-time job. Most teens and young adults who are studying full-time want only a part-time job, at least during the school year, but the fact that one-third of young adults aged 20–24 are working part-time is of concern. It is often assumed that such jobs provide a "flexible" way to balance work and school, but part-time jobs often involve highly variable and unpredictable schedules.

One big change in the job market in recent decades has been the rise of temporary or contract jobs, that is, jobs with a defined end date. As employers have restructured work to make jobs more precarious and contingent, and less secure, they have often done so by making changes that principally affect new hires. In other words, much of the impact falls on young workers entering the job market. More than one in five (21%) of youth new hires have recently been in temporary jobs, double the proportion of 1989 (Morissette and Picot 2005). In 2007, almost one in three (29%) of young workers were in temporary jobs with a fixed end date. It remains to be seen if the young workers who replace retiring baby boomers will enjoy the same terms and conditions of employ-ment—including an expectation of ongoing employment—or if more contract and temporary jobs have become a permanent feature of the economic landscape.

The fact that young workers are likely to be in part-time and temporary jobs means that they are much less likely than adults to qualify for Employment Insurance benefits when they do become unemployed, even though they pay premiums for every hour worked. To qualify for benefits, new entrants to the workforce must meet an initial threshold of working more than 910 hours in a year (or about six months in a steady, full-time job), and even after that, it is hard for part-time and seasonal workers to qualify. As noted above, one in three unemployed workers are young workers, but young people under age 25 make up only about 10% of new claims for regular EI benefits.

A very high proportion of young workers who are mainly working full-time and are not students are earning low wages. In a Statistics Canada study, a low-wage worker can be defined as someone earning less than $375 per week, or less than $10 per hour for a 37.5-hour week (in inflation-adjusted dollars for the year 2000). This is approximately the low income threshold or poverty line for a single person living in a larger city. In 2000, almost half or 45% of all young workers aged 15–24 working mainly full-time and who were not students were low paid (39.9% of men and 52.4% of women), up from 40.7% in 1990, and up from less than one-third or 31.2% of young workers in 1980 (Morissette and Picot 2005). While most are protected by family incomes, one in four young low-wage workers lived in households falling below the poverty line. As of 2007, about one-half of all young workers were still earning less than $10 per hour (in 2007 dollars, not adjusted for inflation). Low youth wages translate into a very high risk of poverty for young workers who form their own households and live away from home, particularly young families with children.

Some full-time, young, low-wage workers are in entry-level jobs that eventually lead to ladders to better jobs, but many others—especially those who do not complete post-secondary education—face a high risk of being trapped in low-pay jobs for life. Too many of today's young workers—mainly those who fail to gain post-secondary qualifications—will become tomorrow's working-poor adults. Research shows that the probability of young women workers moving up the wage ladder over time is relatively low compared to men, and that the chances of young male workers moving up the job ladder have been falling compared to previous generations (Beach and Finnie 2004). The ongoing polarization of the job market between reasonably secure and well-paid jobs and insecure, poorly paid jobs puts more and more entry-age workers at risk, facing much more unequal futures than did their parents. Post-secondary qualifications do offer a cushion, but many employed graduates find that they are overqualified for the jobs that they manage to find (OECD 2008).

Conclusion

Despite falling unemployment rates, young workers continue to face major problems in the job market, including insecure work and low wages. Governments and policy-makers tend to assume that most young workers are students in transition to better jobs. Some will certainly make this transition, and this may be made easier by the job vacancies opened up as baby boomers retire. However, the trend is now for older workers to remain in the workforce longer, and young adult workers lacking qualifications in demand and desired job experience will face a high risk of insecure and low-paid employment. There are a number of policies that could improve the situation of youth in the job market. Given very low unionization rates among youth (13% in 2007), governments could help even the playing field between employers and young workers by increasing the minimum wage and improving basic employment standards.

Recommended Reading

- Beaujot, Roderic, and Don Kerr. 2007a. *The Changing Face of Canada: Essential Readings in Population.* Toronto: Canadian Scholars' Press. A reader edited by two Canadian demographers. Organized into five sections: fertility; mortality; international migration, domestic migration, and population distribution; population aging; and population composition. Vital issues covered include the role of immigration in Canada's future; the deteriorating economic welfare of immigrants; globalization, undocumented migration, and unwanted refugees; Aboriginal population change; implications of unprecedented low fertility; and the astonishing demographic transformation of Canadian cities.
- Beaujot, Roderic, and Don Kerr. 2007b. *Emerging Youth Transition Patterns in Canada: Opportunities and Risks.* Ottawa: Government of Canada Policy Research Initiative. An interesting look at how the life-course and patterns of transition to paid work vary between generations.
- Organisation for Economic Co-operation and Development (OECD). 2008. *Jobs for Youth: Canada.* Paris: OECD. A very detailed and comprehensive, but not very critical, look at youth employment and transitions from school to work in Canada, highlighting differences among OECD countries.

References

Beach, Charles, and Ross Finnie. 2004. *A Longitudinal Analysis of Earnings Change in Canada.* Statistics Canada Cat. 11F0019MIE, No. 127.

Beaudry, Paul, Thomas Lemieux, and Daniel Parent. 2000. "What Is Happening to the Youth Labour Market in Canada?" *Canadian Public Policy* XXVI, Supplement.

Beaujot, Roderic, and Don Kerr. 2007. *Emerging Youth Transition Patterns in Canada: Opportunities and Risks.* Ottawa: Government of Canada Policy Research Initiative.

Boudarbat, Brahim, Thomas Lemieux, and W. Craig Riddell. 2003. *Recent Trends in Wage Inequality and the Wage Structure in Canada.* Mimeo.

Gunderson, Morley, Andrew Sharpe, and Steven Wald. 2000. "Youth Unemployment in Canada, 1976–1998." *Canadian Public Policy* XXVI Supplement.

Morissette, René, and Garnett Picot. 2005. *Low Paid Work and Economically Vulnerable Families over the Last Two Decades.* Statistics Canada Cat. 11F0019MIE, No. 248.

Organisation for Economic Co-operation and Development. 2008. *Jobs for Youth: Canada.* Paris: OECD.

Picot, G., A. Heisz, and A. Nakamura. 2001. *Job Tenure, Worker Mobility and the Youth Labour Market during the 1990s.* Statistics Canada Cat. 11F0019MPE, No. 155 (March).

PART III

Contemporary Canadian Unions

This part of the book looks at the role of unions in Canada and in other advanced industrial countries, and at the potential future of unions as a force in the modern Canadian workplace. In looking at the role of unions, this part of the book takes up some of the key issues developed in parts I and II, such as precarious work, growing inequality, and barriers to inclusion.

Unions have historically been a major force for improving the quality of jobs, countering low pay, and promoting greater equality in the job market between women and men, between younger and older workers, and between minorities. However, this role is being undercut by declining union strength, particularly among blue-collar male workers. In Canada, union coverage is stable, but very low among private service workers, particularly lower paid women and minority workers who would gain the most from union representation. Unions can be and are a positive force for better jobs, but a key challenge for unions today is to win support among, and to make gains for, unorganized precarious workers.

Chapter 9, "The Impact of Unions," discusses the role and importance of collective bargaining, describes what kinds of workers belong to unions, and closely examines union impacts on wages, low-wage jobs, benefits, access to training, and other dimensions of job quality. It also discusses how unions affect the way in which the economy and the labour market operate, dealing with the often-heard argument that strong unions may be good for their members, but are a negative for economic performance.

Chapter 10, "Is There a Future for Canadian Unions?," provides a detailed look at the changes in union membership, and some challenges facing unions in attempting to organize and represent workers in today's job market. There is a major ongoing process of union renewal, but whether it will be enough to ensure a continuing major role for unions in the workplaces of the future is an issue that remains to be determined.

Related Websites

- Canadian Labour Congress (www.canadianlabour.ca). The CLC is the largest union federation in Canada, representing some three million workers in its affiliated unions, which include all of the largest private- and public-sector unions. The CLC website provides access to a wide range of information on unions and union campaigns, and comprehensive links to the websites of Canadian and international unions. The largest Canadian unions all maintain websites that detail their activities and positions.

- Centre for Research on Work and Society at York University (www.yorku.ca/crws/) publishes research papers and an electronic journal, *Just Labour*, which carries many articles on the theme of union change and renewal, with a major focus on Canada.
- Global Union Research Network (GURN) (www.gurn.info/). GURN was established in January 2004 as a follow-up to the millennium debate of the Global Unions Group, the major international organizations bringing together trade unions around the world. After a request from the international labour movement, the initiative to establish the network was taken by the ILO's Bureau for Workers' Activities (ACTRAV) in co-operation with the International Trade Union Confederation (ITUC), the Trade Union Advisory Committee to the OECD (TUAC), the Global Union Federations (GUF), and the ILO's International Institute for Labour Studies (IILS). The aim of the research network is to give union organizations better access to research carried out within trade unions and allied institutions while enabling them to exchange information on matters of joint concern and to develop the capacity to make analyses and take part in debates and policy formulation.
- Inter-University Research Centre on Globalization and Work (CRIMT or Centre de Recherche Interuniversitaire sur la Mondialisation et le Travail) is a Canadian-based inter-university research centre on the theoretical and practical challenges of institutional renewal for work and employment in a global era (www.crimt.org). The website seeks to stimulate debate and research exchange between researchers working on the project as well as with a broader community of researchers and practitioners interested in the challenge of understanding and developing institutions that promote both equity and efficiency outcomes in the world of work.
- The Labour Program of Human Resources and Skills Development Canada (www.hrsdc.gc.ca/eng/labour/index.shtml). This branch of the federal government publishes a wide range of information and studies on unionized workplaces and collective bargaining issues.

CHAPTER 9

The Impact of Unions

Introduction

This chapter discusses the role of unions in Canada and in other advanced industrial countries. It discusses the role and importance of collective bargaining; briefly summarizes what kinds of workers belong to unions; and examines union impacts on wages, wage differences, benefits, and other dimensions of job quality. Generally speaking, unions are a force for better jobs and greater equality in the job market, and this is shown not to come at the price of economic growth and job creation. However, unions can be a strong force for better jobs only if a high proportion of workers at risk of being in low pay and precarious jobs are unionized. This is not the case in much of the private services sector in Canada, where most low-wage and precarious jobs are to be found.

What Are Unions and What Do They Do?

"Unions reduce wage inequality, increase industrial democracy and often raise productivity.... [I]n the political sphere, unions are an important voice for some of society's
weakest and most vulnerable groups, as well as for their own members" (Freeman
and Medoff 1984, 5).

Unions are organizations that define, promote, and fight for the collective interests
and rights of workers or a group of workers, especially in relation to employers, but
also in relation to governments, the media, and other social groups. Unions emerge
from and are a product of the fundamental difference of interests between workers
and employers.

The key defining feature of all capitalist societies—including today's post-
industrial societies—is that the great majority of working people gain their livelihood
through paid work—that is, by selling their labour to employers. The basic terms of
any employment relationship are that workers agree to work under the direction of
an employer (with respect to place of work, hours of work, methods of work, etc.)
in return for a wage. If it were not for unions, workers would have to negotiate the
terms and conditions of their employment (wages, benefits, hours of work, work
schedules, conditions of work, etc.) as individuals, protected only by minimum legal
standards. And, if it were not for unions, individual workers would be on their own
when it came to dealing with arbitrary and unfair treatment by employers, such as
dismissal without just cause, harassment, discrimination in hiring, promotion and
layoffs, favouritism by employers and managers in setting pay and assigning jobs,
and so on. Of course, there are many decent non-union employers, but it is usually
only in unionized workplaces that there are formal rules governing what an employee
must do and workplace procedures, and a formal process for filing and investigating
complaints if the rules are broken.

Unions have been formed out of the fundamental recognition that there is strength
in numbers, and that workers are stronger when they unite and bargain together
with employers and have a common voice to represent their interests. Individual
workers have less power in determining the content of the employment relationship
than employers because many workers are capable of doing a given job and can be
hired to do so. The bargaining power of individual workers is particularly weak in
times when unemployment is high and many workers are seeking any available job.
Unfortunately, the norm is for the demand of workers for jobs to exceed the number
of jobs that are available at any given time in any particular place. This is particularly
true for good jobs with decent wages and working conditions. Relatively unskilled
workers benefit most from unionization, since they have little bargaining power as
individuals.

Historically, unions have been a major force for humanizing and democratizing
capitalist societies by balancing the power of employers, which results from their
control over production. Unions are an important source of human dignity in the
workplace and a wider force for social justice. Unions promote higher levels of economic equality and, in some ways, also make labour markets work better from the
point of economic growth and efficiency.

Box 9.1: Labour Rights Are Human Rights

Freedom of association and the right to free collective bargaining are well-established as fundamental human rights, and have been enshrined in numerous important international human rights declarations, most notably the United Nations' *Universal Declaration of Human Rights* of 1948. Canada has, unfortunately, formally ratified only five of the eight so-called core conventions of the International Labour Organization (ILO), but these include Convention No. 87 on "Freedom of Association and Protection of the Right to Organize," which establishes the right of all workers to form and join unions of their own choosing without prior authorization, and guarantees the free functioning of labour organizations without interference by governments, including the right to engage in free collective bargaining.

Canada has, unfortunately, been found by the ILO to have frequently violated the core labour conventions we have ratified. In fact, according to www.labourrights.ca, "in the past 25 years Canadians have endured a serious erosion of a fundamental and universal human right: our right to free collective bargaining and the right to strike. Our governments—federal and provincial—are to blame. Rather than protect our labour rights, they are more and more likely to provide the legal means to abuse or ignore them."

Since 1982, Canadian governments have passed 175 pieces of legislation that have restricted, suspended, or denied collective bargaining rights for Canadian workers by denying workers the fundamental right to join a union, outlawing the right to strike, imposing collective agreements on workers that represent the employer's last offer, and allowing employers to engage in union-busting activities. Over 70 complaints have been filed with the ILO, which has determined in over 90% of these cases that Canadian governments had violated basic labour rights. (See *Collective Bargaining in Canada: Human Right or Canadian Illusion* at www.labourrights.ca.)

On June 8, 2007, in a landmark decision, the Supreme Court of Canada ruled for the first time that Canadian workers' rights to free collective bargaining are constitutionally protected by the freedom of association provisions of the *Canadian Charter of Rights and Freedoms*. In striking down British Columbia legislation, which essentially ignored the provisions of collective agreements then in force, the Court ruled that the right to free collective bargaining predates labour relations legislation, and that the Charter should protect human rights at least as much as the international legal conventions that Canada has ratified. The Court concluded that free collective bargaining enhances the human dignity, liberty, and autonomy of workers by giving them the opportunity to influence the establishment of workplace rules and thereby gain some control over a major aspect of their lives, and also ensures the rule of law in the workplace.

At a minimum, the Supreme Court ruling will make it far more difficult for governments to interfere in free collective bargaining. At a maximum, it may support the argument of some human rights experts that Canadian employers are legally obliged under international human rights law to recognize and bargain with unions, and cannot avoid that obligation through restrictive labour laws.

Canadian unions form a democratic labour movement fighting for better wages and better working conditions, as well as for democratic and human rights and better social programs for all workers. The labour movement has been a central part of the wider social-democratic movement to make Canadian society more democratic, both inside and outside the workplace, more secure from the perspective of working people who are vulnerable to unemployment and low income, and more equal in terms of the distribution of income and economic resources between social classes. More recently, unions have joined the fight for women's rights and the fight against racial discrimination. Most big historical breakthroughs in union recognition and in collective bargaining—such as the eight-hour day and the five-day workweek—have come when many groups of workers were pursuing the same goals at the same time. Of course, unions vary a great deal in terms of how internally democratic they are, and to what extent they are committed to wider social goals and not just the narrow interests of their current members. Commonly, a distinction is made between business unions—which focus on the interests of their own members in the workplace—and social unions—which seek to broaden the labour movement, to find and build common cause among a broad range of workers in the job market, and engage in collective political action. Some speak of a difference between social unionism—the tradition of many large industrial and public-sector Canadian unions in the post-World War II era—and social movement unionism, characterized by a commitment to radical social and economic change through mass mobilization and political action above and beyond electoral politics.

Union strength varies a great deal between countries, including the advanced industrial countries, ranging from collective bargaining coverage of 80% or more of workers in many continental European countries to less than 15% in the U.S., and to even lower levels in the formal labour markets of most developing countries. Outside of public and social services, where union coverage is typically high, the key bastions of union strength are typically among mainly blue-collar workers in larger companies in primary industries, manufacturing, utilities, communications, transportation, and construction. Union coverage usually extends to only a minority of workers in most private service sector industries, such as finance, retail trade, accommodation and food, and personal services. The main exception is in some European countries where unions and employers sign broader based agreements covering workers in many smaller workplaces. (Very high union coverage in some European countries also flows from the fact that unions are a key point of access to government programs, notably Unemployment Insurance, as is the case in Denmark and Belgium.) Unions will clearly be a greater force for equality and social justice only if union coverage is extended to the many low-paid and precarious workers, many of them women and workers of colour, who are currently excluded from the benefits of union representation. The existence of a large, informal sector in developing countries and of a precarious, secondary labour market in most developed countries poses major challenges for union organization and representation.

As documented in the next chapter, union coverage now extends to just one in three Canadian workers. There is a big difference between very high union coverage in the public sector (almost 80%) and low coverage in the private sector (now just below 20%). Union representation for men and women is now about equal, but the great majority of union women work in public and social services, while the majority of unionized men work in the private sector.

Collective Bargaining

In Canada today, unions are almost always organized on the basis of a certification by a provincial labour board, which allows a union or bargaining agent to represent a specific group of workers in a specific workplace. (About one in 10 workers are covered by federal labour legislation.) Bargaining units are usually quite narrowly defined, so different groups of workers working for the same employer often belong to different unions and/or bargaining units. For example, at Air Canada, different unions represent and bargain separately for the pilots, customer service agents, baggage handlers, flight attendants, mechanics, and so on. Managers and even lower level supervisors are typically excluded from these bargaining units, which are meant to represent communities of interest. The norm is for union locals to belong to one of a few major national or international unions, which, in turn, primarily represent either private- or public-sector workers, but are now usually spread across different industrial sectors. These national unions may or may not coordinate bargaining among the locals they represent, and may or may not co-operate with other unions in bargaining.

It used to be the case, from the 1940s through to the 1970s, that similar kinds of workers in the same industry were represented by the same union. For example, the United Steelworkers (USW) represented workers in the steel industry. Today, most large industrial unions, such as the USW, the National Automobile, Aerospace, Transportation and General Workers Union of Canada (CAW-Canada), and the United Food and Commercial Workers (UFCW) are the product of mergers between what used to be separate industrial unions, and represent workers across different sectors of the economy. There are often several unions representing similar kinds of workers in the same industry. For example, there are at least two major unions in the mining sector, and employees in long-term care homes belong to different unions in different provinces, and often to different unions in the same province and even municipality. Unions that used to represent mainly blue-collar men in manufacturing have now branched out into different parts of the private sector and even the public sector. For example, the auto workers (CAW) and the steelworkers (USW) are now general unions. The USW, for example, represents not only miners and steelworkers, as in the past, but also security guards, clerical and support workers at universities, and retail workers. The CAW represents not only auto workers, but also hotel workers, airline customer-service agents, fish plant and railway workers, among others.

Almost all major unions in Canada belong to the Canadian Labour Congress (CLC). (The main exceptions are two labour centrals in Quebec, but not the FTQ, which is the largest Quebec central labour body, and some smaller professional unions.) The CLC tries to make sure that its member unions do not fight each other for members, a practice known as raiding. It is quite rare, but not unknown, for unions to get into fights with each other for the right to represent already unionized workers, and there is certainly a fair bit of rivalry in trying to organize non-union workers. Unlike central labour bodies in many other countries, the CLC generally leaves collective bargaining and union organizing activities to its affiliated unions. The primary role of the CLC and its affiliated provincial federations of labour and local labour councils is to advance the interests of its members and all workers at the political level; to wage broad-based labour movement campaigns—often involving community partners; to provide services such as research and education to affiliated unions; and to represent Canadian workers internationally through the International Trade Union Confederation (ITUC).

Box 9.2: Labour and Political Action

This chapter concentrates on the role of unions in the workplace. However, the CLC and its member unions, as well as other unions, play a major role outside of the workplace in terms of social advocacy and political action on behalf of all workers. To take one example, in recent years, unions have joined forces with anti-poverty groups and community organizations to fight for higher minimum wages and better employment standards, as well as improvements to Employment Insurance and other income security programs. Unions have lent organizational and financial support to organizations fighting for public health care, and the causes of international development and peace.

Labour political action is often associated with electoral support for the New Democratic Party, and many unions do continue to actively endorse and support the NDP, which is the most labour-friendly party, and was co-founded in 1961 by its predecessor party, the Co-operative Commonwealth Federation (CCF), and the CLC. However, many unions support other parties (notably the Liberals or the Bloc Québécois), or are formally neutral. The CLC, while still endorsing the NDP, supported new political party financing legislation, which has eliminated direct labour financing of political parties and has recently focused its political action efforts on issue-based campaigns in advance of federal elections, seeking to push all parties to support labour's political priorities. The following is taken from the Political Action section of the CLC website:

Politics is about choices. Political Action is about organizing working people and giving them the tools they need so when they vote, they elect politicians and parties who are truly on their side. It's also about giving workers the tools they need to make sure the people who get elected continue to make better choices for working people, our families, and our communities every day.

At the Canadian Labour Congress, we are focused on building the capacity for positive political change nationally and locally through worker education, community campaigns, and direct advocacy with elected officials. Our plan for doing this is outlined in the document *Building Capacity for Change*. Here are a few examples of what we do:

- We help voters sort through the issues and the candidates at election time, so they can make better choices when they vote and elect people who will support the priorities of working people. We did this during the last federal election through our Better Choice campaign. We'll do it again this autumn in Saskatchewan, Manitoba, Ontario, PEI, and the Territories with our municipal campaign.

- We coordinate ongoing meetings between workers and their local Members of Parliament through local labour councils to discuss issues of national priority to working people like child care, health care, and passing anti-scab legislation.
- In 2005, we organized a national weekend of action against Wal-Mart Canada to draw consumer attention to its anti-worker business practices. Thousands of flyers were handed out over a single weekend by hundreds of workers in front of stores across the country.
- Our anti-sweatshop campaigns help workers convince municipalities, school boards and universities to change the way they purchase products, like clothing and uniforms, to guarantee they are not made by companies that violate worker rights and human rights.

It's a different way of doing politics from the past and a different way for unions and labour councils to get the results working people need. What matters is that it works!

Source: canadianlabour.ca/index.php/political_action.

After a union is certified to represent a group of workers, its central activity is to bargain and enforce a collective agreement covering such issues as wages, benefits, hours of work, and working conditions with the employer. Literally thousands of such agreements are in force, with most being re-negotiated every two or three years. The members of a union local must elect an executive and bargaining committee to take responsibility for bargaining and union affairs, and usually union members also elect stewards to represent members to managers and employers on a day-to-day basis when conflicts arise. Local union officers are typically assisted by full-time, paid union staff, particularly in collective bargaining, and help resolve complaints or grievances arising over the term of an agreement that cannot be resolved at an early, relatively informal stage of discussions. Naturally, the quality of service to members can and does differ between unions, but all have a legal responsibility to bring forward reasonable member grievances against an employer. Unions can and do also differ a great deal in terms of internal democracy and the extent of member involvement, but collective agreements are almost invariably ratified by a vote of members, and a vote will be held before a strike is conducted. Usually members are closely consulted before bargaining begins so as to identify key issues, and most union locals have regular membership meetings to discuss issues that arise during the course of a collective agreement.

A great deal of media coverage of union issues focuses on work stoppages or strikes, but these are actually very rare events. In recent years, in all of Canada, there have only been 300 to 400 stoppages per year, involving 100,000 to 400,000 workers. One-third of all employees are union members but, in a typical year, time lost due to strikes has been well under one-tenth of 1% of total working time. That said, the right to strike is a key ingredient in Canada's system of free collective bargaining and it is often the threat of a strike—and the prospect of lost pay for the workers involved—that leads to a negotiated settlement. In Canada, unlike the U.S., employers cannot permanently replace striking workers, and in Quebec and British Columbia, employers cannot replace striking workers during the course of a legal strike.

Most bargaining with employers takes place at the local union level, and some employers bargain with several unions. Industry-wide bargaining was always quite weakly developed in Canada, and has eroded in recent years. It remains important in the auto and pulp and paper sectors, and construction agreements are also often negotiated centrally. This very decentralized bargaining system tends to weaken the bargaining power of Canadian unions compared to unions in countries such as Germany and the Scandinavian countries where bargaining across whole industries is still common, and where there is some coordination of bargaining aims between different unions at the national level. Fragmented bargaining also reflects the reality of very different issues and economic circumstances in different workplaces and sectors of the economy, as well as Canada's diverse regional economies.

Collective agreements are formal and legally binding documents that can run to many pages. The fact that unionized workers are covered by the terms of a collective agreement means that they have rights. Unions are legally obliged to take up (through a grievance) reasonable complaints by members that the terms of an agreement have been violated, and employers are legally obliged to change their practices if they are found to violate the terms of an agreement. Workers join unions at least as much to ensure this due process at the workplace as for the economic objective of higher wages. Indeed, the ongoing role of unions in workplace governance makes them a crucially important democratic institution.

Probably the most important aspect of unionization for individual workers is that they have a formal contract of employment that can be readily enforced through the grievance and arbitration process. Members can readily grieve dismissal, disciplinary actions and harassment by supervisors, and can often grieve being passed over for promotion, favouritism by managers and supervisors, unwelcome changes in work assignments, hours of work, work schedules, and so on, depending upon the wording of the agreement. By contrast, non-union workplaces are usually more informal, which can mean arbitrary and capricious exercise of managerial authority. Some large non-union employers do adopt formal, written workplace rules and formal complaint processes and procedures, in effect mimicking union workplace rules. These can be effective, but it is also the case that they do not have the binding legal force of a collective agreement. Of course, minimum employment standards laws do provide for minimum wages, maximum hours of work, and safe working conditions in all workplaces (with some important exceptions). However, it is striking that very few complaints about wages or working conditions are filed with government labour standards officials while an employment relationship still exists. The vast majority of individual complaints under employment standards laws, usually well over 90%, are lodged only after a worker has been dismissed, usually for non-payment of wages. Very few complaints are filed against a current employer, most likely because of fear of reprisals, since the evidence shows that many employers do not comply with basic legal standards. (The best recent study is the Report of the Federal Labour Standards Review, *Fairness at Work*, Human Resources and Skills Development Canada, 2006.) It is union members who generally benefit most from legal protections, since unions have the resources to effectively bring forward and prosecute complaints on behalf of members. For example, pay equity legislation formally applies to all workers, but large settlements such as those covering federal public-sector workers and Bell Canada workers were the result of literally years of expensive legal action paid for by unions.

Table 9.1 provides information on the proportion of unionized employees covered by selected provisions in collective agreements.

Typically, collective agreements define the following.

Wages

Wages are usually set by the hour, week, or pay period. Sometimes there is an element of performance pay, but this is much less common than in non-union workplaces where piecework, commissions, and bonuses based on individual or group performance are more common. Wages are usually set for defined jobs and job classifications, so there is a formal system of pay by position. The union wage advantage is detailed below.

Non-Wage Benefits

Collective agreements commonly specify benefits, such as employer pension plan coverage, health care, and paid or unpaid time off for family and personal reasons. As detailed below, such benefits are quite expensive and make up a major part of the union advantage in economic terms.

Job Security and Protection

Collective agreements formalize the norm that individual dismissal shall only be for just cause, so individual discipline and dismissal can be appealed through the grievance and arbitration process.

There are usually provisions for layoff for economic reasons to be based upon seniority by date of hiring, so long-tenure unionized workers effectively have a high degree of job security. As shown in Table 9.1, 68% of union members are protected from layoff by seniority. Sometimes seniority provisions are opposed by younger workers. Seniority is usually justified by reference to the fact that long-tenure workers have invested a lot in a specific job and employer, and thus deserve greater protection from job loss. In the absence of seniority provisions, there is also greater potential for purely subjective and arbitrary factors to come into play.

Often, agreements have formal provisions to prohibit or limit an employer's contracting out of work to other employers, and to provide advance notice of technological and organizational change. Sometimes there are formal no-layoff provisions for the term of a contract, and often layoffs become subject to formal negotiation. Sometimes

Table 9.1: Selected Provisions in Collective Agreements, 2006

	% of Union employees covered
Job security and protection	
Layoffs based on seniority	67.8%
Some restriction on contracting out	61.2%
Advance notice to union of technological change	55.6%
Training to deal with technological change	49.2%
Severance on layoff based on years of service	51.4%
Opportunities for job progress	
Promotion based on seniority:	
Primary criterion	20.8%
Tie-breaker	42.2%
Specific to job	50.4%
General	17.0%
Apprenticeship program	29.5%
Employer contributes to training fund	29.9%
Joint committee on training	32.8%
Equity	
Employment equity program	22.8%
Harassment complaint procedure	52.8%
Workplace conditions	
Joint committee:	
Broad mandate	62.6%
Organization of work	38.4%
Working conditions	39.9%
Working-time	
Normal hours of work 37.5 hours or less:	
White-collar	48.7%
Blue-collar	15.9%
Some limit on overtime	11.2%
Paid holidays:	
10 days or more	76.8%
12 days or more	32.5%
Annual vacation:	
Four weeks after 10 years or less	74.6%
Four weeks after 5 years or less	34.5%
Five weeks after 15 years or less	33.7%
Provision for job-sharing	15.7%
Provision for flex-time:	
White-collar	23.3%
Blue-collar	6.0%
Compressed workweek:	
White-collar	27.8%
Blue-collar	13.8%

Source: Human Resources Development Canada, Bureau of Labour Information, 2006.

Note: Collective agreement provisions vary widely re the precise content.

unions have even bargained for employers to commit to new investments to maintain and increase employment.

Opportunities for Job Progress
Most, but certainly not all, agreements provide for at least some consideration of seniority in promotions, so that a worker who has the skills and abilities to fill an available job will get the job if she or he is the most senior candidate. Job vacancies usually have to be posted, and are subject to formal competitions. Often, agreements provide defined opportunities for training. These provisions mean that union members are generally able to access better jobs through formalized internal labour markets. Formal structures for promotion can exist in larger non-union firms, but collective agreements typically provide much stronger rights for workers.

Equity and Human Rights
Only a minority of collective agreements provide for formal employment equity programs (sometimes because legislative provisions exist), but harassment complaint procedures have become much more common and now cover a majority of unionized workers. Harassment—often directed at women and racialized workers—is not normally covered by employment standards legislation, though Quebec now requires employers to maintain anti-harassment workplace procedures. These usually require independent investigation and swift resolution of any complaints.

Workplace Conditions
Many agreements contain provisions—sometimes very detailed—on the content of jobs, workloads, and proper working conditions. Often agreements also set up labour/management committees to informally discuss working conditions. However, almost all agreements also contain management rights clauses that give management the right (subject to specific exceptions) to assign tasks to workers, to direct work, etc. Unionized workers generally enjoy much higher levels of protection in terms of health and safety, since health and safety committees are common in unionized workplaces, and because union involvement gives life to such committees when they are mandated by law.

Working Time and Hours of Work
Agreements usually specify regular hours of work, shift schedules, maximum hours, and provisions for overtime pay, as well as provisions for paid time off. Again, this contrasts to informal schedule arrangements (such as highly variable weekly hours, on-call arrangements, and unpaid overtime) in many non-union workplaces. It is not uncommon for unionized workers in public and social services to work unpaid overtime due to the demands of the job, but unpaid overtime is uncommon among unionized workers outside of professional and managerial job categories.

Unionized workers generally enjoy far more paid time off the job than do non-union workers. Provincial employment standards legislation gives workers access to a minimum of two weeks of paid vacation (or vacation pay) after one year of service. There is no entitlement at all to a third week in three jurisdictions—Ontario, PEI, and Yukon—while workers have to put in five or more years of service (15 years in Newfoundland, and eight years in Quebec, Nova Scotia, and New Brunswick) to reach three weeks of paid vacation. The exception is Saskatchewan, where every worker has access to three weeks after one year of service, and four weeks of paid vacation after 10 years of service.

On top of fixed paid holidays (which often add to the list of provincial statutory holidays), the great majority of unionized workers get at least three weeks of paid vacation time, and 70% get four weeks, usually after 10 years of service. One in three (31%) unionized workers gets five weeks of paid vacation, usually after 15 years of service.

What Are the Impacts of Unions?

Unions Raise Wages

In Canada, as in almost all countries, it is well established that unionized workers earn higher wages than non-union workers. This is referred to as the union wage premium, or union wage advantage. Usually the wage advantage is greatest for workers who would otherwise be low paid.

Table 9.2 provides data on the union wage advantage in Canada in 2007. The average union worker earned $23.58 per hour, or $4.59 per hour (24.2%) more than the average non-union worker, who earned $18.98 per hour. The difference is somewhat distorted by the fact that non-union workers are a mix of higher paid professionals and managers, and lower paid workers. The median union worker (50% earn more and 50% earn less) made over $6 per hour more than the median non-union worker in 2007. The union average hourly wage advantage is greater for women ($6.08 per hour) than for men ($3.18 per hour). The union advantage, measured in terms of average hourly wages, is greater in the private sector than the much more highly unionized public sector, and tends to be highest in relatively low-paid occupations. As shown in Table 9.2, measured in percentage terms, the union wage premium is well over one-third in many low-wage private service occupations and blue-collar occupations, but is quite low in some professional occupations.

It is important to take into account that union and non-union workers are different, and also hold different kinds of jobs. Union members are, on average, older and more experienced than non-union members, and are much more likely to work in public and social services and, if they work in the private sector, for large firms. And, more union members are highly trained and educated. Public-sector wages tend to be higher than in the private sector, not just because of higher union coverage, but also because of the high proportion of professional jobs. In other words, the apparently very large union wage advantage reflects many factors other than union coverage. Economists have tried to calculate the union wage premium (the difference between the union and non-union wage) for comparable jobs, holding constant all the other factors that determine wages. Calculated this way, the premium has still been generally estimated to be in the range of 7% to 14% (Fang and Verma 2002).

It seems that the union hourly wage advantage has fallen over the past decade. Between 1997 and 2007, the average hourly wage of a union member barely increased at

Table 9.2: The Union Average Hourly Wage Advantage, 2007

	Union	Non-union	Union advantage	Union advantage as % of non-union
All	$23.58	$18.98	$4.59	24.2%
Men	$24.38	$21.20	$3.18	15.0%
Women	$22.79	$16.71	$6.08	36.4%
Age 15–24	$14.45	$11.63	$2.82	24.2%
By occupation:				
Professionals in business, finance	$30.03	$28.94	$1.09	3.8%
Secretary, administration	$22.00	$19.05	$2.95	15.5%
Clerical, supervisors	$20.12	$15.92	$4.20	26.4%
Natural sciences	$29.61	$28.32	$1.29	4.6%
Health, nursing	$29.96	$29.22	$0.74	2.5%
Assist health occupation	$21.05	$18.94	$2.11	11.1%
Social sciences	$26.13	$21.64	$4.50	20.8%
Teacher, professor	$30.45	$23.44	$7.01	29.9%
Art, culture, recreation	$24.42	$19.33	$5.09	26.3%
Mainly low-wage private services:				
Retail, sales, cashier	$13.02	$11.40	$1.62	14.2%
Chefs, cooks	$15.22	$11.42	$3.80	33.2%
Protective services	$23.68	$16.81	$6.87	40.9%
Child care	$17.88	$11.56	$6.32	54.7%
Sales, service, travel	$15.18	$11.26	$3.92	34.8%
Blue-collar:				
Construction trades	$24.76	$18.50	$6.26	33.8%
Other trades	$25.76	$19.60	$6.16	31.4%
Transport equipment	$21.62	$17.00	$4.62	27.2%
Trades helpers	$21.01	$14.41	$6.60	45.8%
Primary industry	$22.29	$16.69	$5.60	33.5%
Machine operators	$20.75	$17.10	$3.65	21.3%
Process, manufacturing	$17.38	$13.07	$4.31	32.9%

Source: Statistics Canada. *Labour Force Survey*, 2007. Calculated from microdata files.

all when adjusted for inflation, meaning that the average of wage settlements in collective agreements just matched inflation over the course of an entire decade. Meanwhile, the average non-union wage adjusted for inflation rose by about $1.50 per hour over the entire decade. However, this increase mainly reflected high earnings gains by non-union senior managers and professionals. It is also important to note that the cost of a typical union benefits package increased significantly over this period. Holding everything else constant, unions still have a very significant impact on wages. And, wages are only one part of the union pay advantage, which includes much higher benefits and more paid time off the job than is the case for non-union workers.

The union wage premium is impossible to determine precisely. It may reflect a compensating differential for more difficult working conditions than those of non-union workers. On the other hand, the union wage premium may be understated to the extent that it takes no account of the positive impacts of unions on the wages of non-union workers. Many non-union employers more or less match union wages in order to avoid unionization.[1]

The union wage premium has been found to be lowest in countries where union density is high, and highest where union density is low. Thus, it is much higher in the U.S. than in Sweden. This is surprising on the surface, but it reflects the fact that non-union employers will be more likely to be forced to match union wages where unions are very strong. The main impact of unions in countries like Sweden, where the unionization rate is well over 80%, is to raise wages for lower paid workers compared to other workers, rather than to raise union wages compared to the wages of non-union workers.

While wages are obviously a key concern in union bargaining, the key goal of labour movements is—or should be—to expand the range of collective bargaining and to increase union density. The goal is to improve the working conditions of all workers rather than raise the wages of a small union elite. A very high union wage premium and low union density is likely to promote very strong employer resistance to unions, as in the U.S. and Canada, as opposed to Germany and Sweden where employers generally take dealing with unions as a given, and perhaps even as an advantage. Widespread unionization is likely to promote weaker employer opposition, at least once high density has been established. That is because, in highly unionized environments, wages are effectively taken out of competition since all employers in a sector or region pay roughly the same union wage and benefits. Employers must then compete with each other on the basis of non-wage costs, productivity, and quality.

The union wage premium can be paid for from several different possible sources. Part of it may come from lower management salaries and lower profits than in comparable non-union firms. The major part comes from higher productivity. (Higher output produced per hour worked supports a higher hourly wage.) And, part may come from higher prices that unionized firms charge in order to cover higher wages. The impacts of union wages on jobs and growth are discussed below.

Unions Counter Low Pay and Make Wages More Equal
Economic research has consistently shown that the union wage advantage is greatest for people who would otherwise be lower paid workers, notably workers

with less formal education and skills, younger and less experienced workers, and women and workers of colour who are vulnerable to discrimination. In Canada, unions have been shown to raise the pay of lower paid workers compared to higher paid workers, to reduce the incidence of poverty, and to make wages more equal (Chaykowski 1995; Chaykowski and Slotsve 1998). This is partly because unions compress the distribution of wages within unionized firms. For example, highly skilled trades workers in the auto industry make more per hour than regular assembly-line workers, but the difference is not as great as it would be in non-union firms. Because unions bargain for all workers in a bargaining unit, the tendency is to negotiate relatively flat, across-the-board wage increases that benefit all members. Over time, this reduces pay differences in the unionized sector. Unionized establishments have lower wage differentials among workers, and probably between union workers and supervisors and lower level managers, and also make less use of performance pay and bonuses, which increase overall pay differences. As shown in Table 9.2, the union advantage is very significant among low-wage occupations, such as childcare workers (54.7%) and sales and service workers (34.8%).

Being low paid is often defined as working in a job that pays less than two-thirds of the economy-wide median wage. In 2002, the median wage was $15.65 per hour, so a low-paid worker was someone earning less than $10.42. By this definition, 33% of non-union workers were low paid in 2002, but just 8.4% of unionized workers were low paid. By raising the wages of traditionally disadvantaged groups the most, unions typically lower pay differences in the unionized sector between women and men, and between workers of colour and other workers.

Unions and Equality-Seeking Groups

Unions have not only raised pay for the lower paid, but have also often attempted to promote pay and employment equity for their members. Many collective agreements contain non-discrimination clauses, and some call for formal pay and employment equity procedures above and beyond those mandated by law. In practice, unionized workers are also most likely to benefit from legislated pay and employment equity laws because unions have been prepared to fight long and costly cases through the courts. For example, after many years, the Public Service Alliance of Canada (PSAC) won a landmark, multi-billion-dollar pay equity settlement for women workers and, in 2006, the Communications, Energy and Paperworkers (CEP) finally concluded a major pay equity settlement with Bell Canada.

It is clear that unions play a major role in closing the wage gap between women and men, and in countering low pay among working women.[2] However, this role needs to be strengthened by increasing union representation for women, especially lower paid women in the private services sector.

By 2006, the unionization rate for women had risen above that for men. However, the unionization rate for women in the private sector is, at 14.1% in 2007, very low and still well below the 22.6% rate for men in the private sector. (The unionization rate for women in the public sector is high and stable at 75.8%. Two-thirds of unionized women work in the public sector, and just one-third in the private sector.) Unionization is especially low for women working in low-paid private service industries, such as retail trade (12.8%), and accommodation and food services (7.9%).

In 2007, unionized women earned an average of $22.79 per hour, or 93.5% of the wage of unionized men. Non-union women earned an average of $16.71 per hour, or 78.8% of the wage of non-union men. Unions raise the wages of working women and narrow the gender wage gap. In the public sector, union coverage is high for women, raises wages, and significantly narrows the gender wage gap. In the private sector, union coverage is much lower for women than for men, raises wages more modestly (with a greater impact on part-time workers), and does not close the gender wage gap as much as in the public sector. However, unionization does have a major impact on the wages of women in the lowest paid occupational category, sales and service workers.

As shown in Table 9.3, the union wage premium for women in this category in 2003 was $3.87 per hour, or a very substantial 38.1% of the wage of non-union women, and unions closed the gender wage gap within this occupational group since the union wage premium is significantly higher for women than men (38.1% vs. 27.3%). Union coverage for women in sales and service jobs ranges from highs of 60.8% in protective services (security guards), to 40.1% in child care and home support (mainly in the broader public sector), to 28.6% in travel and accommodation jobs, to 21.3% of cashiers, 14.6% of chefs and cooks, and just 9.9% of retail clerks, and 6% of food and beverage servers. Clearly, the unionization rate of women must be significantly increased in low-paid private services jobs if the significant union advantage is to be enjoyed by more working women.

Table 9.3: Union Coverage and Wages in Sales and Service Occupations in the Private Sector, 2003

		Average hourly wage			Union wage premium	
	Union coverage	All	Union	Non-union	$	%
All	14.4%	$12.34	$15.41	$11.47	$3.94	34.3%
Men	15.7%	$14.29	$17.07	$13.41	$3.66	27.3%
Women	13.5%	$10.95	$14.02	$10.15	$3.87	38.1%

Source: Gender and Work database: www.genderwork.ca.

Unionization among workers of colour is lower than for the Canadian workforce as a whole. Between 1998 and 2003, the unionization rate among workers of colour (visible minorities) averaged about 22%, well below the 30% overall average, with the unionization rate being about the same for women and men workers of colour. Unions have a positive impact upon employment outcomes. Cheung (2005) and Reitz and Verma (2003) find that unionization (controlling for other factors) closes the wage gap between workers of colour and other Canadians, particularly among men.

Table 9.4: Union Impact on Hourly Wages, 2003

	Workers of colour	All other workers*
Total		
Covered by a union	$17.13	$20.07
Not covered	$14.70	$15.73
Union premium	$2.43	$4.34
As a %	**16.5%**	**27.6%**
Men		
Covered by a union	$17.86	$21.19
Not covered	$16.14	$18.01
Union premium	$1.72	$3.18
As a %	**10.7%**	**17.7%**
Women		
Covered by a union	$16.44	$18.79
Not covered	$13.19	$13.38
Union premium	$3.25	$5.41
As a %	**24.6%**	**40.4%**

Source: Gender and Work Database, York University: www.genderwork.ca, accessed August 8, 2005.
Data from Survey of Income and Labour Dynamics (SLID).
* "All Other Workers" included Aboriginal workers.

Workers of colour with no union coverage make an average of $14.70 per hour, lower than the average hourly wage of all other non-union workers of $15.73. With union coverage, the average hourly wage of workers of colour in Canada jumped to $17.13, an increase of 16.5%. The union wage premium was greater for women (24.6%) than men (10.7%).

Although unions raise wages for workers of colour, the union wage premium is less than for other workers, and there is a larger racial gap in unionized workplaces than in the non-union sector. This is probably mainly due to differences in the distribution of workers of colour by sector and occupation, and a relative concentration of unionized workers of colour in lower paid sectors and jobs. Most workers of colour are relatively recent immigrants, meaning that relatively few are workers with long job tenure. Workers of colour are greatly under-represented in skilled blue-collar jobs and in teaching jobs, both of which are highly unionized occupations. While unions have little direct control over who is hired, some have pushed for more inclusive recruiting and formal employment equity procedures. The racial pay gap among unionized workers may also reflect lack of sufficient attention to pay and employment equity for workers of colour in collective bargaining.

While working-age persons with disabilities are greatly under-represented in the workforce, the unionization rate for the minority of workers with disabilities who do work on a full-year basis is about the same as for the workforce as a whole. This is probably because workers with disabilities are most likely to find jobs in public and social services, and in large firms where employment equity programs are most likely to be in place. Again, unionization helps close the pay gap between people with and without disabilities, and has particularly large impacts on the pay of lower paid women with disabilities (CCSD 2004).

Unions Provide Much Greater Access to Non-wage Benefits

In Canada, there are very significant gaps in public programs covering health and welfare issues. Public pensions do provide a minimum income in retirement, but maximum benefits from Old Age Security, plus the Canada/Quebec Pension Plan, fall far below what most pension experts see as reasonable wage replacement levels for average and higher income workers. Unlike the U.S., doctor and hospital services are covered by public health care, but this still leaves dental care, drugs, and other services to be paid for privately. Only very limited life and disability insurance is provided through public programs. While advocating broader public programs in all of these areas, unions have also traditionally filled the gap by negotiating employer-provided benefits (sometimes on a cost-shared basis). A good pension and benefits package can easily make up 20% and more of the total compensation package, and this is rising fast with the growing costs of drug plans. Most union pension plans are defined benefit plans, which replace earnings with a guaranteed percentage of previous earnings. Such plans are far superior to RRSPs since expenses are much lower and there is no uncertainty.

Table 9.5: Benefits Coverage: Union vs. Non-union

	Medical plan	Dental plan	Life/Disability insurance	Pension plan
All employees	57.4%	53.1%	52.5%	43.3%
Unionized	83.7%	76.3%	78.2%	79.9%
Non-unionized	45.4%	42.6%	40.8%	26.6%

Source: Akyeampong, Ernest. "Unionization and Fringe Benefits," *Perspectives* (August 2002: 3–9).

The impact of unions on benefits is far greater than on wages, particularly in smaller firms. As shown in Table 9.5, union members are three times more likely than non-union workers to be covered by an employer-sponsored pension plan, and twice as likely to be covered by a medical or dental plan. Some 80% of union members have an employer-provided pension plan, which usually provides a defined pension based on salary and years of earnings. Virtually all large pension plans in Canada represent the savings of unionized workers, and typically only a small layer of non-union workers are covered. Only one-third of non-union workers are covered by pension plans, and many of these are managers and other excluded workers covered by public-sector and large unionized company plans. Pension coverage is extremely rare (and rapidly declining) in the non-union private sector outside very large firms. There has likely been some slippage of pension coverage among both union and non-union workers in recent years, but the very strong union advantage in the pension and benefits area persists (Informetrica 2007).

Unions are associated with high benefits coverage mainly because this has been given a very high priority in bargaining. Also, some employers recognize that good benefit plans help retain workers. Not all newly unionized workers manage to gain pension and benefits coverage, but the vast majority of new plans are initiated through collective bargaining. Of course, union members differ in their priorities, with younger members with children being most concerned with health benefits, and older workers being most concerned with pensions. Workplace pensions mean that younger workers often gain significant pension entitlements long before they start thinking about this as a serious issue. Unions have sometimes facilitated benefits coverage as well by providing the means for smaller employers to join with larger groups. Construction unions typically directly sponsor pension plans for members who move from employer to employer.

From the point of view of union members, union jobs are good jobs because they generally provide for a decent pension in retirement, and protection against the costs of ill health and disability. However, it also has to be recognized that private benefit plans are expensive and come at the cost of foregone current wages, and have to be paid for out of the total employer wage bill. In some ways, bargaining for income and social security at the workplace is also a second-best solution to public programs, such as good public pensions and public health care. This is particularly the case when jobs become more unstable. The rapid growth of health benefit costs in particular has become a very acrimonious factor in collective bargaining, leading the labour movement to strongly advocate the extension of public health care insurance to prescription drugs.

Job Security and Working Conditions

Unionized workers enjoy greater job security than non-union workers. In 2001, 9% of men and women non-union workers experienced an involuntary job separation, meaning that they were laid off or dismissed. Just 5.5% of unionized men and 2.6% of unionized women experienced such a separation.[3] This difference reflects the fact that unionized workplaces tend to be either in the public sector, or are larger and more stable than small businesses in the private sector. Individual union members also have greater-than-average job security because of the norm of seniority in layoffs, which protects workers who have been in a specific job longer. Unionized members are less likely to be dismissed because of formal grievance procedures, and are also much less likely to quit their jobs. Unionized workplaces thus tend to be more stable, though many have shut down or experienced layoffs due to economic restructuring.

Only limited information is available on the impact of unions on workplace conditions due to a lack of regular government surveys. One might expect that, other things being equal, unions would help improve conditions at work. However, it is also the case that a higher-than-average proportion of unionized workers are employed in jobs with unsocial work schedules (shift work, night work), in jobs with dirty and dangerous working conditions (e.g., exposure to noise, poor air and fumes, dust), and in jobs that are very stressful in terms of the pace and intensity of work and long hours. Manufacturing, resources, and construction jobs, as well as many jobs in social services, can be very stressful and demanding. Surveys suggest that there is little overall difference between union and non-union workers in terms of perceived job stress, though unions may well be making some difference in very demanding workplaces.

As shown in Table 9.1, above, many union members now have standard workweeks of less than 40 hours. Union members are much more likely to be paid for overtime hours than non-union members (though unpaid overtime is on the increase in unionized public services). Some union members work a lot of paid overtime, particularly in blue-collar jobs. Because of the nature of unionized jobs, unions have little impact upon the overall incidence of shift work and night work in sectors like manufacturing and public services. About one-third of both union and non-union workers do not work a regular daytime schedule, but work evenings, nights, or weekends, or on an on-call basis, but union work schedules are generally more stable and predictable, and there is often premium pay for unsocial hours. More social hours, such as regular day and non-weekend shifts, may be available to higher seniority workers in unionized workplaces even where work is organized on a shift basis.

Box 9.3: Unions and Working Time

Historically, unions led the fight for the eight-hour day and the five-day workweek, which became the standard in industrial jobs only in the late 1940s and 1950s. Since then, there have been only modest reductions in regular working time, and there has been an increase in overtime and long hours for many workers since the 1990s. For employers, it often makes economic sense to schedule overtime instead of hiring new workers and assuming the cost of training and benefits. Many workers also want higher pay from overtime where there is premium pay, such as time-and-a-half and double-time. Long hours are obviously attractive to employers who don't pay for overtime, which is often the case for salaried workers.

In Europe, some unions have seen shorter working time as a way to avoid layoffs and create new jobs while expanding the quality of life of workers. Some Canadian unions have also put working-time issues front and centre in negotiations. Most notably, the Communications, Energy and Paperworkers Union has limited overtime in pulp and paper mills, and the Canadian Auto Workers has bargained for more time off the job in the auto sector. These initiatives have helped protect jobs for younger members who might have been laid off. It has also been shown that shorter work schedules can help boost productivity. In many industries, it is cheaper to run a plant for more hours per day with three short shifts instead of two long shifts.

Unions and Training

Unions commonly bargain education and training provisions, including paid and unpaid time off the job for training, apprenticeship programs, and provisions for on-the-job training to help workers deal with technological and organizational change. About one-half of all unionized workers enjoy some rights to training through their collective agreements. Craft unions, such as the construction trades and some industrial unions, have played a major role in the development and delivery of apprenticeship programs, and some unions provide direct skills training to their members. Indeed, unions are increasingly engaged in workplace learning activities, sometimes independently and sometimes in partnership with employers. A number of unions also actively participate in joint employer-union sectoral training bodies. Generally, unions promote training that gives workers formal, portable qualifications, as opposed to training that is very narrowly geared to the needs of a single workplace. In addition, the union wage and benefits advantage pushes employers to invest in work processes that raise productivity and thus skill requirements, which are generally filled by training the current workforce. Data from the *Adult Education and Training Survey* and several studies show that—as a result—unionization helps significantly reduce the major gap in available training opportunities between well-educated workers and those with less formal qualifications (Livingstone and Raykov 2005).

The Impact of Unions on the Economy and Labour Markets

To summarize, unions raise wages for union compared to non-union workers, and compress wage differences within unionized firms and sectors. In Canada, research has shown that unions significantly reduce wage inequality among men, and also reduce the gender wage gap. The overall impact of unions is to significantly reduce wage inequality (Card et al. 2003; Dinardo 1997; Lemieux 1993). Research has also shown that wage inequality in Canada is significantly lower than in the U.S. partly because of higher union density. However, declining unionization has been a source of growing wage inequality in Canada as well as in the U.S.

Studies show that countries with very high levels of collective bargaining coverage have much less pay inequality than lower union-density countries, such as the U.S., Britain, and Canada. In the social democratic countries of Scandinavia and the social-market countries, such as Germany and the Netherlands, collective bargaining coverage is very high (and generally quite stable) because of high union membership in combination with the *de facto* or sometimes legal extension of agreements on a sectoral or regional basis. Wage floors set by bargaining protect the great majority of non-professional and/or managerial workers, including most part-time and even temporary workers. While direct union membership is slipping, bargaining still covers more than 80% of workers in Germany and the Scandinavian and Benelux countries, as well as in France and Italy. Also, unions and legislatively mandated works councils mean that there are strong elements of joint workplace governance over such issues as training and working conditions in these countries.

Countries with high levels of bargaining coverage have relatively equal wages and high wage floors, so that the incidence of low pay and earnings inequality are much lower than in Canada (OECD 1996, 2006). About one in four full-time workers in Canada in 2003 was low paid—defined as earning less than two-thirds of the median national full-time wage—compared to just over one in 20 in Sweden and one in six in Germany and the Netherlands. The minimum earnings gap between the top and bottom 10% of workers is about three to one in the Scandinavian countries compared to about four to one in the U.S. and Canada. This is mainly because of institutional differences, notwithstanding common exposure to the forces of globalization and technological and organizational change.

Most mainstream economists see unions as almost exclusively concerned with raising the wages of their members, distorting wages compared to free-market levels, and they see this as damaging to the economy as a whole. In the standard economic model, union wage gains come at the expense of other workers and/or society as a whole, since they are paid for through higher prices or through fewer jobs in union-ized firms. In the standard model, higher union wages force union employers to hire fewer workers, pushing more workers into competition for non-union jobs, thus forcing down non-union wages. In fact, the most authoritative surveys of the economic literature conclude that the positive impacts of unions in terms of reducing low pay and inequality and giving workers a voice at the workplace do not come at a significant economic price. Indeed, there is a strong argument to be made that unions promote economic prosperity as well as social justice. A major recent study by the World Bank on the economic impacts of unions (Aidt and Tzannatos 2003) finds that there is no relationship between union density and the economic or employment per-formance of countries. A major review of economic studies by the OECD also found no valid statistical relationship between trade union membership and the economic or employment performance of advanced industrial countries in the 1980s and 1990s. Union density is, overall, related neither to higher- nor to lower-than-average rates of unemployment or economic growth (OECD 1996).

The International Labour Organization (ILO 1995) argues that high employment growth and strong economic growth can be achieved in a very wide range of labour market settings. Recent studies by the ILO and others (Auer 2000; ILO 2003; Jackson 2000) have shown that some countries with very high rates of union coverage, notably Denmark, the Netherlands, and Sweden, have also been able to achieve high levels of employment and strong rates of economic growth since the mid-1990s. High unioniza-tion at the economy-wide level is quite compatible with good economic performance because unions can and do bargain for jobs as well as for wages. Unions and labour movements understand that bargaining outcomes have an economic impact. At the firm level, at which most bargaining in Canada (and, increasingly, elsewhere) is con-ducted, it is also far from clear that the gains of unionization in terms of higher wages, more benefits, and better working conditions come at the price of fewer jobs. A key problem with the standard economic model is that unions do not bargain purely for higher wages without any concern for the jobs of their members. Some elements of the union advantage, such as paid time off the job and restrictions on unpaid over-time, actually increase employment. And, keeping jobs is usually a major priority in local bargaining. Often unions will bargain early retirement provisions for older workers and job-sharing arrangements in order to preserve jobs. Very few unions will raise wages to such a level as to push an employer into severe financial difficulties. Research has found that newly organized firms (in the U.S.) are no more likely to go out of business over the long term than are firms in which unions lost representation elections (Dinardo and Lee 2002), and that unionized firms have similar closure and bankruptcy rates to other firms, controlling for other characteristics (Freeman and Kleiner 1999). As noted above, union wages have stagnated in Canada over the past decade, strongly supporting the case that unions have not imposed major costs on employers.

It has to be borne in mind that employers as well as unions have to agree to collective agreements. Wage settlements must and do reflect market realities. In most bargaining situations, both sides understand that the rough limit for increasing total wage costs is set by productivity and employer profitability. Unions can and will push for improvements in real wages if worker productivity is increasing and firms are profitable. This implicit bargain was much more explicit in industry-wide bargaining in the 1960s and 1970s when wages often rose on the basis of an annual improvement factor based on productivity. Sometimes it is argued that this market discipline on wages does not apply in the public sector, but public-sector wage settlements basically follow the trend that is set in the private sector. (In the 1990s, union wage settlements in the Canadian public sector have, in fact, more or less consistently lagged behind those in the private sector because of statutory or informal wage control programs.)

The union wage premium may be higher than average in highly unionized sectors of the economy. If an industry is highly unionized, such that all employers pay the same union wage and benefit package, the union impact puts no single employer at a significant competitive disadvantage. If union wages are built into the cost structure of all employers, wages are taken out of the competitive equation, forcing firms to compete with one another on the basis of non-cost issues, such as quality and customer service. Indeed, some economists argue that strong unions are a force for positive competition since they force firms to compete with one another on issues that are positive for consumers, but not negative from the workers' point of view. The high road of firm competition on the basis of high productivity, training, and production of high-quality goods and services is often contrasted to the low road of competing on the basis of low wages and poor working conditions.

Box 9.4: Unions and Productivity

The major part of the union advantage in terms of pay, benefits, and paid time off the job is earned through higher productivity or higher output per hour. Higher productivity comes from a firm's investment in capital equipment and technology, as well as investment in worker training and skills. The fact that unionized firms are under constant pressure to pay good wages and benefits and to invest in training may lead them to invest more in new equipment and technologies than would otherwise be the case. Moreover, and most importantly, unionized firms tend to be different from non-union firms in ways that raise productivity.

The important work of Freeman and Medoff (1984) on the economic role of unions emphasizes the importance of voice. Unions provide a collective voice for workers in unionized workplaces, which make them function quite differently than most non-union workplaces. By organizing the internal labour market, unionization can lower the management costs of firms. Formal rules counter discrimination and petty abuses of managerial authority, which can be costly to firms and not just workers. Most importantly, the existence of a union stimulates and facilitates joint labour-management discussion of workplace problems. In this discussion, management listens to the union not just because it is an important source of information, but also because it has some power behind it. Union workplaces have formalized systems in place to govern issues like promotion and technological change, and work organization and training, which means that there is some joint determination of the work process.

As Freeman and Medoff note, a good labour relations climate is essential to the productivity effect: "the extent to which a union is a liability or an asset depends crucially upon how management responds to it." Good labour-management relations can and do lead to limited workplace conflict and high levels of workplace co-operation. This is enormously important to productivity because production is always a social process and not just a technical process. If individual workers are treated with dignity and respect; if workplace rules are perceived as fair; if workers can raise concerns and issues and have them resolved; and if workers have a say in working conditions, training, and health and safety issues, then workers are likely to work co-operatively with management. True labour-management co-operation is much more difficult, if not impossible, to achieve in non-union environments since labour has no formal voice and no real power behind its voice.

There are some very tangible and direct links from a union voice in the workplace to higher productivity. The participatory benefits of unions, combined with better wages and working conditions, greatly reduce the incidence of quits in unionized compared to non-union workplaces (Swidinsky 1992). Fewer resignations and much longer job tenure mean that most unionized workers make a long-term commitment to a particular employer, giving an employer the benefit of experienced workers. Long job tenure also means that unionized employers have a major incentive to invest in the skills of employees in the knowledge that they are unlikely to leave the firm, but will use new skills over a long period. Non-union employers can strive to create more attractive workplaces and to retain workers by paying higher-than-market wages, but it is very difficult for them to give workers the same real stake in the enterprise that comes from workers having their own voice.

The union voice also gives management greater knowledge of workplace conditions, which can result in more efficient work organization. And, job security means that unionized workers have an incentive to share their knowledge of production and co-operate to increase productivity. If workers know that changes in work organization will not cost them their jobs or lead to poorer health and safety or working conditions, then they will co-operate in workplace change. After all, the existence of a union means that the gains of higher productivity will be available to be shared at the bargaining table. A host of studies have shown that the path to higher productivity lies in the effective combination of new technologies, training, and changes in the organization of work to maximize the use of skills. Many of these studies also show that unions and good labour relations can make a major contribution to the success of workplace restructuring. Far from being inflexible, many unionized workplaces can and have implemented new technologies in a much more effective way than non-union workplaces (Black and Lynch 2000).

Conclusion

Unions are an important force for democracy inside and outside the workplace: for better wages, working conditions, social protections for all workers, and for a more equal distribution of wages. Unions improve workplace conditions for their own members and balance the power between employers and employees. The significant union advantage does not come at the price of fewer jobs or slower growth because unions have significant, positive effects on productivity.

Recommended Reading

- Aidt, Toke, and Zafiris Tzannatos. 2003. *Unions and Collective Bargaining: Economic Effects in a Global Environment*. Washington: The World Bank. A major summary of the economic literature on union impacts that finds little support for the common view that unions have negative impacts upon growth and job creation.
- Bantjes, Rod. 2007. *Social Movements in a Global Context: Canadian Perspectives*. Toronto: Canadian Scholars' Press. An original book on social movements in Canada with a global perspective. The chapters are organized around an explanatory framework, such as class analysis or a core analytical question. The author makes connections between movements and the state, focusing on the dynamic of co-optation/coercion and movements' use of a global framework to evade that dynamic. The author also pays attention to the spatial dimensions of movement formation and tactics, which are particularly relevant in the present era of globalization.
- Black, Errol, and Jim Silver. 2008. *Building a Better World: An Introduction to Trade Unionism in Canada*. Black Point and Winnipeg: Fernwood. An excellent short introduction to Canadian trade unions, covering union roles and structures, labour history, and challenges facing the labour movement.
- Freeman, Richmond, and James Medoff. 1984. *What Do Unions Do?* New York: Basic Books. Now dated, but the introductory chapters are still the classic work on the economic impacts of unions.
- Gunderson, Morley, Allen Ponak, and Daphne Taras (Eds.). 2001. *Union-Management Relations in Canada*, 4th ed. Toronto: Addison-Wesley Longman Publishers Ltd. The standard Canadian industrial relations text.
- Yates, Michael D. 1998. *Why Unions Matter*. New York: Monthly Review Press. An introduction to the role of unions from a pro-union, U.S. perspective.

Notes

1. For example, non-union Dofasco Steel matches unionized Stelco wages, and non-union Honda matches the Big Three auto sector wages.
2. For Canadian evidence on the role of unions in closing the gender wage gap, see Doiron and Riddell (1994) and Jackson and Schellenberg (1999).
3. Custom data from Statistics Canada, *Survey of Labour and Income Dynamics,* 2001.

References

Aidt, Toke, and Zafiris Tzannatos. 2003. *Unions and Collective Bargaining: Economic Effects in a Global Environment.* Washington: The World Bank.

Auer, Peter. 2000. *Employment Revival in Europe: Labour Market Success in Austria, Denmark, Ireland, and the Netherlands.* Geneva: ILO.

Black, Errol, and Jim Silver. 2008. *Building a Better World: An Introduction to Trade Unionism in Canada.* Black Point and Winnipeg: Fernwood.

Black, Sandra, and Lisa Lynch. 2000. "What's Driving the New Economy: The Benefits of Workplace Innovation." National Bureau of Economic Research Working Paper No. 7479. www.nber.org.

Canadian Council on Social Development (CCSD). 2004. Disability Information Sheet No. 15. www.ccsd.ca.

Card, David, Thomas Lemieux, and W. Craig Riddell. 2003. "Unionization and Wage Inequality: A Comparative Study of the U.S., the U.K. and Canada." National Bureau of Economic Research Working Paper No. W9473. www.nber.org.

Chaykowski, Richard. 1995. "Union Influences on Labour Market Outcomes and Earnings Inequality." In *Labour Market Polarization and Social Policy Reform School of Policy Studies,* ed. Keith Banting and Charles Beach, 95–118. Kingston: Queen's University Press.

Chaykowski, Richard, and George Slotsve. 1998. "Economic Inequality and Poverty in Canada: Do Unions Matter?" Paper presented to the Centre for the Study of Living Standards Conference on the State of Living Standards and the Quality of Life in Canada, October. www.csls.ca.

Cheung, Leslie. 2005. "Racial Status and Employment Outcomes." Canadian Labour Congress Research Paper No. 34. canadianlabour.ca/updir/racialstatusEn.pdf.

Dinardo, John. 1997. "Diverging Male Wage Inequality in the United States and Canada, 1981–1988: Do Institutions Explain the Difference?" *Industrial and Labor Relations Review* 50, no. 4 (July): 629–651.

Dinardo, John, and David S. Lee. 2002. "The Impact of Unionization on Establishment Closure." NBER Working Paper No. W8993. www.pber.org.

Doiron, D.J., and W.C. Riddell. 1994. "The Impact of Unions on Male-Female Earnings Differences in Canada." *Journal of Human Resources* 29 (2): 504–534.

Fang, Tony, and Anil Verma. 2002. *The Union Wage Premium: Perspectives on Labour and Income* (Winter). Ottawa: Statistics Canada.

Freeman, Richard, and Morris M. Kleiner. 1999. "Do Unions Make Firms Insolvent?" *Industrial and Labor Relations Review* 52, no. 4 (July): 510–527.

Freeman, Richard, and James Medoff. 1984. *What Do Unions Do?* New York: Basic Books.

Informetrica. 2007. *Occupation Pension Plan Coverage in Ontario: A Study for the Ontario Expert Commission on Pensions.*

International Labour Organization (ILO). 1995. *World Employment Report.* Geneva: ILO.

———. 2003. *Decent Work in Denmark: Employment, Social Efficiency, and Economic Security.* Geneva: ILO.

Jackson, Andrew. 2000. *The Myth of the Equity-Efficiency Trade-Off.* Ottawa: Canadian Council on Social Development.

Jackson, Andrew, with Grant Schellenberg. 1999. "Unions, Collective Bargaining and Labour Market Outcomes for Canadian Working Women." In *Women and Work*, ed. R. Chaykowski and Lisa Powell, 245–282. Kingston: Institute for Economic Policy, Queen's University.

Lemieux, Thomas. 1993. "Unions and Wage Inequality in Canada and the United States." In *Small Differences That Matter: Labor Market and Income Maintenance in Canada and the United States*, ed. David Card and Richard Freeman, 66–107. Chicago: University of Chicago Press.

Livingstone, D.W., and M. Raykov. 2005. "Union Influence on Worker Education and Training in Canada." *Just Labour* 5 (Winter).

Organisation for Economic Co-operation and Development (OECD). 1996. "Earnings Inequality, Low Paid Employment, and Earnings Mobility." *OECD Employment Outlook*: 59–108.

———. 2006. *Society at a Glance: OECD Social Indicators.* Paris: OECD.

Reitz, Jeffery, and Anil Verma. 2003. "Immigration, Race and Labour: Unionization and Wages in the Canadian Labour Market." Mimeo.

Swidinsky, R. 1992. "Unionism and the Job Attachment of Canadian Workers." *Industrial Relations/Relations Industrielles* 47: 729–751.

CHAPTER 10

Is There a Future For Canadian Unions?

Introduction

This chapter looks at some of the challenges facing Canadian unions as a result of economic restructuring and the changing workforce. It analyzes trends in union coverage, especially between women and men and the public and private sectors, and details the sharp decline of unions among blue-collar men and the much lower but more stable coverage in private services. It concludes with an overview of the process of union change and renewal in Canada.

Unions face enormous challenges in many advanced industrial countries, and are often seen as increasingly powerless, if not irrelevant, in post-industrial societies and the so-called new global economy. There can be little doubt that the power of unions to influence wages, benefits, and working conditions through collective bargaining has been eroded by much more competitive national and international markets, and the resulting hostility of many employers to unions. In the 1950s and 1960s, strong industrial unions in North America and Europe were able to take wages and labour conditions out of the competitive equation by ensuring that major employers in a specific sector, such as auto or steel or rubber, provided the same basic conditions of employment. This ability to shape the economics of whole sectors has been greatly eroded by increased international trade and by deregulation and privatization of sectors like transportation, communications, and health, which were once insulated to at least some degree from the forces of competition. A traditional key bastion of union strength—male blue-collar workers in manufacturing—has been greatly undercut by the shift to a post-industrial, knowledge-based economy, and the restructuring of global production. More recently, public sector unions have been challenged by the shift to contracting out and privatized delivery of services.

As unions have declined in numbers, their political influence has weakened compared to that of employers, and the legislative climate has become much more hostile. In some countries, notably the U.S., unions have been marginalized to a remarkable degree. American unions now represent only one in eight workers compared to about one in three in the 1960s, and it has become extremely difficult for them to recruit new members due to strong employer resistance and weak labour laws. In Britain, union strength has also declined greatly, from about one-half to less than one-third of the workforce. Even in continental Europe, where the majority of workers are still covered by collective agreements negotiated by unions and employers, individual trade union membership has tended to decline outside the very high union density Scandinavian countries (OECD 2004, Table 3.3). Canada has been a modest exception, with the overall unionization rate declining more gradually than elsewhere, and actual union membership even rising over the past two decades (Jackson 2006, 62). In 2007, Canadian unions had 4.5 million members, up from 3.8 million a decade earlier.[1]

Unions have been forced to confront major changes, not just in the economy, but also in the wider society. The emergence of a more diverse and more highly educated workforce—which is now almost equally divided between women and men, and includes many racialized workers—has posed challenges for labour movements that were once made up mainly of skilled and semi-skilled, white, male, manual workers. Unions were once a powerful expression of tightly knit working-class communities, but old solidarities and forms of class consciousness eroded with the decline of heavy industry and the shift of population to the suburbs, which began even in the early days of postwar prosperity. What workers expect of unions has also changed, with quality of work and work-life balance issues becoming more important than the traditional (and still important) emphasis on wages and benefits.

Yet, even if employers and governments have become more hostile and the workforce has changed dramatically, unions can and often do adapt to change. Unions change in order to survive and because of pressures from members and activists. The alternative to union decline is union renewal, and there is no shortage of workers in today's so-called new economy who are still attracted to unions, and no shortage of active and engaged union members who want to build a vital labour movement to address the pressing problems of the workplaces of today. Against the gradual trend of declining union density, innovations are occurring within the labour movement, which might represent and spark a new move forward. That said, union survival will likely require much more profound changes to unions as they exist today than has taken place to date.

This chapter documents trends in union strength, in union organizing efforts, and in workers' attitudes to unions. It makes an assessment of the forces driving union density and briefly flags some of the things that unions could do to turn things around.

Trends in Union Density

Union density or coverage refers to the proportion of all employees who are covered by a collective agreement. (Note that a small proportion of workers, usually lower level supervisors, are not union members, but are still covered by a collective agreement.) Canadian unions today represent about one in three workers (31.5% in 2007) and 18.7% of private-sector workers, well above the current level of just 13.1% overall, and 8.1% in the private sector in the U.S.[2]

Unlike the U.S., the absolute number of union members in Canada has continued to increase, to a new high of more than 4.5 million union members in 2007. However, while far from marginal and still a powerful force in many sectors of the economy, the best available data suggest that union density in Canada has fallen quite sharply from a peak of almost 40% in the mid-1980s (Jackson 2006, Table 2). Union density has fallen to below 20% in the private sector from a peak of about one-third or more in the mid-1980s, and less than 1% of all non-union workers are currently organized into unions each year. While many workers join unions each year because they are hired into already unionized workplaces, new organizing is insufficient to stop future decline. Canadian unions themselves generally see no room for complacency. In opening a major conference on organizing in September 2003, Canadian Labour Congress president Kenneth V. Georgetti stressed that the labour movement must greatly expand its organizing efforts if it is to avoid marginalization and remain a major force in Canadian workplaces and in Canadian society. A paper on organizing presented to the 2008 CLC Convention struck the same note: "Every other part of our work, from bargaining collective agreements, to fighting for health and safety protection, to campaigning for economic justice and equality, depends, in the final analysis, on the size and strength of the organizations making up our movement" (Canadian Labour Congress 2008, 1).

Table 10.1 provides data on union coverage in 1988, 1997, and 2007. Union density overall has fallen by eight percentage points since the late 1980s, by about six percentage points from the late 1980s to the late 1990s, and by a smaller two percentage points over the past decade. The decline has been gradual rather than sudden, and was concentrated in the private sector in the recession and slow recovery period of the late 1980s through the mid-1990s when many jobs were lost in already unionized workplaces, particularly in the manufacturing sector. The decline slowed with the economic recovery that began in the mid-1990s.

The decline in union coverage has been much more pronounced among younger than older age groups, probably because there was little or no new hiring in union workplaces in the 1990s. As a result, young people entering the workforce have tended to be hired mainly into non-union jobs, while the average age of the union-

Table 10.1: Trends in Union Coverage (percentage)

	1988	1997	2007
All	39.5	33.7	31.5
Men	43.2	35.2	31.2
Women	35.2	32.1	31.8
Public	n/a	74.6	74.5
Private	n/a	21.3	18.7
Full-time	43.1	36.0	33.0
Part-time	30.5	23.6	24.5
Age 15–24	21.7	13.0	15.0
Newfoundland/Labrador	45.8	40.7	37.7
PEI	36.0	29.1	30.0
Nova Scotia	37.3	30.2	29.4
New Brunswick	39.1	29.9	28.2
Quebec	46.2	41.5	39.7
Ontario	35.5	29.8	28.2
Manitoba	40.0	37.6	37.1
Saskatchewan	39.8	36.0	34.8
Alberta	38.0	25.8	23.8
British Columbia	40.0	36.3	32.1
Utilities	73.9	72.1	70.8
Transportation	57.8	45.2	42.9
Construction	35.2	32.4	32.6
Manufacturing	45.5	36.3	29.9
Trade	16.0	14.8	14.3
Accommodation/Food	13.2	8.6	8.2
Finance	12.2	10.4	11.2
Education	75.8	73.5	70.7
Health/Social assistance	61.6	55.7	55.5
Public administration	75.8	71.4	72.4

Source: Statistics Canada. *Labour Force Historical Review.* 2007. Cat. 71F004XCB, CD1t42an for 1997 and 2007 data.

1988 data from J. David Arrowsmith, *Canada's Trade Unions: An Information Manual.* Industrial Relations Centre. (Kingston: Queen's University, 1992.) Note: Industry categories may not be strictly comparable.

Table 10.2: Composition of Union Membership

Percentage of all union members who are:	1997	2007
Men	54.7%	50.0%
Women	45.3%	50.0%
Public sector	51.7%	54.4%
Private sector	48.3%	45.6%
Full-time	87.1%	86.2%
Part-time	12.9%	13.8%
Age 15–24	6.4%	8.3%
Age 25–44	56.7%	46.7%
Age 45+	36.9%	45.0%
Goods	26.4%	22.4%
Services	73.6%	77.6%
Manufacturing	18.1%	12.9%
Total number of union members (000s)	3828.6	4491.5
Public sector	1878.5	2445.3
Private sector	1850.1	2046.3

Source: Statistics Canada. Labour Force Historical Review. 2007. Cat. 71F004XCB, CD1t42an.

ized workforce has increased. The decline has also been far greater among men than among women. The coverage rate for men is now under one-third, down from a high of close to one-half in the mid-1980s. The rate for women, after rising rapidly through the 1970s and early 1980s, has slipped much less, and the difference in union coverage between women and men has now completely disappeared. In 2006, for the first time, more women than men belonged to unions.

Stable union coverage for women compared to the continued decline among men arises mainly from the fact that women are more likely than men to work in public and social services, where the level of union representation is much higher than in the private sector. The majority of all union members are now employed in the public sector rather than in the private sector. Union coverage is much higher in the public sector (74.5% compared to 18.7% in the private sector in 2007), and women in the public sector are even more likely than men to be union members (75.8% vs.

72.3%). Union coverage in public and social services (public administration, education, and health and social services) has remained high, and, while perhaps slipping a bit from the mid-1980s to the mid-1990s, has even increased in recent years. More than two-thirds of union women (68%) work in the public sector (defined as direct government employment, plus employment in directly government-funded institutions, such as schools, universities, colleges, and hospitals), and less than one-third work in the private sector. By contrast, 60% of unionized men work in the private sector.

Union coverage is very high (above 70%) in both education and public administration, and also high (56.5%) in health and social services. These sectors alone now account for well over one-half of all union members. Education and health services make up a large and increasing share of total employment, and jobs in these sectors are predominantly held by women. It is notable that union coverage is quite high, at 28%, even in the private, not-for-profit part of health care and social services, which are not considered to be part of the core public sector by Statistics Canada. Many social services not directly delivered by governments—such as publicly subsidized child care centres, elder care services, and long-term care homes—are often unionized, and the broader public sector has been a key arena for new union organizing. Union coverage is very high in direct government jobs (public administration). This sector shrank slowly as a total share of employment in the 1990s, though some new hiring began thereafter.

In sum, the large public and social services labour force has continued to be a key bastion of union strength, partly because the direct public sector is now stable in size, and partly because of union strength in private and non-profit, often contracted out services, such as long-term care, child care, and home care. Public services unions, such as the Canadian Union of Public Employees (CUPE), the Public Service Alliance of Canada (PSAC), and provincial government workers unions (united at the national level in the National Union of Public and General Employees (NUPGE)), have actively organized within and outside the formal public sector, and have had notable success, particularly among women workers. Some formerly private-sector unions have also organized in this area. For example, one of the largest locals of the United Steelworkers consists of support staff at the University of Toronto. It should be noted that the unionization rate is also very high, at 73%, among part-time workers in public services, contrasting sharply to a unionization rate of just 13.5% among part-time workers in the private sector.

It was sometimes the case in the past that public-sector unions gained voluntary recognition from government employers, but the overall labour relations climate in public services has become much more like the business sector in recent years. In the direct public sector, wage settlements for unionized workers have generally not exceeded private sector settlements since the early 1990s, despite the enduring myth that public-sector workers enjoy greater bargaining power. Privatization and contracting out of many services, from refuse collection to elder care, means that public-sector wages come under competitive pressure, and that employers funded from the public purse have to compete with one another for contracts, putting downward pressure on broader public-sector wages and benefits. Continuing high union density in the direct public sector and broader public sector reflects not so much insulation from market forces as union success in efforts to keep contracted out jobs unionized, and success in new organizing efforts. For example, the Canadian Union of Postal Workers (CUPW) has organized rural mail route carriers even though they were considered not to be direct employees, and many personal support workers and other staff in long-term care homes working for private employers have been unionized in recent years.

Unfortunately, there is no consistent long-term data on union coverage in the private sector. Union density outside public services was probably quite close to 30% in the mid-1980s compared to just under 20% today (Morissette et al. 2005, Table 2). The process of decline has slowed, but not completely halted, in the economic recovery period since the mid-1990s. This was a period of strong private-sector job growth, but new hiring seems to have taken place more in non-union than in union workplaces. The total private-sector paid workforce grew by 2.2 million or 26% between 1997 and 2007, while the union-covered private-sector workforce grew by only 196,000 or by 8.6%. It should be noted that union density in the private sector is much lower for women than for men (14.1% compared to 22.6% in 2007), reflecting the fact that unions are still stronger among mainly male blue-collar workers.

Looking at longer term changes within the private sector, there has been a marked decline in union density in the traditional bastions of male blue-collar unionism. Density has fallen from about one-half to well under one-third of all workers in manufacturing since the mid-1980s. This is still a big enough sector for the drop to have had a major impact on overall union density as well as on union density in the total private sector. About one-third of the fall of private-sector union density since the late 1980s is explained by the fall within manufacturing. As of 2007, just 13% of the unionized workforce were in manufacturing, down from 18% in 1997, and well down from the 1980s.

The decline has been pervasive across most subsectors and occupations within manufacturing, and is almost certainly closely linked to a huge turnover in manufacturing establishments since the mid-1980s and the shift of jobs to small and non-union plants. For example, a lot of the job growth in the auto industry has been in non-union Japanese assembly plants and in smaller non-union parts suppliers. Widespread industrial restructuring in response to free trade with the U.S. after 1988, and the rise of China in recent years, likely drove down union density through a combination of large job losses in union plants because of plant closures and layoffs, and much greater employer hostility to new organizing in a highly competitive environment. Under free trade, workers in Canadian manufacturing were more directly exposed to competition from mainly non-union, lower cost American and Mexican manufacturing operations. The major shift of manufacturing production to Asia, especially China, has produced even more severe competitive pressures on non-resource-based manufacturing, and consequent pressures on wages, benefits, and working conditions of unionized workers. Rather little successful new organizing activity took place in the manufacturing sector in the period of recovery from the mid-1990s to 2002, while job losses since then have disproportionately been in unionized plants. Generally speaking, unionized manufacturing workers have seen only very limited gains in wages and benefits, and representation has been maintained by moving closer to a workplace partnership relationship with employers. For example, the CAW has modified traditional collective agreements in the auto sector to win new investments. As argued earlier, union representation does not necessarily place employers at a competitive disadvantage, provided a business is prepared to adopt a high-productivity strategy and to build a good working relationship with its workforce through the union.

There has also been a marked decline of union density in other industries that have undergone similar restructuring—primary industries, transportation, and, to a lesser extent, communications and utilities. Deregulation saw the rise of competition from lower cost non-union airlines and telecommunications companies, forcing unions at union airlines and telephone companies on the defensive. Many large, unionized companies have contracted out non-core functions to smaller, non-union suppliers, reducing overall union membership and putting intense competitive pressures on their suppliers. By contrast, union coverage in construction has been quite stable at about one-third since the late 1980s. The industrial construction sector remains highly unionized in some provinces, and construction union employment has benefited from the housing and commercial building boom in some cities. Many of the skilled trades have been in high demand, and the pay premium for unionized workers is paid for in significant part by higher skills and higher productivity. Construction unions are typically based on crafts or specific occupations, and the union often plays a major role in directing members to jobs and providing training, pensions, and benefits. Craft unions in construction and in the cultural sector (e.g., unions representing actors, writers, and film technicians) can promote better wages, benefits, and access to training for workers who typically move frequently from one job to another. Their resilience in the 1990s suggests that a very old model of union representation remains quite relevant today, and one could imagine new craft unions emerging to represent workers in, for example, the software development industry.

Union coverage has always been very low in private consumer services like stores, hotels, and restaurants, as well as in financial and business services, but seems to have held up much better than in the traditional high union-density, blue-collar industries since the late 1980s. As shown in Table 10.1, coverage is low (14.3% in 2007) in trade, but fairly stable. Many workers in large grocery stores, alcohol beverage outlets, and a few department stores are represented by unions. Coverage is very low (about 8%), but has always been very low in accommodation and food services (i.e., restaurants and hotels), though many big city hotels and a few restaurants are organized. Coverage is extremely low in business services, though unions have organized some groups of workers like security guards and building cleaners in recent years. Unions are very weak in the financial sector outside of Quebec, but some insurance companies and a few bank branches and credit unions are unionized. Unlike some European countries, Canada has a very weak tradition of union representation among professional and skilled white-collar workers in the private sector, a relatively fast-growing part of the workforce. Since the mid-1990s, union density has been quite steady, but at low levels in private services. This probably reflects a combination of stable employment in some traditionally unionized sectors, and some successful new organizing more or less matching job growth. Union organizing is especially difficult in high worker turnover sectors, and many unions in private services, such as the United Food and Commercial Workers Union (UFCW), typically organize quite a high proportion of their total membership each year. Private service sector organizing has taken place predominantly among lower paid and more precariously employed workers, especially women and recent immigrants.

Turning to geographical trends in union coverage, Ontario and Alberta, where national job growth was relatively concentrated over the past decade, experienced larger-than-average declines in density from already well below-average levels. Traditionally, union density has been low in the Maritime provinces. In 2007, as in 1988, the highest union density provinces were Quebec (39.7%), Newfoundland and Labrador (37.7%), Manitoba (37.1%), Saskatchewan (34.8%), and British Columbia (32.1%). Relative union strength is self-reinforcing to a degree because of the organizational resources it gives to unions, bargaining strength, and, probably most importantly, the union movement's ability to influence governments.

Labour laws in the high union-density provinces were relatively friendly to unions for extended periods in the 1990s, not least because of unions' ties to the New Democratic Party (NDP) in British Columbia, Manitoba, and Saskatchewan, and the Parti Québécois in Quebec. It was more difficult for employers to resist a worker choice for unionization in Quebec than in the rest of Canada, and was harder for unions to mount successful organizing campaigns in Ontario, Alberta, and much of Atlantic Canada through much of the 1990s. Unions generally benefit if labour law requires employers to recognize a union on the basis of a majority of workers in a proposed bargaining unit signing cards, or on the basis of a genuinely free vote, and operate at a significant disadvantage if the law allows employers to fight an active anti-union campaign before a vote (Panitch and Schwartz 2003). A lot also hinges on whether a first contract can be won through arbitration, and whether employers can replace workers who go on strike for a first or later contract. It is not uncommon for a group of workers to win union certification, but to fail to get a first collective agreement because of employer resistance. New union organizing in Ontario surged under the NDP (Rae) government to a high of over 37,000 new members in 2000–2001, but has fallen to well under half that level since, and the same has been true of the NDP and post-NDP government periods in British Columbia. One of the first acts of the newly elected Saskatchewan Party government in that province, in 2008, was to change the law to shift from card check certification of unions to votes. Government attitudes to unions also matter a lot in terms of representing social services workers. Contracting out services to low-bid, often private-sector providers, as is the case with home care services in Ontario, works against union representation, as opposed to service delivery through the public or non-profit sector. One reason for the strength of Quebec unions has been that recognition was given to unions as the broader public sector expanded into areas like child care services.

Public-sector union density is high across all provinces, while private-sector density is much more variable, ranging from a low of just 10% in Prince Edward Island and 12.3% in Alberta, to 16.6% in Ontario, to highs of 19.5% in British Columbia, 20.6% in Newfoundland and Labrador, and 26.3% in Quebec. Only Quebec and Newfoundland and Labrador now have private sector unionization rates above 20%. Union density is also very variable across cities, but is notably lower than the national average in two fast-growing cities, the huge Toronto Census Metropolitan Area (23%) and Calgary (21.7%). It is higher than average in the two other very large urban centres of Montreal (36%) and Vancouver (30.7%).

Forces Driving Union Density

Canadian union representation is usually achieved through a labour board's certification of a union to represent workers in a particular workplace. Almost always,
unionization is a collective rather than an individual choice, and it continues unless
and until there is a vote to decertify the union. Most union members become members
by being hired into a job in an already unionized workplace rather than by actively
joining or supporting a union campaign to organize a non-union workplace. Most
non-union members stay that way simply because there is no active union campaign
to certify the workplace in which they work. Changing union density is thus a function
of three things: changes in employment in already certified workplaces as a result of
establishment closures, layoffs, and new hiring; changes in employment in non-union
workplaces; and the rate at which non-union workplaces are organized into unions.
Unfortunately, it is impossible to fully separate out these factors. Obviously unions
have a direct influence only on the last factor.

At a broader level, the growth of union membership will be strongly influenced by
structural change in the economy, which influences the relative growth of employment by industrial sector, by occupation, by firm or establishment size, and by form
of employment. This is especially true in Canada given that union density varies a lot
along all of these dimensions. Union membership is still concentrated among full-time
workers in larger private-sector firms in resources, manufacturing, transportation, and
utilities, as well as in the public sector. Union density will also be influenced by the
changing composition of the workforce, especially by age, gender, and race, which
is overlaid upon the changing industrial and occupational mix.

Declining unionization has often been associated with the shift to a post-industrial
economy, with a shrinking share of male blue-collar jobs, and a rising share of private
services jobs, especially for women, in growing but low union-density sectors like
business and consumer services. Structural change has brought into question the continued relevance of the labour laws and kinds of unions that emerged in the postwar,
so-called Fordist, era when a high proportion of the workforce could be found in large
industrial workplaces like steel mills and auto assembly plants. Unions, it is often
argued, cannot easily organize workers in small workplaces or in very precarious
forms of employment, and also win little support from well-educated professionals
in the private sector. They thus face the risk of being squeezed by two of the fastest
growing areas of employment.

Other forces of change working against unions include the shifting balance of power
between labour and employers in workplaces and the job market as a result of fiercer
competition, and squeezed profitability in the private sector as a result of globalization
and deregulation, as well as restructuring of public and social services through privatization and contracting out to the private sector. Structural social and economic change
also influences the balance of power between labour and employers at the political
level, and with it the legal and regulatory climate that influences union strength. Studies
of Canada–U.S. density differences have often stressed the importance of facilitative
labour legislation to new organizing. Finally, density will clearly be influenced by the
attitudes of individual workers toward unions, and by the capacity of unions and the

labour movement to attract and mobilize the unorganized, as well to retain the loyalties and commitment of the already organized. At a broad, cultural level, there has probably been a shift to greater individualism among workers, and less of a sense of working-class identity than may have been the case in the 1950s and 1960s.

The idea that declining union density is strongly associated with the changing industrial and occupational composition of employment is plausible and has some elements of truth given the extent to which deindustrialization, privatization, and the growth of knowledge-based work have eroded former bastions of union strength. However, as was shown earlier in this book, the total employment share of blue-collar men who traditionally supported unions has not fallen dramatically since the late 1980s. Employment in high union-density public and social services has been growing as a share of all jobs, and will continue to do so. Looking at sectors of traditional union weakness, it is true that sales and service jobs are a big share of employment, but this has been the case for a long time. One big change that has indeed taken place, however, has been the shift of jobs to business services, partly in professional, scientific, and technical services, which employ mainly higher skilled, very infrequently unionized workers. That said, business services include many less skilled occupations, such as building cleaners and security guards, who have joined unions.

Without denying the long-term trend toward higher skilled jobs (at least as measured by education) or the emergence of new economy information technology occupations, it is hard to see why occupational and industrial shifts should have had a big negative impact on overall union density. A technically sophisticated analysis of the decline in union density from 1984 to 1998 indeed finds that shifts of employment by industry and by occupation, taken together, have had only a modest impact on the unionization rate, and that the decline is explained more by downward shifts within industries and occupations (Riddell and Riddell 2001). For example, the decline of unions within formerly strong union sectors like manufacturing and blue-collar jobs explains more of the fall in union density than a shift of jobs away from manufacturing and blue-collar jobs. That said, unions will obviously have to reach out to more highly skilled new economy workers, as well as to low-paid private services workers if continued private-sector decline is to be halted. A few public-sector unions have attempted to organize private-sector professionals, but with limited success to date.

It is often also believed that unions have become weaker because of the decline of large private-sector workplaces and the rise of small business. It is indeed true that the rate of unionization in the private sector is much higher in large than small establishments. About 40% of workers in large firms with more than 500 workers are unionized, and very large industrial operations are still highly likely to be unionized. It is very difficult to organize and represent workers in smaller businesses under the labour relations practices that generally apply in North America. One problem is that union dues from small workplaces make it practically difficult for unions to effectively represent the workers in them. Another is that small- and medium-sized employers tend to be especially hostile to unions and prefer very informal labour relations practices. Most importantly, it is very difficult for unions to improve wages, benefits, and working conditions in very competitive sectors dominated by smaller firms. High union density in private services in some Northern European countries is made possible mainly by sector-wide agreements, at least at the community or regional level, rather than by North American-style decentralized certification and bargaining. For example, many Scandinavian and German hotel workers are covered by contracts that are bargained centrally and cover almost all hotel workers, placing no single hotel at a competitive advantage, and extending union conditions and protections to workers who are dispersed across many workplaces. Where unions in Canada have gained a foothold among smaller employers, as in the housing construction industry in Toronto, or the child care sector in Quebec, it has often been by developing sector-wide rather than employer-by-employer-by-employer collective agreements and bargaining structures.

All that said, a shift from large to small workplaces does not explain why Canadian union density has declined. In the late 1990s, about 40% of private-sector workers were employed in very small workplaces with less than 20 workers, and about 30% were employed in establishments of more than 100 workers, but this was also the case in the mid-1980s (Drolet and Morrissette 1998). Employment has actually shifted somewhat away from small workplaces. In retailing, for example, there has been a shift from small stores to superstores; in financial services, large call centres have replaced local bank branches; in food services, a lot of food preparation has been contracted out from restaurants to large food processors. And, if anything, recent union organizing successes have been relatively concentrated in small rather than large establishments, and union density has risen (from low levels) in small workplaces while falling in larger workplaces.

Changes in the form of employment have also probably had little impact on union density. Self-employment and part-time employment have become a bit more common, but union density has increased a bit among part-time workers, even in the private sector, since the mid-1990s. The incidence of very low-tenure jobs has not increased since the mid-1980s, and average job tenure has increased. None of this is to deny that many Canadian workers, particularly women, youth, and workers of colour, are employed in precarious and insecure jobs in smaller workplaces, which makes union organization extremely difficult under prevailing labour laws. However, putting all of the emphasis on structural change as a source of union decline can be greatly exaggerated.

New Organizing and Union Renewal

Every year, some non-union workers join unions and gain a collective bargaining relationship with their employer through a labour board certification. Much less commonly, some unions are decertified with the consent of the workers involved. Obviously, if union density is to increase, more workers must be persuaded to build and join unions. Indeed, given that many union employers will shrink or go out of business over time and new businesses will be established, union density will inevitably decline if unions are not organizing many new members. The much slower decline of union density in Canada than in the U.S. in the 1980s and 1990s almost certainly reflects not just more union-friendly labour legislation, but also a greater union commitment to new organizing and movement building. The absolute number of workers organized into Canadian unions each year was, relative to the size of the workforce, probably some five times higher than in the U.S.

Unfortunately, available data from provincial labour boards provide very incomplete information on how many workers are joining unions, and where the new organizing is taking place. From the mid-1970s to the late 1990s, anywhere between 60,000 and 100,000 workers (or as many as 2% of all non-union workers) were organized into unions through new certifications (minus decertifications) each year (Johnson 2002; Katz-Rosene 2003; Martinello 1996). There has been a downward trend since the high point of the mid-1980s, with some ups and downs, and by the late 1990s, just under 1% of all non-union paid workers were joining unions each year. The new organizing rate seems to have slipped even further in recent years. The organization rate has been consistently much higher than average in Quebec and, until recently, in British Columbia. As noted above, the content and administration of labour laws clearly make a major difference.

Box 10.1: "At a Crossroads, Big Labour Digs in"
By Ingrid Peritz, Greg Keenan, and Bertrand Marotte
Canada's labour unions don't exactly follow the words of *Solidarity Forever* when it comes to dealing with each other, but Canadian Auto Workers president Buzz Hargrove has won an ally in the battle against wage concessions.

In the battered forestry sector, where mill closings and job cuts have rivalled if not surpassed those in the auto industry, the Communications, Energy and Paperworkers Union (CEP) of Canada will not allow employers to cut wages, pensions or benefits. But they are ready to start talks a full year before their contract expires and are willing to discuss ways of boosting productivity in a bid to help troubled AbitibiBowater.

But on "wages, pensions and benefits—the answer is no," said CEP national president Dave Coles, standing in solidarity with Canadian Auto Workers president Buzz Hargrove, who drew that line in the sand earlier this week in preparation for talks with the Detroit auto makers later this year.

Unions across the country representing workers in struggling sectors face tough choices as they renegotiate contracts, and those choices have become more stark as the economy has shown signs of slowing. Should they consider wage cuts, as did a local of the United Auto Workers at a Magna International Inc. plant in New York State, to save their jobs? Or should they toe Mr. Hargrove's line?

"Our experience has been that where local unions caved in and made major wage concessions, the mill goes down anyways," Mr. Coles said. "We could give them a 20-per-cent wage reduction and it wouldn't solve the problem."

Those words echoed Mr. Hargrove's statements that his members could have agreed to work for free at a General Motors Corp. plant in Oshawa, Ont., but that would not have saved 1,000 jobs.

Leaders of CEP locals echoed their leader's views.

At the AbitibiBowater plant outside Quebec City, union delegate Jacques Bouchard has already watched 40 workers lose their jobs since last year, with another 45 to follow within a few months.

With that kind of downward trend, he knows the future for workers in Quebec's reeling forestry industry rests with finding common solutions with management. He said the pulp-and-paper union's decision to sit down with AbitibiBowater was a signal of openness, though workers are only willing to go so far.

"Some people are really worried," Mr. Bouchard, president of Local 253 of the SCEP, the French-language acronym for the union, said at the AbitibiBowater plant in Beaupré yesterday afternoon. "We all know the situation in Quebec. Do we keep up our militancy and give up nothing, when we know we'd just hit a wall? Or do we sit down with employers and decide how to keep plants open?"

But he and other union representatives said they favour increasing productivity to cutting wages. "We think it's better to optimize these plants than to cut salaries."

At the Kruger paper mill in Trois-Rivières, union representative Michel Proulx also sees the future through increased efficiency rather than lower pay for workers.

"We're ready to do our share but we're not crazy," Mr. Proulx, president of the SCEP's Local 234, said at the plant yesterday afternoon. "We've already made concessions, by having jobs cut."

The tough stance by the two unions against wage cuts, two-tiered wages and other concessions is the opposite of the tactic adopted by one of North America's oldest unions, the United Auto Workers, which agreed last year to a landmark deal that creates two tiers of wages and benefits at the U.S. operations of the Detroit Three.

The Canadian labour movement "is a venerable institution badly in need of a new mission," said Prem Benimadhu, vice-president of governance and human resource management research at the Conference Board of Canada. "The situation for the labour movement is hugely problematic," Mr. Benimadhu said. "It is very tough to be in the space that Buzz is in and the CEP leaders are in because [of] the economic environment. How do you deal with this issue?"

Mr. Hargrove said he sees his mission to fight concessions as a fight he's leading for the entire Canadian labour movement, not just 35,000 workers at the Canadian units of GM, Chrysler LLC and Ford Motor Co.

He said he had the backing of Canadian Union of Public Employees president Paul Moist, noting that the city of Windsor and other employers of public sector workers will go after their employees if the CAW caves in to the big auto makers.

There is little love lost between Mr. Hargrove and many other national labour leaders, who attacked the CAW head most recently over the Framework of Fairness agreement with auto parts giant Magna, which includes a no-strike clause at any of the company's plants the union is able to organize.

While other labour leaders may oppose that initiative, some of their unions have taken similar hard-line stances.

Forestry workers who are part of the United Steelworkers union went on a three-month strike against B.C. forestry companies last year when the industry was already being devastated by the high Canadian dollar and the beginning of the U.S. housing slowdown.

Nonetheless, the union won wage increases and improvements to benefits and health and safety, Ken Neumann, the United Steelworkers' national director for Canada, said yesterday.

Negotiations with Companhia Vale do Rio Doce, which took over Inco Ltd. last year will begin soon in Sudbury, Ont., and it's a highly profitable location with lucrative bonus schemes for workers that Vale doesn't have at its other operations, Mr. Neumann said.

"I'm not that naive to not think for a moment that they're going to come after that," he said.

Two-tiered wages hit the forestry sector in the United States last summer even while the Detroit Three were still negotiating such deals with the United Auto Workers.

The United Steelworkers signed a deal in August with International Paper Co. that creates a two-tiered wage as well as prohibiting strikes and lockouts at that company's mills for four years. But it also provided wage increases.

*****

Struggling sectors

Makers of cars, forest products and steel are closing plants and demanding concessions from labour to keep other facilities open. A look at recent examples:

FORESTRY

AbitibiBowater closed its plant in Dalhousie, N.B. At last count, only 16 of the 61 mills in New Brunswick were operating at full capacity. According to one estimate, the forestry sector in the province has shed one-quarter of its 20,000 jobs in the past few years.

Canfor Corp., Canada's biggest lumber producer, has closed two mills in Fort Nelson, B.C.—putting 435 people out of work.

TimberWest Forest Corp. announced the permanent closing of its Elk Falls sawmill in Campbell River, B.C., as well as the associated shipping operations at Stuart Channel Wharves located in Crofton, B.C.

AUTO MAKING

GM and its U.S. work force in the fall reached a landmark deal that slashed wages for new workers and handed the responsibility of health care to the union.

UAW workers at Magna's plant in Syracuse, N.Y., voted to reduce wages by about 25 per cent.

Workers at Magna's Integram seat-making plant in Windsor, Ont., are facing non-wage cuts of about $2-million.

PPG Industries Inc., wants a 25-per-cent wage cut, a two-tiered wage structure, and major reductions in benefits at a glass-making plant in Oshawa.

STEEL MAKING

The domestic steel industry has been marked by bankruptcy filings and foreign takeovers.

Algoma, Dofasco, Ipsco and Stelco have all been purchased by foreign companies in recent years.

Source: Peritz, Ingrid, Greg Keenan, and Bertrand Marotte, "At a Crossroads, Big Labour Digs in," *Globe and Mail,* February 22, 2008, B3.

The average size of new bargaining units is small: 50–70 members in Ontario since the mid-1990s, and just 30–40 members in B.C. There is evidence of relative success among women workers and workers of colour, and more new organizing in services, especially health and welfare services (Yates 2000, 2003). In B.C. (where the data are most complete), more than 50,000 workers were organized into unions from 1997 to 2002, of whom just one in six worked in the resource and manufacturing sectors. Large private-sector industrial unions, like the CAW-Canada and United Steelworkers (USW), have continued to add new members alongside the Canadian Union of Public Employees (CUPE), the National Union of Public and General Employees (NUPGE), and other public-sector unions, but many of these new members have been in services, especially the broader public sector, rather than in areas of traditional blue-collar industrial jurisdiction. Large unions have also grown through mergers.

In most years, from the mid-1980s to the mid-1990s, union growth from new certifications offset stagnant or declining union membership in already unionized workplaces, accounting for almost all absolute membership growth. Since the mid-1990s, union membership in already unionized workplaces seems to have grown as well. New organizing in Canada has been far from negligible and has made an important difference to union density, but it has been a case of rowing against the tide of forces working against unions in the job market as a whole.

Observers have often drawn a contrast between an organizing as opposed to servicing model of trade unionism related to a social movement, as opposed to a business union model of what unions are about. While overdrawn, the servicing and business union model stands for the bureaucratic, top-down structures, member passivity, and lack of activism and interest in organizing that were often the results of stable industrial relations in long-unionized firms and sectors in the 1960s and 1970s. Some unions were not particularly concerned about an overall fall in union density or building links to the wider community so long as their own membership was stable and members were making gains at the bargaining table. However, falling overall union strength tends to reach a tipping-point, at which time even long-unionized employers will take a much harder line in bargaining or will seek to become non-union because of increased competition from lower cost, non-union employers. In the U.S., the central labour body, the American Federation of Labor-Congress of Industrial Organizations (AFL-CIO), was quite complacent about union density decline through much of the 1970s and into the 1980s, but this turned to alarm as the absolute number of union members began to fall, and as slipping density began to turn into a downward spiral. By the mid-1990s, almost all American unions recognized that new organizing was absolutely key to survival.

The commitment of unions to organizing new members will be strongly influenced not just by threats to union security in already unionized sectors, but also by whether leaders, activists, and members see themselves as part of a broader labour movement linked to a wider movement for social and economic change. At their best, unions have been concerned about improving conditions for all workers, not just the narrow union elite. Historically, union expansion has come in big waves as a growing labour movement has rapidly expanded into many workplaces over a very short period. In Canada, there were two big waves of union growth. The first was during and just after World War II when hundreds of thousands of blue-collar industrial workers joined unions like the auto workers and the steelworkers. In the process, they transformed a small labour movement that had hitherto been made up of unions mainly representing skilled tradespeople. Indeed, for some years, there were two rival labour central bodies. The second big wave came in the 1960s and into the 1970s when public services unions grew very rapidly, bringing many women and professional workers, such as teachers and nurses, into the labour movement. It is notable that both of these big waves of union expansion coincided with periods of major social reform. One of the big questions today is whether unions are fated to experience a slow and steady decline, or if there will be another big wave of union organizing in the future, perhaps on a very different organizational basis than in the past.

Since at least the 1980s, there has been a gradual process of union renewal in Canada (Kumar and Murray 2002, 2003; Schenk 2003; Yates 2000, 2002, 2003; Kumar and Schenk 2006). The process of renewal is about much more than just organizing new members, and is much more complex than just turning from servicing current members to organizing new members. Organizing is important, but unions abandon servicing of current members at their peril since active and mobilized members are a necessary base for a growing movement. Most people first hear about unions, about what they are like and what they can do, from family and friends. At one level, renewal has been about making unions more democratic and responsive to changes in the workplace and to the changed needs and interests of union members. This has involved changes in leadership and staff with an emphasis on making unions more representative of a changing workforce through the inclusion of more women, workers of colour, and younger workers who are better placed to connect with the new workforce both within and outside unionized workplaces. While the shift has been partial, more women in particular have moved into top leadership and key staff positions.

There have been some changes in structures to make unions more accountable to more active and engaged members. There has been a greater emphasis on internal education and on rank-and-file member involvement in union activities, including bargaining, representing members at the workplace, and sometimes in organizing. There has also been at least a limited shift in bargaining priorities and in workplace activities to issues of interest to the new workforce, including training and work-family balance (Kumar and Murray 2002). There has also been a revival of some of the social movement dimensions of unions, which had atrophied to some degree in the days of greater employer and government acceptance of a major union role. Unions have led major campaigns on issues of interest to all workers—such as the need to protect public health care and public services, pensions, employment and pay equity, human rights, and minimum wages and employment standards—and have built stronger links with community organizations and other social movements.

Many unions have changed rather dramatically as a result of declining membership in some sectors, offset by mergers with other unions and expansion into other sectors. The former big blue-collar industrial unions, such as the auto workers and steelworkers, have become much more like general worker unions, representing a very broad range of workers, including more women, while the main public sector unions have expanded from an original base of direct government employees into the much broader social services sector. Many unions now devote significant resources to new organizing within and outside their traditional areas of jurisdiction. However, resources and staff directed to new organizing are still a relatively small fraction of the total, and many unions still do little organizing outside their areas of traditional jurisdiction (Kumar and Murray 2003). There is also often intense union rivalry in organizing and bargaining, which can be counterproductive in terms of building a stronger movement. Organizing practices continue to vary a great deal, with some unions relying on rank-and-file members and activists much more than others. While there is no magic formula for success, the evidence shows that successful organizing campaigns tend to be those in which there is a great deal of rank-and-file member involvement and close ties to community groups (Bronfenbrenner and Friedman 1998).

A renewal of activism and renewed emphasis on organizing new members help explain some recent successes, particularly among workers in services who would otherwise be in relatively low-paid and precarious jobs. In recent years, there have been notable successes in organizing security guards, hotel workers, workers in long-term care homes, teaching assistants in universities, and even some workers in retail trade and restaurants. Unions have thus had some success in organizing precarious workers. The greater difficulty seems to have been in reaching out to core workers.

Box 10.2: Do Workers Still Want to Join Unions?

Public opinion surveys and academic studies have found evidence of significant, if qualified, continuing worker support for unions. The Canadian Labour Congress (CLC) has commissioned independent surveys, which find that about two-thirds of current union members are satisfied with their own national union, rising to three-quarters who are satisfied with their local union. In 2003, one in seven non-union workers (14%) would "very likely" vote for a union tomorrow if they had the chance. Another 19% would be "somewhat likely" to vote yes, indicating probable one-third support even before any union campaign for certification. Forty-three percent of non-union workers would be "very or somewhat likely" to join a union if there were no grounds for fear of employer reprisal. Underlying support for unions is even higher among young workers aged 18 to 29 (52%), visible minorities (54%), and women (50% vs. 37% for men), showing that the shift to a new workforce is much more positive than negative for the future of unions. Support is somewhat higher from workers in lower income households and much higher for people from families with a union member.

Workers, both union and non-union, see unions as positive vehicles for workplace representation, protection from discrimination and favouritism, better health and safety, job security, higher benefits and pay, and also support unions that are active in community issues. However, non-union members in particular have concerns about the seniority principle, which gives preference in promotions and layoffs to long-tenure workers, and also have concerns about the degree of member control of unions.

Both union and non-union workers, despite the differences one might expect, are generally quite satisfied with their jobs across most dimensions. One of the big gaps, however, is in terms of worker representation. More than 70% of non-union workers would like to see an association represent them at work. There is strong evidence of a major representation gap in the contemporary workplace, even if workers are divided on whether unions, as they now exist, are the best answer for the future.

Future Prospects for Unions

Union density has fallen slowly in the private sector, particularly in the traditional stronghold of male blue-collar industrial workers. It has held up much better among women than among men, mainly because of union strength in public and social services combined with the impact of organizing efforts among lower paid workers. Unions are weak in some important parts of the new knowledge-based economy, but are not doomed to extinction because of structural change or the emergence of a new workforce. There is still substantial worker support for unions as a vehicle for improving pay and benefits and, even more important, for representation of workers in the workplace.

A factor in union weakness in terms of recruiting new members has probably been the fact that unions have had great difficulty making major gains at the bargaining table for their current members, and have been thrown on the defensive by extensive restructuring in both the private and public sectors. This suggests that if unions are to grow, organizing strategies must be linked to finding a new economic role.

In the workplace, unions have often actively co-operated in changes that improve firm productivity, especially by promoting more training and business strategies that rely on higher skills. As noted before, unions are not an anachronism just because union employers face much more competitive markets than in the past. Yet, unions will be much more likely to grow in the business sector if they can again find ways to take wages and working conditions out of the competitive equation to at least some degree.

Organizing a handful of workplaces in a low-density sector is very hard given strong employer resistance, and is unlikely to make a lot of difference for workers. Organizing across an economically relevant labour market is likely to result in greater gains and, beyond a certain threshold, less employer resistance. Bargaining of master agreements with groups of employers also makes union representation in small workplaces more viable. Examples in Canada include a handful of master agreements in hotels, restaurants, and the retail sector. In community social services in British Columbia and Quebec, organizing success has been achieved in part by promoting sector-wide bargaining between all employers and unions.

Broader based organizing and bargaining can also be based on unions working with community organizations. In recent years, notable broader based organizing and bargaining successes in the U.S. have included large groups of low-paid, predominantly minority group workers. For example, the Service Employees International Union (SEIU) has organized downtown office cleaning services in several cities through community-based Justice for Janitors campaigns. The hotel workforce in Las Vegas is highly unionized as a result of union renewal and new organizing across the sector, and wages and benefits are now well above the industrial average (Meyerson 2004). Broader based organizing and bargaining are generally hindered rather than facilitated by current labour laws based on the norm of workplace-by-workplace certification and bargaining, but successful union organizing can make change happen in any case. The industrial unions of the 1930s and 1940s forced industry-wide bargaining, and a new legal framework was put in place over what had already happened.

Another possible path forward is community as opposed to, or in advance of, workplace unionism. Associations of workers, most notably an organization known as ACORN in the U.S., have come into existence to fight for workers' rights and interests outside of collective bargaining. Workers can and do unite to fight for their legal rights under minimum wage and employment standards legislation, and some of these efforts have been supported by unions that also engage in collective bargaining. The Canadian Union of Postal Workers, for example, has supported collective action by bicycle couriers in Winnipeg. The United Food and Commercial Workers has organized and advocated for the rights of migrant farm workers, even though these workers are currently not allowed to organize for purposes of collective bargaining in some provinces, notably Ontario. In the United States, some unions accept associate individual members and act as a vehicle for access to benefits and minimum employment standards. In Canada, to date, there have been only small experiments along these lines, but they remind us that unionism is not confined to any one legal or organizational form.

Conclusion

No one can say with certainty that there will be a future big wave of union organizing in Canada, but unions will remain a presence, in one form or another, as long as there are conflicts of interest between employers and workers, and a desire for dignity and respect as well as more democracy at the workplace. The Canadian labour movement has remained relatively strong, still representing close to one-third of all workers, but most unions agree that change and renewal are essential if a slow decline is to be reversed.

Recommended Reading

- Fairbrother, Peter, and Charlotte A.B. Yates (Eds.). 2003. *Unions in Renewal: A Comparative Study*. New York: Continuum. This study provides an excellent series of articles on union renewal in the U.S., Canada, Britain, and Australia, with good articles on Canada by Pradeep Kumar, Gregor Murray, Chris Schenk, and Charlotte Yates.
- Kumar, Pradeep, and Christopher Schenk (Eds.). 2006. *Paths to Union Renewal: Canadian Experiences*. Toronto: Broadview Press, Garamond Press, and CCPA. The editors provide an excellent review of the process of union renewal with a Canadian focus, and contributors detail aspects of union adaptation and change based on Canadian examples.

- Meyerson, Harold. 2004. "Las Vegas as a Workers' Paradise." *The American Prospect* (January). A lively account of Las Vegas's unusual status as one of the strongest union towns in the U.S., and the difference this has made for hotel and hospitality industry workers.
- Panitch, Leo, and Donald Schwartz. 2003. *From Consent to Coercion: The Assault on Trade Union Freedoms*. Aurora: Garamond Press. A good account of legal restrictions and barriers to union organizing and union action.
- *Studies in Political Economy* 74 (Fall/Winter 2004) contains a forum on "Reorganizing Unions," with an overview by Andrew Jackson, which is one basis for this chapter, and lively and provocative contributions from Pradeep Kumar, Gregor Murray, Chris Schenk, and Charlotte Yates.

Notes

1. Unless otherwise indicated, all unionization data in this chapter are from Statistics Canada's *Labour Force Historical Review*, 2007, or *Labour Force Survey* microdata. From 1962 to 1993, the major ongoing source of data on unionization was the *Companies and Labour Unions Returns Act* (CALURA) return, which was filed annually by most unions with Statistics Canada. CALURA data show that union density in the last year of the survey was, at 32.6%, virtually unchanged from the peak of 33.5% in 1983, giving rise to a general impression of stability. (See Diane Galerneau, "Unionized Workers," *Perspectives on Labour and Income*, Cat. 75-001-XPE (Ottawa: Statistics Canada, 1996) and "Unionization in Canada: A Retrospective," Cat. 75-001-SPE (Ottawa: Statistics Canada, 1999)). However, CALURA data underestimated union coverage due to under-reporting by small unions, particularly prior to the early 1980s, and other sources indicate a decline in density. Labour Canada (now Workplace Information Directorate) data—calculated annually from the reported national membership of unions—show a peak unionization rate of 40% of non-agricultural paid workers in 1983 and 1984, falling to 34.8% in 1990, and to 30.4% in 2003. Comparable household surveys by Statistics Canada (the source of the data in Table 10.1) also suggest a significant decline in density, defined as the proportion of paid workers covered by a collective agreement.
2. Data for 2006, available at www.trinity.edu/bhirsch/unionstats.

References

Bronfenbrenner, Kate, and Sheldon Friedman (Eds.). 1998. *Organizing to Win: New Research on Union Strategies*. Ithaca and London: ILR Press.

Canadian Labour Congress. 2008. "Organizing: Growth and Strength." Available from www.canadianlabour.ca/updir/organizingGrowthStrengthEn.pdf.

Drolet, Marie, and René Morrissette. 1998. *Recent Evidence on Job Quality by Firm Size*. Ottawa: Statistics Canada.

Jackson, Andrew. 2006. "Rowing against the Tide: The Struggle to Raise Union Density in a Hostile Environment." In *Paths to Union Renewal: Canadian Experiences*, ed.

Pradeep Kumar and Christopher Schenk. Toronto: Broadview Press, Garamond Press, and CCPA: 61–79.

Jackson, Andrew, and Sylvain Schetagne. 2003. "Solidarity Forever? Trends in Union Density." Research Paper No. 25. Ottawa: Canadian Labour Congress. www.clc-ctc.ca.

Johnson, Susan. 2002. "Canadian Union Density 1980 to 1998 and Prospects for the Future." *Canadian Public Policy* XXVIII (3): 333–349.

Katz-Rosene, Ryan. 2003. "Union Organizing: A Look at Recent Organizing Activity through Analysis of Certification across Canadian Jurisdictions." CLC Research Paper No. 26. Ottawa: Canadian Labour Congress.

Kumar, Pradeep, and Gregor Murray. 2002. *Innovation and Change in Labour Organizations in Canada*. Ottawa: Department of Human Resources Development Canada.

———. 2003. "Strategic Dilemma: The State of Union Renewal in Canada." In *Trade Unions in Renewal: A Comparative Study*, ed. Peter Fairbrother and Charlotte A.B. Yates, 200–221. New York: Continuum.

Kumar, Pradeep, and Christopher Schenk (Eds.). 2006. *Paths to Union Renewal: Canadian Experiences*. Toronto: Broadview Press, Garamond Press, and CCPA.

Martinello, Felice. 1996. *Certification and Decertification Activity in Canadian Jurisdictions*. Kingston: Industrial Relations Centre, Queen's University.

Meyerson, Harold. 2004. "Las Vegas as a Workers' Paradise." *The American Prospect* (January). www.prospect.org.

Morissette, René, Grant Schellenberg, and Anick Johnson. 2005. "Diverging Trends in Unionization." *Perspectives on Labour and Income*. Statistics Canada Cat. 75-001-XPE (Summer). 1–8.

Organisation for Economic Co-operation and Development (OECD). Chapter 3 "Wage Setting Institutions and Outcomes", 2004. *OECD Employment Outlook*. Paris: OECD: 128–177.

Panitch, Leo, and Donald Schwartz. 2003. *From Consent to Coercion: The Assault on Trade Union Freedoms*. Aurora: Garamond Press.

Riddell, Chris, and W. Craig Riddell. 1998. "Changing Patterns of Unionization: The North American Experience, 1984 to 1998." Department of Economics Working Paper. Vancouver: University of British Columbia.

Schenk, Christopher. 2003. "Social Movement Unionism: Beyond the Organizing Model." In *Trade Unions in Renewal: A Comparative Study*, ed. Peter Fairbrother and Charlotte Yates, 244–263. New York: Continuum.

Yates, Charlotte. 2000. "Staying the Decline in Union Membership: Union Organizing in Ontario, 1985–1999." *Relations Industrielles/Industrial Relations* 55 (4): 640–674.

———. 2002. "Expanding Labour's Horizons: Union Organizing and Strategic Change in Canada." *Just Labour* 1. www.crws.ca.

———. 2003. "The Revival of Industrial Unions in Canada." In *Trade Unions in Renewal: A Comparative Study*, ed. Peter Fairbrother and Charlotte A.B. Yates, 221–244. New York: Continuum.

PART IV
Canada in a Global Perspective

This part of the book looks at how Canada's increasing integration in the global and North American economy has changed the labour market and the world of work, and the extent to which the forces of free trade and global economic integration limit our choices in terms of labour market alternatives.

Chapter 11, "Canadian Workers in a Changing World," focuses upon the impacts of globalization and the Free Trade Agreement (FTA) with the U.S. on Canadian workers and on social programs, arguing that there have been some pressures toward downward harmonization of labour and social standards.

Chapter 12, " Improving Work," compares and contrasts Canada's labour market and workplace institutions to those of some European countries, and argues that the high-inequality and high-insecurity liberal labour market model is not universal, and that there are viable alternatives that Canadians could consider.

Related Websites

- Canadian Centre for Policy Alternatives (www.policyalternatives.ca) is a left-leaning, labour-supported think-tank that has published many studies critical of the Free Trade Agreement (FTA), the North American Free Trade Agreement (NAFTA), and the World Trade Organization (WTO).
- C.D. Howe Institute (www.cdhowe.org) is a right-leaning, business-supported think-tank that has published many studies broadly supportive of the trade deals and trade liberalizations, including even deeper economic integration with the United States.
- European Industrial Relations Observatory (EIRO) (www.eiro.eurofund.ie) monitors trends in work in the European countries. Searches can be undertaken by topic or by country. See "Non-permanent Employment, Quality of Work and Industrial Relations," "Lifelong Learning and Collective Bargaining," "Low Wage Workers and the Working Poor," and "Collective Bargaining Coverage and Extension Procedures."
- International Labour Organization (www.ilo.org) is the UN specialized agency that promotes social justice and internationally recognized human and labour rights. The ILO formulates international labour standards in the form of conventions and recommendations and undertakes and publishes research on many aspects of work.
- Organisation for Economic Co-operation and Development (www.oecd.org) is a Paris-based policy think-tank and research centre supported by the governments

of member countries, which are almost all advanced industrial countries. The website—particularly the sub-site of the Directorate of Labour and Social Affairs (DELSA), contains numerous statistics on member countries and comparative research studies on labour market and social issues.

CHAPTER 11

Canadian Workers in a Changing World: The Impacts of Globalization and Free Trade

Introduction

Earlier chapters of this book have detailed increased precariousness of employment, rising wage inequality, increased income insecurity, and declining union bargaining strength. This chapter looks at the impacts on working people that have resulted from Canada's increased degree of integration into the North American and global economy in terms of trade and investment flows, and how "globalization" in this sense has contributed to negative trends in the job market and the wider society. It sets out some reasons why closer trade and investment ties with other countries, particularly low-wage developing countries, would lead to a process of downward harmonization to lower wages and social standards, and argues that globalization has indeed been a force working against better wages, working conditions, and labour standards. However, globalization is only one element of broader neo-liberal policies that have contributed to negative impacts on workers, including privatization and deregulation, and the consequent shrinking of relatively protected areas of employment, as well as labour market deregulation. Pressures to downward harmonization can be exaggerated, and can be countered by better economic and labour market policies. This theme is taken up in the next chapter.

Globalization: A Race to the Bottom?

In textbook economic theory, increased trade between countries leads each country to concentrate its productive resources in areas of greatest comparative advantage, and this leads to higher national income. The basic idea is that access to larger markets and increased competition will lead to economies of scale, specialization, and higher productivity, and thus to rising living standards. Certainly trade openness has been sold to Canadians on the promise that it would lead to growth, better jobs, and rising incomes.

However, the classical theory of free trade is based on a number of assumptions that are not necessarily true in the real world, not least the assumption that capital does not flow between countries, only goods and services, and that all resources in a country are fully employed. In the real world, a country might be a net exporter of capital, and workers who lose their jobs due to increased imports might not necessarily find comparable or better jobs quickly due to a shortage of expanding sectors. Many economists have noted that the reality of international trade often fails to fit the theory in that governments can and do intervene to shape and create comparative advantage, rather than leave it all to the market. For example, many of today's advanced industrial countries, including the U.S., Germany, and Canada, industrialized behind high-tariff walls, and extended significant government support to the development of infant industries. Many of today's more successful East Asian economies, such as China and South Korea, have similarly industrialized and moved up the value-added ladder, not just by exporting to global markets, but also by actively managing trade and investment flows so as to develop their own industrial capacities. In this context, while few economists today promote relatively closed national economies, at least beyond a certain stage of development, it is something of an open question if it is greater openness to trade and investment that leads to growth and better jobs, or openness twinned to successful national, industrial, and economic policies that build strong export capacities (Prestowitz 2005).

Further, it could be expected that the impacts of trade and capital flow between countries at similar stages of economic development, such as the OECD advanced industrial countries, might be more favourable than those between such countries and low-wage developing countries. The latter have grown quite rapidly from quite low levels over the past two decades. Most economists would argue that there are still gains from trade, but concede that there are "losers" as well as "winners" as industries in high-wage industrial countries restructure, and jobs in labour-intensive manufacturing are shifted to those countries that have the strong comparative advantage of abundant cheap labour. The conventional wisdom of economists has shifted in recent years, to some degree, and many now concede that the rise of China, India, Brazil, and so on as major industrial powers over the past 15 years or so has been a significant factor behind stagnant wages for many workers, rising wage inequality, and the decline of unions (Freeman 2007). The fact that national income may rise due to increased openness also does not mean much to working people if most of the gains flow to much higher profits and to the incomes of the very rich.

Finally, the metaphor of mutually advantageous trade between countries based on specialization and comparative advantage is increasingly misleading in a world economy dominated by large transnational corporations that have few loyalties to any one country, and allocate different elements of their production chains across countries in order to minimize costs while maximizing productivity and quality. Some one-third of U.S. corporate profits are earned outside of the U.S., meaning that the relatively few Americans who own most U.S. corporate assets and the senior managers of U.S.-headquartered transnationals have a rather different take on the costs and benefits of globalization than American workers whose jobs are vulnerable to offshoring and to higher U.S. imports from foreign affiliates of U.S.-owned corporations. To ask if increased free trade is good or bad for the United States misses the point that some gain, and others lose.

There have been many important changes in the global economy over the past three decades and more, driven by new communication and transportation technologies that have sharply cut costs, and by trade and investment liberalization agreements, such as the GATT (now World Trade Organization or WTO) which began after the Second World War, and the Canada–U.S. Free Trade Agreement signed in 1988. The fundamental principle behind such agreements is that countries should not require companies selling into a national market to produce in that market, and should treat domestic and foreign producers in the same way. While many exceptions still exist, this means that corporations are generally free to produce where they want without losing market access. National economies have become more closely integrated as trade and investment flows across borders have grown much more rapidly than the growth of the world economy as a whole (Glyn 2006). Many of those investment flows take place through transnational corporations. These may be based in one country, but offshoring means that many services and component inputs to final products are sourced globally, and final product assembly may also be widely dispersed so as to access different national markets at the lowest cost. Markets for most manufactured goods and at least some services (notably business, financial, and information services) have become much more competitive. In the 1960s, the noted U.S. economist John Kenneth Galbraith described a world in which a handful of large companies dominated national markets for auto, steel and the like, engaged in restrained "oligopolistic" competition with one another, and were generally content to share the wealth generated by their protected market position with workers and, through taxes, with governments. While a very few global industries (such as production of large passenger jets and pharmaceutical drugs) are similarly dominated by a very few companies, the reality in most manufacturing industries and in some service industries is fiercely contested national and global markets, especially in the advanced industrial countries that maintain low tariffs, and have dropped most significant regulatory barriers to imported goods and services.

Companies facing intense competition for market share (and also under increased pressure from the financial sector to maximize short-term profitability) will try to lower wages and benefits along with other costs to match those of their lowest cost competitors; to raise productivity or output per hour, with potentially negative implications for hours of work and working conditions; and will consider shifting production and new investment to jurisdictions where wages are lower. It is true that wages are only one element in total costs, and that what really counts is the level of wages in relation to worker productivity, which is a function of skills and capital investment. That said, corporations very much seek the lowest cost of labour at a given level of technology and productivity.

Industrial restructuring in response to increased global competition has pushed the manufacturing industries in the advanced industrial countries to become much more capital-intensive and productive, and some market share has usually been lost to imports from new global producers. Globalization has thus been one factor behind the slow shrinkage of the manufacturing sector in almost all advanced industrial countries, including Canada (Informetrica 2007). It is very hard to estimate the impacts of increased global competition on jobs and wages based solely on looking at the level of imports in a given sector in a given country, since wages may have fallen and productivity may have increased by working harder or for longer hours in order to avert a rise in the import share. Increased global competition also results in major incentives for companies to move to jurisdictions that levy low business taxes and impose few costly regulations on business, including strong employment standards. This often means lower levels of social protection for working families. Many observers see so-called liberal globalization as prompting a race to the bottom in which mobile global corporations play off workers and governments against each other to the detriment of working people. This has undermined the major gains made in the period after World War II of managed, regulated national capitalism in which unions were strong and comprehensive welfare states were constructed (Teeple 2000; Harvey 2005).

The basic problem of greatly increased competition is compounded by the fact that regulation of the economy at the national level to promote the rights and interests of workers has not been replaced by positive regulation at the international level. To be sure, the conventions of the International Labour Organization (ILO) require governments to promote labour rights and standards, and the *Universal Declaration of Human Rights* ratified by most states protect a wide range of social rights, but no one enforces these commitments. When China joined the WTO, for example, the government was not required to recognize the rights of workers to form independent trade unions or, for that matter, to hold free elections. The only requirement was to provide free access to its market to foreign imports and investments. Companies can thus effectively choose to operate under one set of social rules in Canada, or another in China, while governments must apply the same set of economic rules to domestic and foreign corporations and investors alike.

Globalization is often associated with especially strong pressures to downward harmonization of wages and labour and social standards because of increased trade and investment ties between the developed and developing, low-wage countries. There are certainly grounds for concern that increased North-South trade has impacted negatively on Canadian jobs and wages. The shift of manufacturing to developing countries in Asia and elsewhere in the Americas has been an important cause of plant closures and layoffs in the manufacturing sector, and there are signs of a growing impact on services as telecommunications technology increases the capacity of developing countries to serve our market from a considerable distance for everything from software, to back-office operations, to call centres. Wages in developing countries are, at best, only a small fraction of Canadian wages, including for quite highly educated and skilled workers. The average industrial wage even in large export-oriented and foreign, transnational-owned plants in China is less than one-tenth of that in Canada.

Box 11.1: "Mexico Ready to Eclipse Canada as Continent's No. 2 Auto Maker"
By Greg Keenan
Mexico is riding a boom in small-car sales that has put the nation's vehicle production on track to pass Canada for the first time and become the second-largest vehicle manufacturer in North America this year.

The country, home of the Volkswagen Beetle in North America for decades, saw production begin to take off after the North American free-trade agreement came into effect in 1994.

Now, based on five months of production data, auto industry analyst Dennis DesRosiers estimates auto makers in Mexico are on target to crank out 2.26 million vehicles in 2008, while production in Canada is on pace to plunge 19 per cent to 2.09 million vehicles, its lowest level since 1992. In the U.S., output is falling even faster, with the Big Three companies in Detroit in the middle of their weakest production in 47 years.

While Chrysler LLC and General Motors Corp. [GM-N] have throttled back production in Canada this year—with GM's announcement earlier this week of eight weeks of shutdown at its Oshawa, Ont., truck plant just the latest example—output in Mexico is scheduled to increase even before major investments that are planned for later in the decade come on stream.

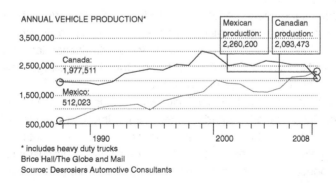

ANNUAL VEHICLE PRODUCTION*

Mexican production:	Canadian production:
2,260,200	2,093,473

Canada: 1,977,511
Mexico: 512,023

1990   2000   2008

* includes heavy duty trucks
Brice Hall/The Globe and Mail
Source: Desrosiers Automotive Consultants

"Mexico is doing quite well in all of this," said Mr. DesRosiers, president of DesRosiers Automotive Consultants Inc.

Longer-term trends also favour Mexico over Canada.

The key factor among those is a dramatic rise in sales of passenger cars, particularly subcompacts. The only subcompacts assembled in North America are built in Mexico because sharply higher labour costs in Canada and the United States combined with the low profit margins on such vehicles make them expensive to build in those two countries.

There's more investment in small cars under way in Mexico. Ford Motor Co. [F-N] will spend more than $3-billion (U.S.) in the biggest single automotive investment yet in the country, which will begin producing subcompact Ford Fiesta cars for North America in 2010.

GM is spending $650-million and hiring 2,000 workers to build its Chevrolet Aveo and Pontiac Wave subcompacts.

One major factor in Mexico's favour is labour costs, and the country is maintaining that edge with further wage reductions. Mexican workers agreed this month to a two-tier wage system that cuts hourly pay for newly hired workers to about half the current level of $4.50 an hour.

The country also has a diverse roster of vehicle manufacturers that exceeds the broad assembly footprint in Canada, which is home to five vehicle manufacturers.

Mexico boasts plants from those same five companies, but also major factories for Nissan Motor Co. Ltd. [NSANY-Q] and Volkswagen AG, which do not assemble vehicles in Canada.

The country's auto sector now resembles Canada's. Autos are its most important manufacturing industry and its largest source of exports. The number of vehicles exported is greater than the number sold domestically and the largest market is the United States, although some auto makers export vehicles to parts of South America as well.

Auto industry investment and exports have grown to such an extent that Volkswagen is establishing a bank in the country.

The prohibitive costs of such new technologies as fuel cells and plug-in hybrids are also expected to favour Mexico in the next decade. As auto makers seek to offset those cuts, countries with lower labour rates will loom large.

"I really do believe we're heading into a decade of opportunity in automotive," Mr. DesRosiers said. "The question is: Who will benefit from that opportunity? Will it be Canada, the U.S. or Mexico?"

At the moment, the soaring price of gas and the U.S. housing crisis are battering Detroit to such an extent that Chrysler, Ford and GM are on track to produce just 7.96 million vehicles this year, which would be their lowest production total since 1961.

But it's not just truck production that has fallen. Output of passenger cars is on pace to drop 5 per cent from year-earlier levels, too.

The slide in trucks and sport utility vehicles will show up in the second-quarter financial results of Canada's largest parts maker, Magna International Inc., RBC Capital Markets analyst Nick Morton told clients yesterday in a research note.

"Given Magna's size, [approximately $26-billion in revenues], its customer concentration and its product mix weighting, it is unlikely to escape unscathed the retrenchment in the auto market," Mr. Morton wrote as he cut his target price for Magna shares to $92 from $110. The stock closed yesterday at $63.52 on the Toronto Stock Exchange.

Mr. Morton noted, however, that Magna's status as a global supplier to Ford and GM could give it a boost as those two auto makers use European and Asian subcompacts as part of their small-car strategies in North America.

Source: Keenan, Greg. "Mexico Ready to Eclipse Canada as Continent's No. 2 Auto Maker," *Globe and Mail*, June 25, 2008, A1.

Canadian workers and unions often face plant closures and layoffs due to rising imports, as well as demands for lower wages and other rollbacks at the bargaining table to compete with lower wages and labour standards in other countries. The jobs that are most vulnerable to relocation are often considered to be those in relatively low-skill and labour-intensive sectors, such as clothing and light assembly consumer goods industries, which have indeed massively contracted as the share of the Canadian market for these goods accounted for by imports has grown. It is now unusual to find an item of clothing, footwear, or even more so, a toy, appliance, or a consumer electronics product in a Canadian store that is made in North America or Europe. Developing countries have also built quite sophisticated industries, such as aerospace in Brazil, where Embraer competes directly with Canada's Bombardier in global markets; auto assembly and auto engine manufacturing in Mexico, which competes directly with our domestic auto industry in both Canada and the U.S. market; and more recently, information technology services and software development in India. Even if only a relatively small proportion of workers in Mexico, India, or China have the education and skills needed in these kinds of industries, their absolute numbers are large, and the advanced industrial countries now have absolutely no monopoly in higher education, skills, or ingenuity.

To take one concrete example, wages in manufacturing in Mexico—which enjoys ready access to the Canadian market under NAFTA—average about one-quarter the Canadian and U.S. level. Mexico entered NAFTA with a significant auto assembly and parts industry oriented mostly to its domestic market, including plants operated by the Big Three North American producers, Volkswagen and some Japanese companies. While wages are far lower, auto assembly plants and many sophisticated parts and engine plants in Mexico employ basically the same technology and work practices as in Canada, though the best Canadian plants are generally seen to enjoy at least a modest productivity and quality advantage. Under NAFTA, the Mexican share of North American auto and auto parts production has steadily grown. In 2008, the shift of the industry to Mexico became even more pronounced when the Mexican unions—in the context of a major wave of threatened North America-wide capacity reduction—agreed to cut the wages of new hires in assembly plants to just $2.50 per hour. It appears that new investment to produce the more fuel-efficient vehicles sought by U.S. and Canadian consumers will disproportionately be undertaken in Mexico, which can produce essentially the same products using the same technologies at a far lower labour cost.

Globalization entered a new phase in the 1990s when the global economy grew enormously in scale and space. Until that time, international trade and investment flows took place overwhelmingly between the advanced industrial countries of Western Europe, North America, and Japan, though an increasing role in manufacturing was being played by the East Asian Tigers—South Korea, Taiwan, Singapore, Hong Kong—as well as Brazil. China and the Soviet Bloc had only modest trade and investment links to the OECD countries, while much of the rest of the world, such as Latin America and Africa, had low levels of both imports and exports even when they had industrially developed. From about 1989, however, there was a massive increase in effective world labour supply as the Soviet Bloc collapsed and as China in particular liberalized and followed the path of industrialization-driven manufacturing for export (Glyn 2007; Freeman 2007). Even pro-globalization economists, such as former U.S. Federal Reserve Chairman Alan Greenspan, have conceded that massively increased foreign production and competition from low-wage countries has resulted in lost jobs and very significant downward pressures on wages.

"Well over a billion workers, many well-educated, all low paid, began to gravitate to the world competitive marketplace from economies that had been almost wholly or in part centrally planned and insulated from global competition. The IMF estimates that in 2005 more than 800 million members of the world's labor force were engaged in export-oriented and therefore competitive markets, an increase of 500 million since the fall of the Berlin Wall in 1989, and 600 million since 1980, with East Asia accounting for half of the increase.... [M]any hundreds of millions of people, mainly in China and India, have yet to make the transition.... [T]his movement of workers into the marketplace reduced world wages.... [E]ven though the aggregate payroll of the newly repositioned workforce was only a fraction of that of developed nations, the impact was pronounced. Not only did low-priced imports displace production and hence workers in developed countries, but the competitive effect of the displaced workers seeking new jobs suppressed the wages of workers not directly in the line of fire of low-priced imports" (Greenspan 2007, 382–383).

Over the past two decades, Chinese exports—almost all manufactured goods—grew by about 20% per year, driven by huge investments in industrial capacity. China has invested a staggering one-fifth or so of its national income in new machinery and equipment investment every year, and trebled its share of global output to over 15% in the last 25 years. Its exports have grown rapidly at the expense of the OECD countries (Glyn 2006). Of course, the global economy has greatly expanded as the Chinese share of that market has grown, but the fact remains that the share of the domestic markets of the OECD countries accounted for by imports from low-wage countries has grown very rapidly, especially in the U.S., which runs huge trade deficits with China and other Asian countries. At least one-half of these Chinese manufactured exports come from the Chinese operations of transnational corporations, as assembly and other relatively low value-added, labour-intensive activities have been shifted from the U.S., Japan, Taiwan, and Korea to China and other low-wage, fast-developing Asian countries. Workers are paid well under $1 per hour even in the more sophisticated export-oriented plants, and engineers and other highly educated workers can be hired at a fraction of North American wages.

> **Box 11.2: Why Can You Buy a DVD Player for under $30?**
> At Christmas time in 2003, American Wal-Mart shoppers found they could buy a
> DVD player for U.S. $29, made by the world's fastest-growing consumer electronics
> company. A report in the *Globe and Mail*, "Employees Boost Earnings with Overtime,"
> June 14, 2004, found that workers at the Chinese plant in Zhenjiang manufacturing the
> low-price players were earning a basic monthly wage of Canadian $74, just enough
> on which to survive. To bring their incomes up to $135 per month, and to meet rigidly
> enforced production quotas, most workers were routinely putting in 12-hour days and
> six-day weeks. One employee reported that he had once worked for 42 consecutive
> hours.

As China has rapidly industrialized by shifting workers from farms and the old
state sector to the export-oriented manufacturing sector in the coastal regions, the
"China price" has fundamentally changed the economics of entire industries, such
as toys, clothing, textiles, consumer electronics, and a wide range of other consumer
goods (Prestowitz 2005; Fishman 2006). By 2005, China produced about one-third to
one-half of total global production of a significant range of consumer goods.

Prestowitz and other observers note that China is not just the world's location of
choice for low-cost commodity manufacturing, but it is also rapidly becoming the
location of choice for high-tech manufacturing and even research and development.
China is now at the point of developing export capacity in the auto assembly sector,
has given birth to at least a few indigenous high-tech firms partnered with world-
leading companies in aerospace and other high-tech industries, and has even induced
some companies such as Microsoft, IBM, and Motorola to locate leading-edge research
in that country.

Limits to Downward Harmonization

All that said, there are limits to the logic of the argument that, in a globally integrated
economy, production and mobile investment capital will inevitably flow overwhelmingly to those countries where investors and corporations find low wages, weak
unions, low taxes, and low social and environmental standards, setting in motion a
competitive race to the bottom in terms of wages and labour and social standards.
This is certainly true to a degree, and very real forces work in this direction. But
sometimes the proponents and critics of globalization alike exaggerate the power of
corporations and the weakness of labour and governments.

Despite all of the rhetoric of globalization, many areas of the contemporary economy
are not very highly exposed to international competition at all, let alone to competition from developing countries. The possibility of relocation of production is largely
confined to manufacturing, still with a bias to labour-intensive production of final
products. It makes sense for corporations to ship clothing production and components
of a laptop to China for final assembly, but transportation costs and time still count
against the offshoring option within complex production chains, which still often

take place in a concentrated geographical area. The fact that parts of a production chain can be profitably offshored may also help sustain the future of the higher value activities that remain in high-wage countries, ultimately limiting the loss of market share to offshore producers. Very capital-intensive manufacturing is also less vulnerable. If industries like auto and aerospace shift in a major way from North America and Europe, it will be a gradual process, driven by new investments at the margin given the large sunk capital investments already in place. Offshoring of services is happening, but service imports still account for well under 10% of the huge markets for private services in advanced industrial countries. Low-wage "McJobs" are better explained by high youth unemployment and low minimum wages than by low wages in China. Most service jobs—from health care to hotels, stores and restaurants, to business consulting, to public services—can be offshored only with great difficulty, if at all. It is true that India has developed a very fast-growing offshore service industry, and that call centres, data analysis, software development, and the like are being relocated, but the overall impacts on jobs and wages are still modest.

There is also some reality and not just rhetoric to the idea that the advanced industrial countries must and can shift to a knowledge-based economy built on innovation, high productivity, and highly skilled and educated workers. These countries, now including countries like Korea and Taiwan, continue to hold an overwhelming comparative advantage in many major and growing industries, from software development, to entertainment, to aerospace and biotechnology, to the manufacturing of sophisticated machinery and equipment of all kinds. Computers may be assembled in China, but advanced computer-controlled machinery in Chinese factories is imported from Japan, Europe, and the U.S. Mobile phones are assembled in developing Asian countries, but new generations of communications technology are mainly designed, developed, and often first manufactured in Japan, Europe and North America. A lot of manufacturing production in terms of a huge physical volume of cheap goods has shifted to the South, but very high-valued goods and services are still overwhelmingly produced in the North. While their manufacturing sectors have shrunk in terms of their overall share of employment, Germany, Japan, and, to a lesser extent, the U.S. still dominate global markets for sophisticated capital goods and global technology development. Only a handful of developing countries, notably Korea and Taiwan, have built genuinely innovative transnational corporations of their own. Because of all of these factors, the volume of North-South trade is still eclipsed by trade among the advanced industrial countries. The Organisation for Economic Co-operation and Development (OECD) countries (basically the advanced industrial countries, plus Korea) still generate about two-thirds of both world exports and imports, and most long-term investment flows are still among these countries. However, there are big differences within the OECD. Western Europe, Japan, and the Asian Tigers hold a strong edge over North America when it comes to balancing their growing imports with higher sophisticated exports to China.

It is also important to bear in mind that, although there is a higher labour content in goods manufactured in the low-wage global South, a large share of the manufacturing export earnings of the South are recycled in the form of imports of goods and services from the North. The problems of globalization posed by low wage-based exports could be ameliorated to a significant degree if global trade were more balanced between regions, and countries like China were to run much smaller trade surpluses. This could be accomplished if currencies were realigned, and also if developing countries could be persuaded or pressed to place more emphasis on the growth of domestic consumption as opposed to trade surpluses and new investment. As production shifts to the South, living standards and wages should gradually rise, feeding the growth of the global market as a whole. This process is far less automatic than pro free trade economists assume. For long periods of time, wages in developing countries can be kept at very low levels because of huge reserves of unemployed and rural workers seeking industrial jobs, and because of severe government and employer repression of unions. Still, wages have increased in South Korea and other developing countries in Asia, including coastal China, and the internal markets of the most successful developing countries have grown more or less in line with exports. The problem of large export surpluses being run by China and other developing countries is not inherent in North–South trade, but results in large part from unstable and highly speculative financial markets, and the legitimate fear of developing countries that they could face devastating currency crises if they do not bank large foreign currency reserves.

The logic of relentless downward harmonization to the lowest common denominator because of global competitive pressures is also suspect to the extent that highly productive and innovative economies rest on a high level of labour and social standards. As detailed in the next chapter, since the mid-1980s, some advanced industrial countries in Europe with very high levels of social spending and unionization did quite well in terms of job growth. The evidence for OECD countries is that there is no clear link from low taxes, weak unions, and low levels of social spending to higher levels of business investment, job creation, and economic growth as one would expect if it was necessary to win a relentless race to the bottom in order to survive global competition (Arjona 2001).

The Impacts of Free Trade Agreements and North American Economic Integration

From the earliest days of European settlement, Canada has been very closely integrated with the changing international economy. Economic historians, such as Harold Innis, have seen our national economic development as a process driven mainly by foreign demand for Canadian resources, from fur and fish, to wheat and forest products, to minerals and energy resources. We have always traded a lot with the rest of the world, and relied on foreign capital to finance new investment until very late in the 20th century. Over time, close trade and investment links with Great Britain and the British Empire gave way to gradual incorporation into a North American economy, with the U.S. becoming by far the most important destination of Canadian exports and source of imports and new investment by the 1940s. It is true that Canada built up a manufacturing sector behind tariff walls from the late 19th century in order to create stable jobs and to limit dependency upon exports of resources, and that Canadian governments helped shape economic development through policies such as the national energy policy and the auto pact through the 1970s. But, the Canadian and U.S. economies were very closely tied together through trade and major U.S. corporate investments in Canada long before the Canada–U.S. Free Trade Agreement of 1988.

For Canadians, globalization was, until quite recently, more about greater economic integration with the U.S. than increased openness to the developing world. The FTA marked a further and important stage in continental economic integration and liberalization. It not only phased out most remaining tariffs and trade barriers, which were modest, but also explicitly prohibited Canada from ever returning to nationalistic economic policies of the kind that had been pursued from time to time in order to actively shape the economic development process. Most notably, the FTA limited the federal government's ability to review, prohibit, or place conditions on U.S. corporate takeovers of Canadian companies, or to block new U.S. corporate investments, or set up new Crown corporations, or give favourable treatment to Canadians when it came to pricing our natural resources or giving out government contracts. While subject to numerous exceptions, the guiding principle of the FTA was that Canadian governments would dismantle barriers to the free flow of goods, services, and investment between the two countries, and treat U.S. and Canadian companies in almost exactly the same way. These same principles have been gradually incorporated, not just into NAFTA, which was created when Mexico joined the FTA, but also into the rules of the World Trade Organization, which now govern Canada's economic relations with most of the rest of the world.

NAFTA and WTO rules did not just liberalize trade and investment flows, but also restricted the ability of governments to regulate corporations in the public interest and to maintain a public sphere outside of the market economy. Critics of these agreements, such as Stephen Clarkson (2002), point out that they form a new constitution that entrenches not only the principle of non-discrimination against foreign corporations, but also the free market or neo-liberal ideological principle that governments should intervene in the market to only a very limited degree. Trade rules tend to reinforce the currently dominant view that governments should not intervene too greatly in the decisions of business on where and how to operate, and should not insulate large sectors of the economy from the forces of the so-called free market.

The General Agreement on Tariffs and Trade (GATT), which governed liberalization of Canadian trade before the FTA, NAFTA, and the recently concluded WTO agreement, used to be almost exclusively about trade in goods and lowering tariffs, and had few (if any) implications for the boundary between the market and the state outside of a limited set of industrial development policies. But new agreements, such as NAFTA and the General Agreement on Trade in Services (GATS), which is an extension of the WTO, intrude much more deeply into the sphere for democratic choice by restricting the ability of governments to maintain a non-market sector or to change the boundaries between the market and non-market sectors in line with the shifting winds of democracy. Pushed actively by transnational corporations, the fundamental premise of these agreements is that commercial providers should, subject to certain exemptions, have the right to establish in national markets, and be given the same treatment as domestic providers (the principle of national treatment). NAFTA broke new ground by codifying investment rights and extending trade liberalization rules from goods to services like communications, finance, and culture, and by creating (through Chapter 11) a means through which foreign corporations could directly challenge government decisions outside of domestic legal processes (through investor-state disputes settlement as opposed to GATT provisions for the resolution of state-to-state disputes). While GATS does not have investor-state provisions, it does envisage setting up domestic tribunals to which transnational corporations could turn for redress. Agreements have increasingly effective enforcement mechanisms, usually based on narrow constructions of rules arrived at in private sessions of trade specialists. The central point is that privatization and the erosion of the public and not-for-profit sectors are already being promoted through binding trade and investment agreements to some degree, and that the pressures are mounting.

Box 11.3: Trade Deals and Public and Social Services

While the underlying presumption of trade and investment agreements is that all sectors should be liberalized and opened up to transnational corporations and investors, exemptions are provided for in general terms and under the specific terms through which states adhere to particular agreements. In the case of GATS, the general exemption for public services is very narrow. Only services "provided in the exercise of governmental authority" are exempt in principle, and this is narrowly defined to make it clear that services provided by governments on a commercial basis, or in competition with private suppliers, are included. Under NAFTA, services such as health, education, child care, income insurance, and welfare services are excluded "to the extent that they are social services established or maintained for a public purpose." The meaning of this phrase has never been definitively established, but the U.S. government's position has been that, like GATS, this excludes only monopoly government services and does not exclude government services delivered in competition with the private sector.

Neither the GATS nor NAFTA general exemption are clear on the potential application of trade and investment rules to areas of mixed public, private, and not-for-profit delivery, yet health care in Canada is a mixed system, with not-for-profit hospitals and private doctors and private laboratories delivering services paid for by governments. The same can be said increasingly of education and skills training, of child care, and of many community services, such as home care and elder care. The Canadian social welfare system is a patchwork of public services, private services contracted for by governments or delivered in competition with government services, and not-for-profit services provided on contract to governments or provided with the support of government grants and subsidies. There is a range of means through which government support is provided, from grants and contributions, to subsidies, to exclusive contracts, to contracts awarded on the basis of competitive bidding.

The position of the Government of Canada as of 2004 was that health and social services should be excluded from trade and investment agreements on the still-untested NAFTA model. However, the report of the Romanow Royal Commission on Health Care argued that if privatization advanced beyond a minimal stage, the NAFTA-type exemption would no longer be adequate. For example, if the government of Alberta begins to seriously experiment with delivery of public health care through private hospitals, it will be difficult, if not impossible, for future governments to return to a not-for-profit system without paying compensation to U.S. health corporations that had entered the Canadian market.

The Free Trade Debate

The great national debate in the late 1980s over the Canada–U.S. Free Trade Agreement split Canada down the middle. While the Mulroney Conservative government won the 1988 election, which was fought almost entirely on the FTA deal, a majority of voters backed the Liberals and NDP who opposed the deal. Supporters, such as the Business Council on National Issues and many economists and conservative think-tanks, argued that there would be significant economic gains from trade and investment liberalization that would be shared with workers in the form of higher wages in better jobs, and that a stronger economy would support and sustain social programs. In line with the economics textbook argument for gains from trade, tariff elimination was expected to lead to higher productivity and a stronger manufacturing sector (Department of Finance 1988). Labour adjustment was seen as a small, manageable problem because it was assumed that there would be a small overall job gain as workers moved from shrinking to expanding sectors and firms.

For their part, critics such as unions and the nationalist Action Canada Network feared major job losses and argued that closer trade and investment ties with the U.S., and the reduced power of government to control those ties, would increase the bargaining power of mobile corporations compared to workers, unions, and governments. Threats to move investment, production, and jobs to the U.S. would work toward downward harmonization of social standards that add to business costs. Free trade was seen as a threat to the more progressive and more equal Canadian social model of stronger unions, higher levels of income protection, and broader access to public and social services (Cameron 1988; CLC 1987). Critics also argued that the FTA risked freezing the status quo of excessive resource dependency and a relatively weak manufacturing sector. The difference was not so much over whether trade with the U.S. was a good or bad thing as over how much policy space was needed to manage trade and to shape the economy in the interests of Canadian workers and communities.

Structural Economic Change

Canada–U.S. economic integration in terms of two-way trade flows proceeded extremely rapidly in the wake of the FTA, far faster than anyone on either side of the debate had anticipated. Exports and imports both almost doubled as a share of the economy over the 1990s. Most manufacturing industries have become even more strongly oriented to the North American rather than domestic market to the extent that the U.S. is now a larger market for Canadian-based manufacturers than is Canada itself, and most of the Canadian market for manufactured goods is now met from imports. Some industries, such as auto and telecommunications, are now so closely integrated that components cross and recross the border as they move between different productions sites of the same companies.

The FTA was expected to help close the long-standing Canada–U.S. productivity gap, but at best, the gains were modest in the most heavily liberalized sectors. Many smaller plants went under, but the plants that survived did not necessarily expand. The overall Canada–U.S. gap in terms of productivity or output per worker has actually widened since the late 1980s, mainly because Canada has been relatively weak in the knowledge-based sectors where productivity growth has been most rapid. A plethora of reports from the OECD (e.g., OECD 2008), the Conference Board of Canada, and other business think-tanks have documented and lamented the growing Canada–U.S. productivity gap that free trade was expected to narrow, while generally favouring even more trade and investment liberalization.

Because of weak productivity growth, Canada's healthy export position in the U.S. market through the economic recovery of the 1990s until 2002 was almost entirely due to stagnant real wages and the continuing fall of the Canadian dollar rather than to building up a more sophisticated industrial economy. The long-standing structural problems of Canadian industry remain with us: too many small, undercapitalized plants; relatively low business investment in machinery and equipment, research and development, and worker training; and overdependence on production of resources and low value-added industrial materials as opposed to finished goods. Deeper integration of the manufacturing sector in the North American economy has done little to decisively shift the structure of the economy toward the more dynamic and faster growing, higher wage, knowledge-based industries capable of withstanding growing global competition and tapping into developing country markets. Canada certainly has some strength in a few high-tech industries like communications, biotechnology, and aerospace, and our auto industry is large and important. But, business investment in research and development is confined to a very few firms and sectors, and is less than half the U.S. level as a share of the economy.

While it was hoped that free trade would support a higher value-added industrial economy, resources and resource-based, low value-added products like oil and gas, lumber, pulp and paper, and minerals have continued to make up a large share of our exports, and resource dependency has grown significantly since 2002. Resources are an important and continuing source of wealth and jobs, and help sustain regional economies, but sectors like mining and energy are extremely capital-intensive and provide very few direct jobs. It will be very hard to raise Canadian living standards and to sustain and create well-paid jobs over the long term if we do not shift production toward more unique or sophisticated goods and services that can command a price premium in world markets, and are better placed to withstand competition from producers in low-wage countries.

The immediate labour adjustment costs of the FTA turned out to be much greater than had been forecast, partly because the Canadian dollar was very overvalued against the U.S. dollar just as the deal came into effect. Between 1989 and 1991, more than one in five manufacturing workers lost their jobs through a massive wave of layoffs and plant closures that devastated industrial communities throughout Ontario and Quebec. The adjustment programs that had been promised were not delivered, and many older workers were forced into premature retirement. Other workers found new jobs, but at much lower wages. The lost jobs in manufacturing were, over time, more than offset by gains in the firms and sectors that survived restructuring, and eventually began to grow as the Canadian dollar fell against the U.S. dollar after 1992. The scale of change in manufacturing that disrupted the lives of so many working people is underlined by the fact that half of all the plants in existence in 1988—accounting for more than one-quarter of all jobs—had closed by 1997, while 39% of all plants in 1997—accounting for 21% of all jobs—did not exist at all in 1988 (Baldwin and Gu 2003).

Globalization and Canadian Workers Today: The Resource Boom and the Manufacturing Jobs Crisis

As of 2007, manufacturing continues to be an important direct source of almost two million good jobs due to above-average productivity, the result of higher-than-average capital investment per worker and a strong base of skilled workers. These jobs pay about $21 per hour on average compared to hourly wages of perhaps $15 per hour in private services where most of the net new jobs in the business sector are being created. Manufacturing jobs are also more likely to be full-time jobs, to provide pension and health benefits, and to be unionized. Displaced workers must compete for other jobs, lowering wages in other sectors in periods of layoffs, and usually face significant pay cuts in new jobs. Even though the manufacturing sector has been shrinking as a share of employment over time due to rising productivity and increased imports, it still supports many good jobs in both private and public services, and tends to set a wage standard that spills over into other sectors. The state of manufacturing is thus important to the overall health of the job market. While often denigrated as part of an "old economy" that must be replaced by a new "knowledge-based economy," it should also be noted that the majority of all business research and development in Canada, in fact, takes place in manufacturing, especially in industries like aerospace and electrical machinery and equipment (Informetrica 2007).

After 10 years of relative stability, the manufacturing sector entered a new period of crisis and restructuring in 2002. More than 300,000 direct manufacturing jobs were lost over the five years through 2007. The major cause has been a competitiveness squeeze caused by the high dollar and a huge and growing trade deficit with Asia. Jobs have been lost to plant closures and layoffs caused by lower production, a corporate drive for intensified productivity in remaining operations, and increased outsourcing of production inputs, especially services to other countries as part of the creation of global value chains. By sector, job losses have been greatest in auto, forest products, and clothing and, in the capital goods sector, computers and telecom equipment, which never fully recovered from the dot-com bust of 2000. The impact has also been greatest in the unionized manufacturing sector, which has accounted for half of the job losses even though only one-third of manufacturing jobs are unionized.

The Canadian economy is being driven by a geographically and sectorally concentrated resource boom. Prices of oil and gas and many base metals have soared, leading to increased production and major investments in new capacity, most notably the Alberta tar sands and new mines. These higher commodity prices, along with the huge U.S. balance of payments deficit, led to a major appreciation of the Canadian dollar against the U.S. dollar from a low of 62 cents U.S. in 2002 to parity in 2007. Since major Asian currencies (notably those of China, Japan, and Korea) are closely tied to the U.S. dollar, Canadian competitiveness with Asia has been severely eroded. The higher Canadian dollar has led to further losses of the Canadian market to imports, and to the loss of Canadian market share in the U.S. to Asia. In 2007, China accounted for 16.3% of U.S. imports, up from 10.7% in 2002. Over the same period, the Canadian share of U.S. imports fell from 18.2% to 16.3% (Informetrica 2007).

A large deficit in the trade of manufactured goods, defined as non-resource-based goods, opened up from 2002, and by 2007, the Canadian trade deficit with China and developing Asia was even greater as a share of the economy than that of the U.S. Canada's overall merchandise trade surplus, once quite high, had shrunk to almost zero by 2007 despite high energy and mineral prices, and Canada imported about $1.30 worth of manufactured goods for every $1 of manufactured exports. The deficit in trade of manufactured goods rose from $22.4 billion in 2002 to $59.9 billion in 2007. (Manufactured goods are defined as machinery and equipment, consumer goods, and auto products combined, as opposed to resource-based and industrial goods, such as pulp and paper, ore concentrates, chemicals, and fertilizer, which are at best only semi-processed.) In 2007, Canada imported $35 billion worth of goods, mainly consumer goods and machinery and equipment from China, but exported just $7.7 billion worth of goods, mainly resources, to that country in return. Canada also ran large trade deficits with Korea, Japan, and virtually every country in the world except the U.S., which is the almost exclusive buyer of our oil and gas exports. (Canadian trade data by commodity, country, and year can be found at www.strategis.ca.)

Relatively few Canadian manufacturers have taken advantage of the high dollar to purchase machinery and equipment in an effort to restructure their operations in a more positive way for workers. The dominant response to a more competitive global market has been to shift non-resource production out of Canada, rather than to upgrade the productivity and innovativeness of production capacity in Canada. New Canadian business investment has instead been concentrated in the oil and gas and mining sectors, accounting for over 40% of all business investment in 2007. Since 2002, our exports have become even more dominated by resources and industrial materials, such as ores and concentrates, chemicals, potash, etc. The share of manufactured goods in our exports has fallen from 52% to 42%. There has, then, been a major reversion to Canada's traditional role in the global economy as a resource producer, rather than a more inward driven and controlled path of economic development.

The conventional wisdom has been that the shrinkage of the manufacturing sector is not a major problem. But, the rising manufacturing trade deficit is troubling in that resource exports can finance only about one-fifth of our imports, and services exports make up only 13% of our exports. It is far from clear that Canada can pay its way in the world if it becomes a highly specialized resource producer for the global market. More importantly, good new jobs have not been created in sufficient numbers to replace lost manufacturing jobs. While there are certainly good jobs in the resource sector, mines and oil and gas production are extremely capital-intensive operations that, once built, will require relatively few workers. There are potential problems down the road if manufacturing shrinks too much, especially if growth is driven by an energy sector that is based on non-renewable resources being extracted far too fast in an environmentally unsustainable fashion, with little value added in Canada. Resource-led economies are prone to boom-bust cycles and to having a relatively narrow core of good jobs, as opposed to diversified economies with a strong manufacturing base, which are more stable and have relatively more jobs in higher productivity sectors.

Harmonization to the U.S. Social Model?

In the free trade debate of the late 1980s, advocates argued that a stronger economy would support better social programs. However, after the deal was signed, business increasingly argued that high social expenditures, financed from progressive taxes, made Canada uncompetitive in a shared economic space. Competitiveness came to be defined as lower taxes, lower social spending, and more flexible labour markets. Experience has shown that there are indeed downward pressures from North American economic integration on progressive, redistributive social policies that arise mainly from the tax side.

Canada used to have a very different social model than the U.S., which was valued by most Canadians. Among the elements of difference, Canada had—and indeed still has—a significantly more equal distribution of both earnings and after-tax/transfer (disposable) income, which reflects higher unionization, somewhat higher minimum wages, and a smaller pay gap between the middle and the top of the earnings spectrum. More equal after-tax incomes and lower rates of after-tax poverty than in the U.S also reflect the impacts of a more generous system of transfers acting upon a somewhat more equal distribution of market income. Until the changes of the mid-1990s, the Canadian Unemployment Insurance system was notably more generous than that of the U.S., and Canadian welfare programs benefit a larger share of the non-elderly, non-working poor. All Canadian provinces, but no U.S. states, provide welfare to singles and families without children, and social assistance benefits, while low and falling in real terms, are generally higher than in the U.S. In the mid-1990s, the Canadian poverty rate for all people was just over half the rate in the U.S., using a common definition of less than half of median household income, and the minimum distance between the top and bottom 10% of families ranked by income was four to one compared to almost 6.5 to one. The level of services provided on a citizen entitlement basis is also higher in Canada than the U.S., reducing dependence on market income for some basic needs. Medicare is the key example, but Canada also provides a somewhat higher level of community services, such as not-for-profit child care, home care, and elder care services. Greater equality has sustained better social outcomes in terms of health, crime, and educational attainment.

Economic Integration and Income Inequality

As detailed earlier in this book, there has been a significant increase in income inequality among working-age Canadian families over the past decade, driven by stronger wage growth for high-income earners and cuts in social transfers. While many factors have been at play, there is a link between increased global competition and the stagnation of average wages, with part of that linkage running through a weakened labour movement. Real wages have failed to rise in line with productivity, and the decline in unionization and labour bargaining power has been greatest in the manufacturing sector, the most exposed to the reality and threat of disinvestment. There is also a link between continental integration and the increased market incomes of the most affluent Canadians. Closer trade and investment links and more investment by Canadian and U.S. transnationals on both sides of the border have led to convergence of salary and stock options for highly mobile professionals and managers in the corporate sector upwards to U.S. levels. This has driven the increased income share of the top 1%. Interestingly, this has not happened to the same degree in Quebec, where senior corporate executives are, for cultural and linguistic reasons, much less likely to be tempted to move to the U.S.

Economic Integration and Social Programs

Closer integration can be linked to the erosion of income transfers to the working-age population and cuts to social programs. Many people would argue that the Employment Insurance (EI) cuts imposed by the Liberal government in 1995, cuts in federal transfers to the provinces for social programs, and provincial welfare cuts were driven primarily by deficit reduction goals, which is true to a degree. However, the Department of Finance, the OECD, and the International Monetary Fund (IMF) have long argued that Canada's supposedly generous welfare state is associated with a stronger tendency to wage-driven inflation than in the U.S. The basic argument is that income benefits strengthen the bargaining power of workers and their willingness to hold out for better wages if and when they become unemployed. Cuts to transfers, particularly EI, were consciously intended to promote greater labour market and wage flexibility (Jackson 2000; Sargent and Sheikh 1996). In short, closer integration with the U.S. and increased low-wage competition made the U.S. model of a more minimalist welfare state attractive to those who worried about the relative strength of Canadian workers.

Competitive pressures to social policy convergence are exaggerated to the extent that progressive and redistributive social models have significant economic pluses. A good economic argument can be made that integration per se does not mean that Canada has to harmonize down to lower levels of social spending and public services in order to build a productive economy. Further, Canada–U.S. tax differences in the mid-1990s were quite small, and slightly higher business taxes in Canada were offset by other cost factors for business, such as lower energy prices and lower health costs for workers. Yet, all that said, the operative, endlessly repeated argument of business organizations and the policy mainstream in the era of free trade has been that economic success will go to countries that most closely copy the U.S. model of weak unions, low taxes, and low social spending. Over the 1990s, particularly after the elimination of the federal deficit in 1997, the political argument was constantly advanced that taxes had to be cut to U.S. levels to maintain competitiveness and fuel economic growth and job creation. The argument was that Canadian business taxes (corporate income taxes and capital taxes) and personal income taxes on higher earners were too high compared to the U.S., making the U.S. a more attractive location for mobile corporations to invest and produce. A great deal of stress was placed on the need to cut corporate taxes and taxes on high-income earners by business lobby groups, such as the Canadian Council of Chief Executives and the Chamber of Commerce, and conservative think-tanks, such as the C.D. Howe Institute.

The extent of "fiscal discipline" imposed in Canada during the 1990s was by far the greatest of any major OECD country, including countries with worse deficit and debt positions at the start of the 1990s (Stanford 2004). In fact, between 1992 and 2002, total government program spending in Canada fell by 10 percentage points of GDP compared to an OECD average of just one percentage point. Of this reduction, about half came from federal program spending cuts. The major impact was on social programs and public services. Spending cuts were not reversed after budgets were balanced since the business lobby for deep tax cuts won the day. Driven by personal and corporate income tax cuts that began in 2002, the federal government's share of national income has been cut by more than two full percentage points of GDP, or the equivalent of $25 billion since 1997–1998 (Department of Finance 2007). Provincial tax revenues have also fallen as a share of the economy. Among the personal income tax cuts was the elimination of the high-income surtax, and a major reduction (from 75% to 50%) in the proportion of capital gains income that is subject to income tax. (More than half of capital gains income goes to very high-income people earning more than $250,000 per year.) The federal corporate tax rate was cut by one-quarter, from 28% to 21%, and will be further cut after 2008. Thus, after the federal deficit was eliminated, much of the growing federal surplus went to the tax cuts that business argued were needed for competitive reasons rather than to reinvestment in social programs.

While Canadian governments still spend a bit more on social programs and public services than U.S. governments, the difference has shrunk dramatically. Between 1992 and 2001, total Canadian government spending on programs other than defence fell from 42.9% to 33.6% of GDP, while U.S. government spending on non-defence programs remained almost the same (increasingly slightly from 27.7% to 27.9% of GDP). Thus, the once very large gap between the two countries fell from about 15 percentage points of GDP in 1992 to just six percentage points in 2001(Department of Finance 2003). A more recent study by Ferris and Winer (2007) concludes that government spending, when corrected for accounting differences, is now almost exactly the same size in both countries, 38.5% of Canadian GDP compared to 37% of U.S. GDP in 2004. Non-defence-related government spending is, according to the authors' estimates, still more than 5% of GDP higher in Canada than in the U.S. (37.5% vs. 32.7% in 2004), though that is down very sharply from the huge 16% of GDP (50% vs. 34%) peak gap between the two countries in 1994. In fact, they find that government transfers to people now account for *less* of GDP in Canada than in the U.S. (11.9% vs. 10.1% in

2004). This reflects deep cuts to Employment Insurance and social assistance, combined with the fact that the U.S. spends more on public pensions and on income supports for the working poor. The key point is that the once very significant Canada–U.S. differences in the relative priority given to social spending or lower taxes have greatly eroded in the era of greater economic integration.

Public opinion surveys show that there was a deep class cleavage over the key issue of tax cuts or social reinvestment after the federal budget was balanced in 1997. Polling in 1998 for the Department of Finance found that lower income groups were most supportive of social spending, and that all but the very highest income groups placed a greater priority on social investment than on tax cuts, and rejected harmonization of Canadian and U.S. tax policies. A survey that regularly charts differences between elite and non-elite opinion found that only the former very strongly favoured corporate and personal tax cuts as the best use of the emerging federal surplus (Mendelsohn 2002). In the final analysis, corporate elite views on the need for tax cuts for competitiveness were the most influential, and the desire of middle and lower income Canadians for significant social reinvestment went largely unheeded.

This cleavage between elite and non-elite views has probably been influenced by the cultural and not just the economic implications of North American integration. In an ever more closely integrated economic space, corporate executives see their personal prospects and future in continental terms, and make comparisons of their personal well-being to their American peers rather than to other Canadians. Career prospects have been continentalized through transnational corporations operating on both sides of the border. The Canadian trade-off of higher taxes for better services and greater security is also less relevant to high-income groups who can afford to buy what they need on the market. By contrast, for middle-class and lower income families, the trade-off of higher taxes for social programs is still relevant, and comparisons to U.S. disposable income are not very relevant.

There continues to be space for autonomy in social policy, and the Canadian social model is not doomed to extinction just because of ever closer trade and investment ties with the U.S. But there are strong downward pressures on our capacity to finance social spending, which arise from strong pressures to lower business taxes and taxes on high-income earners to U.S. levels. This compounds inequality in Canada, particularly at a time when earnings are becoming much more unequal.

Conclusion and Implications

Globalization, the FTA, and NAFTA have significantly increased competitive pressures on Canadian corporations, and resulted in erosion of the bargaining power and living standards of working people. The new trade agreements also pose major issues for the future capacity of governments to regulate corporations in the public interest and to maintain a public sphere outside the market. The issues posed by these developments will remain very much with us in the years ahead given business proposals for still deeper continental integration, plus further liberalization of the international trade and investment rules. The services sector will be increasingly affected by liberalization, especially under the GATS, and developing countries, especially China, will become much more important players in the global economy of the future. In response to these developments, critics have advanced a range of alternatives. The so-called anti-globalization movement embraces a very wide range of views, from supporters of economic nationalism who want democratic national governments to have much greater control over corporations operating within their borders, to progressive internationalists who support a more global economy, but want it to operate under a different set of international rules. The former argue that economic and political space has to be reconnected at the national level to make democracy a continuing reality. The latter argue that globalization is here to stay, and that it is possible to build a different kind of global economic order. The international trade union movement, for example, has called for provisions in trade and investment agreements to require countries to respect and enforce basic labour rights, and there have been a number of initiatives to establish binding rules of conduct on transnational corporations in their worldwide operations. In Europe, the ongoing economic integration process has had an explicit social dimension, and there are European Union-wide common standards in a few key areas, such as hours of work and health and safety rules.

It is argued in the next chapter that small, open economies such as Canada still retain considerable capacity for political choice at the national level, and countries can certainly work together to shape a different international agenda. In short, globalization is a powerful force, but it remains a force that can be shaped by citizens and governments.

Recommended Reading

- Clarkson, Stephen. 2002. *Uncle Sam and US.: Globalization, Neoconservatism, and the Canadian State.* Toronto: University of Toronto Press. A very detailed analysis of the impacts of the free trade agreements with the U.S. on living standards and on a wide range of Canadian public policies. The author tries to carefully separate out the impacts of what he describes as the "new constitution" of trade rules from other forces for change.
- Glyn, Andrew. 2006. *Capitalism Unleashed: Finance, Globalization, and Welfare.* Oxford: Oxford University Press. A readable, critical overview of contemporary global capitalism with some consideration of the impacts on living standards of working people.
- Macdonald, Ian L. (Ed.). 2000. *Free Trade: Risks and Rewards.* Kingston: McGill-Queen's University Press. A collection of papers that are broadly supportive of the FTA based on the first 10 years.
- Teeple, Gary. 2000. *Globalization and the Decline of Social Reform: Into the Twenty-first Century.* Toronto: Garamond Press. A critique of the impacts of globalization on workers.

References

Arjona, Roman, Maxime Ladaique, and Mark Pearson. 2001. "Growth, Inequality, and Social Protection." Draft OECD paper presented to the IRPP-CSLS Conference on Linkages between Economic Growth and Inequality, Ottawa, January 26–27. www.oecd.org.

Baldwin, John, and Wulong Gu. 2003. *Plant Turnover and Productivity Growth in Canadian Manufacturing.* Ottawa: Statistics Canada.

Cameron, Duncan (Ed.). 1988. *The Free Trade Deal.* Toronto: Lorimer.

Canadian Labour Congress (CLC). 1987. *Canadian Labour Congress Submission to the House of Commons Standing Committee on External Affairs and International Trade,* December 4.

Clarkson, Stephen. 2002. *Uncle Sam and U.S.: Globalization, Neoconservatism, and the Canadian State.* Toronto: University of Toronto Press.

Department of Finance. 1988. *The Canada–U.S. Free Trade Agreement: An Economic Assessment.* Ottawa: Government of Canada.

———. 2003. *Government Spending in Canada and the U.S.* Working Paper 2003–05. Ottawa: Government of Canada.

———. 2007. *Fiscal Reference Tables.* www.fin.gc.ca.

Ferris, J. Stephen, and Stanley L. Winer. 2007. "Just How Much Bigger Is Government in Canada? A Comparative Analysis of the Size and Structure of the Public Sectors in Canada and the United States, 1992–2004." *Canadian Public Policy* 33 (2): 173–206.

Fishman, Ted. 2006. *China Inc.* New York: Scribner.

Glyn, Andrew. 2006. *Capitalism Unleashed: Finance, Globalization, and Welfare.* Oxford: Oxford University Press.

Greenspan, Alan. 2007. *The Age of Turbulence: Adventures in a New World.* New York: Penguin Press.

Harvey, David. 2005. *A Brief History of Neo Liberalism.* Oxford: Oxford University Press.

Informetrica. 2007. *Structural Changes in Manufacturing.* www.informetrica.com/IL_ManReport1_Final.pdf.

Jackson, Andrew. 2000. "The NAIRU and Macro-Economic Policy in Canada." *Canadian Business Economics* (August): 66–82.

Mendelsohn, Matthew. 2002. *Canada's Social Contract: Evidence from Public Opinion.* Ottawa: Canadian Policy Research Networks. (See charts 56, 118, 119, 123, 124, 149, and 152.)

Organisation for Economic Co-operation and Development (OECD). 2003. *Economic Survey of Canada,* Table 29. Paris: OECD.

———. 2008. *Economic Survey of Canada.* Paris: OECD.

Prestowitz, Clyde. 2005. *Three Billion New Capitalists: The Great Shift of Wealth and Power to the East.* New York: Basic Books.

Sargent, Timothy C., and Munir A. Sheikh. 1996. *The Natural Rate of Unemployment: Theory, Evidence, and Policy Implications.* Department of Finance, Economic Studies and Policy Analysis Division. August.

Stanford, Jim. 2004. "Paul Martin, the Deficit, and the Debt: Taking Another Look." In *Hell and High Water: An Assessment of Paul Martin's Record and Implications for the Future*, ed. Todd Scarth. Ottawa: Canadian Centre for Policy Alternatives.

Teeple, Gary. 2000. *Globalization and the Decline of Social Reform into the Twenty-first Century*. Toronto: Garamond Press.

CHAPTER 12

Improving Work: Could Canada Look More Like Denmark?

Introduction

This chapter compares Canada's liberal labour market model to the social democratic Scandinavian countries. It draws on recent European experience to suggest that there is no inevitable trade-off between high employment and job creation on the one hand, and improving the quality of jobs and promoting equality on the other.

Labour Market Models

The experience of some European countries shows that low wages and precarious jobs are not a necessary condition for job creation, and that improving job quality at the bottom of the labour market does not inevitably come at the price of unemployment. This is a significant conclusion, since Canadian policy-makers' major argument against

271

labour market regulation aimed at protecting workers in precarious employment has been that such policies will hurt those whom they are intended to protect.

The experience of Scandinavian social democratic countries over the past decade and more suggests that a combination of high employment, relatively equal wages, and real opportunities for workers in precarious employment is possible, and that different varieties of capitalism can continue to exist even in a highly competitive and integrated global economy. This depends on regulating the labour market to create a wage floor and a low level of wage inequality, achieved primarily via collective bargaining; keeping the non-wage costs of employment low by providing social and economic security primarily through public programs financed from general taxation; providing significant investment in active labour market policies to upgrade the skills of those at greatest risk of engaging in precarious employment; and building a distinct kind of post-industrial service economy based on a large non-market sector and high-productivity private services. Success in securing high rates of employment in good jobs also depends on appropriate macroeconomic policies and good labour relations.

The social democratic labour market model, found in its most developed form in the Scandinavian countries, is based on high levels of paid employment for both women and men, high levels of collective bargaining coverage, and universalistic social welfare programs and public services financed from taxes, which reduce reliance on wages. (This model has persisted in broad outline despite the occasional defeats of ruling social democratic parties.) The model has limited precarious employment by socializing some caring responsibilities of households, such as child and elder care. This has reduced the double burden of household and paid work on women, directly created many jobs of reasonably high quality for women in social services, and reduced the importance of low-wage jobs in private consumer services. However, women still perform a highly unequal share of caring work, and, as in Canada, there is a highly gendered division of paid labour between women and men, with women having only limited access to higher level jobs in the private sector. In short, the social democratic model is progressive from the standpoint of limiting precarious employment and holds lessons for Canadians, but it still falls short from the standpoint of promoting full equality between women and men. Also, there have recently been some signs of rising inequality in the Scandinavian countries, which are by no means exempt from competitive pressures that prompt employers to demand greater "flexibility."

This chapter is organized as follows. The first section, "War of the Models," summarizes the orthodox economic argument for deregulated or flexible labour markets as the key to job creation for workers deemed to be low skilled. It demonstrates that levels of low pay and earnings inequality are high and rising in countries that have embraced this model, but with no evidence of superior job creation performance compared to countries with high levels of collective bargaining coverage. The second section, "Social Foundations of Job Creation," shows that high levels of collective bargaining coverage coexist with other labour market policies that have different implications for the extent of low-wage and precarious employment, notably employment protection legislation, the division of responsibility between the government and employers for financing social programs, and the extent of active labour market policies. The social democratic labour market model is the most employment friendly.

The third section, "The Economics of Labour Market Regulation," argues that high labour standards can raise productivity in what would otherwise be low-wage jobs. The final sections, "The Scandinavian Social Democratic Model" and "A Closer Look at Denmark," show that some countries have been able to achieve very high rates of good quality employment with very low levels of precarious work.

"War of the Models": Liberal vs. Regulated Labour Markets

In what has been termed the "War of the Models" (Freeman 1998, 2007), the Great American Job Machine has often been contrasted to high unemployment Eurosclerosis. The highly influential *OECD Jobs Study* (1994) argued that more labour market regulation in continental Europe compared to the U.S. and the U.K. was a major factor behind higher unemployment. The orthodox view is that overly generous unemployment benefits create barriers and disincentives to work by leading workers to expect wages that are higher than wages in available jobs, particularly for low-skilled workers who would qualify only for low-wage jobs. Further, it is argued that high wage floors set by minimum wages and/or collective bargaining mean that low-skilled workers will be priced out of the low-productivity jobs that could otherwise have been created. The ideal labour market is one in which wages rapidly adjust to changing economic circumstances and closely reflect the relative productivity of different groups of workers. The dismal message to governments has been that there is a trade-off between the quantity and quality of jobs for lower skilled and vulnerable workers, and that protective measures such as generous unemployment benefits, unions, and minimum wages come at the significant cost of high unemployment.

Table 12.1: Earnings Inequality (full-time workers)

	U.S.	Canada	Sweden	Denmark
Decile ratios				
9:1				
2006	4.84	3.74	2.31	2.67
1996	4.63	3.53	2.27	2.49
9:5				
2006	2.30	1.87	1.67	1.73
1996	2.20	1.76	1.63	1.70
5:1				
2006	2.10	2.00	1.38	1.54
1996	2.10	2.00	1.40	1.47
Incidence of low pay (less than 2/3 median)				
2006	24.2%	22.2%	6.5%	9.3%
1996	25.1%	22.0%	5.7%	7.3%

Source: *OECD Employment Outlook*. 2008. Table H.

The orthodox view has been a major influence on Canadian labour market policy. Employment Insurance and welfare benefits have been substantially cut and entitlements restricted; minimum wages have fallen behind average wages; employment standards have been eroded; and labour laws have generally become much less facilitative in terms of providing access to collective bargaining. The argument has been that a less regulated job market would lead to lower unemployment. The Canadian policy debate has largely ignored viable alternatives to U.S. and British-style deregulated labour markets. In fact, there are still profound differences between the labour markets of advanced capitalist countries; regulated labour markets work far better for vulnerable workers, and there is no clear-cut link between the extent of labour market regulation and employment performance.

As shown in previous chapters, Canada has done reasonably well in terms of job creation in the economic recovery that began in the mid-1990s. Compared to other OECD countries, the employment rate for both women and men is high, and the long-term adult unemployment rate is very low. However, labour market inequality has increased since at least the mid-1980s, in that earnings inequality has increased sharply, and in that there has been a rise in the incidence of precarious and low-paid jobs. Indeed, Canada stands out as an exceptionally high-earnings-inequality and low-wage country among advanced industrial countries, particularly when compared to the Scandinavian countries. Table 12.1 provides some key indicators of earnings inequality. As shown, the ratio between the 9th decile and the 1st decile—that is the minimum gap between the top 10% and bottom 10% of the workforce (looking only at full-time workers)—was 3.74 in Canada in 2006, meaning that the top 10% earned at least 3.74 times as much as the bottom 10%. This is lower than the 4.84 ratio in the U.S., but a much greater pay gap than in Sweden and Denmark where the minimum gap between the top and bottom 10% is more like 2.5. (Countries like Germany, France, and Italy generally stand about halfway between the high-inequality North American and low-inequality Scandinavian ends of the spectrum, with the U.K. being close to the North American end.) As shown, there are also significant differences in the gap between the top 10% and the middle 10% of full-time earners, and between the middle 10% and the bottom 10%. In fact, the latter gap—between the middle and the low paid—varies rather more between countries than that between the top and the middle of the earnings spectrum. Further, the incidence of low-paid work—defined as a full-time worker earning less than two-thirds the median wage of a full-time worker—was 22.2% in Canada in 2006, a bit lower than in the U.S., but for higher than the 6.5% rate in Sweden. (Directly comparable Danish data are not available, but earnings differences are only slightly larger in Denmark than in Sweden.) One in three Canadian women workers is low paid compared to less than one in 10 women in Sweden. Moreover, upward earnings mobility for low-paid workers is greatest in those countries with the lowest levels of earnings inequality, with Sweden and Denmark performing notably better than the U.S. (OECD 1996). As further shown in the table, earnings inequality as measured by the 9:1 ratio has increased in all countries over the past decade, but less so in the Scandinavian countries, which have seen top earners grow a bit away from the middle. A detailed analysis by Pontusson (2005, 39–43) shows that earnings inequality in the Scandinavian social democratic countries has increased modestly since the 1980s, but not nearly as dramatically as in the U.S., the U.K., and Canada, which have the most deregulated job markets.

Labour market institutions—wage floors set by collective bargaining and legislated minimum wages—play a major role in accounting for different levels of low pay and earnings inequality. Advanced industrial countries differ rather little in terms of the big structural forces shaping job markets. All are exposed to increased international competition from low-wage countries and technological change, widely believed to be tipping the scales against relatively low-skilled workers. But, there is a strong consensus that labour market institutions still significantly shape outcomes for workers (Aidt and Tzannatos 2003; Freeman and Katz 1995; OECD 1996, 1997; Freeman 2007). As has been shown, collective bargaining raises the relative pay of workers who would otherwise be lower paid—women, minorities, younger workers, the relatively unskilled—and narrows wage differentials. Due to declining unionization, increases in wage inequality from the mid-1980s have been much greater in liberal labour markets than in the Scandinavian or continental European countries (Freeman and Katz 1995; OECD 1996).

The deregulated or liberal labour market model of Canada, the U.S., and the U.K. differs profoundly from that in most continental European countries. It is common to divide countries into different "social welfare regimes" based upon the level of income transfers, taxes, and public services, as well as the extent of labour market regulation (Esping-Anderson 1999; Pierson 2001; Scharpf and Schmidt 2000; Pontusson 2005). The social democratic countries of Scandinavia and the social market countries such as Germany and the Netherlands differ significantly in terms of the degree of development of public services and the extent of labour force participation by women. But, they are both distinguished from "liberal" countries by the relative generosity of income support programs, such as unemployment insurance, and by the fact that the labour market and the workplace are still regulated by the "social partners." Collective bargaining coverage is very high and generally quite stable in the social democratic and social market countries, covering close to 80% of workers, because of high union membership in combination with the *de facto* or sometimes legal extension of collective agreements to non-union workers. Wage floors protect the great majority of non-professional and/or managerial workers, including most part-time and even temporary workers. The more equal after-tax distribution of income and the lower poverty rates in these countries reflect the fact that the distribution of wages is much more equal than in liberal welfare states, even before more generous social transfers are added to the mix (Smeeding 2002; Pontusson 2005). It is interesting to note that support for high levels of equalizing social spending is greatest in countries where earnings are more equal to begin with.

If the orthodox view of how the labour market works was correct, generous unemployment benefits, high wage floors, and low earnings inequality would come at the price of jobs. The social democratic and the social market models with their regulated labour markets would lose the "War of the Models" hands down, particularly in terms of employment rates for the relatively unskilled. But, major recent summaries of the research by the World Bank and OECD find that there is no relationship at the country-wide level between collective bargaining coverage and economic or employment performance in the 1980s and 1990s (Aidt and Tzannatos 2003; OECD 1997). The OECD's updating of its earlier mid-1990s *Jobs Study* has conceded that there are, in fact, different routes to high employment and low unemployment, and that some countries with more regulated job markets have done as well or better than the highly deregulated countries like the U.S. and the U.K. (OECD 2006). Union density, generous unemployment benefits, and relatively equal wages are, overall, related neither to higher- nor lower-than-average rates of unemployment or economic growth (Baker et al. 2002).

To be sure, the larger continental European economies such as France, Germany, and Italy in the 1990s and today have high unemployment rates compared to the U.S., and employment rates for women and young people lag well behind those in North America. But, a number of smaller European countries with high levels of bargaining coverage and still quite generous welfare states, notably Denmark, Sweden, and the Netherlands, performed very well in the 1990s. The International Labour Organization highlighted the experience of some smaller European economies, particularly Denmark, in a counterattack on the orthodox prescription for jobs (Auer 2000; ILO 2003). The European Commission has also rejected the idea of a job quality/job quantity trade-off for lower skilled workers, and also highlighted the experiences of Denmark and the Netherlands as a desirable alternative to the U.S. model (European Commission 2001, 2002). The fundamental message has been that the liberal labour market gives rise to unacceptable levels of wage inequality and social exclusion, and that a new European labour market model can provide high levels of quality employment with low levels of insecurity.

Social Foundations of Job Creation: Labour Market, Regulation, and Social Welfare Regimes

Labour market regulation combines with different key building blocks of social welfare regimes. The social market and social democratic models have similarly high rates of collective bargaining coverage, but differ greatly in terms of the extent of social services and the extent to which women participate in the workforce. The social democratic countries have very high proportions of their workforce employed in social services, have given much more priority to worker training and active labour adjustment programs, and tend to pay for social programs from general taxes rather than by requiring a lot from individual employers. These features all make the model more employment friendly, despite a very high commitment to equality in the job market.

Some countries, notably Germany, France, Italy, and Spain, impose serious restrictions on employers' ability to lay off workers. A high level of job security can perpetuate an insider/outsider labour market, since the incentive is for employers to hire the minimum number of permanent workers and to achieve flexibility by contracting out and hiring temporary workers. (That said, employment protection laws also limit layoffs during downturns.) But, tight job security has never been a major feature of the Scandinavian countries, which have stressed employment security through active labour market policies and high levels of worker training, as well as generous unemployment benefits as workers move between jobs in a constantly changing labour market. Similarly, some European countries have frowned on the creation of part-time jobs, but others have seen part-time jobs as valuable so long as they are taken voluntarily and provide a decent level of pay and benefits. The very strong job-creation performance of the Netherlands in the 1990s owed a lot to part-time job creation.

The more successful European countries emphasize not strong job security regulation or strict limits on part-time and temporary work, but "flexicurity," striking a better balance between the flexibility needs of employers and the security needs of workers. Part-time work is not seen as undesirable so long as it conforms to certain minimum standards of non-discrimination compared to full-time work. Accordingly, the European Union (E.U.) has implemented binding directives mandating member countries to legislate non-discrimination against part-time workers (1997) and temporary workers (1999) with respect to pay and access to permanent jobs and training. The directive on fixed-term work requires states to set limits on the maximum duration of contracts or the number of renewals. If Canadian workers were covered by E.U. directives, significant wage and benefit gaps between otherwise comparable full- and part-time workers would be narrowed.

There are other major differences between the labour markets of advanced industrial countries. The extent to which employers are expected to finance social security through payroll taxes or private pension, health, and other benefits varies greatly. Loading social welfare costs onto employers is common in the social market model, where social security has been primarily financed by employer and employee contributions rather than general taxes. Non-wage costs can also be significant in liberal labour markets like that of Canada, where modest public programs have been supplemented by bargained health care and pension benefits for core workers, increasing the divide between insiders and precarious workers. High non-wage costs for employers are likely to lead to greater use of temporary and contract workers with no benefits, and perhaps to lower rates of overall job creation. The social democratic model of services for all citizens financed from general taxes lowers these levies on employers. Countries also differ greatly in terms of the extent to which they invest in public education and active labour market policies to promote labour adjustment and lifelong learning. Training for the unemployed and workers in precarious employment helps equalize access to job opportunities and also creates a base for higher quality jobs. As shown earlier, training can be a force for better jobs in low-wage private services. Active labour market policies directed to the relatively unskilled have long been a major feature of the social democratic model, but have been much less emphasized in the liberal and social market countries.

Finally, advanced industrial countries differ a lot in terms of the structure of the service sector, depending on the extent to which the caring needs of households, such as child and elder care, and a wide range of community services, such as health, have been assumed by the market or by the state (Esping-Anderson 1999; Pierson 2001). Traditionally, women's low rates of labour force participation in social market countries went hand in hand with the assumption that children and the elderly would be cared for mainly by women in the home. Both social market and liberal countries have less developed social services than the Scandinavian countries. Here, state delivery of caring services has expanded the public sector, enabled women to work, and created new jobs that have gone mainly to women. Jobs in social services tend to have higher skill requirements than private consumer services jobs, and working conditions are usually covered by collective bargaining. Thus, a country's decision to tax and spend on social services has had direct implications for the quality of services jobs. Moreover, higher taxes to pay for these social services means that households have less after-tax income for consuming private services, in turn, limiting the growth potential of low-productivity/low-wage sectors. The structure of services employment differs quite profoundly between social democratic and liberal countries. The ratio of private-to-public-sector jobs ranges from six to one in the U.S., to four to one in Canada, to 2.5 to one in Sweden and Denmark. One in six of the total working-age population in Canada and the U.S. are employed in the retail trade, restaurants, and accommodation sectors combined, compared to just one in 10 in Sweden and Denmark (Scharpf and Schmidt 2000, Data Appendix, Vol. 1; OECD 2000).

It is important to recognize that, while the social democratic labour market model is progressive from the point of view of limiting the incidence of precarious employment among women, it is still problematic from a wider equality perspective. Denmark and Sweden have the lowest gaps in employment rates by gender among OECD countries, and a slightly smaller than average gender wage gap (OECD 2002a). The high level of social services means that children or elderly relatives pose few barriers to women's labour market participation. However, there are an even higher proportion of women employed in female-dominated occupations in Sweden and Denmark than in Canada, and women still perform a very unequal share of work in the home. Glimpses of a more progressive model are to be found in Scandinavian initiatives to share domestic work more equally by promoting longer parental leaves for men, and in the Netherlands model of reduced working time for both women and men to make a more equal division of both paid and domestic labour possible. The growth of part-time work in the Netherlands has seen the emergence of a new model among some younger families with children, in which both women and men work four-day weeks and men undertake a relatively high share of caring and domestic work.

The Economics of Labour Market Regulation: Positive Employment Effects of Labour Standards

As noted, high rates of collective bargaining coverage do not necessarily lead to poor employment outcomes. Denmark, the Netherlands, and Sweden have done well, partly because widespread bargaining has produced wage outcomes that have preserved cost competitiveness for employers and maintained low inflation. Unions in Denmark and the Netherlands have consciously bargained, within a framework of loose national guidelines, to promote job growth. The ILO has underlined the importance of wage moderation in employment success, while noting that this has been consistent with real wage growth and reductions of working time in line with the growth of productivity. By bargaining for jobs rather than just for higher wages for employed insiders, some labour movements have helped counter unemployment and precarious employment.

Many economists argue that relatively high wages for lower skilled workers destroy jobs that could have been created. However, social democratic countries have tended to think that low-paid jobs should be squeezed out of the system. The famous Swedish labour market model developed by union economists Rehn and Meidner from the 1950s through the 1970s featured the negotiation of solidarity wages with the idea that wage differentials by gender, skill, occupation, industry, or enterprise profitability should be very limited. Swedish union economists argued that low-productivity firms and sectors should raise productivity by investing in capital or skills to justify higher wages, or go out of business. Solidarity wages meant that wages would be lower than they would otherwise have been in very profitable firms, which would then hire more workers. The policy of solidarity wages was twinned with measures to retrain workers for jobs in the expanding sectors. The solidarity wage model has been difficult to maintain because it effectively requires higher skilled (mainly male) workers to lower their wages for the benefit of others, and creates tensions between public- and private-sector workers, but it still remains a factor in wage negotiations in the Scandinavian countries and the Netherlands.

Rather than just destroying private services jobs, high labour standards can raise job quality and pay by raising productivity. Wage floors can lower worker turnover and increase experience and skills, reducing employer costs. A common wage standard can also take wage costs out of the competitive equation. If all employers pay the same wage and benefit package, firms must compete with one another on the basis of non-labour cost issues, such as quality and customer service. There is good evidence that decent wages and high labour standards raise productivity. The fact that employers come under pressure to pay good wages will lead them to invest more in capital equipment and training than would otherwise be the case. Further, high labour standards can raise productivity by improving the social relations of production. If workers know that changes in work organization will not cost them their jobs, will not lead to poorer health and safety or working conditions, and that the gains of higher productivity will be shared with them, then workers will co-operate in workplace change.

Box 12.1: Labour Conditions and Productivity

In a major defence of labour rights and standards, Werner Sengenberger, a retired senior official with the ILO, argues that the orthodox view of the labour market is profoundly misleading since it does not take account of the fundamental fact that "labour is not a commodity" or a "factor of production" (Sengenberger 2003). Rather, labour is a productive potential linked to human beings with individual and social needs. Productivity—what a worker delivers in return for a wage—depends upon what the ILO has termed "decent work." "A worker will be more or less productive, co-operative and innovative depending on how he or she is treated; whether the wage is seen as fair in relation to the demands of the job; whether the worker gets equal pay for work of equal value; whether training is provided; whether grievances can be voiced. In short, what the worker delivers is contingent on the terms of employment, working conditions, the work environment, collective representation, and due process" (Sengenberger 2003, 48).

The Scandinavian Social Democratic Model

Table 12.2 provides comparative data for the U.S., Canada, Denmark, and Sweden to draw out some key contrasts between the liberal and the social democratic models. As shown, Sweden, Denmark, and Canada have comparable levels of GDP per person, and have remained at about the same level of GDP per person compared to the U.S. since the mid-1990s. (The slight slippage compared to U.S. GDP per capita indicates that they grew at a slightly lower rate.) It should be noted that the significant U.S. advantage in terms of GDP per capita reflects much longer working hours, especially compared to the Scandinavian countries. For example, the average full-time Danish worker has a workweek of 37 hours, long hours are very uncommon, and all workers now enjoy six weeks of paid vacation per year. Also, the modest U.S. growth advantage over the past decade was likely built on an unsustainable trade deficit and high levels of foreign borrowing.

On top of more or less equal economic performance compared to the U.S. and Canada, the Scandinavian countries have achieved somewhat higher employment rates than the U.S. or Canada, and have especially high employment rates for women. Notably, employment rates for workers with low levels of formal education are also significantly higher in Denmark and, especially, Sweden than in the U.S. or Canada, disproving the idea that it is low-skilled workers who are squeezed out of jobs if the wage floor is set too high. If high levels of participation in paid work are seen as key to social inclusion, the development of individual capabilities, and gender equity, then the social democratic countries are the winners compared to Canada and the U.S. High employment has also been twinned with very low unemployment rates, especially in Denmark, and, as in North America, by a low incidence of long-term unemployment. (Unemployment in Sweden was at or below Canadian levels through most of the 1990s.)

Sweden and Denmark have very low levels of after-tax income inequality and rates of poverty compared to North America, reflecting much lower levels of earnings inequality and low pay, and also higher levels of publicly funded social investments as a share of GDP. Cash benefits paid to households (i.e., public pensions, unemployment, welfare, and disability benefits) are about double the North American level. Unemployment compensation is also much more generous than in North America. The income replacement rate for unemployed workers (an average of different household types over different time periods) is notably more generous. Pontusson (2005) details how relative earnings equality combined with high levels of cash transfers by governments produce a strikingly more equal distribution of after-tax family income. As shown, the minimum gap between the top and bottom 10% of households in Sweden and Denmark is 2.8 to one (or about three times as much) compared to four times as much in Canada, and five times as much in the U.S. Because transfers have risen to offset modestly rising earnings inequality, household income inequality in Sweden and Denmark has remained more or less unchanged over the past decade. As shown, poverty rates—especially for children—are also strikingly lower than in Canada and the U.S. (Poverty is defined as living in a household with less than half the median household income.) Not only is income much more equally distributed than in North

Table 12.2: North America vs. Scandinavia: Key Economic and Social Indicators

	U.S.	Canada	Sweden	Denmark
1. Economic performance				
GDP per person in 2005 (U.S.=100)	100	81.5	76.8	81.7
GDP per person in 1995 (U.S.=100)	100	82.7	78.1	82.4
2. Employment performance (%)				
Employment/Population ratio in 2005:				
All (Age 15–64)	71.5	72.5	73.9	75.5
Men	77.6	76.7	75.9	80.1
Women	65.6	68.3	71.8	70.8
Less than upper secondary education	56.5	57.1	67.0	62.0
Unemployment Rate in 2005:				
All (Age 15–64)	5.1	6.8	7.8	4.9
Men	5.1	7.1	7.9	4.2
Women	5.2	6.5	7.6	5.6
3. Social investment (%)				
Public social expenditure as % GDP:				
a. Cash benefits	8.4	7.4	16.0	14.8
b. Health and social services	7.6	9.5	13.9	11.1
Unemployment compensation as % GDP	0.2	0.6	0.9	1.5
Income replacement rate–unemployed (as % wage)	31%	50%	73%	78%
Active labour market spending (% GDP)	0.14%	0.31%	1.36%	1.85%
4. Social outcomes				
Household income inequality (90/10 ratio, after taxes/transfers):				
2000	5.7	4.2	2.8	2.8
1987	5.7	3.9	2.7	3.2
Poverty rate (less than 50% median):				
2000	16.8%	12.4%	5.6%	7.5%
1987	17.8%	11.4%	7.5%	10.1%
Child poverty rate:				
2000	22.3%	15.5%	4.7%	3.9%

Source: Except as indicated, data are from OECD Social Indicators. 2006.

1. OECD Fact Book. 2007. 26. GDP per capita measured at purchasing power parity.

3. "Active Labour Market Spending," *OECD Employment Outlook*. 2007. Table J.

4. Luxemburg Income Survey. www.lisproject.org/keyfigures.htm.

America, Swedish and Danish households rely much less on cash income because they get a lot of social services at modest cost. Taxpayer-funded health and social services as a share of GDP are at 14% in Sweden and 11% in Denmark, far more developed than in the U.S. (7.6%) or Canada (9.5%). High levels of spending on social services mean that the share of national income spent on private consumption (i.e., household spending) is correspondingly much lower. A lot of the difference in spending is accounted for by much higher spending on child care, elder care, and community social services, all of which also account for significant areas of employment.

A Closer Look at Denmark

While in very broad terms a variation of the Scandinavian social democratic model, Denmark differs from Sweden in many ways. It has an economy based much more on small firms in services, food processing, and light industry, and less on large-scale industry. The Social Democratic Party, while in government most of the time until 2002, has been less dominant than in Sweden, and the unions a somewhat weaker social force. Like Sweden and the Netherlands, recent employment success contrasts to experiences of high unemployment, fiscal crisis, and very strained labour-management relationships at various times in the 1980s and early 1990s. Like the Netherlands, crisis led to a renewal of the social partnership model and major reforms.

The incidence of low-wage work in Denmark is very low because of the high-wage floor set by collective bargaining. More than 80% of all workers and about 70% of private-sector workers are covered by collective agreements (EIRO 2002). Coverage is almost universal in community and social services, and collective agreements cover the majority of workers even in normally low-wage consumer services sectors such as retail trade (57%) and hotels and restaurants (50%). Bargaining coverage is stable or even increasing, despite erosion among some higher paid professionals, and unions and employers have maintained that employee protection legislation is largely unnecessary because of continued high union coverage of potentially vulnerable workers. Bargaining is conducted on a sectoral basis between employer associations and unions within a loose framework of centrally agreed wage guidelines, with some enterprise flexibility to pay higher wages. The wage determination system has been characterized as "centralized decentralization." While wage moderation has been a feature of Danish success, LO, the major union federation of non-professional workers, recently conducted national strikes to win a sixth week of paid vacation and real wages have increased more or less in line with those in Germany (Ploughmann and Madsen 2002). Wage inequality has not increased in the 1990s.

The incidence of precarious employment in Denmark is very low. Self-employment (which is disproportionately, though not universally, precarious) accounts for just 7% of total employment compared to about 20% in Canada and an E.U. average of 15%, and has been declining from 9% in 1990 (European Commission 2002). Temporary or fixed-term contract employment accounts for 10.2% of all jobs and is higher for women than for men, but less than one in three temporary workers report that this status is involuntary. The status of temporary workers generally compares very well to other E.U. countries and to Canada (OECD 2002-b). Temporary workers are covered by collective agreements; qualify for paid holidays, parental leave, and sick leave if they have worked for just 72 hours in the past eight weeks; and earn 78% of the hourly wage of permanent employees (more when controlled for other differences in work status). However, they have much less access than permanent employees to training. Similarly, the low incidence of part-time work (at 14.5%) is falling (from 19.2% in 1990), and is generally voluntary (European Commission 2002).

The European Commission judges Denmark to have the highest overall quality of jobs in the E.U. (European Commission 2001, Chapter 4). Measured by pay, working conditions, subjective job satisfaction, and opportunities for advancement, 60% of Danes are in good jobs (the highest proportion in Europe), 20% are in jobs of reasonable quality, and just 20% are in jobs of poor quality (of which less than half qualify as really bad, dead-end jobs). There are also very high rates of transition from lower quality to higher quality jobs, with 35% of workers in low-quality jobs moving to better jobs one year later, and 50% in better jobs three years later (compared to 35% in the U.K.) (European Commission 2002, 93). Subjective job satisfaction is the highest in the E.U. Data from the *European Survey on Work Conditions* also suggest that jobs in the Danish services sector are, on average, much better than elsewhere in the E.U. in terms of levels of work autonomy and the incidence of monotonous work (OECD 2001). It seems probable that the high level of social services jobs and high incidence of training have militated against dead-end (very low-skill/low-productivity) consumer services jobs.

The Danish labour market is remarkable in terms of its high level of labour mobility. Annual worker turnover is as high as 30%. About one-half of annual job turnover is due to job destruction, but the level of voluntary resignations to seek or take new jobs is also very high (Madsen 2003, 64; Ploughmann and Madsen 2002, 21). Only about two-thirds of workers have been in their current job for more than two years, the lowest proportion in the E.U., and one-quarter have been in their current job for less than one year, the highest proportion in the E.U. (European Commission 2001, 72). There is a very low level of job protection by law or collective agreement. On the OECD scale of strictness of employment protection, Denmark ranks very low, just above Canada. Collective agreements typically specify two to three months' notice of layoff for long-tenure workers. The main union central, LO-Denmark, has not called for stronger job protection, arguing that generous unemployment benefits and access to training serve workers better.

Despite quite high rates of entry into unemployment, perceived employment security is very high. A 2000 survey found that only 9% of Danish workers were afraid of losing their current jobs, the lowest in the E.U. (Ploughmann and Madsen 2002, 12). By contrast, one-quarter to one-third of Canadian workers have reported fear of job loss in recent years according to the CCSD Personal Security Index. The annual incidence of unemployment is as high as one in four workers, but for the majority, unemployment is very short term (less than 10 weeks). Madsen, who has written extensively on the Danish model for the ILO, talks of the "Golden Triangle" of the Danish labour market. As in liberal labour markets, there is a very low level of job protection, which has encouraged job creation. However, in line with the principle of flexicurity and the traditional social democratic model, unemployment benefits replace a high proportion of wages, and there is much more emphasis on training and active labour market policy to promote employment security.

The great majority of unemployed workers belong to an Unemployment Insurance Fund administered by the unions, and are eligible for benefits if employed for one year in the last three. The OECD calculated the relative generosity of benefits for unemployed workers for different family types and earning levels and found that the Danish and Swedish systems are by far the most generous. The income replacement rate for an average production worker is at least 70%, rising to 90% for relatively low-paid workers (Madsen 2003, 74). For an estimated one-third of unemployed men and one-half of unemployed women, benefits just about match prior earnings (Benner and Vad 2000).

Reforms to the unemployment insurance system in the mid-1990s modestly trimmed benefits and introduced individual employment plans. It is now mandatory for beneficiaries to participate in an active labour market program after one year, and after six months for younger workers. While this has been seen as akin to North American-style workfare in some critiques and is deliberately intended to counter dependency, the carrots of good benefits and meaningful training opportunities are much more important than the stick of potential sanctions. Moreover, unemployed workers are clearly being trained for jobs at decent wages. As shown in Table 12.2, public expenditures on labour market training and other active employment measures are even higher in Denmark than in Sweden, and six times higher than in Canada. The main focus is on training for the unemployed, and about two in three unemployed workers or 6% of the total workforce receive some public training each year. This can be in private firms with a wage subsidy, with a public-sector employer, or in training or educational programs to fill future labour market vacancies. In addition, about 10% of the workforce benefit each year from government training programs directed to employed workers compared to almost zero in Canada. There has been skepticism in Canada about the effectiveness of skills training for unemployed and vulnerable workers, but Danish studies judge their programs to be effective in job placement and raising skills (ILO 2003; Madsen 2003). Credit has been given to the decentralization of public training to the regional level since the mid-1990s, where it is run by the social partners.

In addition, the Danish system features high levels of education and training for the currently employed. On top of a strong base of universal public education and high participation in post-secondary studies, the rhetoric of lifelong learning in a skill-based economy has been translated into reality through rights to individual educational leaves and opportunities to take education leaves funded by unemployment benefits. These were quite popular when used to address high unemployment in the early to mid-1990s. Unions bargain access to training, and help run employer-sponsored training. Denmark has recently ranked very high among OECD countries in terms of the extent of adult participation in training and equality of access for women (OECD 1999). Average hours spent in training per worker are double the OECD average. Such training extends to workers in private consumer services, with participation rates of 70% in hotels and restaurants, and 49% in retail trade (European Commission 2001, Table 9).

In the discussion above, emphasis was placed on the importance of public and social services as a source of quality employment for women. Such services account for about one-third of Danish employment, and fully one-half of employment for women, but private services employment has grown faster since the mid-1980s, and two out of three new jobs created between 1993 and 2002 were in the private sector (Madsen 2003). The importance of not loading too many non-wage costs onto employers was also noted. In Denmark, tax reform in the mid-1990s trimmed already low payroll taxes, and sharply reduced employer responsibility for funding active labour market programs. According to Madsen (2003, 60), "[t]he direct costs of protecting the employee are borne to a large extent by the state and not by individual firms." Workplace pensions play a modest role compared to universal state pensions and the state-run, work-based pension system. As a result, the proportion of social expenditures financed by employers is the lowest in the E.U.—8.7% compared to 46.5% in France and 37.4% in Germany (ILO 2003, 58), and the percentage of non-wage costs in total labour costs is just 6.3% compared to 31.8% in France and 20.7% in the U.S. (ILO 2003, 61).

Denmark figures as a particularly interesting case study in a major comparative study of low-wage work in advanced industrial countries commissioned by the Russell Sage Foundation (Westergaard-Nielson (Ed.) 2008). The study shows that a high "wage floor" set by collective bargaining makes a real difference for workers in sectors that are low wage in other countries. Set at about $20 Canadian per hour (14 Euros per hour in 2005), the minimum wage floor negotiated centrally between employers and the unions means that the incidence of low-wage work in Denmark is just 8.5% of the workforce compared to 25% in the U.S. (Low-wage work is defined here as earning less than two-thirds of the national median hourly wage.) In all advanced industrial countries, there are strong downward pressures on wages on working conditions at the bottom of the job market, since low-skilled workers are easy to replace and lack ready access to better employment alternatives, but Denmark has managed to improve the quality of jobs that would be low paid in a North American context.

In two of the sectors studied—retail trade and housekeeping work in hotels—the overall structure and functioning of the industry and the way in which work is organized do not seem to be radically different from in Canada. There is intense competition between large chains, which increasingly dominate the sector, and employers seek to compete, in part, by "flexibly" hiring many part-timers on variable hours. Danish unions are not especially strong in these sectors, particularly at the workplace level, but the wage floor is still generally maintained, and working conditions and work schedules seem to compare extremely well to North American standards, notwithstanding employer demands for increased flexibility. These jobs tend to be held by transient workers such as students, and many work in the sector for only short periods of time. One interesting facet of low-wage work in Denmark is that it is rarely a continuing condition, with most low-wage workers managing to find better jobs over time. The most notable exception is immigrants. The retail sector study emphasizes that those people who seek a career in retail trade usually manage to acquire managerial jobs quite quickly, moving rapidly from sales associate, to assistant manager, to manager. Training for these job ladders is provided by large chains.

While the minimum wage floor is probably the key reason why there is such a low prevalence of low-wage jobs in Denmark, there are also indications that work in what would be low-wage sectors in a North American context is structured quite differently in such a way as to raise wages. As Robert Solow notes in his introduction to the study, raising productivity in low-wage sectors can both improve the quality of jobs and increase the output of the whole economy. Employers can, as in the U.S. and Canada, follow a low road of using disposable low-pay/low-skill workers, or they can organize the work differently so as to improve productivity and pay while earning a similar profit. Two of the Danish case studies bear out this argument that decent wages can lead to higher productivity as well as better jobs. While a low-wage industry in the U.S. and Canada in the wake of a frontal attack on unions, Denmark's relatively large food processing sector has pursued a classic "high road" strategy, raising productivity and producing high-quality products by investing in new equipment, processes, and worker skills. There has been a major shift from manual work to automation in meat processing and other subsectors, with skills rising as a result. The workforce—which includes many recent immigrants—is highly unionized, which helps sustain not just decent pay, but also safe working conditions. An industry focus on high quality as well as on high productivity has helped maintain strong national brands, and a large share of the domestic and European market.

In health care, low-wage work has been virtually eliminated not just through high unionization, but also through a concerted strategy to raise worker skills at all levels and to create coherent and well-planned ladders to better jobs. Given shortages of very highly skilled workers, physician work has been shifted to nurses, from nurses to nursing assistants (two levels of which exist), and from nursing assistants to a new category of ancillary workers. At the lowest level of the job ladder, a category of "hospital service assistant" has jobs that combine cleaning and food preparation tasks with some tasks formerly performed by the lower level of nursing assistants. They receive training in a range of tasks, and have the opportunity to train so as to take on more basic nursing assistant tasks. Many of the workers who were previously employed in the lowest nursing assistant category have been re-trained to work at the level requiring higher skills. In short, a serious attempt has been made to create job ladders so those at the bottom of the ladder can and do move up. As a result, very few workers remain at the bottom of the ladder. Examples of such programs do exist in a North American context, but they cover almost the entire Danish health care sector.

In summary, higher wages at the bottom can and do raise skills and productivity in such a way as to make a decent wage floor an economically viable proposition. Work in food processing and in ancillary health care seems to be organized quite differently in Denmark than in the North American context, with gains to workers and to productivity and efficiency. In retail and hotels, the differences in work organization do not seem to be especially marked, but workers certainly benefit from higher wages and better working conditions than in North America. The studies do not go into great detail, but higher wages at the bottom in these sectors are likely paid for by relatively lower wages for managers, and some combination of higher prices and lower profits compared to North America.

The Danish model is not without flaws. In common with other socially homoge-neous small countries, the values of social solidarity tend to be racially and culturally defined. Unemployment is relatively high among recent immigrants from developing countries, and the recently elected (conservative) government has limited immigrant access to full welfare benefits. As noted, occupational segregation of women and men is very high. Also, many observers question if the social democratic countries can continue to create such a large share of new jobs in tax-financed public and social services, as opposed to lower skilled and usually lower paid jobs in consumer services. Ultimately, the social democratic model does depend on a high political commitment to low inequality achieved through narrow pay differentials and high taxes—not least by those who might do better in a liberal context.

Conclusions and Lessons for Canada

The central conclusion to be drawn from this chapter is that it is possible to have high levels of employment at decent wages and with decent working conditions. There is no inevitable trade-off between job quantity and job quality, even at the low end of the job market. Several European countries have achieved very high employment rates and low unemployment even with generous welfare benefits and wages that are extremely equal compared to Canada.

The Danish example is unique in some respects, but has wider lessons. First, a wage floor and the virtual elimination of low pay do not preclude job growth in private services. Good labour standards can raise productivity, though a high wage floor probably works best when combined with training policies that raise the skills of workers. The Danish example also suggests that high levels of public services, financed from general taxes, can make a positive contribution to high-quality, post-industrial employment.

Canada is a far more diverse society than Denmark, but this makes more difficult rather than impossible political projects linked to values of equality and solidarity. Canada is also highly integrated with the deregulated U.S. economy. This poses limits on policy, particularly with respect to the level of taxes, as was noted in the last chapter, but the experience of Denmark and Sweden strongly suggests that precarious work is not a precondition for success in today's changing international economy.

Recommended Reading

- Auer, Peter. 2000. *Employment Revival in Europe: Labour Market Success in Austria, Denmark, Ireland, and the Netherlands*. Geneva: ILO. This study by the International Labour Organization draws on the experience of four smaller countries to sug-gest that improving the quality of jobs can be consistent with high levels of job creation.
- Freeman, Richard B. 2007. *America Works: Critical Thoughts on the Exceptional U.S. Labor Market*. New York: Russell Sage Foundation. This short and accessible book

by one of America's leading academic labour economists argues that the highly deregulated U.S. job market is exceptional, and gives rise to high levels of inequality and insecurity compared to European countries.

- Pierson, Paul (Ed.) 2001. *The New Politics of the Welfare State*. Oxford: Oxford University Press. Both Esping-Anderson and Pierson provide good accounts of the major differences in labour markets and social programs between the advanced industrial countries, and how this affects their relative performance in terms of meeting economic and social goals.
- Pontusson, Jonas. 2005. *Inequality and Prosperity. Social Europe vs. Liberal America*. Ithaca and London: Cornell University Press. A comprehensive account of key differences between the different labour market and social policy models to be found in advanced industrial countries, which systematically compares and contrasts European and U.S. experiences.

References

Aidt, Toke, and Zafiris Tzannatos. 2003. *Unions and Collective Bargaining: Economic Effects in a Global Environment*. Washington: The World Bank.

Auer, Peter. 2000. *Employment Revival in Europe: Labour Market Success in Austria, Denmark, Ireland, and the Netherlands*. Geneva: ILO.

Baker, Dean, Andrew Glyn, David Howell, and John Schmitt. 2002. "Labor Market Institutions and Unemployment: A Critical Assessment of the Cross-Country Evidence." Centre for Economic Policy Analysis Working Paper 2002-17. www.newschool.edu/cepa.

Benner, Mats, and Torben Bundgaard Vad. 2000. "Sweden and Denmark: Defending the Welfare State." In *Welfare and Work in the Open Economy: Vol. II Diverse Responses to Common Challenges*, ed. Fritz Scharpf and Vivien Schmidt. Oxford: Oxford University Press.

Esping-Anderson, Gosta. 1999. *Social Foundations of Post-industrial Economies*. Oxford: Oxford University Press.

European Commission (Employment and Social Affairs). 2001. *Employment in Europe*. Brussels: European Commission.

———. 2002. *Employment in Europe*. Brussels: European Commission.

European Industrial Relations Observatory (EIRO). 2001. "Annual Review for Denmark." www.eiro.eurofund.ie.

———. 2002. "Annual Review for Denmark." www.eiro.eurofund.ie.

Freeman, Richard B. 1998. "War of the Models: Which Labour Market Institutions for the 21st Century?" *Labour Economics* 5 (1): 1–24.

———. 2007. *America Works: Critical Thoughts on the Exceptional U.S. Labour Market*. New York: Russell Sage Foundation.

Freeman, Richard B., and Lawrence F. Katz (Eds.). 1995. *Differences and Changes in Wage Structures*. Chicago: The University of Chicago Press.

International Labour Organization (ILO). 2003. *Decent Work in Denmark: Employment, Social Efficiency, and Economic Security*. Geneva: ILO.

Madsen, Per Kongshoj. 2003. "'Flexicurity' through Labour Market Policies and Institutions in Denmark." In *Employment Stability in an Age of Flexibility*, ed. Peter Auer and Sandrine Cazes, 59–105. Geneva: ILO.

Organisation for Economic Co-operation and Development (OECD). 1996. "Earnings Inequality, Low Paid Employment, and Earnings Mobility." *OECD Employment Outlook*, 63–92. Paris: OECD.

———. 1997. "Economic Performance and the Structure of Collective Bargaining." *OECD Employment Outlook*, 133–175. Paris: OECD.

———. 1999. "Training of Adult Workers in OECD Countries." *OECD Employment Outlook*, 133–175. Paris: OECD.

———. 2000. "Employment in the Service Economy: A Reassessment." *OECD Employment Outlook*, 79–126. Paris: OECD.

———. 2001. "The Characteristics and Quality of Service Sector Jobs." *OECD Employment Outlook*, 89–127. Paris: OECD.

———. 2002a. "Women at Work: Who Are They and How Are They Faring?" *OECD Employment Outlook*, 61–125. Paris: OECD.

———. 2002b. "Taking the Measure of Temporary Employment." *OECD Employment Outlook*, 127–183. Paris: OECD.

———. 2006. *OECD Employment Outlook, Boosting Jobs and Incomes*. Paris: OECD.

Pierson, Paul (Ed.). 2001. *The New Politics of the Welfare State*. Oxford: Oxford University Press.

Ploughmann, Peter, and Per Madsen. 2002. "Flexibility, Employment Development and Active Labour Market Policy in Denmark and Sweden in the 1990s." CEPA Working Paper 2002-04. New York: Centre for Economic Policy Analysis, New School University.

Pontusson, Jonas. 2005. *Inequality and Prosperity. Social Europe vs. Liberal America*. Ithaca and London: Cornell University Press.

Scharpf, Fritz, and Vivien Schmidt (Eds.). 2000. *Welfare and Work in the Open Economy: Vol. I From Vulnerability to Competitiveness*, and *Vol. II Diverse Responses to Common Challenges*. Oxford: Oxford University Press.

Sengenberger, Werner. 2003. *Globalization and Social Progress: The Role and Impact of Labour Standards*. Bonn: Friedrich Ebert Foundation.

Smeeding, Timothy. 2002. *Globalization, Inequality, and the Rich Countries of the G-20: Evidence from the Luxemburg Income Study*. Luxemburg Income Study Working Paper No. 320. www.lisproject.org.

Westergaard-Nielson, Neils (Ed.). 2008. *Low Wage Work in Denmark*. New York: Russell Sage Foundation.

Copyright Acknowledgments

Box 4.5

Immen, W.,"'Role Overload' Makes Workers Sick," *The Globe and Mail*, October 22, 2003, C3. Copyright © CTVglobemedia Publishing Inc. Reprinted with permission.

Chapter 5

Opening photo ©istockphoto.com/stock-photo-3366646-engineering-student-reads-blueprints

Figure 5.1

"Earnings Ratio Female/Male, 1980-2006, Full-time, Full-year," adapted from the Statistics Canada publication *Work Chapter Updates 2006, Women in Canada*, Catalogue 89F0133XIE, Table 11, 2007. Copyright © Statistics Canada. Reprinted with permission of Statistics Canada.

Figure 5.2

"Distribution of Annual Earnings of Men and Women, 2006 (all earners)," adapted from the Statistics Canada publication *Income Trends in Canada*, Catalogue13F0022XIE, Table 2020101, 2008. Copyright © Statistics Canada. Reprinted with permission of Statistics Canada.

Box 5.1

Map, K., "Workers 'cut' family for jobs: study," *Ottawa Citizen*, October 3rd, 2007, p. A1, A4. Copyright © Ottawa Citizen Group Inc. Material reprinted with the express permission of "Ottawa Citizen Group Inc.," a CanWest Partnership.

Table 5.1

"The Pay Gap: Earnings of Women vs. Men," adapted from the Statistics Canada publication *Income Trends in Canada*, Catalogue 13F0022XIE, Tables 2020102 and 2020104, 2008. Copyright © Statistics Canada. Reprinted with permission of Statistics Canada.

Table 5.2

"Average Hourly Wage of Women as Percentage of Men," adapted from the Statistics Canada publication *Labour Force Survey 2006*, Catalogue 71F0004XCB, Table cd3t01an, 2008. Copyright © Statistics Canada. Reprinted with permission of Statistics Canada.

Table 5.3

"Average Hourly Wages, by Occupation, 2006," adapted from the Statistics Canada publication *Labour Force Survey 2006*, Catalogue 71F0004XCB, Table cd3t01an, 2008. Copyright © Statistics Canada. Reprinted with permission of Statistics Canada.

Table 5.4

"Distribution of Annual Earnings of Women vs. Men, 2005," adapted from the Statistics Canada publication *Income Trends in Canada*, Catalogue 13F0022XIE, Table 2020101, 2008. Copyright © Statistics Canada. Reprinted with permission of Statistics Canada.

Table 5.5

"Employment of Women and Men, by Form of Employment, 2006," adapted from the Statistics Canada publication *Labour Force Historical Review 2006*, Catalogue 71F0004XCB, Tables cd1t07, 08, 44an, 2008. Copyright © Statistics Canada. Reprinted with permission of Statistics Canada.

Table 5.6

"Part-time Worker in 2006 Among Core-age Workers (age 25-54)," adapted from the Statistics Canada publication *Labour Force Historical Review 2006*, Catalogue 71F0004XCB, Table cd1t08an, 2008. Copyright © Statistics Canada. Reprinted with permission of Statistics Canada

Table 5.7

"Distribution of Employment of Women and Men, by Occupation (%)," adapted from the Statistics Canada publication *Women in Canada, Work Chapter Updates 2006*, Catalogue

89F0133XIE, Table 11, 2007. Copyright © Statistics Canada. Reprinted with permission of Statistics Canada

Table 5.8

"A Closer Look at Professionals, 2006," adapted from the Statistics Canada publication *Women in Canada, Work Chapter Updates 2006*, Catalogue 89F0133XIE, Table 11, 2007. Copyright © Statistics Canada. Reprinted with permission of Statistics Canada

Chapter 6

Opening Photo ©istockphoto.com/stock-photo-2201928-man-is-on-the-telephone-behind-a-laptop

Box 6.1

Jimenez, M. "We Are All Capable People," The Globe and Mail October 25, 2003, F9. Copyright © CTVglobemedia Publishing Inc. Reprinted with permission.

Table 6.1

"Median Earnings of Immigrants and Non-Immigrants (persons aged 25-54, in constant 2005 dollars)," adapted from the Statistics Canada publication *Census of Canada 2006, Income and Earnings, Topic Based Tabulations*, Catalogue 97-563-X2006059, Table 44, 2007. Copyright © Statistics Canada. Reprinted with permission of Statistics Canada

Table 6.2

"Unemployment Rate in 2005" adapted from the Statistics Canada publication *Census of Population 2006*, Catalogue No. 97-562-XCB2006013, Table 3, 2008. Copyright © Statistics Canada. Reprinted with permission of Statistics Canada

Table 6.3

"Median Annual Income of All Visible Minority Persons in 2005," adapted from the Statistics Canada publication *Census of Population 2006*, Catalogue No. 97-562-XCB2006013, Table 3, 2008. Copyright © Statistics Canada. Reprinted with permission of Statistics Canada

Table 6.4

"Median Annual Income in 2005 (persons aged 25-44) with a University Degree," adapted from the Statistics Canada publication *Census of Canada 2006, Income and Earnings, Topic Based Tabulations*, 97-563-XWE2006060, Table 45, 2008. Copyright © Statistics Canada. Reprinted with permission of Statistics Canada.

Table 6.5

"Median Employment Income of Aboriginal Identity Persons," adapted from the Statistics Canada publication *Census of Canada 2006. Income and Earnings, Topic Based Tabulations*, 97-563-XWE2006061, Table 46, 2008. Copyright © Statistics Canada. Reprinted with permission of Statistics Canada.

Table 6.6

"Types of modifications required in order to be able to work, by severity, Canada, 2006," adapted from the Statistics Canada publication *Participation and Activity Limitation Survey, 2006*, Labour Force Experience of People with Disabilities in Canada, no. 7, Catalogue 89-628-XWE, Table 6, 2008. Copyright © Statistics Canada. Reprinted with permission of Statistics Canada.

Chapter 7

Opening photo ©istockphoto.com/stock-photo-4408214-human-need-portraits

Box 7.1

Avery, S., "Canada Faces Challenge to Keep Aging Economy Engine in Tune," Globe and Mail, Wednesday March 5th, 2008, p. B6. Copyright © CTVglobemedia Publishing Inc. Reprinted with permission.

Table 7.1

"Tax Filers with Contributions to a Registered Pension Plan (%)," adapted from the Statistics Canada publication Morrissette, R., and Ostrovsky, Y., *Pension Coverage and Retirement Savings of Canadian Families, 1986 to 2003*, No. 286, Catalogue 11F0019MIE, 2006. Copyright © Statistics Canada. Reprinted with permission of Statistics Canada.

Table 7.2

"Incomes of Persons Aged 71 to 73, 2000," adapted from the Statistics Canada publication LaRochelle-Cote, S., Myles, J., and Picot, G., *Income Security and Stability During Retirement in Canada*. Statistics Canada Analytical Studies Research Paper No. 306, 2008. Copyright © Statistics Canada. Reprinted with permission of Statistics Canada.

Chapter 8

Opening photo ©istockphoto.com/stock-photo-3134043-strategy

Box 8.1 Maclean's Pending

Kirby, J., "A Generation of Failure," *Maclean's*, February 12, 2009, 41–44. Copyright © Rogers Publishing Limited.

Table 8.1

"Average Hourly Earnings (in 2007 dollars)," adapted from the Statistics Canada publication *Labour Force Historical Review 2007*, Catalogue 71F0004XCB, Table CD 3T03, 2008. Copyright © Statistics Canada. Reprinted with permission of Statistics Canada.

Chapter 9

Opening photo ©istockphoto.com/stock-photo-3183059-human-chain

Table 9.1

"The Union Average Hourly Wage Advantage, 2007," Based on the Statistics Canada *Labour Force Survey* Microdata files, 2007. Copyright © Statistics Canada. Reprinted with permission of Statistics Canada.

Table 9.2

"Selected Provisions in Collective Agreements, 2006," Based on the Statistics Canada *Labour Force Survey* Microdata files, 2007. Copyright © Statistics Canada. Reprinted with permission of Statistics Canada.

Table 9.3

"Union Coverage and Wages in Sales and Service Occupations in the Private Sector, 2003," Based on the Gender and Work Database, York University. http://www.genderwork.ca, accessed August 8, 2005. Data from Labour Force Survey, 2003.

Table 9.4

"Union Impact on Hourly Wages, 2003," Based on the Gender and Work Database, York University. http://www.genderwork.ca, accessed August 8, 2005. Data from Survey of Labour and Income Dynamics, 2000.

Table 9.5

"Benefits Coverage: Union vs. Non-union," adapted from the Statistics Canada publication Akyeampong, E., *Unionization and Fringe Benefits*, Perspectives, August 2002: 3-9. Copyright © Statistics Canada. Reprinted with permission of Statistics Canada.

Chapter 10

Opening photo ©istockphoto.com/stock-photo-3067922-student-demonstration

Box 10.1

Peritz, I., Keenan, G., and Marotte, B., "At a Crossroads, Big Labour Digs In," Globe and Mail, February 22, 2008, p. B3. Copyright © CTVglobemedia Publishing Inc. Reprinted with permission.

Index

Abella, Rosalie, 134
AbitibiBowater, 235–36, 237
Aboriginal Canadians, 4, 6, 97, 146–48
  earnings gap of, 147, 148t
  and economic development projects, 147–48
  in precarious work, 36
Adult Education and Training Survey, 60–61, 215
age. *See* older workers; younger workers
Alberta, 15, 64, 101, 114, 137
  employment/unemployment in, 30, 31t
  health care privatization in, 259–60
  resource boom in, 263
  union coverage/density in, 226t, 231
  workplace accident underreporting in, 78
  younger workers in, 186
Alternative Mortgage Transaction Parity Act (U.S.), 22
Amalgamated Transit Union (Toronto), 85
American Federation of Labour–Congress of Industrial Organizations (AFL-CIO), 238
apprenticeship programs, 34, 54, 58, 60, 125, 186, 187, 215
Arthurs, Harry W., and report on employment standards, 92, 128
asbestos, exposure to, 77, 80
Assembly of First Nations (AFN), 98
Association of Community Organizations for Reform Now (ACORN), 242
Australia, immigration policy of, 141
auto industry, 235–37
  in Mexico, 251–53
  non-union workplaces of, 220n1, 229
automation, 56, 286
bad jobs, 5, 35–38, 73

banks and financial institutions
  and executive pay, 20, 26, 42
  and global economic crisis, 13–14, 20–26
Bell Canada, 114, 203, 209
"Big Three" automakers, 235–37, 251–53
Black Canadians, 136, 143
Bloc Québécois (BQ), 200
blue-collar jobs, 55, 56, 82
  and injuries/fatalities, 78, 79
  men in, 10, 32, 78, 79, 106, 124–25, 125t, 128, 193, 199, 229, 232, 241
  racialized workers in, 211
  and training, 62, 62t, 63–64
  unionization of, 193, 198, 199, 224, 229, 230, 232, 233, 238, 239, 241
  wages of, 39, 106, 106t, 206, 207t
  women in, 100, 106, 106t, 125, 127, 128
  working time of, 83, 204t, 214
British Columbia, 114, 137, 202
  and contracting out of health care jobs, 123–24, 197
  employment/unemployment in, 30, 31t
  unions in, 226t, 231, 235, 241
  workplace injury reporting in, 78
budgets, federal
  and deficit reduction, 265–67
  and EI, 12–13, 19
Bureau for Workers' Activities (ACTRAV), of ILO, 194

Canada Pension Plan (CPP), 4, 162, 163, 166, 167, 169–70, 173, 212
Canada-U.S. Free Trade Agreement (FTA), 9, 74, 245, 249, 258, 267
  see also North American Free Trade Agreement